Versions of Election

ReFormations

MEDIEVAL AND EARLY MODERN

Series Editors:
David Aers, Sarah Beckwith, and James Simpson

RECENT TITLES IN THE SERIES

VERSIONS
of ELECTION

From Langland and Aquinas
to Calvin and Milton

DAVID AERS

University of Notre Dame Press
Notre Dame, Indiana

University of Notre Dame Press
Notre Dame, Indiana 46556
undpress.nd.edu

Copyright © 2020 by the University of Notre Dame

Published in the United States of America

Library of Congress Control Number: 2020947047

ISBN: 978-0-268-10865-6 (Hardback)
ISBN: 978-0-268-10866-3 (Paperback)
ISBN: 978-0-268-10868-7 (WebPDF)
ISBN: 978-0-268-10867-0 (Epub)

To Christine Derham Aers

Yet doubt not but in valley and in plain
God is as here, and will be found alike
Present, and of his presence many a sign
Still following thee, still compassing thee round
With goodness and paternal love, his face
Express, and of his steps the track divine.

—John Milton, *Paradise Lost*, XI.349–54

CONTENTS

PREFACE

---

*Narrative history of a certain kind turns out to be the basic and
essential genre for the characterization of human actions.*

—Alasdair MacIntyre, *After Virtue*

*And it is perhaps the principal task of the political and moral theorist
to enable rational agents to learn from the social and cultural tradition
that they inherit, while becoming able to put in question that particular
tradition's distortions and errors, and so, often enough, engaging in a
quarrel with some dominant forms of their own political and moral culture.*

—Alasdair MacIntyre, *Ethics in the Conflicts of Modernity*

This book emerged from a web of substantial questions that have long
preoccupied me, ones that cross habitual divisions between the study of
literature, theology, ethics, and politics. They also cross the divisions between medieval and early modern studies, between the Catholic Middle
Ages and the Protestant Reformation, divisions firmly institutionalized
in modern universities. So it is inevitable that *Versions of Election* should
be both cross-disciplinary and diachronic. This may make it seem of a
kind with the recent grand narratives of modernity, narratives in which
the Middle Ages play an important role, albeit often a fabular one.[1] Yet
it is no such thing, nor is it a historical survey of doctrinal topics. It does
not even always follow the time of chronometers (see the relationship
between chapters 1 and 2, for example). And it certainly has no encyclo-
pedic aspirations. What *is* it then, and why does it study the texts on
which it concentrates in the way it does?

As the title indicates, this book is an exploration of some (not all) versions of predestination and reprobation in Christian traditions of the Middle Ages and the Reformation. It considers some medieval versions composed by well-known writers (Aquinas, for example) and some by far less well known ones (Bromyard, for example). It also studies some early modern versions generated within predominately Calvinist traditions. But which versions? And why are these particular versions discussed, given the plethora of relevant materials? After all, the topic was routinely addressed by most medieval theologians since their apprenticeship involved commenting on Peter Lombard's *Sentences*, a text that offered an eclectic but recognizably Augustinian account of the subject (chapter 2). Nor was interest in this topic confined to medieval universities, as we shall see (chapters 1 and 2). In the Reformation issues of predestination and reprobation became central, especially within Calvinist churches (chapters 3 and 4). The issues generated an immense range of writing in a wide range of genres: doctrinal treatises, contemplative writing, pastoral work, sermons, poems, and Protestant accounts of a person's spiritual life.

From this cornucopia accumulated across five hundred years of Christian writing I have chosen to explore a few versions that embody the strikingly different paradigms of election and reprobation generated within Christian tradition. The medieval versions I discuss help one see how the late medieval church could make and live with doctrinal diversity, conflict, and fragmentation in this important area. By the end of the Middle Ages we find that the church included paradigms that were unequivocally anti-Augustinian alongside paradigms that were hyper-Augustinian (proposing unambiguous forms of double predestination) together with those representing a Thomist form of Augustinianism (chapter 2). Such was the complex legacy of the medieval church to the Reformation. The second half of the book (chapters 3–5) addresses what the Reformation did with this legacy, especially in predominantly Calvinist churches.

But my aim is not merely to observe the presence of such variety, perhaps writing an extensive footnote to James Halverson's fine work, *Peter Aureol on Predestination* (see chapter 2). For in this study I am also exploring just how Christian tradition is made, unmade, and remade. I am fascinated by its complex modes and paths; its forms of memory, amnesia, and often gross misrepresentation of other participants in the tradition; its losses and recoveries of past arguments. To follow a tradition is to elucidate its ways of responding to changing circumstances. Such a mode of elucidation must attend to the minute particulars of specific texts, including their images, allegories, and grammar. Where appropriate, it may consider the transformation of one image or allegory across time and in differing contexts. For example, throughout the book I consider several responses to Paul's recollection of a text that ascribes to God hatred and love of unborn people (Rom. 9:11–14); I also return at various points to the strikingly different treatments by several authors of Jesus's comparison of himself to a hen who desired to gather her chickens under her wings but was rejected by them (Matt. 23:37: "O Jerusalem, Jerusalem, thou that killest the prophets, and stonest them which are sent unto thee, how often would I have gathered thy children together, even as a hen gathereth her chickens under her wings, and ye would not!"). In addition to providing an illuminating lens through which the ethical and theological implications of differing models of election become sharply apparent, the various responses to the latter passage that I consider here also inspired the choice of cover image to the present volume. I am grateful to Lindsey Larre for suggesting this illustration from a fifteenth-century French manuscript of a mother hen collecting her chickens, Christ-like, under her protective wings. That this image of mercy was not the only interpretation of this passage available to writers in the seventeenth century becomes a telling indication of the chasm between Calvinist versions of predestination and reprobation and traditional exegesis, as chapter 3 will show.

In pursuing this inquiry it has become clear that one must not assume that tradition is unidirectional. It has also become clear to me that even those who most vehemently deny their participation in human traditions, a distinctive feature of many writers throughout the Reformation, often turn out to be recovering strands of the very traditions they reject. This is especially striking when such rejection is combined with blazing confidence that their own position depends solely on scripture and spirit. John Milton, the poet, revolutionary, and theologian, came to exemplify this paradox in some especially fascinating ways (chapter 5), but the paradox was common enough in the Reformation. How could it not be when the makers of the Reformation belonged to a living

tradition that enabled distinctively Christian lives, disputes, and reformations across time and across diverse communities and polities?

Not even John Henry Cardinal Newman in *An Essay on the Development of Christian Doctrine* has illuminated this subject better than
Alasdair MacIntyre did many years ago in *After Virtue*.

> A living tradition then is an historically extended, socially embod-
> ied argument, and an argument in part about the goods which con-
> stituted that tradition. Within a tradition the pursuit of goods ex-
> tends through many generations. Hence the individual's search for
> his or her good is generally and characteristically conducted within
> a context defined by traditions of which the individual's life is part,
> and this is true both of those goods which are internal to practices
> and of the goals of a single life. Once again the narrative phenome-
> non of embedding is crucial: the history of a practice in our time is
> generally and characteristically embedded in and made intelligible
> in terms of the larger and longer history of the tradition through
> which the practice in its present form was conveyed to us; the his-
> tory of each of our own lives is generally and characteristically em-
> bedded in and made intelligible in terms of the larger and longer
> histories of a number of traditions. I have to say 'generally and
> characteristically' rather than 'always', for traditions decay, disin-
> tegrate and disappear.[2]

It is true enough that, as I have acknowledged, unlike MacIntyre I am
only exploring one aspect of a particular "living tradition" and its "his-
torically extended, socially embodied argument." But versions of predestination and reprobation were neither marginal nor esoteric subjects without existential and political relevance.

Teaching about predestination and reprobation informed the versions of the God worshipped by Christians. Inevitably this had major
consequences for Christian ethics and politics. If, as the Augustinian tradition claimed, God hated and reprobated some unborn people (such as
Esau) while he loved and predestined others to eternal beatitude (such as
Jacob), how, without sinking into a marsh of double-think and double-
talk, could Christians make sense of scriptural assertions that "God is

love" (1 John 4:8, 16) and God is just ("are not my ways right [*aequae*]?" [Ezek. 18:29]), one who proclaims, "I am the Lord that exercises mercy, and judgement, and justice [sum Dominus qui facio misericordiam, et judicium, et justitiam]" (Jer. 9:24)? Furthermore, Jesus plainly told his disciples to imitate God the father: "Be ye therefore perfect, even as your father which is in heaven is perfect" (Matt. 5:18); or, "Be ye therefore merciful [*misericordes*], as your Father also is merciful [*misericors*]" (Luke 6:36). How would Augustinian traditions of predestination and reprobation affect the language and understanding of *liberum arbitrium* (free decision) or *voluntas* (will), the source of love? How would it affect understanding of the human virtues that are intimately bound up with models of divine and human agency? The versions of predestination studied in this book display some of the ways in which the immense force of Augustine's teaching in this area was accepted, elaborated, or resisted. They have also enabled me to follow the consequences particular versions could have for people's understanding of social relations in a Christian polity, whether town or village or parish. This is why I devote a chapter to Arthur Dent's immensely popular Calvinist dialogue, *The Plaine Man's Path-way to Heaven: wherein every man may clearly see whether he shall be saved or damned* (chapter 4). Here we can follow the social and political ramifications of this tradition of election in the specific situations of early seventeenth-century England.

There are, inevitably, some versions of election that I do not consider in detail here. One of the book's early readers observed that the so-called radical Reformation occupies far less of the book's attention than the magisterial one, and mused that it would have been very interesting to explore, for example, Gerard Winstanley in the contexts provided by chapter 4 and by the book as a whole. I do not demur. But while figures of "the radical Reformation" have long engaged my attention and do appear in the margins of chapter 5, to give them anything like appropriate attention is, as the reader acknowledged, the task for another book. To attempt to treat them here would have had two consequences I did not want: it would have diffused the argument I make, and it would have encouraged me to set aside my commitment to following the implications of St. Thomas's view that "from the mode of speaking the teaching is given us."[3]

Versions of Election was written from within both a divinity school and an English department, both at Duke University. This rather unusual context encouraged me to offer graduate classes across works of literature and theology from Anselm to Langland, from Calvin to Milton. I came to think the history of theology was impoverished by restricting itself to works of formal theology and that it should incorporate literary texts. I also came to understand a little better how a few literary works have made distinctive contributions to theology. In doing so their forms and their specific modes of writing did theological work, something we will see from reading *Piers Plowman* (chapter 1). In this approach theology is not treated as a background for literature, nor is literature treated as a response to a theological background. I do appreciate that this may upset the disciplinary assumptions of some, and perhaps many, scholars. But here I recall MacIntyre's reflections on the reception of *After Virtue*, first published in 1981: "My thesis was deeply incompatible with the conventional academic disciplinary boundaries, boundaries which so often have the effect of compartmentalizing thought in a way that distorts or obscures key relationships, even if *that* entailed some large inadequacies from the standpoint of those immersed in each of the academically autonomous disciplines."[4] I quote this not because I harbor some strange delusions that my own work is even remotely comparable to MacIntyre's extraordinary writings from 1981 to 2016. I do so because the passage identifies so lucidly contexts that remain relevant in the contemporary academy. All I would add to MacIntyre's description of "conventional academic disciplinary boundaries" is that these include the distribution of jobs and the formation of coteries with guildlike structures largely defending synchronic and even single-author studies. Diachronic, cross-disciplinary work necessarily crosses the boundaries of such guilds and considers their subjects from different perspectives than those shaped by synchronic and single-author institutions. It was in this context, to encourage diachronic work that also maintains commitments to analysis of specific texts, that the series called ReFormations was invented at the University of Notre Dame Press.

One text on which I focus in this book poses some quite peculiar difficulties in a work not written for the guild of Langlandians. This is the great late fourteenth-century poem known as *Piers Plowman*. It is a dazzlingly complex and profoundly dialectical work, one read quite widely in the later Middle Ages and also in the English Reformation. It is studied in the first chapter but returns at many points throughout this book. Indeed, *Piers Plowman* actually becomes a major source for meditation on changes and continuities between the Middle Ages and the Reformation. The chapter on Dent's Calvinist *Path-way* needs to be read alongside the chapter on *Piers Plowman*. This is not only because the chapter makes some direct comparisons but also because Langland's work, too, includes agrarian settings in which to explore "the plain man's pathway to heaven." These agrarian settings explicitly refract contemporary English politics over two hundred years apart. What difference does it make that the guide in Dent's work has become a Calvinist minister, teaching and applying Calvinist doctrines of predestination and reprobation and displacing an agricultural laborer, the Plowman Piers? What can be learned about Christian traditions and the lives they constitute by this displacement? In my view, we can learn some things here we are unlikely to learn in a study that is synchronic and restrictive to the archive of one academic discipline.

What then are the "peculiar difficulties" I have in mind as I address *Piers Plowman* and give it such a prominent place in this diachronic work? In a nutshell, the difficulty is how to concentrate on its distinctive treatment of predestination and reprobation without shattering the poem's dialectical form and crushing its dialectical and visionary processes. *Hoc opus, hic labor.* Langland shows through the figure of Wille (figuring both the poet and *voluntas*, the power of the soul) how Christian teachings about predestination and reprobation can become sources of panic and despair. And, we note, how they did so in the fourteenth century. Such teaching, Langland shows, can occlude the fact that the God Christians worship is *Deus caritas*: "God is charity/love" (1 John 4:8, 16; *Piers Plowman* I.82).[5] But he also draws us into a dialectical process that leads to visions of Christ liberating humanity. These visions dissolve the terrors and perplexities that Wille had experienced in his encounters with doctrines of election. What Langland shows is that when the teaching of such doctrines becomes unmoored from Christology and the church's liturgy the omnipotent God is likely to be experienced as arbitrary and unkind, profoundly lacking in charity: the antithesis of *Deus caritas*. Langland's poem offers a luminous example of the unique way poetry can contribute to what has proved to be an extremely challenging area of Christian tradition.

Because *Piers Plowman* is exceptionally complex and little known outside medieval literary studies, I have done two things to encourage readers who have not yet read it to engage seriously with the poem. First, whenever quotations from *Piers Plowman* are extended I have added a translation in modern English; second, I have included Derek Pearsall's summary of the whole poem in its final version, the version known as the C-text, which I use in this book (for this, see the appendix). I am grateful to him and the current publishers of his edition (Liverpool University Press) for permission to quote; likewise, I thank the University of Pennsylvania Press for permission to use George Economou's translation of Derek Pearsall's edition. I should also probably note here one thing I do not do in my discussions of *Piers Plowman* or other works: I make no attempt to summarize how my readings differ from those of other laborers in the vineyard. In the notes and bibliography I try to acknowledge my debts to others in writing this particular work. But as noted above, I am engaged in a diachronic inquiry crossing many specialisms rather than making a text for a guild of Langlandians, or Thomists, or Miltonists. The consequences of this include just those spelled out by Alasdair MacIntyre in his reflections on *After Virtue*, quoted above. So be it.

I am very grateful for the way Duke University has facilitated my rather idiosyncratic commitments to theological and literary studies. I am also very grateful to the graduate students in both the divinity school and the English department who have worked with me in seminars that have crossed the division between medieval and early modern studies as well as the division between theology and literacy criticism. I am especially indebted to the superb research assistants I have had throughout the researching and writing of this book: first, Jessica Ward, now at Mercy University; then, Lindsey Larre, currently a postdoctoral scholar in the Center for Medieval and Renaissance Studies at Duke University. In addition to her meticulous copyediting, I also want to thank Lindsey for suggesting the book's title, and for reading it so closely that she followed some recurrent images into what became the cover for the book. I am also grateful for help received from Grace Hamman and Chandler Fry. I have learned much from ongoing conversations with Sarah Beckwith and James Simpson: my continuing debt to these extraordinarily gifted and learned scholars is boundless. I should also acknowledge that James Simpson is the person most responsible for encouraging me to pursue this inquiry when I was having acute doubts about its possibility. Both he and Sarah Beckwith have helped me understand the questions I seek to address in this book. Both James and Sarah read the manuscript with the closest engagement any writer could desire. For this, too, I am very grateful. I am also grateful to Nicky Zeeman for many conversations about *Piers Plowman* over many years, as well as for her always illuminating writing on the poem and its cultures of discourse. I also thank her for an exceptionally careful and helpful reading of the manuscript that became this book. I would also very much like to thank Joanna Picciotto. As an initially anonymous reviewer for the University of Notre Dame Press she provided an extraordinarily attentive and wonderfully engaged close reading. She did so not only in the areas that overlap with her own work on early modern culture, but with the whole text treated as a diachronic study of Christian tradition. I have tried to meet some of her questions and suggestions in what follows, but her reading became a conversation drawing us beyond the scope of the present work. I am deeply grateful to her—not only for the specific commentary, but also for her commitment to a common inquiry despite theological differences. I am very glad she emerged from the reviewer's anonymity to continue the conversation. My thinking about working across the great divide has been greatly aided by working as an editor of the *Journal of Medieval and Early Modern Studies*, a labor continually supported by the journal's exceptional managing editor, Michael Cornett. Once more I am grateful to the judicious editor at the University of Notre Dame Press, Stephen Little, and to Sheila Berg for her meticulous eye. Much reading for this book was done in the Rare Books Room of the University Library at Cambridge University, and I would like to thank Claire Welford-Elkin and all who work there for making it such a superb and welcoming place to study.

Finally, yet once more, I thank my closest friend and my wife, Christine Derham. To her this work is dedicated.

CHAPTER ONE

"Predestinaet" or "Prescit"

Langland's Treatment of Election in Piers Plowman (C-text)

*Hence, it is a mark of excessive contentiousness to speak
against predestination or have doubts about it.*

—St. Augustine, *The Gift of Perseverance*

*Sometimes an expression has to be withdrawn from language
and sent for cleaning,—then it can be put back into circulation.*

—Ludwig Wittgenstein, *Culture and Value*

William Langland's *Piers Plowman,* in its longer versions, is a dialectical, often allegorical work. It is driven by an intense commitment to reassess and press back against its own arguments and visions with sometimes remorseless questioning and countervisions. Often this process baffles the dreamer Wille, who is simultaneously a disputatious figure of the poet and a leading power of the soul. Through an extraordinary range of modes, guides, and visions, Langland draws readers into a restless exploration of topics in the theology, politics, and ethics of Christian discipleship in relation to his contemporary church. I hope that some people who have never read *Piers Plowman* and who have never encountered medieval English will read this chapter. The book is, after all, not written for specialists in Middle English literature, and even less for any coterie of Langlandian scholars in English departments. It necessarily works across the disciplines and periods marked out by institutional compartmentalizations. For this reason, I follow quotations of Langland's poetry with translations by George Economou; I also include as an appendix to the book the luminous summary of the poem's final version published by Derek Pearsall in his edition, *Piers Plowman: A New Annotated Edition of the C-text*.[1]

Any reading of *Piers Plowman* that ignores its dialectical modes will not even begin to meet the poem's force, nor can such a reading fully understand the way the poem pursues its specific concerns. This caveat is especially necessary for readings such as the one offered in the present chapter—namely, an attempt to attentively explore what is actually but one moment, one single strand, woven into a complex totality. Inevitably in such a reading, the moment that engages one must be isolated from the whole in order to give attention to its minute particulars, yet this moment's place in the larger conversations that constitute the work must at least be recalled. Even as we attend to the fine details, we should also try to grasp the poem's final understanding of the particular episode under scrutiny, if it does in fact have one. This is always a very demanding task but is perhaps especially so in the present inquiry. Here I concentrate on Langland's dramatic exploration of only one topic: his tradition's teachings on God's predestination and reprobation of human beings. These explorations are focused in Passus XI and XII, but they extend tentacles across the poem and are folded into Christ's great oration in the harrowing of hell in Passus XX.

The title of this chapter is drawn from a troubled and troubling passage in the poem's eleventh passus. The immediate context of the passage is Wille's search for the virtues needed by those who wish to live well, virtues condensed by Wille into a figure he calls "Dowel." This term and the search to which it belongs are initiated earlier in the poem by Wille's encounter with two lines abstracted from the Trinitarian and Christological confession of faith known as the Athanasian Creed: "Dowel and haue wel and god shal haue thy soule / And do yvele and haue evele hope [expect] thow non othere" (IX.287–98). The search for

Dowel becomes increasingly complex as the world becomes stranger and stranger to Wille, but it remains integral to the urgent question he puts to Holy Churche in Passus I: "How Y may save my soule?" (I.80). Holy Churche's answer centers on *Deus caritas* ("God is love" [1 John 4:8, 16]).[2] She shows Wille that the answer he seeks is the revelation of divine love in the Incarnation, together with the insistence that divine love demands human virtues shaped by charity. As she says, even the virtue of chastity, so exalted in medieval teaching, will be "cheyned in helle" if it is not informed by charity (I.175–98; cf. 1 Cor. 13:1–13).

In his search for salvation and a life of Christian virtue (Dowel), Wille receives some lucid maps from many teachers: Holy Churche, Conscience, Reason, Repentance, Piers the Plowman, Wit, Studie, Clergie, and Scripture (I–XII). These figures offer maps that include directions for "the way" to the heavenly city (e.g., I.81–204; VII.205–82; XI.139–59). But however clear the highway initially appears on these maps, the pilgrim nevertheless meets obstacles and arguments that force or lure him into what seem to be uncharitable byways, detours, side roads, and dead ends (II–XI). These explorations of contemporary conflicts and confusions that muddy the path drive Wille toward a sense that the very maps he has been given by apparently authoritative figures lack intelligibility. How can Wille, the source of love in the human person, choose to do well when his maps and guides provide directions that seem to have no obvious bearing on the contemporary landscape? Or when they seem to offer contradictory directions? There are certainly occasions throughout *Piers Plowman* when readers should sympathize with Wille's complaints (at, e.g., X.56–57) that he cannot make sense of the teaching he receives.

Wille's increasing difficulty with reading his maps is encapsulated in a particularly painful exchange with a teacher of great authority whom he encounters in Passus XI. This teacher is Scripture. Reflecting on the authority of scripture in Langland's context, we might recall the conventional account given by Thomas Aquinas at the opening of his *Summa Theologiae*. There he declares that God is the author of scripture ("Auctor sacrae Scripturae est Deus") (I.1.10, resp.).[3] He observes that scripture is thus the supreme authority in the making of Christian doctrine (I.1.8, ad 2). Indeed, all the articles of faith are derived from the truth proposed to us in scripture (II–II.5.3, ad 2).[4] Given this, we might expect the manifestation of scripture in Langland's poem to provide Wille with just the authoritative direction he has been seeking.

But such expectations are not fulfilled. This is perhaps at least in part because neither Langland nor Aquinas participates in one of the shaping commonplaces of the Reformation: the claim that scripture is perspicuous and self-interpreting.[5] On the contrary, in his treatise on faith in the *Summa Theologiae*, Aquinas observes that while the truth of Christian faith is contained in holy scripture, it is so "diffusely, under various modes of expression and sometimes obscurely." To read scripture adequately, Aquinas notes, we need "long study and practice" (II–II.1.9, ad 1). With this, Langland would have no argument. But where Aquinas later foregrounds the unproblematic hermeneutic authority of the Catholic Church, Langland's poem unfolds problem upon problem: early on, he displays the church's interpreters and commentators producing scriptural glosses that are disastrously shaped by contingent material and political interests (e.g., Prol. 56–65); and at the poem's ending, he represents the Catholic Church, including pope and cardinals, as followers of Antichrist (XXII.53–64, 121–28).[6] Despite these scenes of confused and disputed hermeneutic authority, earlier in *Piers Plowman* Wille himself confidently claims that he has been "to scole" and learned how to interpret holy scripture truly (V.35–37, 53–67). Not like those glossing friars we meet in the Prologue (Prol. 56–67)? Perhaps not. But Langland has introduced into the text difficult questions that mean Wille's engagement with Scripture is likely to be more complex than Wille—or, perhaps, the reader—wants.

Wille meets Scripture after following the directions of Studie (his time at "scole" doubtlessly on the way). He then comes to Clergie, a doctor of theology. But what are the relations between Clergie and Scripture in *Piers Plowman*? They are, to say the least, somewhat tricky. Studie tells Wille that Clergie is "over" Scripture and that their relationship can be allegorized in terms of medieval hierarchies of gender: Clergie is the husband, Scripture his wife (XI.96). But while this assertion of hierarchy *might* have produced a strongly ecclesial version of the authority of the church and her theologians presiding "over" the text of scripture, it is not allowed to do so. Instead, Studie tells Wille that her professed ideal of Clergie as an exegetical authority over Scripture would hold only if scribes were truthful makers and transcribers of the canonical text; unfortunately, they are not (XI.94). Where does that leave Clergie, his doctrine, and Wille's pilgrimage? Confronting some profoundly challenging hermeneutic questions in the contemporary church, certainly.

Langland chooses to show some of the consequences of these questions dramatically rather than through scholastic modes of disputation; in this, Langland's mode is closer, perhaps, to Chaucer's much-discussed treatment of clerical glossing in terms of sexual domination in the *Wife of Bath's Prologue* than to Aquinas's systematic reflections in the *Summa Theologiae*.[7] Having suggested, through Studie, that the text of Scripture is too unreliable for Clergie to be "over" her, Langland then shows Scripture exerting authority over Clergie. The latter may well teach Augustinian doctrine on the mystery of the Trinity, but he is simply silenced by Scripture (XI.146–60). Perhaps a good thing, too, as Scripture seems to have no confidence that Wille is a suitable student for Clergie's theological lessons. The narrator writes that Scripture gave many reasons for her disdain of Wille and her interruption of Clergie, but he discloses none of these reasons.[8] Instead of reasoning with Wille, Scripture merely communicates her demand that Clergie dismiss him (XI.160–61). She goes on to address Wille in Latin, choosing words from a beautiful set of meditations on self-knowledge and self-ignorance ascribed in the Middle Ages to Bernard of Clairvaux: "*Multi multa sciunt et seipsos nessiunt* [Many people know many things while they do not know themselves]" (XI.163).

The consequences of Scripture's contempt for Wille and her separation from the doctor of theology seem disastrous. We have already heard Wille lamenting the premature termination of his clerical education because of a crisis of funding (V.35–41). Now, yet once more, he is barred from pursuing what he had taken to be his vocation: laboring among "clerkes Crist for to serve / God and good men" (V.61–62). But if he is only a partially trained clerk, not called to complete his education and become (like Clergie) a theologian, what *is* Wille's calling? His own reason and conscience worried away at this question in Passus V but offered him no answer. At this point perhaps Wille, like Chaucer's uncloistered monk, might well wonder, "How shal the world be served?"[9]

But scripture, as we have seen, was recognized to be a central guide on the journey to God. It was "the word of God" and as such could well be "more piercing than any two-edged sword . . . reaching into the division of the soul and the spirit, of the joints also and the marrow[,] . . . a discerner of thoughts and intents of the heart" (Heb. 4:12). To be rejected by Scripture is a devastating moment for any *viator*; especially so for this *viator*, Wille, who as a youth had already received formal training in the interpretation of scripture (V.35–37). Perhaps he also now, in the midst of his rejection, recalls the moment in Passus I when Holy Churche dismisses his question to her about the location of "treuthe and trewe love" in the human soul. There she accused him of being a "dotede daffe [muddle-headed fool]" who learned too little Latin in his youth (I.139–40). Be that as it may, Wille's Latin is good enough to grasp Scripture's piercing words: he is charged with accumulating external knowledge while failing to explore the world within.

In his *Confessions*, Augustine recalls a similar moment wherein God worked through the Platonic books he was reading: "I was admonished to return into myself [*admonitus redire ad memet ipsum*]. With you as my guide I entered into my innermost citadel [*intravi in intima mea duce te*], and was given power to do so because you had become my helper."[10] But despite this admonition to introspection, again and again Augustine shows how opaque we are to ourselves. So while Scripture's scorn of Wille's lack of self-knowledge may be a true judgment, it is also one that is lacking in charity. After all, Augustine acknowledges that "there is something of the human person which is unknown even to the 'spirit of man which is in him' [1 Cor. 2:11]" (X.5.7). However hard he labors to know himself, he is to himself a "soil which is a cause of difficulty and much sweat" (X.33.50). He remains a question to himself. Augustine confesses that whatever self-knowledge he may have depends on the light God has granted him (X.5.7). Self-knowledge is a gradual process enabled by the help of divine grace, itself hidden and only recognized retrospectively. Although Langland unfolds a theology of grace congruent with Augustine's dramatization of the interactions between human and divine agency in the *Confessions*, Wille himself has no such vision as he responds to Scripture's rebuke.[11] On the contrary, he weeps "for wo and wrathe" at her words (XI.164).

If grace is at work within Wille's misery and rage, it is well hidden, for in his passions he abandons his pursuit of virtue. Separated from Clergie, rejected by Scripture, with Holy Churche having disappeared many passus ago, Wille yields up in despair his pursuit of moral questions and abandons the search for his vocation, his calling.

* * *

As he had been ravished by Mede in Passus II, in Passus XI Wille now finds himself "ravysched [ravished]" by Fortune (XI.166). Scripture's hostile judgment of Wille is about to receive confirmation as he wanders "into the lond of longyng and love" (XI.164–86; cf. II.16). As many have noted, Langland makes a haunting move here, invoking Christ's parable of the prodigal son, a text replete with centuries of meditative exegesis (Luke 15:11–32).[12] In that parable, a man's younger son demands "the portion of his substance [*portionem substantiae*]" due to him. Having received his share of the paternal substance, the son "went abroad into a far country [*peregre profectus est in regionem longinquam*]: and there wasted his substance, living riotously." Translating "in regionem longinquam" as "into the lond of longyng," Langland beautifully echoes the Latin scripture. Wille's journey in Passus XI, as we will see below, echoes the path of the prodigal.

Because Langland has so carefully invoked Jesus's parable and because Langland reads this text within a rich exegetical tradition, it is worth first recalling some of the characteristic late medieval commentary on this scriptural passage.[13] Let us consider the parable's statement that the prodigal son wasted his portion of his father's substance (Luke 15:12–13). How did conventional allegorical exegesis read this passage? Nicholas of Gorran, a thirteenth-century Dominican, sees the son dissipating his portion of divine gifts (natural and supernatural) in vices. This reading is a version of the way the twelfth-century *Glossa Ordinaria* explicates the son's abuse of the divine gift of *liberum arbitrium* (free judgment), an abuse that involves forgetting God. The immensely influential early fourteenth-century exegete Nicholas of Lyra sees the son's actions as representing humanity's withdrawal from God, addiction to mortal sins, and consequent subjection to the devil in the land of the shadow of death. Later, the theologian and contemplative Denis the Carthusian reads the father's gifts as the grace that makes someone pleasing to God (*dona gratiae gratum facientes*). The son loses this grace as he consumes the goods of fortune and poisons the goods of nature.[14]

Langland's Wille follows this same path: he has been given the gifts of baptism and, in a deeply moving episode in Passus V, has been drawn to conversion (I.72–75; V.1–108). He has indeed received a "portion" of his Father's substance. Yet once he is "in the lond of longyng" Wille, like the prodigal, dissipates it. Just as the latter "wasted his substance, living riotously [*dissipavit substantiam suam vivendo luxoriose*]" (Luke 15:13), so Wille pursues "*Concupiscentia carnis* [lust of the flesh]" and "Coveytise-of-yes [lust of the eyes]," encouraged as he is by another personification, "Pryde-of-parfit-lyvnge [Pride of Life]" (see 1 John 2:15–16). This new life involves forms of desire that are in total denial of the horizons of human temporality and the processes of bodily disintegration that Langland invokes here (XI.186–95) but addresses at length in the poem's final passus (XXII).[15]

In Jesus's parable, once the younger son has dissipated his gifts, he is confronted with a great famine and begins to be in need (*coepit egere*)—or, at least, he begins to notice his neediness (Luke 15:14). The son goes to work for a citizen in the far country where he is employed to feed swine, and although he would gladly have eaten the swine's husks, he is not given any (Luke 15:15–16). Exegetes tend to see the famine as a hunger for the word of God or as hunger for grace and the salvific virtues.[16] To Nicholas of Gorran (following Augustine in a passage quoted in the *Catena Aurea* of his fellow Dominican, Thomas Aquinas), the husks symbolize not only the emptiness of worldly knowledge in the far country but also the vanity of beautiful poetry and prose written in praise of idols and those fables belonging to the gods of the Gentiles in whom the devils are delighted.[17]

Langland does not incorporate this parable into his poem in the detail with which he later incorporates the story and traditional exegesis of Jesus's parable of the compassionate Samaritan, but the connections are clear.[18] He has already had Studie associate Wille with hungry swine who "lovyen lond and lordschipe and lykynge of body / More then holynesse or hendenesse or al that seyntes techeth" (XI.7–13). There, Studie was enraged that Wit (understanding, mind) had been teaching wisdom to Wille (XI.1–6). Alluding to Christ's warning about throwing pearls to swine who will only trample them underfoot and attack the giver (Matt. 7:6), she counts Wille among those Christians figured as "hogges" who naturally feed on hawthorn berries—"han hawes at wille," a phrase replete with puns (XI.8). A few lines later, before she allows Wille to go on to meet Clergie and Scripture, she warns Wit about the dangers of disclosing scripture to people who, hog-like, prefer hawthorn berries: "be waer [beware] holy writ to shewe / Amonges hem [them] that haen [have] hawes at wille." She immediately glosses these "hawes" as "a lykyng and a luste, the love of the world" (XI.78–80). Were Wille, at the point where he is abandoned by Scripture and Clergie and lost in "the lond of longyng," to recall these words, his misery would be compounded by such a prophetic warning. For Wille's encounter with Scripture has indeed led to the fulfillment of Studie's doubts about his readiness for the next stage of his journey. Despite Dame Studie's initial suspicions, she has enabled Wille's pursuit of Clergie and Scripture, and it is this encounter with Scripture that pushes Wille toward a place where "unkyndenesse and coueytise" form "hungry contreys bothe" (XV.187–88). He is now indeed lost among the husks and the hawthorn berries, far from the fruit of charity he so desperately needs but is not yet ready to discern (he will not, in fact, be ready to taste the fruit of charity until Passus XVIII).

What can one do as one rummages among husks in "the lond of longyng"? Wille, like the prodigal son, is apparently now enclosed in a hopeless circle where the only available food must exacerbate his hunger and tighten the trap holding him in a famished land. How can one return from this far country? The answer given in Christ's parable is actually related to Scripture's apparently harsh challenge that catalyzed Wille's fall into "wo and wrathe": "*Multi multa sciunt et seipsos nessiunt* [Many know many things and do not know themselves]" (XI.163–64). The answer is conversion. For the prodigal this involves "turning to himself [*In se autem reversus*]." Having done so, he determines his next action: "I will arise, and will go to my father and say to him: Father I have sinned against heaven, and before thee" (Luke 15:17–18). First he returns to himself, then he determines a path of penitent return to his father. In Scripture's terms, he turns away from the endless pursuit of many things in the world ("*multa*") in an act of self-knowledge that is simultaneously an act of remembrance. He remembers his forgotten father, the source of self and figure of God. In the *City of God*, Augustine references this parable when he observes that we are "created in the image of our Creator."

> Contemplating this image in ourselves, therefore, let us, like the younger son of the Gospel, come to ourselves, and arise and return to him whom we had forsaken by our sin. In him our being will have no death, our knowledge will have no error, and our love will know no check.[19]

Returning to himself, the younger son finds the image of God showing him the way from the far country to the source he had abandoned. Such a turning is the antithesis of the introspection of solipsism and soliloquy. But how can one driven by the anarchic and delusive loves that imprison Wille return to oneself without falling into yet further forms of deranged solipsism? Let us look at some of the answers to this question given by late medieval exegesis on Jesus's parable.

Commenting on the prodigal son "returning to himself," Nicholas of Lyra observes that in sinning the son had gone out of himself (*extra se*) and that his return is accomplished through penitence. Importantly, Lyra understands the son's initial turning as a form of contrition that needs divine grace for its perfection, a grace that Lyra sees figured in the father's actions: "And when he [the son] was yet a great way off, his father saw him, and was moved with compassion, and running to him fell upon his neck and kissed him" (Luke 15:20). Although the Franciscan Lyra does not explicate his theology of grace at this point, it can certainly be construed: it is an example of that prominent late medieval strand that maintained that if we do that which is within us, if we do the best that we are capable of, then God will not withhold the grace he has freely covenanted to extend to us.[20] The Dominican Nicholas of Gorran offers a different inflection in his exegesis of the parable, one that introduces the concept of *predestination*. In the father's actions (seeing the son while he was still far away [longe], being moved with compassion, running to the son, kissing him), Gorran finds a figuration of God's predestination. He discerns here a representation of the preparation of grace and glory together with its gift of prevenient grace to the predestinate.[21] I will be returning to such discourse in chapter 2.

In the fifteenth century, Denis the Carthusian shows that late medieval theologies might combine both Lyra's and Gorran's approaches. Denis glosses the son "returning to himself" as the recovery of right reason in an act of self-examination. This act leads to the decision to return to his father's house. Like many others, the Carthusian glosses this house as a figure of the church militant. There, one finds that bread abounds (Luke 15:17). This bread is read as the sacramental bread, concerning which Christ said, "I am the bread of life" and "my flesh is meat indeed" (John 6:35, 56). When he reaches the verse describing the son's approach to his father, Denis (like Nicholas of Lyra) sees a figure of *attrition*, a stage of penitence that disposes the sinner toward true contrition. In this early stage of penitence, the sinner still remains in the chains of sin; he must wait for the grace of charity that will transform attrition into contrition, and which can only be infused by God. Addressing the father's actions, Denis sees a figure of *eternal predestination*.[22] From divine predestination flows *prevenient grace* to help the son who is already returning to God. Like Nicholas of Lyra, Denis writes that when someone does what they can to prepare for grace, God will help and will infuse his grace.[23] Such theology could integrate a discourse of predestination within a covenantal theology in which God responds to human attempts to return to the way. I consider a striking example of this in John Bromyard's *Summa Praedicantium* in the next chapter.

But remaining for another moment with Denis the Carthusian on Jesus's parable, we have seen that the prodigal's conversion involves divine election, right reason, and also the sacramental presence of Christ. How these different strands may or may not cohere will depend on the particular theologian. Langland himself will provide his readers with a distinctly Christological answer to the crucial question of how Wille can, like the prodigal son, return from the far country of "the lond of longyng." Like Augustine in the *City of God*, he will disclose how Christ is our goal as God and our way as man.[24] But this will only emerge much later and only after Wille is made to encounter vexing troubles with the church's teaching on predestination and reprobation.

The contexts I have been describing thus far in this chapter are decisive in understanding how Langland situates and unfolds his exploration of Christian theories of predestination and reprobation as he found them in the fourteenth century. At the moment, Wille remains in the far country, forgetful of Christ and of what Holy Churche has tried to teach him. In this state, he encounters Rechelesnesse, a figure of himself who displays a desire to theologize his current predicament. This will toward theology is of course congruent with Wille's years in "scole" and his alleged education in "what holy writ mened" (V.35–41). The situation the poet has composed may seem desperately unpropitious for doing theology, but throughout *Piers Plowman*, Langland suggests that in his church and culture there may, perhaps, be no circumstances that are not unpropitious.[25] Indeed, in Wille's own desperate hedonism, his anger with Scripture, and his abandonment of ethical inquiry, Langland reminds us that all theologizing is done by humans immersed in one form of delusion or another. No reader is allowed to follow Wille's troubles from a position of condescension.

The theologically inclined figure of Wille's state in the far country, Rechelesnesse, is a brilliantly conceived correlate, added by Langland to the work's final version.[26] Each version of *Piers Plowman* must be read as a work with its own internal dialectical form, narrative, episodes, and preoccupations. Different versions of the poem should not be scrambled together. But they can, of course, be compared. If we do so, we will find that the topics of predestination and reprobation emerge in all versions.[27] In the first two versions of the poem, Langland ascribes the troubled questioning on the issue directly to Wille, while in the final version he introduces Rechelesnesse, the surrogate for Wille whom we will now follow, to pose these difficult questions. As we will see, Langland approaches the topic in a dramatic and dialogic way characteristic of *Piers Plowman* in order to show how the language of predestination and reprobation can be generated from scripture and tradition.

True to his name, Rechelesnesse recklessly encourages Wille to ignore the warnings he has received about human mortality and advises him to continue following Fortune (XI.186–95). Here, the author intercedes and identifies such reckless fantasies of perpetual gratification in the "land of longyng" as illusions of counterfeit immortality proximate to "wanhope [despair]."[28] Having established this relationship, we begin to hear Rechelesnesse's account of Clergie's teaching, an account that mocks the ethical teachings of Clergie and Scripture as absurdly rigorous (XI.194–201). Rechelesnesse initiates a discourse on predestination and reprobation, on the Christian doctrine of election (XI.202–71a). According to Rechelesnesse, Clergie maintains as evangelical doctrine that a person's name is entered in the book of life long before she exists.

> For Clergie saith that he seyh in the seynt evaungelie
> That Y man ymaed was and my name y-entred
> In the legende of lyf longe ar Y were.
>
> (XI.202–4)

———

> [For Clergy says he saw in the holy gospel
> That I was made man and my name entered
> In the book of life long before I was.]

Such a claim is not actually made by Jesus "in the seynt evangelie [holy gospel]" but is rather construed by orthodox traditions from a remark made by St. Paul to some such effect (Rom. 9:13). Setting this aside for the moment, we should note that Rechelesnesse's report does not accurately reflect the teaching we have just heard from Clergie (XI.139–59). What did Clergie actually talk about? He paid attention to the mysteries of the Trinity and the Incarnation. He also acknowledged that humans have the gift of "fyn wit," enabling them to "dispute" doctrine held on faith. Rechelesnesse has ignored what Clergie actually taught and projected alien material onto him. This is certainly a striking response, and one fraught with consequences that are shown to be doctrinally and pastorally disastrous. Rechelesnesse has opened the door to a model of election, of predestination, and reprobation quite independent of the poem's Christology. We should discern the irony in his confident assertion that his source here is "the seynt evangelie."

Equally confident is his claim about contemporary preachers. He declares that they preach about predestination and reprobation in accord with his own version of Clergie's teaching:

Predestinaet thei prechen, prechours that this sheweth,
Or *prescit* inparfit, pult out of grace,
Unwriten for som wikkednesse, as holy writ sheweth:
  Nemo ascendit ad celum nisi qui de celo descendit.
                                    (XI.205–7a)

——————

[They preach men are predestinate, preachers who declare this,
Or beforehand known to be imperfect, thrust out of grace,
Not written down because of some wickedness, as holy writ
  shows.
*No man hath ascended into heaven but he that descended from
  heaven.*]

Rechelesnesse is claiming that contemporary preachers preach the doctrine of election in such a way as to emphasize both predestination (to beatitude) and reprobation (to hell). In "Langland and the Ideology of Dissent," Pamela Gradon refers to "that favourite contemporary topic, predestination," before separating Langland's concerns from those of "Wycliffite thought."[29] Long before that essay, Greta Hort argued in *Piers Plowman and Contemporary Religious Thought* that Langland "writes as a theologian" engaging with other "medieval theologians" concerned with "the question of predestination," even though he does so in a different mode.[30] Similarly, in his recent revision of his book on *Piers Plowman*, James Simpson observes that predestination was a central problem in fourteenth-century Christianity.[31] These statements support Rechelesnesse's account of contemporary preaching. It is certainly true that theologians would have had to engage with this topic during their training. This was so because a central part of their long apprenticeship involved commenting on the twelfth-century *Sentences* of Peter Lombard, and in Book 1 of Lombard's work, distinctions 40 and 41 were devoted to this subject.[32] In chapter 2 of the present book I pursue such directions further.

But Rechelesnesse's claim is more specific: preachers are preaching about predestination *and* reprobation. This claim raises difficult historical questions of the kind very familiar to historians of Reformation England, who have had to explore the relations between Calvinist theolo gies of predestination and reprobation in the Church of England and what was actually preached in the pulpit.[33] This picture is probably much less clear in the later Middle Ages. Predestination is a topic that Wyclif addresses in some of his Latin sermons, and the Benedictine monk Rypon preached on predestination before monks in a sermon surviving in Latin.[34] But how common was such preaching in Latin? How common was it in English? Even the English Wycliffite sermons seem to diminish the opportunities given them to discuss this topic in some of Wyclif's sermons on the Sunday Gospels.[35] My own reading of medieval sermons does not concur with Rechelesnesse's generalization about preaching, but perhaps those who read more widely than I do in this genre will find grounds to accept his assertion. As far as I can see, however, it is Wille's time at "scole"—and not any time he may have spent listening to preaching—that would have introduced him to the theology of election, as the next chapter discusses.

Whatever the putative sources, Rechelesnesse himself seems to imagine the doctrine in terms that belong to some vaguely imagined version of double predestination. By "double predestination" I refer to theologies in which it is alleged that God eternally chose both to bring some to felicity (predestination) and, in a symmetrical eternal decree, to bring some to damnation (reprobation). Standard representations of these two classes in theological writing paired Peter with Judas and Jacob with Esau as figures of those chosen for, respectively, salvation or damnation. God chooses to predestine and reprobate quite independently of any human works. While this model emerged with great clarity in the fourteenth century, it was never the mainstream in medieval theology; not, at least, in explicit teaching. But Rechelesnesse sets up the kind of symmetry we find in versions of double predestination: a symmetry between those predestined to life and those reprobated to damnation through God's denial of divine grace. He asserts that the church claims to find "in the seynt evaungelie [in the holy gospel]" that a person is entered into the book of life ("the legende of lyf") long before birth (XI.202–4). But we are not all written in the book of life. In Aquinas's teaching, this book is a metaphorical way of talking about those who are chosen ("eliguntur") to receive the gift of eternal life: "The inscription of their names composes what is entitled the Book of

Life" (*ST* I.24.1, resp.).[36] It represents the divine marking of those God saves, those Rechelesnesse correctly refers to as "Predestinaet" (XI.205). But Rechelessnesse also says that God has foreknown the names of the imperfect, "*prescit* inparfit": these people will be damned forever (XI.206). There seems some ambiguity in this line. Rechelessnesse could be saying that just as God eternally predestined some to salvation, so he eternally damned some, in his foreknowing. This would be the symmetry of double predestination. But he could also be saying that God foresaw the "inparfit" works of some humans for which he would damn them. This was a line of argument often used against double predestination.

But as Rechelesnesse continues, he dissolves the ambiguity introduced here. First, he uses the striking image of God *unwriting* people foreknown to damnation: by God these people are "pult out of grace, / Unwriten for some wikkednesse, as holy writ sheweth" (XI.206–7). The "holy writ" he quotes is Jesus's statement that "no man hath ascended into heaven but he that descended from heaven" (John 3:13). Jesus is referring to himself, "the Son of man who is in heaven," and links this statement to his forthcoming, life-giving crucifixion: "as Moses lifted up the serpent in the desert, so must the Son of man be lifted up" (John 3:13–16). Not surprisingly, Pearsall's annotations criticize Rechelesnesse's use of this text as "very simple-minded." Similarly, Schmidt's annotations describe it as "so arbitrary and extreme" that it "may be meant to be seen as deliberately provocative."[37] Certainly the strongly Christological and salvific contexts of Jesus's statements seem to undermine the directions of Rechelesnesse's theologizing in ways he fails to grasp but which the poem will gradually unfold (XVIII–XXI).

Rechelesnese also fails to quote the text of scripture that actually does stand behind his image of people being "unwriten" from the book of life, Psalm 68:29. Aquinas, however, offers an illuminating article on exactly what troubles Wille's surrogate, one worth considering in relation to Rechelesnesse's speech. Aquinas asks, "Can anyone be struck off [*deleatur*] the Book of Life?" (*ST* I.24.3). As so often in the *Summa Theologiae*, as in medieval commentaries on the *Sentences*, the objections offered in the text against the position the author wants to defend are forceful. The first objection, taken from Augustine, is that God's foreknowledge (*praescientia*) is unerring, so it disallows any contingency (obj. 1). But in his answers, Aquinas quotes the text that Langland alludes to through Wille's troubles: "Let them be blotted out from the Book of Life [*Deleantur de libro viventium*]" (Ps. 68:29). "Unwriten" indeed. As he develops his responses, Aquinas argues that the promises made to holy people about the book of life are not merely figurative. The book of life, he says, "is the list of those enrolled for eternal life." Such people are chosen through divine predestination, which is the prelude to the gift of saving grace. However, part of Rechelesnesse's anxiety is shown to be warranted. For someone who is enrolled in a predestination that is not subject to contingencies and never errs may nevertheless be deleted from the book. Aquinas tries to reconcile this with the claim that when such a deletion is made, God does so in response to the human's mortal sin. So we seem to have both those who are "irrevocably written down in the Book of Life [*simpliciter scripti in libro vitae*]" and are never deleted from the book (*isti numquam delentur de libro vitae*) and those who are written down but only provisionally (*non simpliciter sed secundum quid*). The latter *can* be deleted (*tales possunt deleri de libro vitae*). As Rechelesnesse observes, some mortal sinners (like the adulterous murderer David) are written in the book of life without the possibility of deletion on account of their sins (XI.263–65). Other mortal sinners, however, are written in the book of life but can be deleted and consigned to everlasting hell. Aquinas insists that this orthodox model does *not* imply that God changes his mind, as though the eternal God first foreknew something, writing accordingly, but then did not know it: "quasi Deus aliquid praesciat postea nesciat." On the contrary, according to Aquinas, God's eternal knowledge is such that somebody is first ordained to eternal life but afterward becomes not ordained when the formerly (eternally?) ordained person falls into sin and becomes cut off from grace (I.24.3, resp.: "Deus scit aliquem prius ordinari in vitam aeternam, et postea non ordinari cum deficit a gratia"). True enough, despite the language of "prius" and "postea," things are in God's mind eternally and immutably, but in themselves they are mutable (I.24.3, ad 2). I return to Aquinas and the strategies of late medieval theologies of predestination in chapter 2, but I am not convinced that Aquinas's distinctions and grammar would have persuaded Rechelesnesse or Wille or their maker. But this is certainly the theological landscape within which Langland's explorations are moving. As I shall outline in the next chapter, this field was an immensely complex one by the time Langland was writing. As such, it was certainly not one in which Aquinas or any other theologian could be offered as a key to orthodox theology of the period.

Reflecting on those names written or deleted in the book of life, Rechelesnesse puts forward Aristotle and Solomon as case studies. He has heard that they are reprobates. Yet he also knows they have been of great benefit to humankind. Indeed, Solomon received abundant grace from God and ruled wisely. He also wrote the Book of Wisdom, a book accepted as "holy writ" in the medieval church. Querulously, Rechelesnesse asks, "Aristotel and he, ho [who] tauhte me [men] bettere?" (XI.214). He observes that contemporary theologians who teach about God's mercy witness that the "wordes" and "werkes" of Solomon and Aristotle were "wonder goed and wisest" (XI.216–17). And yet he has heard that the church considers them both damned: "holi churche, as Y here, haldeth both in helle" (XI.215–18). Does Rechelesnesse hear correctly? The answer to this question is not simple. Medieval tradition does not speak with one voice on the final places of non-Christians. Yet Rechelesnesse has got the gist of one dominant strand of the tradition, and, as Pearsall notes, "Langland introduces here the question of the salvation of the righteous unbaptized which remains a preoccupation throughout the rest of the poem."[38] He does indeed, but I shall continue to focus on the topic with which Rechelesnesse set forth: the doctrine of election. Although issues about the salvation of unbaptized people can overlap with questions of election, they are theologically distinct. Certainly Rechelesnesse himself is not pursuing contemporary debates about what people can and cannot do through natural powers (*ex puris naturalibus*). Rather, he concludes that because people as graced and good as Solomon and Aristotle were damned, we would be unwise to imitate their labors and virtues since these ended in catastrophe (XI.218–21). In Rechelesnesse's model of predestination and reprobation, moral virtues as well as intellectual virtues are irrelevant to salvation. Wille is thus given theological and psychological support to continue in his abandonment of Dowel. Somewhat condescendingly, Rechelesnesse tells Clergie and Scripture that he does not impugn their version of Dowel but insists this is nothing in comparison to a tiny portion of God's grace (XI.222–25). He seems to have reached a fideistic predestinationism that sets aside the virtues in the pursuit of salvation. His answer to Wille's earlier question, "How Y may save my soule" (I.80), seems to be continue as you are doing in "the lond of longyng," abandoned to the hidden God, and in despair.

Rechelesnesse has more to say. He unfolds confusions that his discourse conceals from his own perception. We will find that in such confusions and obfuscations he was not alone among the theologians of predestination and reprobation, in the medieval church (chapter 2) and in the Reformation (chapter 3). He has assumed some version of double predestination and has assimilated to this the rumors he has heard about God's utterly arbitrary treatment of Aristotle and Solomon. To these he now adds further examples of what strikes him as incoherent divine decrees, decrees that open yet wider the gate to moral anarchy. He begins this sequence by invoking the thief who acknowledged and confessed Jesus Christ while being crucified. Rechelesnesse is perturbed that this man entered "perpetuel blisse" before Adam, Isaiah, the prophets, or "Seynt John the Baptiste." Rechelesnesse seems outraged at this divine acceptance of a "robbere" whom he claims was saved without penance or passion or pain (XI.252–60). Rechelesnesse's obsession with the moral anarchy God's hidden decrees unleash occludes from himself the distorting effects of his own moralism in his odd claims about the converted thief dying without penance and suffering.[39] It also occludes from himself his own participation in Wille's abandonment of the virtues. Next, he takes critical note of the salvation of Mary Magdalene (allegedly as sunk as Wille "in likyng of lecherye [in delight of lechery]"), of David (a murderer and adulterer), and of Paul (here remembered only as a pitiless persecutor of Christians [1 Cor. 15:9; Phil. 3:6; Gal. 1:13; 1 Tim. 1:13; Acts 8:1–3]). All these mortal sinners are now, according to the church, saints in heaven (XI.261–69). Rechelesnesse seeks to elaborate the grounds for associating the church's teaching on predestination and reprobation with an anarchy that can only exacerbate Wille's despair.

Yet he seems to have qualified his model of double predestination without reflecting on this qualification or its possible consequences.

He follows orthodox teaching in noting that the reprobate are denied the grace of salvation and deleted from the book of life, a book composed long before the birth of its human subjects. But he also says that the reprobate are deleted and damned "for som wikkednesse" (XI.203–4, 207). He implies that God foresees individual vice and punishes the sinful by withholding the grace that would save them from finally falling into endless hell. This model is quite commonplace in the medieval church (as we shall see in the next chapter). But it does not mitigate Rechelesnesse's anger and despair at God's apparent arbitrariness: one adulterous murderer joins the saints in heaven; another joins those being tortured in the hell we can see represented in Autun Cathedral as vividly as in Dante's *Inferno*. The speaker's reactions are perfectly understandable, but the objection he now raises does not depend on double predestination. In fact, it could incline toward subordinating God's eternal will to the contingencies of human will. That is certainly how a proponent of double predestination, whether Gregory of Rimini in the fourteenth century or Calvin in the sixteenth century, would judge Rechelesnesse's assumptions here.

Had Rechelesnesse chosen to read scripture more carefully, he could have found other accounts of Solomon that might have strengthened the position he seems to be sliding toward. He could have found in the book of Kings that Solomon rejected the divine covenant, "loved many strange women," and decided "to follow strange gods" (3 Kings 11:1–4). This is the kind of story that Conscience knew in his earlier account of Solomon in *Piers Plowman* (III.315–32). Conscience, like Rechelesnesse, is convinced that Solomon resides "in helle" (III.328). But he does so not at all because of any hidden decree or because of God's anarchic will. On the contrary, Conscience maintains that God gave Solomon grace, wealth, and wisdom. But he gave it, as all God's gifts are given, conditionally. When Solomon rejects the covenant with God, God withdraws his spiritual gifts, leaving him to live in his apostasy. In a thoroughly Miltonic declaration, Conscience insists that "god gyveth nothyng that *si* ne is the glosse"—that is, God gives nothing that is not *conditional*, nothing that is not covenantal (III.324–32; cf. *Paradise Lost* III.185–202). Grace abounds, but it does not coerce human choices. On the contrary, God's gifts enable the human cooperation he demands in service of ends that belong to human fulfillment. Hence Conscience's formulation, "god gyveth nothyng that *si* ne is the glosse." This is elaborated by Piers the Plowman when he teaches penitent people the way to Truth in Passus VII (205–91). Even when grace leads someone to a consoling vision of Truth in the individual's own heart, the graced person may still be overwhelmed by vices that lead to a reenactment of the first fall (VII.248–69). Addressing those who, like Wille, worry about their eternal destiny, about God's final will for them, Augustine asks, "Are you certain about your own will for yourself?"[40] Like most of us, fallen into "the lond of longyng," deifying Fortune in hedonistic despair, Wille could hardly answer this searching question in the affirmative. The most he can do at this point is confess that he has stumbled into discourses of predestination and reprobation, to confess that he has found in them the terrors of an arbitrary God for whom "love" could not be the name. But speaking through Rechelesnesse, he cannot do this. He has forgotten Conscience's teaching on the Trinity and the divine covenant in Passus III. As for Aristotle, the pagans, and Rechelesnesse's version of God, Langland will not leave the last word with Rechelesnesse—or with double predestination.[41]

Although Rechelesnesse has not yet finished feeding husks to Wille in "the lond of longyng," I now move my discussion to the return of the discourse of election in Passus XII. The seeds sown by Rechelesnesse have yielded bitter fruit to Wille, and these are now mediated in his encounter with the returned Scripture. She seems to be preaching the gospel. Her text is Christ's parable in which the heavenly kingdom is figured as a king who made a marriage feast for his son, the gospel reading for the twentieth Sunday after Trinity in the church's liturgy (Matt. 22:1–14; Passus XII.41–49). Wille relates that the text and sermon he has heard would make the unlearned ("lewed") have less love for the Christian faith taught by the educated ("lettered men"). This is a surprising comment. How could the gospel of Jesus Christ consolidate divisions between the learned and the unlearned Christian? How could attention to Christ's parable make unlearned people have less affection for doctrine they are taught in the Catholic Church? Is this some kind of dissident polemic? Let us see if Langland's dramatization of the exchange between Scripture and Wille answers any of these questions.

Wille claims that he has paid careful attention to Scripture and her sermon (XII.45). Perhaps he did. But Simone Weil and Iris Murdoch have shown with great force how attention is an act of disciplined love. It is, writes Murdoch, "a just and loving gaze directed upon an individual reality."[42] She sees this as "the characteristic and proper mark of the active moral agent." Indeed, "will continually influences belief, for better or worse, and is ideally able to influence it through a sustained attention to reality."[43] Can Wille attend justly to Scripture? Can he give enough attention (which is an act of love) to overcome the unexamined projections of voracious desires and fears? Has the subject Langland discloses in the wrathful, lustful, despairing Wille become able to give "ful good hede" (XII.45)? Langland is exploring this question.

To follow his explorations, it will help to reveal the particularities of Christ's parable as it is given in Matthew's gospel (Matt. 22:1–14). Langland's writing demands that we pay attention to exactly what the figures in the episode do with this text. We should respond carefully to their acts of interpretation. But before we do this, it is worth recollecting a few of the parable's features that may have escaped Wille's attention. First of all, the parable begins with an invitation to a festival, a wedding feast that has been prepared. Second, those called freely reject the invitation. The king responds to this rejection with patience and benevolence: he sends more servants with invitations and the news that dinner is prepared. But people continue to reject the invitation. They prefer other activities. Some of them are so offended by the king's persistent invitations that they abuse and murder his servants. In response, the king punishes the murderers: he kills them and destroys their city (cf. Matt. 21:33–41). He then sends more servants with more and more invitations calling both good and bad until the feast is well attended. Once more, the parable emphasizes that the call of the kingdom is to *all*, just as Jesus had told his disciples that God "makes his sun to rise upon the good, and bad, and raineth upon the just and the unjust" (Matt. 6:45). But there is another turn in the narrative. The lord of the feast finds one guest who is not wearing "a wedding garment." Asked why not, the guest is silent. In response, the king has him cast out from the feast to a place of misery. After all this comes what Karl Barth describes as "an independent saying": "Many are called, but few are chosen [Multi enim sunt vocati, pauci vero electi]" (Matt. 22:14).[44] Jesus's parable develops a version of God in which humans who hold God in contempt are met by God's inclusive generosity. Before commenting on what Wille and his vision of scripture make of the parable, it is worth remembering conventional medieval interpretations of the narrative. This, after all, is a major context for Langland's own reading of the text.

Medieval exegetes love the polysemy of scripture just as the God they worshipped loved allegorical modes in words and events. Commentaries on the parables are as replete with allegory as those on the historical narratives of the Old Testament, so I will only give here a brief summary of conventional readings. There is a tendency to organize details of the parable around an understanding of the wedding as the union of Christ and the church in the mystery of the Incarnation, or as a figure for the marriage of Christ and the human soul, or, anagogically, as a figure of eternal beatitude. The details of the parable tend to figure forth various moments in the history of salvation: the king's invitations represent different forms of divine calling from the time of Abraham to the time of the church's preachers culminating in the Last Judgment. Some exegetes read the rejection of the first invitations as a figure of Israel rejecting God's covenant, understanding later invitations as the calling of the Gentiles. As for the wedding garment, that is charity, or mercy and kindness, or the grace of the Holy Spirit, or the works of the new man done under the law and the gospel. What about the invited and present man not wearing the wedding garment? He is the figure of someone imbued with faith but lacking in charity, the virtue that is the fulfillment of all other virtues, and the one whose absence hollows out all other virtues (1 Cor. 13).[45] And what did exegetes make of the apparently independent comment that echoes an earlier statement in Matthew's gospel, "Many are called, but few are chosen" (Matt. 22:14, echoing Matt. 20:16)? In his *Catena Aurea*, Aquinas provides readings of this statement that stress that *all* are called in God's courtesy. Some, however, refuse the call while others continue in the way of discipleship; these are the "few" people who are chosen. There is in Aquinas simply no assimilation of the many called and few chosen to theories of predestination and reprobation. Nor is there any such gloss in Nicholas of Lyra's commentaries (literal and moral), nor in Nicholas of Gorran's, nor in Denis the Carthusian's.[46] So much then for the text of Jesus's parable and conventional medieval exegesis.

It is in light of this culture of discourse that we should consider Wille's response to the parable. He claims both that he has been trained to read "holy writ" when he was in "scole" (V.35–37) and that he now paid "ful good hede" to Scripture as the latter directed him to Christ's parable (XII.45). But in fact, Wille pulverizes the text and ascribes the pulverization to Scripture. This is a wry Langlandian joke. What grips Wille in Matthew 22:1–14 is the return of the word *multi* (many) and its contrast with *pauci* (few). We need to remember here Scripture's devastating challenge to Wille in Passus XI. This aligned him with *multi* who knew *multa* (many things) but lacked any self-knowledge (XI.10–163). Now Wille hears these terms echoed in the closing comment attached to the narrative: "Multi enim sunt vocati, pauci vero electi [For many are called, but few are chosen]" (Matt. 22:14). Having been recently dismissed as among the erring *multi* and having reacted in a way that confirmed this harsh judgment, Wille now encounters what he sees as an evangelical distinction between the few elect (*pauci electi*) and the many called (*multi vocati*) but not chosen, not elect. Furthermore, his reading or hearing Scripture's teaching has left him with a vivid sense that many who were called but not chosen actually obeyed the divine call and came to the marriage feast only to be arbitrarily and cruelly excluded. Only a few, he tells us, were secretly taken into the banquet, while all the rest, the many, were shut outside the gate and left to wander off.

"*Multi* to a mangerye and to the mete were sompned
And whan the peple was plenere ycome the porter unpynnede
　　the gate
And plihte in *pauci* priueiliche and lette the remenaunt go rome."
(XII.47–49)

———

["*Multi* to a marriage feast were summoned to table
And when the people were all together the porter opened the gate
And let in *pauci* privily and let the rest go roam."]

How is the prodigal from "the lond of longyng," one already marked as among the "many," to receive this memory of Jesus's gospel? What good news, what consoling version of redemption, could he or any reader find here? None.

But then Wille has not been able to give Jesus's narrative the kind of attention Iris Murdoch sees as an act of virtue and love. Had he been able to read the whole parable attentively, he would have found evidence of human contempt and violent resistance to a generous and patient divine calling. Perhaps he could also have drawn on his education in "scole" to read some of the many available commentaries on the text. As I have just shown, there, too, he would have found an emphasis on divine generosity being met by widespread human contempt. Rereading texts and commentaries, he would notice that he, or someone, has not only pulverized Jesus's parable but has also added to it—in fact, rewritten it. For in Christ's parable, it is made explicit that *all* the invited who come, "bad and good," are welcomed into the banquet. There is simply nothing like the porter we meet in Wille's redaction. The porter, in the passage I have just quoted, unlocks the lord's gate and secretly pulls in a few while excluding the many. In contrast, among the many universally called and admitted guests in Christ's parable, only one is not wearing a wedding garment. The king asks why not. Receiving no reply, the king orders his servants to bind the silent man and cast him into outer darkness where "there shall be weeping and gnashing of teeth" (Matt. 22:11–13). Just as Conscience maintained in Passus III, God's gifts are not unconditional: "So god gyveth nothyng that *si* ne is the glose" (III.329). That is, the model for the relations between God and humanity is covenantal. But that has no entailments for any theology of predestination and reprobation. Had Wille followed traditional exegesis, he would not have stumbled into this field of theology and its disputes. Certainly he would not have received encouragement to agonize over personal reprobation.

James Simpson argues that the discourse on predestination ascribed to Wille in the B version of the poem but shared between Rechelesnesse and Wille in the C version takes up an "Augustinian position."[47] He conflates this with his understanding of Bradwardine's "neo-Augustinian predestinarian position." Perhaps so. But let us consider an example of the way in which Augustine reads the text that grips Wille and seems to have encouraged him to transform Christ's gospel to reflect his own despair. Preaching on Psalm 61 (Vulgate) to the people in Carthage around the year 416, Augustine recalls the text that vexes Wille. He introduces it with this comment: "I find it disturbing [*movet me*], and I think you will too."[48] He summarizes the parable justly and without

Wille's extraordinary addition of the porter. He then comments that the one man who was ejected from the feast for not being appropriately clothed is representative of many, quoting the line that troubles Wille: "For many are invited, but only a few are chosen" (Matt. 22:14). He asks, "What does this mean?" and "Who are the chosen ones?" His answer is given in the Christological terms so characteristic of Augustine's preaching on the Psalms. Those who are finally not chosen, symbolized by the man not wearing the wedding garment, are those who value worldly happiness above God and their own ends rather than the gifts given by Jesus Christ. They may be attending the church, but their real loves "belong to that city whose mystical name is Babylon, the city that has the devil as its king." His congregation would have been familiar with this reference to the city of "abominations" from whence Christians are ordered to go out, a city under catastrophic judgment (Apoc. 17:4–6; 18:1–19). In contrast, those who are chosen "ponder the realities of heaven," try to practice Christian virtues (including penitence and humility), and "belong to the one city whose king is Christ." One city began with Cain, the other with Abel. Opposed to each other, they are united throughout history. Only at the end of time will they be separated. Augustine's preaching, like most medieval commentaries, invites its listeners to consider the grand narratives of salvation history, just as *Piers Plowman* will do (XVIII–XXII). But despite the language of the many and the few, the preacher does not seek to catalyze anxieties about predestination and reprobation. Nothing Augustine says could encourage a response such as Wille's agonized "Wher [Whether] Y were chose or nat chose" (XII.50–51). On the contrary, Augustine guides his congregation to see how the sources of disturbance in the parable can be met by a life pursuing the virtues in a community itself devoted to Christ. Christ, as Augustine writes in the *City of God*, is both the end and the way: as God he is the goal, as man he is the way.[49]

Later in this book we will indeed meet a striking contrast to Augustine's preaching. This will be in the guise of a very popular Calvinist work, Arthur Dent's *The Plaine Man's Path-way to Heaven* (1601). In that author's model of conversion, there is certainly a cultivation of terror around the doctrine of election. It seems to me significantly different from the preaching of Augustine and even from his garrulous works against assorted Pelagians. But it has some odd affinities with Wille's anxieties, his version of scripture, and the approach of Rechelesnesse in what, to Langland, was a state of despair, close to wanhope (XI.196–201). Writing putative genealogies across centuries of historical change and cultural transformations can be an illuminating and essential contribution to our self-knowledge, but it can also encourage arbitrary connections based on a complete evasion of textual and historical specificity.[50] At this point, I am not yet sketching a story that goes across the divides between medieval and Reformation Christianity, but I do wonder what forces in medieval culture are being addressed in this episode, and I wonder what the sources of the anxiety displayed by Wille and Rechelesnesse might have been. As I have shown from other medieval responses to the parable that so worried Wille, such trouble does not seem to have been as common as it would become in Calvinist England.

Langland has grounded Wille's panic in a brilliantly conceived dramatic process that is cultural and ecclesiological, social and theological. Through this process, we see how the doctrine of election, at least as Wille experiences it, abstracts divine election from the revelation of God in Christ. Early in the poem, Holy Churche tells Wille that God is love (*Deus caritas*) and that our understanding of love has to come from contemplating the Incarnation and ministry of Christ (I.82–89, 137–40; 1 John 4:2–21). But after Wille's dismissal by Scripture and Clergie, his loss and panic bring him to a doctrine of election that has sidelined Christology. We have followed exegetes discussing the parable of the banquet and found that they gave no encouragement for this theological position, but were there other strands in late medieval Christianity that might do so? Pamela Gradon and James Simpson may be right in remarking that predestination had become a "favourite" or "central topic" in the fourteenth century, and Nicolette Zeeman may be right in asserting that thinking on predestination had long been recognized as "a problem to which those committed to lives of spirituality or learning were particularly prone."[51] In chapter 2 I join this inquiry, attending to a strand of medieval discourses these scholars have not addressed in this context. But even if scholars' claims about the centrality of the topic of predestination are warranted, there remains something peculiar about Wille's responses to Christ's parable. For I do not find representations of such an acute, distressed, and personal response to be commonplace in late medieval writing, and I wish to stay with this reflection for a moment.

Many readers may immediately invoke contemporary work by Chaucer to brush aside the reservations I have just made.[52] After all, in the *Nun's Priest's Tale* there is a much-quoted reference to Thomas Bradwardine concerning the proposition that what "God forwoot [foreknows] moot nedes bee," and Bradwardine is habitually associated with Augustine's teaching on predestination.[53] But Chaucer's invocation of God's foreknowledge, and (through the Nun's Priest) of Augustine, Boethius, and Bradwardine, belongs to a very different register from that in which Langland presents the episode of Wille and Rechelesnesse in *Piers Plowman*. It comes in a gamesome passage around the forthcoming entrapment of Chauntecleer, the cock, by a "col-fox, ful of sly iniquitee," an entrapment prefigured in the cock's dream and then turned into a provocation for extensive hermeneutic debates between the cock and his sibling paramour, Pertelote (VII.2867–3266). The Nun's Priest, telling the fable, speculates that the dream could disclose what God foreknows. In that case, God's eternal foreknowledge seems to determine the cock's future entrapment. This would make forewarning by dreams a warning without any purpose other than terrorizing the dreamer, since the dreamer's knowledge will have no effect on foreknown and foreordained events (VII.3232–35). Observing that "in scole is greet [great] altercacioun / In this matere, and greet disputisoun," the priest acknowledges his limits. He confesses he lacks the discernment of Augustine, Boethius, or Bradwardine on the relations between divine foreknowledge, future contingents, and human freedom.[54] Still, he does know enough to make the conventional distinction between different senses of the term "necessary" before claiming to set aside these metaphysical matters: "I wol nat han do of swich mateere; / My tale is of a cok, as ye may here" (VII.3245–55). Of course, this tale "of a cok" is so densely allusive to so many medieval discourses and texts that it has been able to keep hosts of erudite interpreters busily at work on Chaucer for decades.

But the Christian doctrine of election and its treatment of reprobation is not foregrounded by Chaucer. Nor is there any existential anxiety surrounding "the opinioun of certein clerkis." Nor is there any interest in tracking recent theologizing that might offer thoroughly disturbing versions of double predestination such as that produced by Gregory of Rimini in the early 1340s. The literary and affective modes of the *Nun's Priest's Tale* are far removed from Wille's responses to Christ's parable in Passus XII of *Piers Plowman* or Rechelesnesse's conversation with the prodigal Wille in "the lond of longyng." If Chaucer's writing about these metaphysical issues has any analogies, they may be found "in scole" in the kind of debates explored by Hester Gelber in *It Could Have Been Otherwise.*[55]

The other Chaucerian passage likely to be invoked in the present context is one from the fourth book of his wonderful "tragedye" *Troilus and Criseyde.*[56] In this work, Chaucer gives Troilus extended ruminations on the relations between "fre chois" and divine providence (IV.953–1085). Here, the Trojan prince is philosophizing in "dispite" (IV.954), and James Simpson has drawn parallels between this and Wille's despairing theology.[57] This is certainly an intriguing comparison. But the Trojan knight is in despair at a parliamentary decision to trade his lover, Criseyde, for men captured by the Greek enemy (IV.953–59). Chaucer's hostile representation of parliament and the complete lack of ethical principles among the self-destructive "peple" is an extremely sharp satire against an institution with which he has firsthand experience.[58] The morally corrupt "noyse of peple," as irrational as blazing fire in straw, opposes Hector's insistence that Trojans do not sell women, that is, do not treat women as commodities. The result of the people's voice is that Criseyde is traded for Antenor, the future traitor "that brought hem to meschaunce"— the destruction of Troy (IV.195–210). The "meschaunce" here is thus identified as the consequence of particular political processes directed by the people's supposedly pragmatic decisions devoid of all ethical obligations and any loyalty to their neighbor, Criseyde. In the face of this choice, to which the king of Troy assents, Troilus is politically helpless. His own polity has deprived him of the person through whom he discovered that love which binds together couples in virtue as it binds the cosmos, a love that is erotic and metaphysical (III.1744–71; III.1128–1441). As Troilus confronts his catastrophic loss and helplessness at the hands of Troy's political forces, he projects his hopeless deprivation into a vision of the world that completely displaces his recent Neoplatonic hymn to love that governs all being. Now he generates a picture of humanity in the grip of a "divine purveyance" and "predestyne" totally indifferent to human flourishing. According to Troilus, this predestination leaves us with "no fre chois."

Chaucer has the mourning Trojan recapitulate arguments made by the condemned prisoner in Boethius's *Consolation of Philosophy*, a figure of Boethius who is himself about to be killed by a tyrannical ruler (*Consolation* V.pr. 2 and 3; cf. *Troilus and Criseyde* IV.953–1085). For Boethius, the prisoner's arguments are poor ones, based in philosophic amnesia caused by his unjust punishment and loss of all worldly comfort. He has Philosophy herself respond to these arguments and correct him. Whether Chaucer himself found Philosophy's arguments persuasive, we do not know. We do know, however, that the solutions Boethius offers in the final book of his *Consolation* were part of a thirteenth-century Christian consensus on the relations between time and eternity, human freedom and divine providence. And we do know that Chaucer thought well enough of the *Consolation of Philosophy* to translate the complete text around the time he was writing *Troilus and Criseyde*. He ends Troilus's Boethian soliloquy before he reaches Philosophy's responses (*Troilus and Criseyde* IV.1000–1085). Troilus explicitly worships the goddess Fortune "above the goddes alle." He continues to hope for saving "grace" from Fortune, although he now suspects the goddess of "foule envye" at his joy with Criseyde. He wonders why Fortune, whom he has "honoured" all his life, should be so "cruwel and unkynde" to her worshipper. Why, he asks, did she not rather kill his father, the king of Troy, or his brothers, or himself, than deprive him of Criseyde (IV.260–87)?

What is it to worship Fortune? It is to worship chance (*fortuita*). Fortune is a projection by those who imagine the world emerges by mere chance, who have no knowledge of God the Creator, God the Redeemer, and God the lord of time, the God who raised Jesus Christ from the dead. So Chaucer consistently reminds us that even if Troilus draws toward Neoplatonic metaphysics in his joy (Book III), he philosophizes as a non-Christian worshipper of Fortune and Venus. But if we wish to link the ruminations of Wille and Rechelesnesse in "the lond of longyng" with Troilus and his philosophical soliloquy, then it seems that the common ground is the worship of Fortune. This veneration joins the despairing pagan lover and the despairing Christian. Langland is acutely aware of the potential for Christians, individually and collectively, to de-Christianize, to become secularized.[59] Like Troilus, Wille is ravished by Fortune "into the lond of longyng" and enthralled by *"Concupiscentia carnis"* (XI.167, 171–80). But Wille's submission to Fortune demands that he forget, yet once more, that he was baptized into the body of Christ (I.72–78). True enough, he follows Fortune into a far country, and like Troilus, as Simpson observes, he despairs. But although Wille forgets the God whom he has abandoned, God remains faithful and cannot deny himself (2 Tim. 2:13). Soon the figure of Reason will put a question to the penitent Wille—who is more patient than God? (XIII.197–99)—and we will see how Wille's agonized panic about predestination and reprobation will gradually be dissolved through a process that reveals the misconceptions behind his theologizing.

Chaucer's Troilus, however, inhabits a culture with no recourse to such resources. The gods he worships belong to a civic religion memorably analyzed by Augustine in the *City of God* (especially Books I–X). His city is about to be destroyed, and he himself is finally rejected by Criseyde, who is traded to the Greeks, and imprisoned in the Greek army's camp (*Troilus and Criseyde* IV–V).[60] He ceases to philosophize about Fortune, predestination, and free will. These were not, after all, the sources of his despair but rather a rationalizing projection born from overwhelming grief at the exchange of his lover for Antenor. Even as he faces the evidence of Criseyde's union with the Greek Diomede, he cannot find any inclination to "unloven" her even "for a quarter of a day" (V.1646–1701). Having lost what he experienced as the source and goal of life, he is totally subject to Fortune, who begins to "pulle awey the fetheres breighte of Troie" (V.1541–54). The only resources available in such despair seem to be either stoic endurance (V.1748–50) or the enraged pursuit of death in battle (V.1751–64 and V.1800–1806). For Chaucer, this story is a "tragedye" (V.1786).[61] The multiple endings of the poem focus remorselessly on the way pagans worship gods who are "rascaille," part of "payens [pagans] corsed old rites" that draw people away from their true joy and fulfillment in the triune God (V.1849–53). The latter created them and loves them, as revealed in the crucifixion of

Christ. Along with the Blessed Virgin Mary, the Trinity receives the poem's final stanza, a prayer.

> Thow oon, and two, and thre, eterne on lyve,
> That regnest ay in thre, and two, and oon,
> Uncircumscript, and al maist circumscrive,
> Us from visible and invisible foon
> Defende, and to thy mercy, everichon,
> So make us, Jesus, for thi mercy, digne,
> For love of mayde and moder thyn benigne.
> (V.1863–69)

This ending *places*, with great force, the eclectic forms of philosophizing we find in Troy and diffused among Troilus, Criseyde, and Pandarus, within a context of Christian theology. It also helps readers remember how Troilus's own philosophy shifts from exuberant Neoplatonism to incoherent fatalism to suicidal despair. We are shown how such philosophizing seems to be the unstable projection of contingent passions, utterly subjective and totally anthropocentric. But Chaucer finally emphasizes that all these shifts assume a humanity without a Creator or a Redeemer, without the one person who died "right for love / Upon a crois," one who was both God (the goal) and human (the way).

Troilus *does* have access to natural law, which participates in the eternal law and divine life from which it derives. He seeks to live a life of virtue, albeit one uncritically shaped by Trojan culture. And St. Thomas himself was perfectly clear that a community can make bad laws and bad customs that become normalized. In such a situation, the "good" may become truly wicked, the "good" citizen a perpetrator of evil practices based in evil habits. Aquinas offers an example of this among Germanic tribes where robbery (*latrocinium*) was not considered wrong. A practice against the natural law had been normalized. Vicious customs and habits can become cultural norms, shaping the lives of all citizens. Aquinas thinks of a community of robbers and the constitution of a good robber.[62] He could also have mentioned a society organized around the worship of Moloch and the sacrifice of children. Or we could bring the examples even closer to home: Chaucer did so for his own culture,

as readers could readily see in *Troilus and Criseyde* figurations of their
own chivalric values, virtues, and customs, ones at home in both London (new Troy) and Troy. The poet chose to bring out the disastrous
consequences of these norms. Even the benevolent conversions experienced by both Troilus and Criseyde finally offer no sustainable inner
or outer resistance to the destructive norms of their community.[63]
Chaucer's Troilus is not represented in the same manner as Langland's
confidently assertive yet confused pagan who claims to have been in
hell, yet has been delivered because of his political (cardinal) virtues.[64]
Rather, Chaucer shows Troilus doing the best he can with his passions,
virtues, and vices in Troy, a city deep in the "lond of longyng." He continues to do so when he faces the imminent loss of Criseyde and tries to
theologize. But, of course, he can only draw on reason formed by the
habits of Trojan culture and unformed by Christian revelation. Compassion does not prevent Chaucer from writing an unambiguous final
judgment on the customs normalized in Troy (V.1835–55). In fact, Chaucer's final stanzas offer no hint that we should understand Troilus's
philosophy and his service of "the God of love" (I.206–31, 400–469,
908–38) as a shadowy anticipation of truth revealed as *"Deus caritas."*
The most compassionate response to the materials Chaucer has explored, he tells us, is giving us his "tragedye."

❖ ❖ ❖

How does Langland resolve Wille's very different and distinctly Christian troubles around the doctrine of predestination and reprobation?
How does despair avoid becoming "tragedye"? Langland decides that
the way to deliver Christians from such troubles does not lie in tracking the reasonings of those Troilus invoked as "grete clerkes" (*Troilus
and Criseyde* IV.986). He could have done so by following Wille back
to "scole" so that he could continue his education. There he would have
found the apprentice theologians studying and lecturing on predestination and reprobation as they addressed the first book of their great
textbook, Peter Lombard's *Sentences.*[65] I visit some of this theology
and its modes in the next chapter, but Langland decides that this theologizing would not free Wille from his troubles. This decision manifests

Langland's profound ambivalence to the contemporary theology in which he participates. He suspects that returning to "scole" would mean immersion in the very sources of Wille's transformation of the gospel into a terrifying question overseen by a secretive and arbitrary porter to the kingdom.

Instead of "scole," Langland directs Wille to the sacrament of baptism. Wille suddenly recalls that Holy Churche had accepted him at the baptismal font (XII.52–53). This is a memory of what Holy Churche herself reminded him of many passus earlier.

> "Holy Churche Y am," quod she, "thou oughtest me to knowe;
> Y undirfenge the formeste and fre man the made.
> Thow broughtest me borewes my biddyng to fulfille"
>
> (I.72–74)

———

> ["I am Holy Church," she said, "you ought to know me;
> I received you at first and made you free.
> Godparents pledged you to fulfill my bidding"]

In allowing so many passus to lapse, with so much suffering, Langland shows us how much of the life of Christians is a forgetting of crucial gifts and teaching. As we have just seen in Wille's fall into "the lond of longyng" under the delusion of Fortune, such forgetting tends toward disaster in both the life of the community and the individual life. But in what seems incorrigible amnesia, Wille, baptized and accepted into the body of Christ, is not abandoned even though he himself has no awareness of this. Such amnesia strangely combined with the secret workings of grace is a recognizable strand of Christian tradition. For example, Augustine's complex paths to his own conversion could only be recognized retrospectively, only through conversion.

It is worth recalling here a characteristic example from Augustine's *Confessions* (V.13.23). He remembers visiting Ambrose's cathedral to hear the bishop preach. He vividly recollects his motives and intention. At that time, he was a teacher of rhetoric and had heard of Ambrose's eloquence. He was despairing of the Catholic Church and held its doctrines in contempt, so he only went to Ambrose's sermons to see if

their eloquence matched their fame. He found they did. But concerning the preacher's teaching, he remained uninterested and disdainful
(*incuriosus et contemptor*). So he remained in the far country, for salvation is far off (*longe*) from sinners. He was indeed "in the lond of longyng." But writing retrospectively, after his baptism and calling to the
priesthood, he is able to see what he could not discern before, namely,
that despite the motives he thought he knew—love of rhetoric and disdain of the church—he was actually being led by God, not coerced, to
Ambrose's preaching. Though at the time he knew nothing, *"nesciens,"*
of this, he now understands that he was being led so that through the
bishop he would be drawn to God, knowing: "ad eum autem ducebar
abs te *nesciens*, ut per eum ad te *sciens* ducerer" (I was led to him by
you, unaware that through him, in full awareness, I might be led to
you) (V.13.23; my emphasis). He returns to the play of *nesciens/sciens*
in the last sentence of the paragraph: although he remained in the far
country and although he did not know it (*nesciens*), he was nonetheless
drawing near. He emphasizes that he was not even remotely concerned
to learn what Ambrose was saying, since he despaired that there was
any way from the far country to God. Despite this despair, despite his
formalist frivolity, the words he heard and loved brought with them
the Christian teaching he had disdained. He found he could not pull
apart rhetorical form and doctrine in Ambrose's preaching. Despite his
intentions, as he attended to the language Ambrose spoke so skillfully,
the Christian truth Ambrose was speaking gradually entered Augustine's mind. Little by little, Christian teaching and scripture started to
seem credible, especially as he learned how to read the Old Testament
allegorically. Where literal exegesis had formerly killed meaning, spiritual exegesis was bringing new life (V.14.24; 2 Cor. 3:6). Yet, despite the
way grace was drawing him, he continued to set aside Christian faith.
He was, after all, neither the lord of time nor lord of the processes of
his vocation.

Neither is Langland's Wille in control of his vocation. Wille is led
to find in his memory a very different version of God. Instead of the
terrifying abstraction who makes secret decisions about eternal exclusion (*many*) and inclusion (*few*), Wille recalls Christ calling not only a
few or even *many*, but *all.*

For Crist clepede us alle, come yf we wolde,
Sarrasynes and sismatikes, and so a ded the Iewes,
And bad hem souke for synne saue at his breste
And drynke bote for bale, brouke hit ho-so myhte:
O vos omnes sicientes, venite ad aquas.

(XII.54–57a)

———

[For Christ called us all, come if we would,
Saracens and schismatics and the Jews as well,
And bade them suck for their sins salvation at his breast
And drink health for harm, enjoy it who may:
O all you that thirst, come to the waters.]

God's healing from the ravages of sin is offered by Christ calling us *all*. Editors usually gloss the Latin quotation here by citing Isaiah 55:1: "All you that thirst, come to the waters: and you that have no money make haste, buy and eat: come ye, buy wine and milk without money, and without any price." It is worth observing that this beautiful invitation glances critically at the commodification of the sacraments, interpretation of scripture, and education—commodifications with which Langland's poem has been so preoccupied. The passage is an invitation to *all*, one that will be explicitly fulfilled by Christ at the feast of the tabernacles: "On the last and great day of the festivity, Jesus stood and cried, saying: if any man thirst, let him come to me and drink" (John 7:37). Traditionally, commentators saw in Christ's call an emphasis on the invitation's freedom from coercion, and the drink as one given for an inner thirst. As Augustine remarked, "If we thirst let us come; and not by our feet, but by our affections; let us come, not by removing from our place, but by loving."[66] Here Wille is called away from the "lond of longyng" with its endlessly unfulfilling addictions. He is called through a grammar that reaffirms Conscience's emphasis (which I discussed earlier) that God's calling draws the called into a noncoercive relationship involving a double agency, human and divine. Invited humans respond to a divine call that enables their human response but leaves them free to refuse the call.

Langland's Wille is reassured by his recollection of the sacrament of baptism that he received in the church, the body of Christ from which all can "souke for synne save [healing ointment] at his brest." This image flows from baptism, the door to all the sacraments. He is reassured that Christ and his gifts call "us alle," and certainly "all cristene." While Wille's misreading of Christ's parable had thrown him into agonized disputation as to whether "Y wer chose or nat chose," his memory of Christ and the sacraments brings assurance that Christians should not be preoccupied with a hidden God or metaphysical speculation concerning that God. Instead, they should attend to the revelation given in Christ, the way (as man) and goal (as God). In Christ, in the church, and in receiving the sacramental gifts, Wille can be assured that "Crist cleped us alle," offering freedom from the bonds of sin. He can be assured that "alle" means that he, too, is included as "on of godes chosene."[67] Christ died for all. Christ calls all. In the next two chapters, I address some of the discomfort this "alle," this *omnes*, caused for many theologians as they read Paul's statement to Timothy: God "will have all humans to be saved, and to come to the knowledge of the truth [*omnes homines vult salvos fieri, et ad agnitionem veritatis venire*]" (1 Tim. 2:4). I will study some of the exegetical strategies adopted by those who teach that scripture's "all" does not actually mean "all" but, in fact, means very *few*. Perhaps Wille's terror at the doctrine of election should be related not only to his abandonment of moral virtues, his "wo and wrathe" (XI.164). Perhaps it should also be understood in relation to some of these mainstream teachings and exegesis, strands that culminate in denials that Christ died for all and denials that God had any will that all should be saved. In exploring the possibility of such relations, we will need to go across the great divide between medieval and Reformation Christianity.

But for the moment, I want to return to Wille's recovery from his crisis of faith, hope, and charity. Like any recovery from the kind of moral catastrophe Wille has experienced, this one will be a gradual process involving many lapses and many conversions. In this episode, however, Langland shows us how Wille's agony can be named theologically. He has turned Wille away from being mesmerized by an abstract doctrine of election catalyzed by Rechelesnesse's reckless polemic and by a deeply disturbing misrepresentation of one of Christ's parables. *Sola scriptura*, Langland can already see, is itself a dangerous abstraction when joined to a doctrine of predestination and reprobation floating free from the complex narratives of scripture and from daily obedience to the poem's final divine command: "Lerne to love" (XXII.208). If Langland has turned Wille away from the version of election he faces, to what is this exemplary turning directed? It is toward Jesus Christ and toward the church. Surprising as it may be, we will find in chapters 2 and 3 a perennial tendency in doctrines of predestination and reprobation to sideline and separate Christology and ecclesiology. Langland, however, displays a profoundly critical insight with analytic potential for his own culture and later. Furthermore, he ascribes this insight not to a theologian (whether mendicant, monastic, or secular), not to any of the tradition of "grete clerkes" invoked by Chaucer's Troilus or by the Nun's Priest in the *Canterbury Tales*, but to an educated layman of peculiarly indeterminate status, a true *laicus litteratus*.[68] I mention this in passing because it is intrinsic to the emerging forms and formlessnesses of the poem's ecclesiology.[69]

Despite his decisive shift away from captivity by the picture of election that has ensnared him, Wille still shows the marks of his imprisonment. He does so by displaying a kind of epistemophilia. He no longer trembles at a pulverized fragment of scripture, desperately disputing with himself about his final state (XII.50–52), but he does want certain and absolutely unconditional knowledge about this. Such epistemophilia will reside at the heart of Calvinism, as we shall see in chapter 3. But it was quite alien to medieval theology and pastoral care. Wille does not explicitly deny this medieval norm, but he seeks to set aside the fundamentally covenantal patterns of vocation in the narratives of scripture. As I have pointed out, these were clearly affirmed by Conscience in Passus III, and Conscience affirms them again to a hostile community in Passus XXI. Wille himself seemed to accept this in his initial turn to Holy Churche, Christ, and the sacraments when he acknowledged that Christ's vocation—Christ's calling of all people—is not coercive. It does not crush the will. It comes, as Conscience says all God's gifts do, with *if* (III.329): "Crist cleped [called] us alle, come *yf* we wolde" (XII.54; my emphasis). Wille seems to acknowledge that this *yf* leaves open the possibility that we might choose not to come. This possibility is exactly what Jesus anticipated in a part of his parable of the wedding feast that Wille ignored (Matt. 22:1–6). Perhaps even more worrying for Wille, his surrogate, Rechelesnesse, has recently urged him to continue pursuing the goods of Fortune while ignoring any thought of the end and ends of human life (XII.194–98). Recheles-nesse thus represents the possibility that humans, including Wille, could reject Christ's call.

To rule out this disturbing possibility, Wille invents a theological narrative that goes against the grain of what he has just acknowledged about vocation and the God-given freedom of will. It also goes against the grain of Conscience's teaching about the covenantal relations be-tween God and humanity. Wille's narrative imagines Christian subjects not as freed people but, in an analogy with contemporary bondmen, as villeins (XII.60–65). These people, in theory, could not change their sta-tus or sell their goods without the permission of the manorial lord. Even if villeins abandon their land and lord, wandering about as "recheles" wretches, Wille declares, they can never break the relationship with the lord. Wille applies his analogy to the inherited ties of baptism. If one is baptized, one knows for certain one's fixed status, as a medieval villein did. Thus, he asserts, Christians can be certain that they can never be cast away, never be unbound from the lord however rebellious their ac-tions. The very worst that can happen is that they will serve a limited time in their lord's prison (XII.80–92). Here Wille's epistemophilia brings back a version of election that once again sets aside not only Christology, church, and sacraments but also any distinctly Christian account of the virtues. He has ignored the implications of what he has just acknowledged about Christ's call ("come yf we wolde"), and he has also forgotten what he had seen when he looked at the pardon given to Piers the Plowman in Passus IX.

There he discerned a lucid statement written "in witnesse of Treuthe" (IX.286). This statement was two lines from the Athanasian Creed, one of the church's confessions of the faith: "*Et qui bona egerunt ibunt in vitam eternam; / Qui vero mala in ignem eternum* [And they who have done good shall go into life everlasting; and they who have done evil into everlasting fire]" (IX.287–88). These credal lines are "in witnesse of Treuthe" and are never simply cancelled. Famously, how-ever, Langland also presents them as "a pardoun" from Truth, provok-ing a substantial and discordant scholarly literature.[70] Suffice it to say here that the combination of this credal statement (abstracted from a

creed that concentrates on Trinitarian and Christological teaching) and
the context of "pardoun" only becomes finally intelligible through the
acts of Christ and the Holy Spirit in Passus XVIII–XXI. Nothing here
will support Wille's attempt to remove the final consequences of human
actions and human will.

But the poem also explicitly discredits his analogy of bondman and
feudal lord in ways that are theologically central. It does so after
Christ's harrowing of hell and the celebration of Easter Sunday. Conscience observes that people who are baptized become "fre men" and
"ientel [gentle] men with Iesu, for Iesu was yfolled [baptized]." He was
later crowned king on the cross and conqueror of death (XXI.37–43,
69–194). So Jesus Christ has freed humans from their status as bondmen,
as villeins. Elsewhere in the poem, we have heard that through Christ's
incarnation and crucifixion we have all become siblings. Through the
body of Christ, we have each become as "gentel men," as if new born
(XII.109–12).[71] Wille, in his analogy, is simply denying the liberation
of humanity in Christ's acts and new covenant.[72] However far it may
be from his awareness, this denial negates the purpose of Christ's work.
Why would Wille do this? Because he seeks to deny Christian liberty, to
escape what Aquinas calls the law of freedom (*lex libertatis*).[73] He wants
to avoid the version of predestination/reprobation that has terrified
him, but he also wants to avoid the demands of a life pursuing the virtues, the life he abandoned in despair. In its place, he wants certainty of
salvation, regardless of his moral life. But the poem he inhabits shows
that humans have to renounce epistemophilia, give up the obsession
with certainty and the kind of assurance Calvinists will, in later centuries, demand. Although Augustine may bear a substantial part of the
responsibility for composing the version of election that troubles Wille,
he does have some comments in *The Predestination of the Saints* that
provide a fruitful challenge to the forms of epistemophilia Langland
identifies: "'But,' someone says, 'I am uncertain about God's will for
me.' What then? Are you certain about your own will for yourself?"
Langland shows that Wille, like everyone else, can only answer, "No."[74]

Piers Plowman insists that when Christ "cleped us alle," he called
the whole human being to a life of continuous struggle, thinking, willing, working. It is a call to continuous reformation, to continuing
conversions. In this life, there is only one unforgivable sin, according to

Christ the Samaritan: that is "unkyndnesse," a sin that we are taught actually "quencheth" the Holy Spirit. We are promised that Christ will pronounce the judgment of Matthew 25 on "alle unkynde creatures": *"nescio vos"* (I do not know you) (Matt. 25:12). We are also reminded that Christ's parable of Dives and Lazarus (Luke 16:19–31) teaches us that the rich man was not damned for his justly earned wealth but because he failed in charitable work: "for his unkyndenesse / Of his mete and his mone [money] to men that hit nedede" (XIX.218–43). Unkindness, here manifest as negligence in the practices of charity, cuts us off from our God-given nature ("kynde") and our God-given freedom to Dowel.[75] When Christ took a scourge and drove out of the temple those selling oxen, sheep, and doves along with those exchanging money, Langland writes, he charged these people with being *unkind* (XXIII.152–60: see John 2:13–22). This judgment is powerfully shadowed in Langland's dramatization of the deadly sin known as Covetousness. Repentance calls him "an unkynde creature" who cannot be absolved until he has made restitution of the wealth he accumulated through the deadly sin of usury (V.294–307; V.196–349). And as we will see, the poet returns to this language in Christ's oration in hell (XX).

But before moving on, it seems worth noting that neither in the figure of Christ the Samaritan nor in Christ's speeches in Passus XVIII–XXI is there any mention of the doctrines of predestination and reprobation. Langland has shown how Wille's troubles with this teaching emerge from serious *errors* in practical reasoning and in the direction taken by the wayfarer as he falls into "the lond of longyng." We will find in chapter 3 that the kind of panic that grips Wille becomes a major component in the formation of Calvinist Christians. But in Langland's prophetic figuration of such anxiety, we are led to understand such terror as the product of a false picture, one that has occluded Christ's manifestation of divine love for all humans.

❖ ❖ ❖

Immediately after the episode I have been discussing, Langland has someone interrupt the dialogue between Wille and Scripture in Passus XII. Scripture has just quoted the discussion of God's mercy in Psalm 144. At this moment, a new figure breaks into the text to respond by dismissing *all* books—including, of course, the one personified in Scripture. He presents himself as a person exemplifying the salvation of virtuous pagans (XII.75–80). He claims to be Trajan, "a trewe knyht" who had died and been damned to hell as an unbaptized person. This claim introduces a speech replete with difficult questions that have elicited extensive and dissenting scholarship.[76] For present contexts, it will be enough to recall two topics in this intense but brief episode: first, what is known as "the salvation of the righteous heathen"; and second, what many scholars are convinced is evidence of Langland's "semi-Pelagianism" or even "Pelagianism." Regarding the first topic, Trajan's self-description challenges Rechelesnesse's assumptions that Aristotle must be in hell as an unbaptized person (see XI.214–18). In reference to the second topic, Derek Pearsall declares that "Langland comes close to Pelagianism," assuming that the poet validates a theological position that claims "salvific power" for the pagan's good works.[77] As with every other episode in *Piers Plowman*, this one must be read in its particularity *and* reintegrated in the dialectical totality to which it belongs. I elsewhere sought to do this at ample length in discussing the episode and its interpretations, so here I will merely summarize my reading in *Salvation and Sin*.[78]

Trajan may well have the experience of salvation he claims, but he has not yet discerned its grounds or meaning. His jaunty confidence, explicitly setting the *Golden Legend* over scripture, shows no signs of understanding the source of his salvation in Jesus Christ, whom he does not even acknowledge. He has no inkling of the fall or of the role of Israel in the processes of salvation. Nor does he even pause to wonder why such a paragon of virtue, as he claims to have been, was ever "dampned to dwellen in helle" (XII.76). Nor has he yet received any instruction on the Trinitarian nature of the God who has delivered him (contrast Passus XVIII–XIX). Furthermore, scholars such as Joe Wittig and Gordon Whatley have shown in fascinating detail how varied and contradictory were the accounts of Trajan in the Middle Ages. Even the *Golden Legend* provides a number of these conflicting versions but leaves them in their unresolved incoherence.[79] Langland has followed suit in this episode, leaving himself half his poem to provide searching, dialectical explorations of the issues Trajan's account raises. These explorations will show very clearly some of the central theological resources lacking from Trajan's speech and his understanding. These can be put in shorthand: Jesus Christ; his incarnation, crucifixion, resurrection, and ascension; the Holy Spirit; the sacraments; and the role of divine covenants and grace in the processes of salvation. Through the Trajan figure's energy and incoherence, new questions are generated that will draw Wille toward the crucial allegorical visions of the tree of Charity, the triune God, and salvation history.

At no point in these extraordinarily dense allegorical narratives and doctrinal expositions does the rejected picture of election return to haunt Wille or the reader. On the contrary, Langland's poetic theology is exuberantly Christocentric as it weaves together the past, present, and future with an account of the sacraments of baptism, eucharist, and penance in the divinely given ways of salvation. Wille is drawn to Charity by Liberum Arbitrium, the rational and voluntary power of the soul by which humans choose and judge freely.[80] In this process, Wille is shown some images of the three persons of the one God committed to sustaining and supporting humanity in its fruition (Passus XVIII). The allegorical vision of the fruit of charity elicits in Wille a longing to "savour [taste]." Unlike the self-destroying desire characteristic of "the lond of longyng," this longing is ordered toward charity and fulfillment of humanity. Also, unlike Adam and Eve, Wille's desire is a figure of the just and ecstatic will savoring its proper fruit. This is the desire figured in the Canticle of Canticles: "I sat down under his shadow, whom I desired: and his fruit was sweet to my palate" (2.3).[81] But as Wille laments during his visions of salvation history:

"Allas!" Y saide, "that synne so longe shal lette
The myhte of goddess mercy that myhte us alle amende!"
And wepte for his words.

(XVIII.286–88)

———

["Alas!" I said, "that sin shall hinder so long
The might of God's mercy that might amend us all!"
And wept for his words.]

Langland's most sublime visions of divine love and human capacity to receive this love always immerse us again in the history of human suffering, sin, and death. But in this reimmersion, as Wille confesses, God is *pro nobis*—he is *for* fallen humanity. He is never the hidden and persecutory adversary Wille had imagined in his vision of the malevolent porter and the wedding feast. God is never an abstract figure of absolute power.

In Passus XIX Langland dramatizes this in his refiguration of Jesus's parable of the Samaritan and *semyvief*, the half-dead man (Luke 10:29–37). Attacked by thieves in "a wide wildernesse," this man is stripped, bound, and beaten, unable to help himself. He is the figure of fallen humanity in *Piers Plowman* as he is in the exegetical tradition that Langland so inventively assimilates to his narrative.[82] In Langland's rendering of the parable, the Samaritan is the figure of Christ himself, the quintessence of charity. He is hastening to his crucifixion in Jerusalem, yet he has time and care for *semyvief*. He dismounts from his mule, tends to the man's wounds, sets him on his horse, and leads him to a farmhouse replete with allegorical images of the new covenant, the church, and the sacraments (XIX.48–78). *Semyvief* (*semivivus* [Luke 10:30]), half-dead in the wilderness, discloses the end of "the lond of longyng" into which Wille himself had wandered and where he was being bound and despoiled of his baptismal gifts. Different versions of fallen humanity converge in *semyvief*, now in the presence of this compassionate Samaritan. God has journeyed into the wilderness, into the far country, to take up fallen humanity. He has *chosen* both *semyvief* and Wille, neither said to represent either the "few" or the "many" but all of fallen humanity. Such is the electing God and his elected creatures. The Samaritan continues on his path to Jerusalem.

Langland treats the ministry of Christ in Passus XVIII (122–80) and his crucifixion in Passus XX (1–94). But it is in Christ's long, sinewy oration in the harrowing of hell that we are given what seems to be the consummating vision of election in Langland's work (XX.359–449). Here the God who creates, redeems, and elects speaks. He does so from the place of rejection, the place from which Trajan apparently "was broken out" (XII.75). He is joined in this place by Wille: "Y withdrow in that derkenesse to *descendit ad inferna* [I withdrew in that darkness to *he descended into hell*]" (XX.114). The grammar here is not "integrated," as Pearsall notes.[83] Yet this makes for a striking suggestion:

"Y," who is Wille, has been joined with the subject of "descendit" (he descended)—Jesus Christ. Langland is quoting from the Apostles' Creed: "I believe in God the Father Almighty, maker of heaven and earth: and in Jesus Christ his only Son our Lord. . . . He descended into hell; the third day he arose again from the dead." The line also evokes Wille's own agency: "Y withdrow."[84] This seems an extraordinary act of trust as Wille, like Christ, freely enters hell, the terrifying abyss at the heart of his earlier agonizing about his eternal destiny, "Wher [Whether] Y were chose or nat chose" (XII.50–51).

His choice to join Christ in hell now draws him to hear the only licit source of Christian teaching: God revealing God. Such a revelation, like that received by Julian of Norwich (May 1373, in Norwich) could well bring many medieval and Reformation theologies of predestination and reprobation under a searching judgment. Out of the overwhelming light of Christ in the darkness of hell, Wille hears Christ (XX.127, 269). At the heart of the ensuing oration, we gather the inseparability of the doctrine of reconciliation and the doctrine of election. The God Christians are called to worship manifests himself in Christ's thirst: "Y faught so me fursteth yut for mannes soule sake: / *Sicio*" (I fought so I thirst yet for the sake of human souls: / *I thirst*) (XX.408–408a). He refers to the version of the crucifixion Langland has just figured and quotes from the rendering of the crucifixion in John's gospel: "Afterwards, Jesus knowing that all things were now accomplished, that the scripture might be fulfilled [Ps. 68:22] said: I thirst [*Sicio*]." Langland goes on to show that Jesus speaks both literally and figuratively. He thirsts for humanity, and particularly for the consummation of human history.

> And Y drynke riht rype must, *resureccio mortuorum.*
> And thenne shal Y come as kynge, with croune and with angeles.
>
> (XX.412–13)

> ———
>
> [And I drink fully ripe new wine, *resureccio mortuorum.*
> And then I shall come as king, with crown and with angels.]

In her *Book of Showings*, Julian of Norwich had a similar vision of "the goostly thyrst of Crist." She describes the thirst:

The love longyng that lastyth and evyr shall tyll we se that sight at domys day; for we that shalle be safe, and shalle be Crystes joy and hys blysse, ben yet here, and some be to come, and so shalle some be in to that day. Therfore this is his thurste and love longyng of us, all to geder here in hym to oure endlesse blysse, as to my syght. For we be nott now fully as hole in hym as we shalle be than.[85]

Like Langland's vision of God, Julian sees God loving humanity, thirsting for the joy and bliss of humans as he gathers "us" into the divine life. Langland himself aligns his vision with St. Paul's brief account of being caught up into paradise and hearing secret words that must not be spoken to humans (2 Cor. 12:3–5): "Audivi arcana verba, que non licet homini loqui [I heard words which cannot be told, which man may not utter]" (XX.438a). Quoting this line, Langland does at least three things: First, he reminds us that the vision and word of God can only be heard "per speculum in aenigmate" and only grasped "ex parte," through a glass in an enigma, in part (1 Cor. 13:12).[86] Second, he aligns his vision with the apostle's. Third, he reminds us that whereas Paul's vision was granted when he was caught up into paradise, Wille's is disclosed in the darkness of hell illuminated by the light of Christ. But what has Christ determined to do with "alle mennes soules"?

Christ's answer discloses the appropriate forms of theological language. It offers us a model against which we can discern the focus Langland had imitated and attacked earlier (XI.33–39). Christ's oration draws readers into a process of reflection that provides ways of contemplating divine election and of asking about the possibilities of rejection. In my view, it evokes reserves of silence and suggests how these may become sources of theology. We may perhaps be receiving a lesson on the contemporary norms in which theologians disputed predestination and reprobation, as I discuss in chapter 2.

Repeatedly Christ emphasizes his brotherhood with humankind through the Incarnation. He has assumed the *kynde* of man to the *kynde* of God. As he taught in the form of the Samaritan, his *kynde* now demands the practice of *kindness* in *kinship*.[87] He has elected to put on the form of humanity and journey into the far country, a manifestation of God's love for humanity (1 John 4.7–21, John 3.14–17). Christ addresses

Rechelesnesse's confidence that only baptized people could be saved. On the contrary, the Incarnation makes a difference unimagined by Rechelesnesse. Those who are not baptized have become "brethrene of o bloed" with the incarnate God, whether they know it or not (XX.418). All, baptized and unbaptized, belong to "mankynde," to humanity not only made in the image of God (VII.122–23), but now joined to divine nature in Christ. These considerations are at the heart of the doctrine of election and reconciliation that forms the grounds of hope encouraged by Christ: "Y were an unkynde king bote Y my kyn helpe," especially in their hour of deepest need (XX.441–42a). Of course, Christ has already *shown* that far from being "an unkynde kyng," he is, as we see in the Samaritan, a compassionate one, one whose love for his kindred drew him through the wilderness to crucifixion and now into hell. He does indeed state that his justice will continue to reign in hell. Yet he also declares that at the Last Judgement he will "mercy al mankynde" before him "in hevene," a manifestation of the love he bears his "kyn" as he refuses to be "an unkynde kyng" (XX.440–41).

One needs to emphasize the word *al* in Christ's disclosure that he will "mercy *al* mankynde." This is a careful challenge to orthodox theologies of reprobation.[88] It works in much the same way as a text I discuss on a number of occasions in the next chapter: 1 Timothy 2:4. There Paul affirms that God wanted *all* people to be saved (*omnes homine vult salvos fieri*). Langland's "al," like Paul's, raises the issue of universal salvation, as a number of commentators on Passus XX have observed.[89] This doctrine was completely developed by Origen, not without scriptural encouragement alongside scriptural discouragement. It was unequivocally anathematized by the church.[90] The effects of this rejection were very visible on the walls of every medieval church and cathedral, just as they were in manuscripts, in depictions of the hell that awaited those who were not saved.[91] Nothing in Christ's oration implies Origen's view that through the cycles of worlds there would come final salvation in which the devils would participate.[92] Granting that, does Christ suggest that "al mankynde" will finally be brought into eternal bliss? As I have just remarked, Pearsall is not alone in thinking that Christ offers "a doctrine and means of universal salvation." But he also maintains that Christ "fittingly implies some further qualification of

the apparent promise of universal salvation." Pearsall finds these qualifications in Christ's statement that he will be merciful "to money of my
halve-bretherne," that is, to many of his unbaptized brethren. *Many*—
not, apparently, *all*. He also finds similar qualifications later when we
read that Christ took from hell those "which hym luste" (those it
pleased him to) and left behind those he wanted to leave (XX.449).[93] Is
Christ, as Pearsall's careful note suggests, "evolving" a teaching with
unresolved ambiguities?

Christ's oration surely recalls some questions that have been evoked
elsewhere in the poem. Certainly his oration, and its aftermath, does
not try to address all of them, let alone resolve them. Here are some of
these questions: Does Christ, at this stage of salvation history, deliver
all from hell, including "alle wykkede" (XX.432–35a)? Does he deliver
all unbaptized people from hell or, as he says, *many* (XX.436)? Wille
sees Christ leaving some humans in hell: are they to be delivered later,
at the Last Judgment, by the *kynde* king who has determined he will
"mercy *al* mankynde"? If one were to press the poet for unequivocal
answers to these questions, his answer might well be one that Julian of
Norwich offers time and again when considering orthodox teaching on
divine wrath and reprobation: I wasn't shown this. Or he could invoke,
once again, his own quotation of Paul's ecstatic rapture in which he
heard secret words he was not allowed to speak (XX.438a). These are
divine words in excess of the poet's language, beyond his theological
horizons.[94] But Christian tradition, despite the church's condemnation
of Origen, did not speak with one voice on the issue of universal salvation. A "minority report" persisted.[95]

Yet the fact that Langland rejects a univocal solution to questions
about universal salvation should not distract us from noticing that
Christ's oration has taught us how to address the doctrine of predestination and reprobation. The oration acknowledges the kinds of questions that had troubled Wille, but Wille himself now exhibits none of his
earlier anxieties about election and reprobation. He does not do so even
in the face of death during Passus XXII, a marked contrast to the death
of the Calvinist divine Mr. Thomas Peacock, "Batchelour of Divinity and
fellow of Brasen-nose Colledge in Oxford," whose agonized death I explore in chapter 3.[96] Wille remains free from the false picture that had

previously captured his theological imagination and straitened his ability to read Jesus's parables. He no longer asks, "Wher Y were chose or nat chose" (Whether I was chosen or not chosen) (XII.52). In his journey to the visions of Charity and in his encounters with Abraham (Faith), Moses (Hope), and Christ, the sources of his false picture have dissolved. He is no longer bewitched by the terms of the old paradigm. He has been freed but, conspicuously, not by the forms of disputation cultivated in "scole," forms so richly illustrated in commentaries on the *Sentences* of Peter Lombard, the textbook that all apprentice theologians had to address.

Processes of reasoning and disputation are part of Wille's pilgrimage from the beginning, and they are never abandoned. We can see this in Wille's argument against the orthodox doctrine of the Trinity that Faith/Abraham tries to show him:

"This is myrke thing for me," quod Y, "and for many another,
How o lord myhte lyue o thre; Y leue hit nat," Y sayde.
                    (XVIII.196–97; see this with XIX.27–47)

———

["This is a dark thing for me and for many another,
How one Lord might live in three, I don't believe it," I said.]

Wille even complains about the doctrine of the Trinity to the Samaritan who figures Christ (XIX.96–107). It is made clear that his critical reasoning converges with arguments of "eretikes [heretics]" against Nicene Christianity (XIX.108–12). But unlike earlier anti-Trinitarian disputants (XI.33–39), Wille is not rebuked here by the poet or the Samaritan. Nor are his difficulties argued out of existence. Instead, his teacher produces a cascade of Trinitarian images bound up with discourse on creation, the constitution of human nature, and eschatology. Wille's critical reasoning is assimilated to a process of liturgical and divine vision in which salvation history centers on the incarnation of Christ and the gifts of the Holy Spirit (XVIII–XIX).

This is embodied in the version of election that emerges from Christ's oration. Langland has returned the doctrine to his own vision of salvation history from creation through Abraham and Moses to the nativity, ministry, crucifixion, harrowing of hell, and resurrection of Jesus Christ. In the next passus (XXI), he turns to the ascension of Christ, Pentecost, and the making of Christ's church with the gifts of the infused virtues and sacraments. Obviously enough, I am summarizing a complex poetic process involving a multiplicity of genres, allegorical modes, and disputations. I do so because I want to stress what seems to me especially relevant to the current topic: namely, that Langland has set aside a shaping force in the doctrines of predestination from Augustine to Calvin and Bunyan. That is, he opts not to indulge in a thoroughly abstract version of the electing God, a version that is mesmerized by a habitually abstract model of divine omnipotence as an overwhelming absolute power. This God, whom we encounter in some medieval and early modern versions of predestination and reprobation, is obligated to none of his creatures because any such obligation was seen as a subversion of his absolute power and autonomy. Such a God seems free of everything except the law of contradiction. The discourses of election become subordinate to metaphysical categories of divine causality, freedom, simplicity, and eternity. Anyone who spends even a little time with medieval commentaries on the *Sentences*, in which the doctrine I am discussing is a set topic in the first book, will find a quite remarkable absence of attention to the narratives of scripture. Yet these absent narratives explore the divine covenant with Israel (election) and they display the specificities of Christ's own ministry, including Christ's own teaching in narratives (parables) and commands.

I will examine these features and their consequences in some of the medieval materials discussed in the next chapter. There we will meet a recurrent image that was a favored way of explicating the church's teaching on predestination and reprobation. Although I treat this extensively during the analysis offered in chapter 2, it is also an appropriate bridge here. The image is Paul's assertion that God made an eternally binding decision about the twins, Jacob and Esau, before they were ever born: "Jacob I have loved, but Esau I have hated [Iacob dilexi, Esau autem odio habui]" (Rom. 9:13; Mal. 1:2–3). Paul himself insists there is no injustice in such judgment of the unborn, any more than there is injustice when a potter exercises power over the clay to make one vessel to honor and another to dishonor. Just as the clay does not question the potter's decisions, so humans should not question God (Rom. 9:13–21). This text, habitually abstracted from its context in Paul's often agonized writing in chapters 9–11 of this letter, becomes a major proof text in medieval and Reformation discussions of predestination and reprobation. This constituted a doctrinal tradition that composed a God other than the one revealed in Jesus Christ and the incarnation of God. The latter had eternally elected to reconcile humanity to God through Jesus Christ and to give Christians the ministry of reconciliation (2 Cor. 5:18–20). The epistemophilic panic Langland represents through Wille was not caused simply by the preachers Rechelesnesse named in Passus XI: "Predestinaet thei prechen, prechours that this sheweth, / Or *prescit* inparfit, pult out of grace, / Unwriten [They preach that people are predestined to salvation or foreknown to be imperfect, reprobated, removed from grace, Unwritten]" (XI.205–7). Its sources are the traditions into which theologians were apprenticed in "scole." It is to these traditions that Langland's work offers a profound challenge, as theological as it is poetic.

* * *

I began this chapter (the core of the present book) with a quotation from Wittgenstein's *Culture and Value*: "Sometimes an expression has to be withdrawn from language and sent for cleaning—then it can be put back into circulation."[97] Among the many tasks and achievements of *Piers Plowman* is Langland's "cleaning" of the language of predestination and reprobation, a "cleaning" of the language of election. He brings back such language from its ensnarement in habitual webs woven out of a God of abstract, willful omnipotence hiding behind arbitrary acts of mercy (Jacob) and justice (Esau). Through his poem, Langland has, as it were, rebaptized this language into the history of the covenants between God and humanity that find their center in Christ and the Incarnation, the Word made flesh. Hence the long liturgically shaped encounters with Christ from Passus XVIII to XXI. Wille is drawn into a gospel of loving kindness toward fallen humanity (XVIII–XIX), one recapitulated and sublimely glossed in the harrowing of hell and Easter Sunday (XX). Readers are drawn along with Wille to see that the God who elects humanity is the God whom Anselm called "Deus Homo." On this Christ's oration in hell centers. No wonder that his speech and acts lead directly into the joyful singing of angels, the symbolic reconciliation of Peace, Truth, Justice, and Mercy followed by the celebration of Easter as Wille calls "Kitte my wyf and Calote my douhter" to "go reverence godes resureccioun," accompanying him to church (XX.470–75). Such is the outcome of the mystery of election: God in Christ calling humanity, symbolized here in all its precious particularity. Had Karl Barth read this, he might have suspected that Langland shared his own quite idiosyncratic view that "in the doctrine of election we have to do with the sum of the Gospel."[98]

As I have observed, Langland always moves from the most intense, joyful visionary insights into the history of human sin and humanity's continual resistance to divine gifts. This is exemplified in the grim power of the final two passus of the poem. There we meet the Christian community rejecting the eucharist rather than making restitution for the bonds of charity that have been shattered. There, too, we meet the pope, the hierarchy of the church, and its religious orders in the vanguard of Antichrist's army. But there Langland does not find any reason to revisit the doctrines of predestination and reprobation. The "foles" who resist Antichrist and de-Christianization within the church are joined by Wille, as death draws near. He is instructed by Kynde to go "into Unity" with Conscience and the "foles [fools]," and there continue learning "to love."[99] The language of the many and the few, the predestinate and the reprobate, has been "withdrawn from language and sent for cleaning." Wille has been decisively freed from it.

CHAPTER TWO

Wille Returns "to scole"

Late Medieval Theologians on
Predestination and Reprobation

Sed contra est quod dicitur Malach:1 [Romans 9:13]. Iacob dilexi,
Esau autem odio habui *[Jacob I have loved, but Esau I have hated].*

—Aquinas, *Summa Theologiae*, I.23.3, sed contra

The title of this chapter refers to a passage Langland wrote for the final
version of his poem. In it, Wille reflects on his experience of going "to
scole" to study scripture and theology. But he relates that those who
were funding his education died before he could complete it (V.35–41).
Having considered Wille's troubles regarding ideas of predestination
and reprobation, and Langland's ways of dissolving their sources, I now
want to sample what was being taught on this topic in "scole." How
responsible for Wille's troubles were the doctrines and modes of inquiry taught in late medieval universities? How different was medieval
teaching on this subject from that of the Reformation?[1]

In this chapter I offer an outline and some exemplifications of medieval teaching on predestination and reprobation. The common ground
seems to be an Augustinian legacy that theologians acknowledged as
authoritative even when they generated accounts that diverged from it

in important ways.[2] A summary of this common ground is provided by Marilyn McCord Adams in her monumental work on Ockham: "From eternity, God immutably chose some rational creatures (the elect) to order to eternal life (to predestine) and rejected others thereby abandoning them to eternal punishment. . . . Divine predestination ([like] reprobation) is certain and unobstructable. . . . Whoever dies in a given state of grace will receive eternal life[,] . . . whoever dies in a state of mortal sin will receive eternal punishment."[3] We have already seen that Wille and his surrogate, Rechelesnesse, assumed some such scheme of orthodox theology. Even from this brief outline, we might glimpse how such theology could draw people toward musings on the eternal will of an omnipotent God. True enough, both the Apostles' Creed and the Nicene Creed begin with a confession of belief in God the Father almighty, but this is immediately bound into a confession of faith in Christ, the Holy Spirit, the Catholic Church, the forgiveness of sins, and other constituents of Christian practice. The question I pursue in what follows concerns the version of the predestinating and the reprobating God generated by this theology. To explore this, we will need to move from the general scheme provided by Adams to consider some particularities.

Given that all theologians had to comment on the *Sentences* of Peter Lombard (d. 1160), paying attention to some predecessors and contemporaries, this book seems a sensible place to begin as we follow Wille back "to scole."[4] The first book of the *Sentences* contains a sequence of questions concerning God's knowledge, causation, freedom, eternity, and temporality, questions that lead into distinctions addressing predestination and reprobation. While giving a range of philosophical and theological arguments on this topic, Lombard tends to foreground an Augustinian account. In distinctions 39–41 of the first book, much use is made of Augustine's later works, including *The Predestination of the Saints, Rebuke and Grace, The Gift of Perseverance*, the unfinished work against Julian, and the *Retractions*. All medieval theologians had at least encountered Augustine's teaching that between God's love, grace, and predestination "there is only this difference, namely, that predestination is the preparation for grace, while grace is its actual bestowal." This is a quotation from Augustine's *The Predesti nation of the Saints.*[5] He emphasizes that "the predestination of God which is for the good is, as I said, the preparation for grace, but grace is the result of predestination" (10.19). Lombard himself quotes this passage (I.d.39, c.4.4). Predestination is, in Augustinian terms, God's decision to bestow divine grace on sinners and thus draw them to salvation. Augustine's model of the predestined is the human nature of Jesus Christ. This had no merits of either faith or works but was predestined to be assumed by the divine Word and to become the head of redeemed humanity (*Predestination* 15.30–31). Here there is no question of God choosing to elect because God foresees the elected will deserve the reward of merits. Marcia Colish shows how in this "Peter summarizes the standard late Augustinian teaching that was the consensus position on predestination in [the mid-twelfth century]." Nevertheless, she also discerns an absence in Lombard and the "consensus" he represented: "There is no trace whatsoever of Augustine's doctrine of the irresistibility of grace." Lombard does not draw attention to this, but Colish sees it as "a calculated omission that deserves to be understood as a criticism of Augustine" by Lombard and twelfth-century theologians.[6] Still, she does not actually show Lombard exemplifying what resistance to his thoroughly Augustinian account of predestinating grace would look like, nor is such a resistance easy to imagine within Lombard's account of predestination. For example: is the elect apostle Paul resisting the grace that overwhelmed him in every way as he went to Damascus to persecute Christians (Acts 9:1–6)? Who knows, for Lombard does not tell us.

Perhaps Chaucer's Troilus might have included analogous questions in his ruminations about human freedom and divine providence in his despair at the loss of Criseyde discussed in chapter 1. But such metaphysical speculation is not what most troubled Langland's Wille. His anxiety was intensely focused on his personal election or reprobation (XII.50–52). What if, instead of being chosen before the foundation of the world, predestined, he had been "pult [pulled] out of grace, / Unwriten" from the book of life (XI.203–7)? As discussed in the previous chapter, Langland composed a complex visionary and theological therapy to free Wille from what is revealed to be a false picture. Liberation did not come through disputation within the terms of the received picture. But had Langland sent Wille and his readers to Lombard's *Sentences*, what would they have discussed about reprobation?

They would have found a model of reprobation inextricably bound up with Augustinian theology. God's reprobation is the other side of God's predestination: God "has reprobated some from eternity by not electing them." In such reprobation, God foreknows sinners' malice and prepares "punishment without end" for them (I.d.40, c.2.1). Explicitly following Augustine, Lombard teaches that those thus foreknown have had their hearts *incorrigibly hardened* by God's eternal will not to impart grace to *these* sinners. They are thus treated very differently from sinners like the adulterous murderer David, about whom Rechelesnesse broods in Passus XI. Lombard quotes Augustine: "those to whom it [grace] is not imparted are not worthy nor deserving of it; rather they are worthy and deserving of it not being imparted" (I.d.40, c.2.2; Augustine, *Epistle* 194.3.14). Quite so. Yet by Augustine's own model not even the humanity of Christ was deserving, let alone murderous sinners like David and Paul. As the latter himself confessed, "Christ Jesus came into the world to save sinners, of whom I am the chief" (1 Tim. 1:15). Or as Hamlet justly rebuked Polonius, "Use every man after his desert, and who should scape whipping?" (*Hamlet*, II.2.532–33).[7] Lombard, however, turns from Augustine to Paul and quotes another text that might well have pulled Wille further into an Augustinian quagmire: "he hath mercy on whom he will; and whom he will, he hardeneth" (Rom. 9:11; I.d.40, c.2.2). Lombard comments: "by mercy meaning predestination" and by obduracy the privation of grace. This is precisely what Rechelesnesse suspects in Passus XI.

Yet Lombard has more to say on reprobation. He invokes the statement from Paul I discussed toward the end of the first chapter and cited from Aquinas in the epigraph to this chapter. Lombard cites the disparity between Jacob and Esau as a kind of proof text: "As it is written: Jacob I have loved, but Esau I have hated [*Iacobi dilexi, Esau autem odio habui*]" (Rom. 9:13; Mal. 1:2–3). Lombard thinks this text demonstrates how God's eternal predestination and reprobation have absolutely nothing to do with merits and demerits since the text refers to *unborn twins*: "when the children were not yet born, nor had done any good or evil" (Rom. 9:11). As Adams points out in the passage I quoted at the beginning of this chapter, this was an area of consensus in medieval teaching. The fragment from Paul was regularly cited as the Holy Spirit's warrant for this theology. Lombard asserts that the text shows how "eternal reprobation" simply does "not result from deserving," but from "the privation of grace" eternally determined: "Just as he elected Jacob and reprobated Esau, which was not because of the merits which they had, because they had none, since they did not even exist. Neither was it because of future merits that he foresaw that he either elected the one or reprobated the other" (I.d.41, c.1.2). He then reinforces this line by quoting from Augustine's *Retractions* (I.d.41, c.2.1). He continues to reiterate his major contention: "God reprobated whom he willed, not because of their eventual deserving which he foresaw" (I.d.41, c.2.7). Thinking about God foreseeing virtues or vices and responding appropriately is thus carefully ruled out of order. This would, allegedly, subordinate God's will to humans.

It seems to me that in such locutions Peter Lombard is moving close to a model of double predestination. True enough, it is normally assumed that medieval theology rejected the symmetries between predestination and reprobation found in the Reformation. This is a plausible assumption concerning the putative intentions of medieval theologians before Gregory of Rimini (d. 1358). Yet the maker of the major textbook of medieval theology is insisting that God's eternal reprobation "does not result from deserving" (I.d.41, c.1.2). God reprobated Esau before he had been born and regardless of future actions (I.d.41, c.1.3–c.2.7). Thus Lombard, reluctantly or not, consciously or not, *is* setting aside the lack of symmetry between predestination and reprobation that acted as a block against double predestination for most medieval theologians.

This raises a difficult question. Did God eternally reprobate some humans so that they would "become evil and faithless and hardened to sin," just as he predestined some to become virtuous people? Some to be Jacob, others to be Esau? This was the question Calvinists, like Augustine, had to face: does the God you worship compel people to become sinners for his own hidden purposes? Lombard, like Augustine, *denies* that this is the case. He asserts that "reprobation is *not* the cause of evil in the same way as predestination is the cause of good" (I.d.41, c.2.8; my emphasis). He wants to retain the barrier to a symmetrical model of reprobation and predestination, yet he also sets aside this barrier. Here we meet not mystery, not paradox, but contradiction. However, even if one were to accept the barrier to the symmetry of double predestination, and the risk of making God the immediate author of sin, this might not offer much consolation to those worrying that they might be the theologians' Esau rather than their Jacob. It is this that Langland had discerned in his representation of Wille's panic and Rechelesnesse's questions: *he might be like Esau.* He might be one of the "many" called to the wedding feast but not one of the "few" (like Jacob) chosen from eternity in the hidden will of God. Yet once more I recall how Wille's response to Christ's gospel was utter distress: "Wher [Whether] Y were chose or nat chose" (XII.50–53). That is, am I Jacob, or am I Esau?

Nor would Wille have been much comforted by Lombard's use of Augustine's letter to Simplicianus in his teaching on election. Here Augustine explains that Esau stands for those who have been called but not *effectually (congruenter)* called.[8] After all, in the version of the gospel heard by Wille, many were "sompned [summoned]," obeyed the call, and then were arbitrarily excluded by the king's secretive and silent porter. He pulled in a *few* of those called and shut out the *many* (XII.47–49). Such, we are taught in the Augustinian tradition, is "ineffectual calling." No wonder that Wille's troubled imagination conjured up that secretive and arbitrary porter to the kingdom. True enough, like Augustine, Bishop Peter asserts the justice of God's alleged hatred of the baby in Rebecca's womb, a hatred unknown to the narrator, traditionally identified as inspired by the Holy Spirit, who described the birth of the twins in Genesis (25:19–28). Despite the theologian's unwavering affirmation of divine justice in such hatred, Lombard acknowledges that it is incomprehensible.

Yet, as is the habit with such theological language, this acknowledgment encourages not silence but more talk. Like Augustine and so many later adherents of this tradition, Lombard turns to another passage in Paul's letter to the Romans to celebrate the incomprehensibility: "O the depths of the riches of the wisdom and knowledge of God! How incomprehensible [*incomprehensibilia*] are his judgements and unsearchable [*investigabiles*] his ways" (Rom. 11:33; I.d.40, c.2.3).[9] This famous *O altitudo* plucks the sentence from its contexts, as was normal enough in both medieval and Reformation theology. Yet this habit creates an irony here which neither Lombard nor Augustine discusses. Paul's *O altitudo* brings to a close an intense, often agonized reflection on those he calls "my brethren, who are my kinsmen [*cognati mei*] according to the flesh: Who are Israelites to whom belongeth the adoption as of children, and the glory, and the testament, and the giving of the law, and the service of God, and the promises: Whose are the fathers, and of whom is Christ" (Rom. 9:3–5). Despite Israel's apparent rejection of the Son of God, the crucified and risen Messiah, God's calling is utterly faithful, and he will not finally abandon those who strenuously resist his grace. *O altitudo* indeed. The mystery and Paul's ecstatic contemplation of divine faithfulness in the case of such resistance do not encourage anybody to spin out a discourse on divine "hatred" of the unborn. On the contrary, the long meditation here is on the faithful love of God in a context that seemed to Paul at best unpropitious.

I have been imagining Wille's return "to scole" and how his troubles might fare there. Lombard's *Sentences* was an obvious place to begin, and it has at least made clear the importance of Augustine's later work in shaping conventional teaching on predestination and reprobation. Having just considered the role of a text on Jacob and Esau in this Augustinian tradition, I now want to look at another text constantly discussed in medieval and Reformation ruminations on predestination and reprobation, a text encountered in chapter 1. It is another text ascribed to Paul. In the first letter to Timothy, the author states that God our Savior "will have *all* be saved and to come to the knowledge of the truth [*qui omnes homines vult salvos fieri et ad agnitionem veritatis venire*]" (1 Tim. 2:4; my emphasis). The letter continues with a hymn to this truth: "For there is one God, and one mediator of God and men, the man Christ Jesus: Who gave himself a redemption for *all* [*pro omnibus*]" (1 Tim. 2:5–6; my emphasis). In Wille's moment of despairing panic, we saw (in chapter 1) that the healing word was *alle*: "Crist cleped us alle, come yf we wolde, / Sarrasynes and sismatikes, and so a [he] ded the Iewes" (XII.54–55). Alas, had Wille gone back to "scole," his "alle" would have been sharply challenged by any teachers working within the received consensus. He would have had to learn that Paul's *all* actually means *not all*, that God only wanted to save a few and, in Langland's vivid language, let "the remenaunt go rome" (XII.47–49). How could this be so? Let Augustine begin the answer.

In his *Enchiridion on Faith, Hope, and Love*, Augustine tells us that "we are certain that not everybody is saved." So Paul's *all* cannot be in contradiction to the church's certainty enshrined in its teaching. We must somehow defend the church's certainties while also defending scripture. Augustine thinks there are a number of ways in which we can read the text to achieve the desired outcome. One possibility is that we can take Paul's meaning simply to be a bland tautology: "Nobody is saved except those whom he [God] wills to be saved." Another possibility is to read the words "[God] wills everyone to be saved" as conveying that God wills to save *some* (but certainly not all) from *all* estates, ages, genders, classes—indeed, from humanity "in all its diversity." Augustine is happy for Christians to understand this text in any way that does not maintain that God "willed anything to happen that did not happen."[10] In *Rebuke and Grace,* he is rather more terse than in the *Enchiridion*. He acknowledges that the words of scripture tell us that God wills all humans to be saved (1 Tim. 2:4). But, he argues, we *know* "not all are saved," so let us then understand scripture's unqualified "all" as only meaning "all the predestined."[11] Later in this work he suggests that since we "do not know who are going to be saved," we are encouraged to will that "all" humans be saved. Thus we have yet another way of reading Paul's words, so vexing to orthodox views about the predestination of the few and the reprobation of the many. Paul simply suggests we will the salvation of all even though we know full well that such salvation for all is *not* what God wills (15.47).

I want to conclude this brief consideration of Augustine by returning to Jacob and Esau. Augustine writes about them in *The Enchiridion*.[12] God, Augustine recalls, "has mercy on whoever he chooses, and he hardens the heart of whoever he chooses" (quoting Rom. 9:18). Augustine invites us to think of the paradigmatic unborn twins. He quotes the words ascribed to God by Malachi and Paul, "I have loved Jacob, but I have hated Esau," and then muses that "it seems unfair that God should love one and hate the other without their deserving it by good or bad deeds." But he is adamant that the text does *not* suggest that

God hates Esau because he foresaw Esau's future "evil" deeds. Yet this hatred of the unborn is not unjust: "Who but a fool could think that God is unfair?" Augustine's conviction is that original sin exculpates God. Original sin makes God's alleged hatred of Esau a just hatred and his love of Jacob a merciful love (25.98). After all, the fall of Adam and Eve turned humanity "into one mass of perdition." To this mass both twins belong. But why love one and hate the other? Typical of this tradition, Augustine takes another figure from Romans 9: "O man, who art thou that repliest against God? Shall the thing formed say to him that formed it: Why has thou made me thus? Or hath not the potter power over the clay, of the same lump to make one vessel unto honour, and another unto dishonour?" (Rom. 9:21–22). Augustine objects that some "foolish people" think that Paul (and hence Augustine) is simply at a loss for any plausible answer to the objector. But Augustine, unlike Paul, claims that the answer being given is Augustine's version of original sin, in which all humanity would justly be damned for eternity (25.99). If one turns out to be Esau, a reprobate from before one's birth, this is no more than one deserves. If one turns out to be the loved Jacob, give thanks to the gratuitous mercy of God who has chosen some and cast away many. This is just what Wille and Rechelesnesse suspected and feared. Wille may have been responding to Jesus's parable of the wedding feast with such teaching in his ears.

Lombard and his church placed Augustine's understanding of predestination and reprobation at the core of orthodox teaching on this subject. Had Wille gone back "to scole" he would certainly have read and heard such teaching. As we will see, by the time he returned he might well have met other versions of election. Even so, the Augustinian tradition continued to be integral to theories of predestination and reprobation, exerting pressure on the grammar and ethics of divine agency in the imagination of theologians. The latter, of course, taught, preached, and trained confessors. Reflecting on the formation of orthodoxy, I have every sympathy with a sharp comment made by James Wetzel in a fine study on Augustine, free will, and predestination.

> There is a dark side to Augustine's reading of Rom[ans] 9. It is Esau. Augustine assumes that because Esau is the son not favoured, he is forever cast off. Leave aside whether this reading fits Paul (it does

not); in subscribing to a doctrine of reprobation, Augustine sub-
scribes to the belief that some who feel abandoned by God are, in
fact, abandoned by God. These unhappy souls are the damned, the
sons and daughters not favoured. The doctrine of reprobation has
mixed poison into Augustine's motives for affirming predestination. You do not have to be a Pelagian not to like the taste.[13]

This "poison" was to have a fascinating and tragic history in Christian
tradition encompassing both Catholic and Reformation strands. I have
argued in chapter 1 that Langland grasped something of this tragic potential and included a prophetic exploration of this in *Piers Plowman*. I
call Langland's exploration prophetic because the psychological and
existential consequences of this theological "poison" only seem to have
become common in Calvinist churches of the Reformation.[14]

Even when we read the work on this doctrine that was produced in
"scole" we find an absence of the affective, passionate response we saw
in Langland's Wille. I have not encountered works where the theologian thinks, "*Perhaps I am Esau*, perhaps those I love, including my
family and their children, including those in the womb, might be figured in Esau." Perhaps the fact that those who wrote the doctrine in
"scole" were men, celibate men without children, might have shaped
the available forms through which questions could be disputed or not
disputed. I have not come across the kind of visceral response to the
commonplace presentation of Esau that Langland gives Wille in response to the reading of Jesus's parable of the wedding feast: "Al for
tene [pain, anger, distress] of here [her] tyxst [text] tremblede my herte"
(XII.50). Do the genres of academic theology immunize users from the
human implications of their own theologizing? Do they know not what
they say when they write in its modes and in its exclusively male and
adult institutions?

Indeed, if we were to leave the universities to go out into the world,
might we find more people like Wille, troubled by predestination? Nicolette Zeeman has suggested that "those committed to lives of spirituality" tended to suffer such afflictions.[15] Certainly *The Chastising
of God's Children* takes note of those nuns and monks who "wolen
[would] imagyne of predestinaciouns and of the prescience of the fore-

knowynge of God."[16] The author addresses this trouble most fully after considering the temptation to despair at the recollection of one's sins and the remedies for such despair (151–55). Moving to those troubled "in ymagunaciouns and thoughtis of predestinacioun and of the prescience of God," he immediately explains that predestination concerns salvation, "prescience" concerns damnation. Anxiety is stimulated by doubt as to whether God has predestined one, and also by imagining "the prescience of God" through which one is damned (156). Here one *is* indeed Esau. Instead of dramatizing or narrativizing such doubts and fears, however, the author immediately moves to a cluster of remedies. These focus on the coexistence of divine and human agency, the gift of "fre wil" to act virtuously, the help of the saint's prayers, Christ's wounds (welcoming the anxious), and the compassionate mediation of the Virgin Mary (156–60). He concentrates on the predestined means by which God gives humans good grounds for faith, hope, and love, grounds centered in creation and redemption. While existential anxieties generated by the church's teaching on predestination and reprobation are acknowledged, the mode is far removed from Langland's, the imagined monastic subject very different from the despairing prodigal in "the lond of longyng." Nevertheless, Wille would receive much more help in the community of *The Chastising of God's Children* than by his return "to scole," as he would have if he had he been able to visit the anchoress Julian of Norwich.

But I will return again "to scole." Would not the Angelic Doctor, the Common Doctor of the Roman Catholic Church, free Wille from the "poison" of Augustinian teaching on Esau and Jacob, on God's predestination and reprobation? Thomas Aquinas (d. 1274) writes a careful and lucid exposition of what was undoubtedly the consensus position on this doctrine during his lifetime.[17] He does so in part 1 of the *Summa Theologiae* immediately after he treats questions of God's love (I.20), God's justice and mercy (I.21), and God's providence (I.22). He does not get to the Trinity until I.27–44, while the work's most sustained treatment of Christology and the sacraments occurs in part 3. I mention the location of his treatise on predestination (I.23) because Aquinas explicitly presents the *Summa Theologiae* as a corrective model for teaching beginners in theology. In the prologue, Aquinas states that he intends to teach whatever belongs to the Christian religion for the instruction of beginners (*ad eruditionem incipientium*). He complains that other theologians have cluttered their teaching with a multiplication of useless questions, articles, and arguments. In doing so, they have wearied and confused students even when they are teaching what needs to be known. They have failed to follow the order of theological discipline. He will correct all this.

Before I begin my discussion of *De Praedestinatione* (I.23), I will recall his earlier treatment of a text already encountered on more than one occasion: God will have all people to be saved (*qui [Deus] omnes homines salvos fieri*) (1 Tim. 2:4). He addresses this text in his consideration of "the will of God" (I.19). He asks whether God's will is always fulfilled. It is (I.19.6, resp.). So how do we take Paul's statement that God wills all to be saved? Aquinas's answer follows Augustine, whose own answer we have followed in his *Enchiridion* and elsewhere. We must take "all" to mean only that God wants all to be saved who will be saved. We can also, as Augustine argued, take "all" to mean *not* all people but some from every estate of life. Another way of interpreting this "all" Aquinas takes from John of Damascus's *De fide orthodoxa* (II.29). This reading was widely rehearsed in the late Middle Ages and the Reformation. It maintains that Paul's statement refers to God's "antecedent will [*de voluntate antecedente*]" but not to God's "consequent will [*de voluntate consequente*]." An example is offered: A just judge wills *antecedently* that all people should live. But *consequently* he wills, and does so justly, that a murderer should be hanged.[18] Similarly, God wills *antecedently* that all humans be saved, but he wills *consequently* that some be damned according to the criteria of his justice. Whatever God wills *simply* (*simpliciter*) happens. But what he wills antecedently may not occur (I.19.6, ad 3). In his commentary on Paul's letter to Timothy, Aquinas includes another common definition of divine will to help us see how when Paul says *all* people, he actually means *not* all people. This distinction is between God's "will of good pleasure [*voluntas bene placiti*]" and his "will of sign [*voluntas signi*]." The former is what God truly wills and thus will necessarily occur; the latter refers to the language of divine volition in ways that do not commit God to enacting such language. Paul's statement, says Aquinas, is of the latter kind. God has told humans how he wants them to live. Thus while in a sense he wills them to be saved, he does not actually will all of them to be saved, only *some*.[19] Here and elsewhere in the *Summa Theologiae*, Aquinas's reading of 1 Timothy 2:4 represents the dominant, Augustinian tradition and does so without any reservations. Paul's letter to Timothy must not be allowed to question ecclesiastic decisions to reject Origen's teaching on universal salvation. Perhaps unsurprisingly, Aquinas returns to this Pauline text in his treatise on predestination. He poses a question asking whether the predestined are God's chosen ones (I.23.4). As usual, he begins by composing objections to the position he upholds. One objection argues that the predestined are not the chosen ones of God because this would imply that God discriminates against some people, whereas scripture tells us that God wills all humans to be saved (I.23.4, obj. 3). We are by now very familiar with Aquinas's answer to this objection since he has already dealt with it to his satisfaction (I.19.6, ad 1; I.23.4, ad 3). Only by his *antecedent* will does God want to save all people; by his *consequent* will he does no such thing.[20] So Aquinas continues to affirm Augustinian tradition here, just as Calvin would affirm it in the sixteenth century.

The question on predestination contains eight articles. Aquinas begins by observing that divine providence, the subject of the previous question (I.22), orders everything to its proper end. But the human end is complex: it is twofold (*duplex*). That is because one end (*finis*) is eternal life, the attainment of which exceeds the ability of creatures; the other end is proportionate to created nature and can be attained by a creature's natural powers, whether the creature is a mouse or a human. For humans to reach an end beyond their natural powers they need supernatural help, just as, Aquinas says, an arrow needs an archer if it is to reach its target. In a rational creature, God's direction toward their supernatural end—his nocking of the arrow, drawing of the bow, and aiming toward the mark—is called predestination. For Aquinas predestination is thus "part of providence" (I.23.1, resp.). This calm introduction to the topic seems to contain nothing that would have disturbed Langland's Wille. No wonder that when the distinguished Dominican theologian Herbert McCabe "was a lad," he thought predestination "was a Protestant doctrine, specifically a Calvinist one."

He recollects: "The picture we had was of God planning the world de-
ciding that some people would be the elect, the chosen, the predestined
and others would be damned—to the greater glory of God. It was particularly the notion of people being predestined to damnation that sent
a chill down the spine." He continues: "In those days I was very glad to
be a Catholic, for I thought we don't believe in predestination at all."
As he became a Dominican, a theologian of the church, and an expert
on the work of Aquinas, he discovered that Catholics do "believe in
predestination" but not at all in the "spine-chilling" doctrine of double
predestination. On the contrary, Catholics apparently experience predestination as "a delightful and joyful and liberating doctrine, all about
the love of God and the glorious freedom of the sons of God." And
truly McCabe's version of Aquinas's teaching is all of these things.[21]
Langland and his Wille would surely have embraced it.

But unlike Aquinas, the modern Dominican theologian has nothing to say about reprobation, nothing to say about the unborn Esau and
Jacob, nothing to say about Paul's statement in 1 Timothy 2:4 and traditional exegesis. Neither medieval Catholicism nor Aquinas was reticent
on these issues. A traditional question put by Aquinas in the second article of his treatise on predestination asks whether predestination "places
anything in the predestinated [*Utrum praedestinatio aliquid ponat in
predestinato*]" (I.23.2). Like Augustine and Lombard, Aquinas answers
that predestination is not anything within or imparted to the predestined but only in God, the predestinating agent. Aquinas again emphasizes that predestination is part of providence, an exemplar in the mind
of God (see I.22.1). In the execution of predestination, the human is
passive. This in itself would not perturb Langland's Wille because
Christian worship and scripture acknowledge that God is the creator
and sustainer of life. Indeed, Holy Churche reminded him of this with
great eloquence throughout Passus I. But Aquinas follows this conventional teaching down paths that were part of the labyrinth within which
Wille became lost and terrified.

In the next article on predestination, Aquinas addresses the issue at
the root of Wille's anxiety: the doctrine of reprobation. He poses the
following question: whether God reprobates anybody (*Utrum Deus
aliquid hominem reprobet*) (I.23.3). It is from this article that I took the

epigraph to the present chapter. But before I come to that (in the sed contra), I will consider the objections Aquinas composes against the affirmative answer his tradition gives to the question. The first objection is that nobody reprobates what he loves: as God loves all humans, God reprobates nobody. The objection quotes from a work taken to be scripture in Aquinas's church: "Thou lovest all things that are and hatest none of these things which thou hast made" (Ws 11:25). Aquinas could have strengthened this objection by following the Christological emphasis of Langland's Holy Churche who reminded Wille that "*Deus caritas* [God is love]" and offered an exquisite allegorical lyric on the Incarnation (I.81–82, 146–70; 1 John 4.8–21). Nevertheless, the objection is clear enough and clashes with Romans 9:13, the endlessly rehearsed text concerning God's alleged hatred for the unborn Esau. The second objection argues that the logical consequence of teaching that God eternally reprobates some is a symmetry between predestination to glory and reprobation to damnation—that is, *double predestination*. But the objection concludes that this is false to scripture. Therefore, God does not reprobate anyone. The third objection argues that the doctrine of reprobation favored by Aquinas would be replete with injustice: nobody should be punished for something unavoidable, and nobody can avoid being damned if God reprobates him. As God does not act unjustly, we should not say he reprobates people. How does the Angelic Doctor deal with these substantial objections?

He begins by selecting a grain of scripture within which he finds a very familiar world: "I have loved Jacob, but I have hated Esau [*Iacob dilexi, Esau autem odio habui*]" (Rom. 9:13; Mal. 1:2–3; *ST* I.23.3, sed contra). The contexts in which Aquinas produces this endlessly rehearsed text are thoroughly Augustinian. He argues that divine reprobation is a part of providential beauty: just as the plentitude of God's cosmic providence includes some defects (I.22.2), so his treatment of humanity permits (*permittat*) certain people to be endlessly damned. Reprobation is that part of God's providence which relates to people not ordained to eternal life. That is, God wills to permit some to fall into a guilt for which they will be eternally damned (I.23.3, resp).

I would like to consider this argument based on the beautiful diversity of providence a little more closely. In the treatise on providence,

Aquinas considers an old objection. *Either* God cannot prevent evils (catastrophic natural disasters, terrible suffering of innocent victims, genocide) and therefore is not almighty; *or* he can prevent these evils but chooses not to do so. Why would an almighty God so choose? Perhaps because he doesn't care (somewhat like Epicurean gods); perhaps because he is cruel and enjoys such suffering and evil (I.22.2, obj. 2). Aquinas answers this objection by claiming that a being with the power of universal providence might allow some defects in the service of the good of the totality. For the defect of one thing yields the good of another. If God prevented all evils (*omnia mala*) many good things would be removed from the world. Aquinas gives two examples. The first is the killing of animals: without this, he asserts, the universe would lack lions (I.22.2, ad 2). This is a surprisingly feeble example, but its weakness points to the weakness of the traditional argument (Neoplatonic in assumptions) he is defending. Compare Milton's vision of God's wondrous creation in *Paradise Lost*, Book VII, and the consequences of freely chosen human sins for the flourishing of that creation (shown in Book X). In Milton's paradise, all creatures are vegetarian as befits their foreshadowing of the promised consummation of creation by the Son of God, the Messiah.

> The wolf shall dwell with the lamb: and the leopard shall lie down with the kid: the calf and the lion, and the sheep shall abide together, and a little child shall lead them. The calf and the bear shall feed: their young ones shall rest together: and the lion shalt eat straw like the ox. And the sucking child shall play on the hole of the asp: and the weaned child shall thrust his hand into the den of the basilisk. They shall not hurt, nor shall they kill in all my holy mountain, for the earth is filled with the knowledge of the Lord [*scientia Domini*], as the covering waters of the sea. (Isa. 11:6–9)

Toward the end of the book of Isaiah we are again told that "the wolf and the lamb shall feed together; the lion and the ox shall eat straw; and dust shall be the serpent's food: they shall not kill in all my holy mountain, saith the Lord" (Isa. 15:25). So it is definitely not beyond the wits of the God revealed in scripture to maintain the life of lions and the life of humans without slaughtering animals. Aquinas himself began his

Summa Theologiae by affirming that sacred doctrine, theology, depends not on natural reasoning but on divine revelation, scripture (I.1.2, resp., ad 2; I.1.8, ad 2). For Milton, the slaughter of animals reflects the violence introduced into our world by human rejection of God's peace, a story narrated in Genesis 2–6 and 9–10 (*Paradise Lost* XI.181–207).[22] Aquinas, however, introduces the paradisical slaughter of animals as an example of the beautiful variety in God's (prelapsarian) creation. What seems a defect from the perspective of the slaughtered zebra is a wonderful perfection from the perspective of the lion. Why God apparently forgot this in the eschatological visions revealed in the book of Isaiah Aquinas does not discuss here.

The second example Aquinas provides to illustrate the beauty of providential defects is the slaughter of Christian saints. Without the persecution of Christians by tyrants (*persecutio tyrannorum*), Aquinas reasons, there would have been no patience of the martyrs in world history. In this framework, even persecution by Nero, Hitler, and Stalin can be welcomed as setting off the beauty of their victims' lives and displaying the platitudinous perfections of the totality: no Hitler, but also no Bonhoeffer. Some scholars have placed the invention of theodicies as distinctly postmedieval and probably the consequence of Enlightenment cultures.[23] But what Thomas is doing here certainly seems a form of theodicy, quite as much as does Milton's hope for Paradise Lost: "I may assert Eternal Providence, / And justify the ways of God to men" (*Paradise Lost* I.25–26). We come across a version of Aquinas's theodicy in Langland's *Piers Plowman* where it is ascribed to a personification named Peace. Thinking about human suffering and human rejections of God, she sets these in the light of the reconciliation of humanity to God in Christ.

> For hadde they wist of no wo, wele hadde thay nat knowen;
> For no wiht woet what wele is that neuere wo soffrede
> Ne what is hoet hunger that hadde neuere defaute.
> Ho couthe kyndeliche whit colour descreve
> Yf all the world were whit or swan-whit all thynges?
> Yf no nyht ne were, no man, Y leue,
> Sholde ywyte witterly what day is to mene.
>
> (XX.210–16)

[For had they known no woe, they'd not know well-being;
For no one knows well-being who never suffered woe,
Nor what hot hunger is who never was famished.
Who could naturally describe with color
If all the world were white or all things swan-white?
If there were no night, I believe no man
Should really know what day means.]

Peace offers a conventional account of the way appreciation for goods depends on, or is sharpened by, the lack of such goods. In the grand totality, all sufferings are justified as making us appreciate not-suffering. Did we not have night, we would not know day; did we not have murderous tyrants, we would not appreciate living in peace, nor would we know the patience of the martyrs under intense suffering. Thus the beauty of creation would, allegedly, be diminished.

Aquinas turns from generalizing analogies of providential variety to the order of predestination and reprobation. He now offers more specific replies to the objections he composed in I.23.3. As I outlined above, the first objection centered on God's abundant love of his creatures. To this Aquinas simply asserts that God does *not* want *all* people to be saved. We know this from his preceding explication of 1 Timothy 2:4, where Aquinas writes that when God does not want eternal salvation for people he is said to *hate* them or to *reprobate* them (*dicitur eos habere odio vel reprobare*) (I.23.3, ad 1). He is confident that God does *not* love us all. Does this square with the scripture quoted in the objection affirming God's universal love (Ws 11:25)? Is it congruent with the proclamation in 1 John 4:8–19 that "God is love"? The Angelic Doctor thinks so.

His answer to the second objection tries to stave off the logic of double predestination articulated there. He does so by stating that the forms of causality at work in predestination and in reprobation are not the same. Predestination causes both the grace, which enables fallen humans to live well, and it causes the final reward, the life in glory. God's reprobation, however, causes the abandonment by God of some of those born in original sin, but it does not cause sin itself. This withdrawal of grace means that the heirs of Adam and Eve will stumble from sin to sin, accumulating the demerits which will finally be rewarded with everlasting hell. Aquinas insists (as Augustine had done and Calvin will do) that the guilt of the reprobate is from their own free decision ("culpa provenit ex libero arbitrio ejus qui reprobatur"). But, as Aquinas argues, it is also caused by the fact that these people have been *deserted* by divine grace (*gratia deseritur*) (I.23.3, ad 2).

The third objection outlined above argues that nobody should be punished for what they could not avoid. Aquinas has just acknowledged that while all human beings, derived from Adam and Eve, were born in original sin, the predestinate receive grace which enables a life of virtue, whereas the reprobate are abandoned without any such grace. Aquinas asserts that such abandonment does not diminish the powers of the reprobate. The predestinate and the reprobate equally have *liberum arbitrium*, free choice or judgment. He agrees with the objection that the predestinate must necessarily be saved. Here we might remember Langland's Rechelesnesse: he objected to what he perceived as an arbitrary difference between the salvation of an adulterous murderer such as David, and the damnation of an unbaptized but virtuous person such as Aristotle (XI.205–21, 252–71a). Aquinas's reply is that the necessity with which the predestinate are saved is a conditional necessity (*praedestinatum necesse est salvari necessitate conditionata, quae non tollit libertatem arbitrii*) (I.23.3, ad 3). He agrees that the reprobate cannot do anything to acquire the grace they would need for salvation. He also agrees that without such grace, they are *compelled* to fall into sin through their own free choice (*ex ejus libero arbitrio*). Rather like an addict of any destructive substance, the reprobate can be said to continue his addiction by his own free choice, *ex ejus libero arbitrio*. All those born in original sin and deprived of the grace of conversion and perseverance are damned justly. The Angelic Doctor is apparently satisfied with his reasonings. Whether these would have satisfied Langland's Wille in Passus XI–XII, I very much doubt.

The next article in the treatise on predestination addresses relations between love, election, and predestination (I.23.4). The discussion here includes a reading of 1 Timothy 4, whose theological traditions I have already exemplified, including Aquinas's own exegesis (I.19.6; I.23.4, obj. 3, ad 3). Here, in addition to affirming his earlier approbation of Augustinian interpretations, Aquinas acknowledges that God predestines some to salvation. This "means that God wills their salvation." He thus offers saving love "to some and not to others, for, as we have seen [I.23.3] some he reprobates" (I.23.4, resp.). Aquinas does not venture to quantify his "some," but the prolific and influential theologian Jean Gerson reckoned this "some" would be about a quarter of all human beings, applying Jesus's parable of the sower as his warrant for this figure (Matt. 13:2–23). One can see how such thinking and such wild exegesis could encourage the kind of panic that overwhelmed Langland's Wille as he misheard another of Jesus's parables. No wonder that even Jean Gerson's devout sisters asked their theologian brother what chance they had of being saved when so few are graced to salvation.[24]

Despite Aquinas's assurance that predestination presupposes election and election presupposes love, these articles on predestination seem conspicuously lacking in attention to divine love and redemption (unlike the third part of the *Summa Theologiae*, devoted to Christology and the sacraments flowing from the passion of Christ). Perhaps what at first appears to be a striking lacuna is not, after all, surprising when one considers the essentially Augustinian model of predestination and reprobation that Aquinas defends. The fifth article of Aquinas's question on predestination insists that God does indeed impose a massively unequal outcome (heaven for some, hell for others) on humans who, having all been born in original sin, are essentially equal. As an objection to this, Aquinas presents an argument that seeks to deliver God from the injustice of a doctrine that seems to make God exactly what the apostle Peter was taught that God is *not*: unjustly partial, a respecter of persons (*personarum acceptor*). I am thinking here of the episode related in Acts 10: led by the Holy Spirit to go to the Roman soldier Cornelius and his household, against his ideas of purity, Peter learns that "God is not a respecter of persons. But in every nation, he that feareth him and worketh justice is acceptable to him" (Acts 10:34–35). Aquinas does not cite this challenging text in the objection, but it was frequently used in medieval discourses on election.[25] Instead, the objection Aquinas writes asserts that since God is neither unjust nor arbitrary, he must reward and damn people on account of actions he has foreseen (I.23.5, obj. 3). This view is, of course, anathema to Augustinian Christianity and the orthodox tradition Aquinas defends. It was in the Middle Ages habitually judged to be Pelagian, as it would be in the Reformation. In rejecting it, Aquinas confesses God's goodness and merely asserts that his *justice* is displayed in the eternal damnation of those born in original sin while his *mercy* is displayed in the salvation of predestined sinners (I.23.5, ad 3). Why does God elect some sinners to bliss and reprobate others to everlasting hell? In answer to this question Aquinas acknowledges that no reason can be found except to name the *will* of God: "sed quare hos elegit in gloriam cet illos reprobavit, non habet rationis, nisi divinam voluntatem" (I.23.5, ad 3). He turns to the authority of Augustine, who beats the same drum in his homilies: to predestine one and reprobate another depends not on the actions of human beings but entirely on the simple will of God (*dependet ex simplici divina voluntate*) (I.25.5, ad 3).

Some of the problems germane to this tradition are manifest in an illustration Aquinas provides in an attempt to assuage any ethical anxieties that might by this point be emerging among his students. These students, after all, soon have to become priests and confessors to Christians who, like Langland's Wille and Rechelesnesse, may be deeply troubled by this teaching. I think Aquinas's clarificatory exemplum is worth pausing over both in its own right and because it is later invoked by teachers such as the fourteenth-century Dominican author of the *Summa Praedicantium* to which I will soon turn. Aquinas invites us to think of someone building a wall. The builder has a plan, which requires the use of stones, some here, some there. Aquinas observes that no injustice can be ascribed to the builder for placing different stones in different parts of the wall.[26] How does he want us to apply this example concerning builder, stones, and wall? Aquinas tells us to think of God's unequal distribution of equally sinful humans as akin to the builder of the wall distributing one stone here and another there (I.23.5, ad 3). This is an astonishingly bland analogy in the context of an exploration of our salvation and damnation. But its very blandness seems part of its force: if Aquinas can persuade his students to analogize like this, he will be persuading them to make a major step in accommodating themselves to the Augustinian orthodoxy on predestination and reprobation. Such accommodation will certainly be much easier if the human lives at stake are figured in ways that entirely dehumanize them. Let silent stones replace Jacob or Esau, you or me. Perhaps this substitution will diminish the likelihood of reading such arguments in ways that produce the terrors described by Bunyan in *Grace Abounding* or by Wille in *Piers Plowman*. Yet this strategy is replete with ethical difficulties: if the authorities we reverence teach us to imagine our fellow humans as inert stones, then we are being prepared to theologize about them and treat them as things rather than as living, suffering, hoping images of God. I discern continuities between such language and Aquinas's later arguments defending the church's practice of burning to death those deemed to be obstinate heretics (*ST* II–II.11). A habitual dehumanization in language and imagination serves as preparation for an astonishing cruelty in practice. Indeed, in engaging these modes of thought, we prepare ourselves for practices that Christ the Samaritan in *Piers Plowman* identifies as the primary sin against the Holy Spirit: unkyndenesse (XIX.255–56; see XIX.172–334).

Let us stay a little longer with those who are represented among the stones, the reprobate. Aquinas assures us that these people are preordained (*praeordinate*) by God not only for the beauty of the builder's wall but also for the good of the elect (*in bonum electorum*) (*ST* I.23.7, resp.). Locutions such as this would be quite at home in Calvinist writing. Furthermore, like Jean Gerson, Aquinas is confident that the elect are the minority (*pauciores*), while the reprobate constitute the majority (*plurimi*) who never receive the grace that would enable conversion to a life of virtue (I.23.7, ad 3). As we read these arguments and images, we do not seem far removed from the Catholic theologian who became archbishop of Canterbury before dying in 1349, Thomas Bradwardine. His massive work *De Causa Dei* was printed in 1618 in support of Calvinist theology at the Synod of Dort, dedicated to James I and published under the patronage of the Calvinist archbishop of Canterbury, George Abbot.[27] Bradwardine only devotes four chapters to predestination and reprobation (I.44–47, 420–41). There is enough ambiguity in the grammar of divine agency here to prevent a reader from being sure whether Bradwardine affirms a Thomistic model of election or whether he slides toward one of double predestination.[28] Be that as it may, he concludes his discussion by considering a view that the church's teaching on this subject makes God wicked and cruel (I.47, 440). But Bradwardine affirms that the elect actually profit greatly from the making of reprobates. Indeed, he asserts that the reprobates have been especially created for the elect (*ipsi reprobi propter electos specialiter sunt creati*). Aquinas agrees (*ST* I.23.7, resp.). And, as in Aquinas's analogy of the stones and the wall, Bradwardine's way of thinking discourages attention to the human realities such theology claims to address. Bradwardine asks what wickedness or cruelty could possibly be charged to God for making one human (the reprobate) for the service of another human (the predestined). Both the predestined and the reprobate, like Aquinas's stones, serve the greater good, God's glory. Besides, Bradwardine argues, God's punishments are just and merciful. Even the reprobate should be grateful for their making. Indeed, if God should eternally punish the innocent, we could not accuse him of cruelty and wickedness. Think of all the innocent animals God punishes (I.47, 441). In case a reader might not be persuaded by these assertions, Bradwardine turns not to Aquinas's builder with his stones but rather to Paul's potter with his lump of clay, quoting Romans 9:21.[29] He closes the chapter affirming that the spirit of truth teaches us truth (I.47, 441).

It would be wrong to leave Aquinas's treatment of predestination without considering his return to the topic in his explorations of Christology in the third part of the *Summa Theologiae*. As noted above, the figure of Jesus Christ had hardly been a shaping presence in the treatise on predestination in part 1, but perhaps the new location might make a difference. Considering the grace of Christ, which makes him head of the church, Aquinas takes note of those who are not predestined to union with Christ. At their death, those people who have not received the gift of persevering grace will be totally separated from Christ (III.8.3, resp.). Once again we meet the reprobates. Later in this part, Aquinas addresses the predestination of Christ himself (III.24). Is Jesus Christ among the elect? In *The Predestination of the Saints*, Augustine argued that the man Jesus Christ is "the most brilliant beacon of predestination and of grace." In his human nature, he exemplifies how the elect have no preexisting merits of faith or works, nothing to deserve salvation. So Jesus "was predestined" to be assumed by the Word of God (15.30–31). Aquinas draws explicitly on Augustine's work in his affirmation that Jesus Christ was predestined (III.24.2, sed contra, resp., ad 3). He does so again in the next articles, both on Christ's predestination as the "exemplar" of human predestination and on Christ's predestination as "the cause" of human predestination (III.24.4). Augustine pervades Aquinas's writing on predestination quite as much as he does his treatise on grace (I-II.109–14).[30] A change in location does not seem to make for any difference in approach.

In concluding my discussion of Aquinas and the contemporary consensus on the subject of predestination, I will stay in the third part of *Summa Theologiae* to consider a text exploring Christ's prayers (III.21). This topic had troubled theologians for centuries. It did so because it generated searching questions about what became orthodox teaching on Christ's two natures.[31] My own concerns with Question 21 of part 3 are not on Chalcedonian Christology; rather they center on the fourth article: whether Christ's prayer was always heard. One objection to the orthodox affirmation of this statement is that Christ prayed for the forgiveness of those who crucified him (Luke 23:34). The objection maintains that despite these prayers, "not all were pardoned this sin, since the Jews were punished on account thereof. Therefore it seems that not every prayer of his was heard" (III.21.4, obj. 2). Aquinas's reply to this is as odd as it is illuminating: he simply states that Christ did *not* pray for all who crucified him: "Dominus non oravit pro omnibus crucifixoribus" (III.21.4, ad 2). Let us recall the evangelical text: "Pater, dimitte illis: non enim sciunt quid faciunt [Father, forgive them, for they do not know what they do]" (Luke 23:24). Aquinas feels quite free to add an exclusionary qualifier to Christ's prayer, though there are no traces of this in Luke's gospel. True enough, all traditions of Christian exegesis are replete with examples of theologians bending the wax nose of scripture to prevent it from causing trouble for their version of orthodox dogmatics (whether by church or sect). But what troubles might the Lord's prayer on the cross make for the Common Doctor of the church?

The trouble is that it contains no traces of the binary foundational to the consensus on predestination and reprobation in Aquinas's church. Where in Christ's prayer is there a sign of those included by God's love (the "Jacobs") being separated from those excluded (the "Esaus")? The trouble this gospel text makes for Aquinas here, and for all those sustaining Augustinian orthodoxy, is similar to the trouble made by 1 Timothy 2:4. We recall that in this epistle God is said to will the salvation of all humans, and we will also recall the exegetical and theological strategies normalized in turning *all* into *not all*. Yet Jesus's prayer to the Father from the cross perhaps causes even more trouble for Augustinians than does the verse from 1 Timothy because this prayer is not uncharacteristic of the Gospels' accounts of his ministry. The Gospels often show Jesus Christ being vilified for his failure to support the binary in question and its variants. For example, he is vilified by the guardians of orthodoxy for keeping an open table that failed to exclude notorious sinners: "Now the publicans and the sinners drew near unto him to hear him. And the Pharisees and the scribes murmured saying: This man receiveth sinners and eateth with them" (Luke 15:1–2). Or take the example given in Jesus's rebuke to his disciples who wanted him to display the vengeful violence Elijah had used against those who troubled him (2 Kings 1:9–15):

> And he sent messengers before his face; and going, they entered into a city of the Samaritans, to prepare for him. And they received him not, because his face was of one going to Jerusalem. And when his disciples James and John had seen this, they said: Lord, will thou that we command fire to come down from heaven, and consume them? And turning, he rebuked them, saying: You know not of what spirit you are. The Son of man came not to destroy souls, but to save. (Luke 9:52–56)

Jesus's words from the cross in Luke's gospel are totally congruent with this version of Christ. But they can apparently make an orthodox medieval theologian uneasy enough to gloss them against the grain of the text. Aquinas's gloss asserts, without qualification, that Christ *only* prayed for the predestinate:

> The Lord did not pray for all those who crucified him, and nor did he for all those who would believe in him, *but only for those who were predestined to eternal life through him* [Dominus non oravit pro omnibus crucifixoribus, neque etiam pro omnibus qui erant credituri in eum, sed pro his solum qui erant praedestinati ut per ipsum vitam consequeruntur aeternam]. (*ST* III.21.4, ad 2; my emphasis)

We see a similar gloss later in part 3 when Aquinas discusses Christ's harrowing of hell (III.52). Aquinas asserts that Christ only freed the elect (*electos*) while leaving behind the reprobates (*reprobos*). He does so in an article that asks whether Christ freed any of the damned from hell (III.52.6). Aquinas denies that he did. The first authoritative text he offers for his position is in the sed contra of the article, a text Langland also used in his comments on Christ's crucifixion: "Ero mors tua, O mors, morsus tuus ero, inferne" (O death, I will be thy death; O hell, I will be thy bite) (Hosea 13:14; *Piers Plowman* XX.34). To this text, Aquinas attaches a comment from a medieval gloss to the Bible explaining that Christ achieves his victory over death and hell by leading forth the elect and leaving behind the reprobates. He then concludes this comment by observing that only the reprobates are in the hell of the damned and Christ did not go there, nor did he liberate any reprobates from hell (III.52.6, sed contra). Langland, however, ascribes Hosea's prophecy to a personification called "Lyf" whose concerns are not those of the Dominican. Lyf comments on Christ's crucifixion, which he sees as inextricably bound up with the resurrection, the liberation of "Peres fruyt the plouhman [the fruit of Piers the plowman]" (XX.30–36a, referring to XVII.100–116). For Langland, Hosea's prophecy of liberation does not encourage glosses speculating about reprobation, reprobates, and Christ's exclusion of those he calls his half-brethren, his brethren, his "kyn," and his "kynde" (XX.393–449).

Moreover, unlike Aquinas, Langland does not depict Christ choosing to leave in the hell of the damned all unbaptized children. We have seen that Augustine, Lombard, and Aquinas teach that God's decision to withhold saving grace from most humans is the cause of reprobation. We have seen how this tradition emphasizes that the decision has nothing to do with human vices (*ST* I.23.2). And we have seen how the unborn twins, Jacob and Esau, are frequently deployed as figures of predestination and reprobation (I.23.3). Now, in his discussion of Christ's liberation of humanity, Aquinas speculates on God's judgment of infants (*pueri*) who died without baptism. He determines that Christ refused to deliver these infants from hell (III.52.7). He composes some strong objections to his own orthodoxy. The second of these appeals to Paul's celebration of God's grace abounding to "many" through Christ

(Rom. 5:15) and comments that the unbaptized children are not in hell because of any sin committed but because of Adam's sin (III.52.7, obj. 2). Another objection is that the power of Christ's passion liberates people from the sin of Adam: Christ's liberating presence in hell would thus liberate such children (III.52.7, obj. 3). Aquinas could here have taken note of a promise in scripture:

> In those days shall they say no more: The fathers have eaten sour grapes and the teeth of the children are set on edge. But every one shall die for his own iniquity: Every man that shall come, saith the Lord, and I will make a new covenant with the house of Israel, and with the house of Juda. (Jer. 31:29–31; see also Ezek. 18:1–5, 19–32)

But Aquinas replies to these objections that when Paul wrote that grace abounds to many (*in plures abundavit*), he did *not* mean to suggest that more (*plures*) were saved by Christ than lost by Adam's sin. As for unbaptized infants in hell, Aquinas claims to know that Christ's grace could not have reached them. Why is Aquinas so sure of this? His confidence is that infants who died unbaptized could not have been freed by Christ because his grace could only reach those who became his members by spiritual regeneration (III.52.7, ad 2). This is a rather puzzling assertion, since his own treatises on grace and on predestination make clear that it is God's grace that *enables* spiritual regeneration and is the product of his eternal will. It is also puzzling because he and his church teach that, through the sacrament of baptism, the church's priests (or, in an emergency, even midwives) can communicate Christ's saving grace to dying infants so that they are not damned. Finally, it is puzzling because he later acknowledges, without any equivocation, that God's grace is *never limited* to the sacraments he ordained for the church (III.64.7, resp.).

In his assertions about Christ's inability to deliver unbaptized infants from hell in the harrowing of hell (or at any other time), Aquinas thus contradicts his own acknowledgment that God does not limit his grace to the sacraments or ministers of the church—or even to Christians in the performance of baptism (III.67.5). I think he also goes against his own account of divine power in part 1 (I.25). There he confesses that God is *not* restricted to any particular order that God institutes. God certainly *could* do what God does not do (I.25.5, sed contra). Aquinas writes in this account:

> Whence the divine wisdom is not so restricted to any particular order that no other course of events could happen. Wherefore we must simply say that God can do other things than those he had done [Unde divina sapientia non determinatur ad aliquem certum ordinem rerum, ut non possit alivs cursus rerum ab ipsa effluere. Unde dicendum est simpliciter quod Deus potest alia facere quam quae facit]. (*ST* I.25.5, resp.)

Some readers might be inclined to associate such views specifically with Ockham or Holcot and their emphasis on the contingency of any particular dispensation, but what Aquinas says here is a medieval commonplace. It is often rehearsed by theologians addressing a question found in their Lombardian textbook: could God have made a better world than this one?[32] This response also relates to a much-discussed conception of divine power, understood in its "absolute" mode and in its "ordained" mode.[33] Aquinas himself uses this distinction in the article I am discussing. The wisdom and justice of God cannot be restricted to the present order (*de potentia ordinata*). We must affirm that things could be otherwise, that God could act differently (*secundum potentiam absolutam*) (I.25.5, resp.; see too I.25.5, ad 2). Such statements seem obvious enough reflections of the fact that Christians do not worship Aristotle's first mover but the God disclosed in scripture. Yet when Aquinas thinks about reprobation of unbaptized infants, his confidence in Christ's inability to free them testifies to the hold of Augustinian theology on his thinking. And in this commitment, he was perfectly representative of the consensus in the medieval church of his time.

* * *

Had Wille gone back to "scole" in the later fourteenth century, he would certainly have become familiar with the paradigm I have been illustrating. He would also have become equally familiar with the kinds of objections that theologians were trained to compose as a means of strengthening the position they wished to defend. We have encountered some examples of Aquinas doing this in his treatment of election. But Wille would probably also have met new arguments that went beyond the standard objections rehearsed in the dominant paradigm. Very likely, he would have encountered the emergence of two rival paradigms of divine election. These have been carefully identified and described by James Halverson in his study of predestination in the theology of Peter Aureol (d. 1322).[34] In my view, Halverson has demonstrated that Aureol established a paradigm of predestination and reprobation that was fundamentally opposed to the Augustinian one defended by Aquinas. Indeed, Halverson remarks that "Aureol has developed a doctrine of predestination unlike any in Latin theology."[35] While such claims to originality are precarious (who can be certain that one's confidence in something being unprecedented will not turn out to be merely a sign of one's ignorance about earlier histories?), I remain persuaded by his close reading of Aureol on election, and by his comparisons with the theological tradition in which Aureol was apprenticed.

What are the features that James Halverson identifies in the making of this rival tradition? They are ones that might have given Wille good hope. In Aureol's account, God's electing will is "general." That is why Halverson names this model GE, general election. God does not predestine and reprobate particular individuals like the unborn twins Esau and Jacob. Rather, God offers saving grace to *all* who do not place an obstacle in the way of this grace but simply receive it. If one wants an analogy, think of the sun shining: "The sun shines wherever its rays are not impeded. In a like manner, God's gracious will is effective wherever it is not impeded." In this model, the cause of reprobation is not God's providential plan to make me an Esau-stone rather than a Jacob-stone in his wall. It is rather my freely chosen maintenance of an obstacle to grace, "obex gratiae." We are free, in other words, to resist divine grace. Aureol was confident he was not veering into Pelagianism in his thinking on the resistibility of grace because, he insists, we cannot ever merit God's grace or our salvation.[36] Despite criticism from those who saw Aureol (correctly) as breaking with the consensus that knew itself as orthodox tradition, Halverson shows that there were theologians who responded to this new paradigm with considerable sympathy. He presents examples of such work from William of Ockham, Robert Holcot, and Thomas of Strasbourg (working in the fourteenth century), together with Gabriel Biel, writing in the later fifteenth century.

At the same time, the hegemonic paradigm of predestination received a very different challenge. This challenge took the form of an explicit and unembarrassed version of double predestination, a version extremely close to that espoused in the mid-sixteenth century by Peter Martyr in his conversion from the Augustinian Order to the Calvinist Reformation.[37] The originator of this version of double predestination was Gregory of Rimini, who lectured on the *Sentences* at Paris in 1343–44 and became prior general of the Augustinian Order of hermits in 1357. Halverson acknowledges that other historians argue that Gregory's paradigm was "unique among Scholastics." He agrees, but he also contends that in Gregory's critical response to Aureol and his composition of double predestination, we are witnessing a clash between new paradigms that exemplifies how "the Scholastic consensus concerning predestination was irrevocably shattered. From this point on there would be three doctrinally viable doctrines of predestination in Western theology. The Reformation did not cause this pluralism; it merely reinforced a diversity that was already present in theological discussion" (143).

While I think this a salutary and well-warranted historical claim, it seems to me that Halverson's "merely" may be too abstract, too cerebral to reflect the consequences of a doctrine of double predestination in the lives of at least some of its adherents within the political and cultural conflicts of the Reformation in the sixteenth and seventeenth centuries. Before turning to evidence of some of these consequences in the Calvinist writing of post-Reformation England, however, I want first to offer some brief exemplifications of the new and conflicting paradigms whose origins in the fourteenth century Halverson has identified.

First, I will illustrate the model of double predestination developed by Gregory of Rimini. He is quite clear that there is a perfect symmetry between predestination and reprobation. The fragile block Aquinas and his tradition had carefully erected against such symmetry is swept aside as illogical and unwarranted in an Augustinian theology. Gregory explicitly poses the question that lay behind the discourse of Rechelessnesse and Wille in *Piers Plowman*: "Utrum quilibet homo fuerit ab aeterno praedestinatus vel reprobatus a deo" (Whether anyone is predestined or reprobated by God from eternity).[38] Gregory's answer is unequivocal: there is no cause for eternal life or eternal damnation in the lives and loves of human beings. The good and evil works of human beings are irrelevant to God's eternal will concerning their destiny.[39] Inevitably, Gregory takes up the traditional proof text in this discourse: Esau and Jacob in Romans 9:13. Jacob, affirms Gregory, figures forth the predestinate; Esau figures forth the eternally reprobate.[40] Gregory is confident that in this he follows Augustine, whom he cites copiously and justly. Just as inevitably, he addresses Paul's statement that God wills the salvation of *all* (1 Tim. 2:4). Here he is certainly within the theological mainstream we have been following, for he, too, argues that the text means God does *not* want to save *all* human beings but only some from all estates. He cites Augustine's *The Predestination of the Saints* and *Enchiridion* to show how orthodox and traditional is his exegesis.[41] Like many before him, including Bradwardine, Gregory asks whether the God he describes and worships is wicked, cruel, and unjust. His answer is the familiar *O altitudo* and the assertion that God does no injustice to anyone by reprobating them from eternity.[42] He acknowledges that he is addressing difficult and dangerous matters, but like his predecessors and contemporaries in "scole," he, too, manifests no trace of existential anxiety, no uncomfortable sense that he might be Esau or Judas (Bunyan's fear in *Grace Abounding*). He assures his listeners that he is only mediating Catholic tradition and that nothing he teaches is derived from his own invention: "nihil ex me."[43] Certainly there is no trace of Wille's "tene" (vexation, anger), none of his panic. How would Gregory have consoled the latter? Not, as far as I can see, by any Christological meditation, by any attempt to show Wille how the doctrine of election is gospel.

Having offered this outline of Gregory of Rimini's predestinarian thought, I will briefly illustrate the version of election that Halverson names "general election." While he concentrates on Peter Aureol as the major source for this paradigm, he recognizes the Dominican Robert Holcot as a participant. Halverson shows how Holcot moved from "an unenthusiastic acceptance" of the dominant tradition in his early lectures on the *Sentences* "to an unambiguous endorsement of GE [general election]" in his lectures on the Book of Wisdom.[44] This extraordinarily vivacious and eclectic theologian has attracted some very fine work by historians of medieval theology and philosophy. These scholars have shown how mistaken is the once-common opinion that Holcot was a skeptic, an agnostic, and a fideist. Instead, recent historians have identified Holcot's critical thought with a particular culture of academic discourse that welcomed forms of Christian thought across many genres. This culture grasped the ways in which God's revelation was continually provoking new questions to philosophy and theology, new questions to human beings in changing historical circumstances. He belonged to a theological and philosophical moment in which it was appreciated that received treatments of many topics were not the final word and might actually include mistakes that require correction—even in the work of Aquinas or Scotus. These theologians were active contributors to the continuation of Christian tradition, posing new questions and bringing attention to resources that had been sidelined in earlier versions. Such it is to participate in a living tradition.[45]

Let us briefly consider the version of election developed by Holcot, and let us do so by comparing his approach to a recurrent image we have already encountered in the dominant paradigm Holcot was challenging: the potter, the clay, and the vessels of honor and dishonor. Holcot engages with this image in the course of his massive, often dazzling lectures on the Book of Wisdom, given when he was a master of theology. As John Slotemaker and Jeffrey Witt observe in their recent book on Holcot, this work survived in over 175 medieval manuscripts and was "a medieval bestseller."[46] It is the kind of work that crossed boundaries between academic theology, preaching, and the literate laity. It seems extremely likely, for example, that Chaucer knew and made use of this fascinating work in his *Canterbury Tales*.[47]

During his lectures on this book, Holcot reaches the opening of chapter 12 in Lectio 146.[48] He has already discussed one of the texts given by Aquinas as an objection against his Augustinian teaching on predestination: "For thou lovest all things that are and hatest none of the things which thou hast made" (Ws 11:25; see *ST* I.23.3, obj. 1). Holcot sets out with the remainder of the passage: "And how could any thing endure, if thou wouldst not? Or be preserved, if not called by thee. But thou sparest all: because they are thine, O Lord, who lovest souls" (Ws 11:26–27). Unlike Aquinas's teaching on predestination in part 1 of the *Summa Theologiae*, Holcot discusses the divine call in this passage as an evocation of God's call to humanity through the Word made flesh (Lectio 145, 488). In the next Lectio (146), his text is the opening two verses of the twelfth chapter of the Book of Wisdom: "O how good and sweet is thy spirit, O Lord, in all things! And therefore thou chastisest them that err, by little and little: and admonishest them, and speakest to them, concerning the things wherein they offended: that leaving their wickedness, they may believe in thee, O Lord."

Holcot reads this text as describing the divine sweetness that is infused into the minds of the just as well as God's admirable mildness in correcting the sinners (Lectio 146, 490–91). Although nobody can have the kind of *certainty* regarding one's predestined status that (as I discuss in chapter 3) will become an obsession of Calvin and his followers in the Reformation, Holcot describes signs by which someone may discern whether she is being led by the Holy Spirit in daily life (Lectio 146, 491–92). As he pursues conventional questions about the relations between divine and human agency, he introduces the image of the potter and his clay (Rom. 9:20–23; Jer. 18:6). At first it seems that Holcot will maintain the Augustinian and Thomistic insistence that humans who receive grace do not receive it because they have disposed themselves for the gift—not, that is, because of any merit in themselves, but because of God's will alone. But against this traditional anti-Pelagian teaching, Holcot argues that if humans do the best they can, then God will give them the grace they need for salvation (Lectio 146, 492).[49] God only withholds grace from those who, like Satan, reject God's offer: "ipse non accepit. Quia quicunque se parat ut accipiat, necessario recipit" (Lectio 146, 492). In considering common disputations concerning such claims, Holcot distinguishes different meanings of *necessario*. He observes that in the sense of a necessary compulsion, *necessario* never pertains to God. This is because God has freely given his promise and covenant: "ex promisso suo & pacto, sive lege statuta" (Lectio 146, 492). God freely promises to give grace to those doing the best they can to follow the ways of God. The figure of Cornelius in Acts 10 would be a good example of this. God, however, is not compelled by any antecedent or extrinsic necessity to give his grace: the disposition of humans cannot act as a cause on God "de necessitate" (Lectio 146, 492).

But God is utterly faithful to this promise, that is, to the covenant he has established with humanity, even though this does not prevent him establishing a new covenant.[50]

Finally, Holcot comes to the analogy of the potter and the clay pots. This is clearly an image that has been frequently used in service of a paradigm of divine agency quite alien to the one Holcot is elaborating. That paradigm thus seems to be one supported not only by scripture but also by the authoritative weight of the church's saints and doctors. How can Holcot challenge this authority? He agrees that, of course, in one way, we are indeed as clay in the hands of a creative God. *In one way*. But the simile does not hold *in every way*. Holcot does not name his august predecessors (including the recently canonized theologian of his own order, Aquinas) as he reads the text against the grain of its traditional appropriation. But he observes something the Angelic Doctor failed to note in his use of the simile (*ST* I.23.5, ad 3): namely, that there is no *covenant* (*pactum*) between the potter and the clay. Furthermore, even if there could be a *pactum* between a potter and his clay, or between Aquinas's builder and the stones used in making the wall, the artisan could break the specific covenant (*pactum*) with the clay, leaving the general law that governs all covenants still standing. But God could not break his covenant with humans and leave the covenantal law unbroken. Nor can the clay be promised anything by the artisan, neither *de condigno* nor *de congruo*. Holcot thus totally rejects the analogy as it is applied by Augustine, Aquinas, and many others. In Holcot's view, it simply gives us no relevant picture of the way God relates to human beings through his gracious making of covenants to help them to their heavenly flourishing.

Holcot closes his thoughtful and critical discussion with the kind of warning perhaps more associated with Thomas à Kempis's *Imitation of Christ* than with "scole" work: "In hac tamen quaestione magis pie quam logice est loquendum [In studying this question one should talk more devoutly than logically]" (Lectio 146, 492). John Slotemaker and Jeffrey Witt see this conclusion as Holcot demonstrating "a pastoral sensibility for his audience: that is, preachers should follow the rule of piety and not strict logic when discussing this analogy."[51] That is one way of reading the ending. Another way would concur but further suggest that Holcot is able to do this, against the grain of traditional theology, because he has broken with the hegemonic paradigm defended by the authoritative Dominican teacher, Thomas Aquinas. Only by inhabiting and elaborating an alternative paradigm, as Halverson argues, could Holcot have the resources to make this rhetorical and theological move. Christians, like those figured by Langland's Wille, would have been grateful for such "pastoral sensibility" in this sphere. But in order to access this sensibility, they would need to find a teacher at "scole" who embraced the way in which "the scholastic consensus concerning predestination was irrevocably shattered," one using this fragmentation to enable participation in the paradigm Halverson calls GE, general election.[52] Only in this paradigm did it seem possible to take with utter seriousness, rather than caustic disdain, Paul's statement that God willed *all* people to be saved (1 Tim. 2:4). And if one were even to begin such revisionary work, then one would necessarily also have to rethink the commonplace assumption that Jacob and Esau were figures of the eternally predestined and eternally reprobate.[53] Some in the fourteenth century were ready to do this.

✳ ✳ ✳

I will conclude this chapter by considering the study of predestination and election in a mid-fourteenth-century work. This is the *Summa Praedicantium* by the Dominican John Bromyard, who probably died by 1352.[54] The work is brilliantly designed to make academic theology an accessible resource for preachers and confessors working beyond the walls of the university. Replete with the vivid exempla that so intrigued G. R. Owst in his *Literature and the Pulpit in Medieval England*, it is also a massive encyclopedia of theological and pastoral topics discussed with great thoughtfulness and often surprising thoroughness.[55] The entry on predestination is no exception to this. Although it does not mention by name any fourteenth-century theologians, it is written after what Halverson describes as the shattering of the thirteenth-century consensus and the introduction of a "multi-sided debate" on models of predestination and reprobation.[56] It seems to me that its eclecticism and its genuinely exploratory nature are a testimony to these circumstances.

Bromyard incorporates in his treatise on predestination the Augustinian and Thomistic tradition that insists there is no cause for human salvation other than God's will. Such a confession was not without the kinds of equivocation that academic theology generated and disputed as part of its apprenticeships. But Bromyard is not writing solely for the university coteries that generated over four hundred years of disputative commentaries on Peter Lombard's *Sentences*. He writes also for preachers and confessors—for, that is, the clergy who were charged with caring for the souls of people such as Wille.

He sets out with the language of predestination in the Epistle to the Ephesians. God, the writer says, "hath predestinated us unto the adoption of children through Jesus Christ unto himself: according to the purpose of his will: unto the praise of the glory of his grace, in which he hath graced us in his beloved son" (Eph. 1:5–6). This quotation helps Bromyard address a common question in academic treatments of election. Ockham's formulation of this question is a typical one: "Utrum in praedestinatio sit aliqua causa praedestinationis et in reprobatio aliqua causa suae reprobationis [Whether there is any cause of predestination in the predestined and whether there is any cause in the reprobate of reprobation]."[57] We encountered this question in the earlier treatment of predestination by the Dominican saint, Thomas Aquinas (*ST* I.23.2). Bromyard agrees that human salvation depends entirely on divine goodness, a proposition that no Christian theologian denied (*SP*, 246). Later in his exposition he aligns this common opinion with Paul's statement that salvation "is not of him that willeth, nor of him that runneth, but of God that showeth mercy" (*SP*, 250; Rom. 9:16). But what do such conventional locutions tell us about human agency and its relationship to divine agency?

Like Aquinas and so many others who addressed this topic, Bromyard considers an image from the same chapter of Romans, one that has been prominent throughout this chapter: the analogy of the potter, the clay, and the pots (Rom. 9:17–23). To Bromyard this famous text seems an *objection* to what is one of his firmest convictions: namely, that nothing in Christian doctrine should call into question God's gift of *liberum arbitrium*. Yet if the analogy of the potter is read in the way Augustine, Aquinas, and Gregory of Rimini read it, it surely does so. Indeed,

Bromyard strengthens the opposition he presents to his own position by recalling how God commanded Isaiah to blind the hearts of his people lest they be comforted and healed (Isa. 6:10). He thinks, too, of God's people lamenting that God has made them err and has hardened their hearts against God himself (Isa. 63:10). Alongside this he sets Paul's claim that God delivered idolatrous gentiles "to a reprobate sense to do those things that are not convenient" and so to make them "worthy of death" (Rom. 1:28, 32). Bromyard observes that such texts seem to make God the author of sin, the cause of the acts of reprobates. Following medieval tradition, Bromyard denies that this could be so. God moves our will, but he does so without coercion. He is no tyrant, and he created humans with the gift of *liberum arbitrium*, making its actions central to their destiny (250). But he has already asserted that not everything happens by necessity (249). Those who do wickedly have only themselves to blame.

Why? After all, we have seen that orthodox tradition (Augustine, Aquinas) maintained that we who are reprobates are reprobates not only because we act badly, as all born in original sin are doomed to do, but because God has withheld the grace that he gave our fellow sinners who were predestined (such as the adulterous murderer David). Yet Bromyard does *not* take this conventional line. He says instead that those who enact evil do so because they actually *resist* the light of grace. They resemble people who shut their eyes against the sun, which illuminates the whole world (*SP*, 250). This sounds very like statements Halverson reports from the paradigm generated by Aureol, Holcot, and Biel, the one he designates GE. God pours out grace to all of us, but we are all free to resist such grace, to place *obstacles* in its way, to shut our eyes to its light.

Unlike his Dominican contemporary Robert Holcot, Bromyard does not directly question the relevance of Paul's analogy of the potter and clay to the theology of predestination. Instead, he puts forward another analogy. He asks us to consider the case of a murderer who acted under the influence of alcohol.[58] The killer's drunken state does not excuse his act of slaughter because it, too, is a sin. He became drunk through the exercise of his will (*voluntarie*). In this analogy, the murderer's choice to intoxicate himself is akin to the sinner's choice to refuse the grace of God. Bromyard imagines that such people say to God, "Depart from us. We desire not the knowledge of thy ways" (*SP*, 250; Job 21:14). Bromyard finds such *resistance* to grace an extraordinary act but a free one that leads to compulsive sinning. For such addiction, Bromyard argues, God is not responsible. With the gift of *liberum arbitrium* comes God's permission to use this gift, even if one chooses to do so against one's flourishing. Bromyard acknowledges that we are free to enslave ourselves in self-destructive practices.

As he develops this line of inquiry, he twice touches on a text that, as we have seen, had proved challenging to those writing in the dominant paradigm for discussing predestination and reprobation: 1 Timothy 2:4, God wills *all* people to be saved (omnes *homines vult salvos fieri*). We have already considered the habitual ways of manipulating this text to conform to the favored paradigm, but Bromyard is utterly untroubled by it. He does not strangle "all" by a thousand qualifications. Instead, he seems to follow the path of those constructing a new paradigm, what Halverson calls general election. Bromyard has no problems with Paul's *all* because he is convinced that God does indeed give sufficient grace to all humans for their salvation: *omnes homines vult salvos fieri* (250). He sees no need to turn "all" into "not all." How then does he explicate the difficulties surrounding this text that so troubled the dominant tradition: *either* universal salvation (heresy) *or* divine impotence (heresy)? We must defend divine omnipotence in a way compatible with God's form of foreknowledge (*praescientia*) and future contingencies.[59] Bromyard is sure that we must accept, without casuistic evasions, what is ascribed to God's own proclamation in Deuteronomy and Ecclesiasticus: "Consider that I have set before thee this day life and good, and on the other hand death and evil" (Deut. 30:15); "Before man is life and death, good and evil: that which he shall choose shall be given him" (Eccles. 15:18; *SP*, 251).

Into this context Bromyard assimilates a much-used text from the Epistle to the Ephesians: "As he chose us in him before the foundation of the world, that we should be holy and unspotted in his sight in charity" (*SP*, 251; Eph. 1:4). As far as Bromyard is concerned, the two texts he takes from the New Testament (1 Tim. 2:4 and Eph. 1:4) teach the same lesson as the two texts from the Old Testament (Deut. 30:15 and Eccles.

15:18): namely, that sanctification is placed by God in the human will, either to choose to become sons of God or to choose against divine grace ("Sic tamen in voluntate nostra sit, quod sumus sancti & immaculata, & filii Dei, vel non" [*SP*, 251]). Such is the way God relates to his human creatures; such is the doctrine of election and reprobation.

Bromyard consistently cultivates a model of doubled agency when he addresses the issues that so troubled Langland's Wille. Such a model was eloquently displayed in Augustine's *Confessions* and elsewhere in his preaching and writing. But Augustine was also capable of assuming a very different model of divine agency, one that had coercive implications for his own ecclesiology that were massively amplified in the medieval church. I noted an example of this in Aquinas's justification for burning heretics to death. Augustine based the second, coercive model of divine agency on the account of Paul's conversion in Acts (9:1–20) and on a line taken from one of Jesus's parables, turning these words to a use Luke could never have imagined for them: "And the Lord said to the servant: Go out into the high-ways and hedges, and compel them to come in, that my house may be filled" (Luke 14:23; see 14:16–24).[60]

In contrast to Augustine, Bromyard's model of doubled agency favors a language of *concausality* and *cooperation* (for examples, see 246, 248, 259). How then does his approach deal with the traditional interpretation of Jacob and Esau, unborn twins, viewed as figures of predestination and reprobation? Bromyard accepts the dominant interpretation of that passage as one showing the irrelevance of human works to God's predestination and reprobation. This does not seem to fit his overall approach to the topic. Indeed, it seems contradictory. Bromyard attempts to solve this difficulty by reading God's love and hate for the unborn twins as manifesting God's knowledge of the choices the twins would make when they became adults. He quotes an address of God to Israel as related by Isaiah: "For I knew that transgressing thou wilt transgress, and I have called thee a transgressor from the womb [Scio enim quia praevaricans praevaricaberis, et transgressorem ex utero vocavi te]" (Isa. 48:8). Bromyard deploys his own model of divine and human *concausation*, doubled agency, to explicate both Paul's text and Isaiah's (*SP*, 247–48). God and humans work in ways that are appropriately different, but human agency is intrinsic to the total process (*SP*,

248). He thinks the ways in which the prayers of the saints have effi-cacy is not dissimilar (*SP*, 248).[61] This solution would not have satisfied Augustine, Aquinas, or adherents to the pre-fourteenth-century "con-sensus" described by Halverson. It would have been judged to be Pela-gianizing, to be undermining divine sovereignty. But Bromyard does not feel obligated to follow this paradigm, any more than did Ockham or Holcot.

Elaborating his model, he directs readers to the evangelical parable of the wedding feast that inspired such panic in Langland's Wille (*SP*, 248; Matt. 22:1–4; *Piers Plowman* XII.41–53, discussed in chapter 1). Although Bromyard brings this parable into a discourse of predestina-tion and reprobation, he does so in a manner strikingly different from the one that vexed Wille. For the Dominican does not read the text as an example of an apparently arbitrary and eternal judgment, nor does he imagine the king's porter secretly letting only a few into the feast and letting the many "go rome" (XII.48–49). Bromyard says that all who accept the invitation to the king's feast are welcome if they make the ef-fort to wear the appropriate clothing given to the guests by the generous king (248). True enough, one of the assembled guests is ejected. Why? For not wearing the wedding garment he had been given. Traditionally, the garment was read as a figure of charity or the precepts of God.[62] But Bromyard characteristically reads it as spiritual preparation, the will to cooperate with God's gracious gift. Like Conscience in *Piers Plowman*, Bromyard is teaching that all God's gifts come with a *si*: "So god gyveth nothing that *si* [*if*] ne is in the glose" (III.329). All are welcome to the feast *if* they cooperate with the king by preparing themselves.[63] The only guests expelled are those who, through an act of their *liberum arbi-trium*, itself a divine gift, decide not to cooperate. Bromyard sees no cause for anxiety. He sees no cues in Jesus's parable for imagining an ar-bitrary, hidden will of God displayed in an apparently silent and secre-tive porter. Bromyard, like Holcot, is confident that nobody who coop-erates with God, using the gifts God gives, need fear reprobation.[64]

Developing this argument, Bromyard immediately turns to an-other of Jesus's parables in Matthew's gospel: the parable of the ten bridesmaids (Matt. 25:1–13). Five had not brought enough oil for their lamps in the face of the bridegroom's unexpected delay. By the time these people returned from buying more oil, the bridegroom had arrived and the doors to the marriage celebration were closed. The lesson: "Watch ye therefore, because ye know no the day nor the hour" (Matt. 25:13). Bromyard focuses on the verse that narrates the arrival of the bridegroom and the entrance to the marriage by those bridesmaids who were prepared: "and they that were ready went in with him" (Matt. 15:13). The door is closed, Bromyard observes, only to the unprepared (*et clausa est ianua non paratis*) (248). As in his reading of the parable of the feast (Matt. 22), Bromyard insists that God calls *all* and exhorts *all* to be prepared if they wish to participate in the feast, the symbol of the celestial banquet in the New Jerusalem. He links this parable with Jesus's exhortation in Luke's gospel: "Be you then also ready: for at what hour you think not the son of man will come" (Luke 12:40; *SP,* 248). God calls all, God invites all. Yet, once again in the language of Langland's Conscience, God calls with a "*si*," with a condition belonging to a covenantal theology. God is certainly faithful: both to his invitation and to the explicit conditions humans are called to fulfill through the adequate resources God has given.

Bromyard offers an exemplum for the preachers his work addresses. It is based on contemporary mercantile culture (248). Bromyard thinks of mercantile joint ventures in which some provide the money while some provide the labor: "unus precium & alius laborem apponit" (*SP,* 248). Bromyard observes that it would simply be unjust if one put forward everything and another contributed nothing and yet profit (*lucrum*) was shared between them. He considers this a helpful model for thinking about the covenantal relations between God and humanity. Christ puts forward the *precium*, the price: his blood shed on the cross together with prevenient grace. This outpouring of gifts constitutes predestination, the election of humanity. This seems an example of the paradigm of general election that Halverson identifies in some fourteenth-century theologians and Gabriel Biel. For Bromyard (as for Holcot and Biel), this model of election does not entail an Origenist universal salvation. It belongs to a covenant in which humans have the gift of freedom, a gift that can be used to resist grace. Bromyard is convinced that justice demands we respond to God's generosity by cooperating with our labor (248).

From his own exemplum, Bromyard turns to a passage in Leviticus. There the Lord is teaching Moses the law of the holocaust, which he is to teach Aaron. A fire is to burn on the altar all night. The priest must put on his tunic and linen breeches, then take up the ashes and place them by the altar. Next he is to remove his garments, reclothe himself, and take the ashes outside the camp to a clean place. The fire upon the altar must always be kept alight, and the priest must put wood on it every day in the morning laying on it the holocaust. On this he shall burn the fat of the peace offerings. The fire shall burn perpetually, it "shall never go out on the altar" (Lev. 6:8–13). This is another figure of God's ways with humanity and humanity's with God, another figure of election in Bromyard's favored paradigm. It, too, reveals that humans are called to work by *cooperating* with the gifts God has offered: God pours out the fire of grace and charity, and he wants this fire to culminate in blessedness for the human agents. Bromyard takes special note of the sustained work to which the priest is called, keeping the fire alight and offering sacrifices that belong to the covenant. In the old covenant, these commands are meant literally; in the new covenant that replaced the old, they are meant spiritually. In both covenants, election entails cooperation.

Bromyard links this passage from Leviticus with the parable of the talents (Matt. 25:14–30). This immediately follows the parable of the bridesmaids discussed earlier. A lord going to a far country calls his servants and gives them his goods. One receives five talents, one receives two talents, and the third receives one talent: "to everyone according to his proper ability." After a long time the lord returns. He judges the servants' use of his goods: the servant given five talents had made five more; the one given two had made two more; the one given one had simply preserved one and returned it. This servant confesses to his lord that he was terrified of him, a hard and unjust man, so he had buried the one talent and now returned it. The first two servants are highly praised by the lord and rewarded. The third servant is condemned as a wicked and lazy servant, cast out into darkness and misery. Bromyard observes that the servant who is so severely punished had actually looked after his lord's talent and returned it: what had he done wickedly? The answer Bromyard gives is that this servant had failed to put the talent to good use. He had failed to do good works with the resources given by the lord (*SP*, 248). Clearly enough, Bromyard is again expressing his covenantal theology: God gives with the condition of *cooperation*.

But how does this illuminate the topic ostensibly being explored, predestination? Bromyard is sure it does so. He sees predestination, once again, as the divine offer of grace to humans, which will enable their acceptance by him into glory. But this version of election continues to stress human freedom: election comes with a covenantal "*si* [if]." If one chooses not to cooperate with the Lord's gifts, if one hides them in the earth, then one will finally lose everything. Such is reprobation in Bromyard's paradigm (248). Bromyard offers a further cluster of texts from both the Old and New Testaments to support his model (248–49). Humans have been chosen, elected by God as *coadiutores* (assistants, helpers) on their way to the heavenly city. He is sure that Paul agrees: "with fear and trembling work out your salvation. For it is God who worketh in you, both to will and to accomplish, according to his good will" (*SP*, 248–49; Phil. 2:13). Bromyard is convinced that Paul here shares his own understanding of doubled agency in the processes of salvation.

Even when he cites Augustine as his authority, Bromyard does not read him as he was read by Aquinas in his treatises on predestination and on grace (*ST* I.23; I–II.109–14). In fact, naming Augustine in no way impedes Bromyard's elaboration of a profoundly un-Augustinian paradigm. Take, for example, his comments on the unrepentant Pharaoh. To Bromyard the repentant Nebuchadnezzar *and* the unrepentant Pharaoh show how people respond differently to divine grace. The former repents; the latter resists divine calling and hardens his heart (*SP*, 249). The former uses his *liberum arbitrium* in another way. Bromyard does not use the Augustinian/Thomist scheme of Jacob and Esau to differentiate Nebuchadnezzar and Pharaoh, with the former representing the few predestinate and the latter the many reprobate whose sinful hearts are hardened to justify their imminent and everlasting torture. He has no doubt that just as Nebuchadnezzar repents, so Pharaoh *could* have repented. Nothing God does or does not do prevents Pharaoh. In a strikingly different mode from that of Augustine, Aquinas, and Gregory of Rimini, Bromyard understands divine predestination

in terms of human cooperation or resistance, acts that God foresees
(*SP*, 249). Yet does scripture not state that God hardened Pharaoh's
heart (Exod. 7:13; 9:12; 10:1, 20, 27; 11:10)? Of course, says Bromyard.
Does this not drive us into the paradigms of Augustinianism? Certainly not: God's actions in hardening Pharaoh's heart are a response to
the acts of Pharaoh's own free judgements. God is not bending or co-
ercing the human will but rather confirming decisions freely made.
Even God's punishments leave open the possibility that the punished
person could respond by repentance—just as Nebuchadnezzar did
(*SP*, 249). Truly, Bromyard's God is not a crusher of *liberum arbitrium*
and of human will.

Another of Bromyard's examples illuminates how far his theology
of reprobation and election has shifted from that of Augustine and
Aquinas. In this exemplum, a Lord tells his servant to reach a certain
place on a certain day. When he does so he will receive a great advance-
ment (*promotionem magnam*). The lord knows the servant cannot
fulfill his command without a horse, so he sends the servant a horse, ordering him to come when he receives the gift. Bromyard observes that
in this transaction the servant retains his free will: even after he receives
the horse it is still in his will (*in sua voluntate*) to use the horse or not
to use the horse (*SP*, 249). As usual, Bromyard's model is replete with
both divine generosity and human freedom. He *relishes* the statement
in 1 Timothy 2:4 and quotes it after this exemplum: God wants *all* people
to be saved. A text that caused such embarrassment, vexation, and
casuistic exegesis in the work of earlier theologians causes no problems
for Bromyard.[65] In his study of predestination, he is consistently sure
that nothing in the Christian doctrine of predestination and reprobation should suggest that God undermines his great gift of liberty or that
he is a hidden God who seeks to convert and save his disciples through
terror. This is a vision of God very unlike the one we will encounter in
chapter 4 in the writings of Calvinists such as Arthur Dent.

Bromyard's explorations include a glance toward the model of the
builder and his wall, a story I analyzed in Aquinas's treatise on predestination (*ST* I.23.5). Let us recollect Aquinas's analogy, designed to
stave off the objection that the God he wants us to worship is unjust
(I.23.5, obj. 2). He answers that predestination and reprobation both

come from the goodness of God. As for God's eternal punishment of the reprobates, such as the unborn Esau (I.23.3, sed contra), this is lauded as an act of justice—indeed, the vengeance of justice ("vindictam justitiae"). Musing on why God chose one such as the unborn Jacob and reprobated another such as the unborn Esau, Aquinas decides he can give no reason other than God's will.[66] Despite this confession, Aquinas still wants to go on giving reasons for God's allegedly unaccountable will, and he does so in the analogy we encountered earlier: "Just as from the simple will of the artificer it depends that this stone is in this part of the wall, and that in another; although the plan [*ratio artis*] requires that some stone should be in this place and some other in that place" (I.23.5, ad 3).

So the beauty of creation (the wall) derives from a divine plan in which some folk are predestined to bliss and others are to be denied the grace that would deliver them from everlasting evil. Some stones are like embryo Jacob; some are like embryo Esau. So far as Aquinas can see, the results of this plan involve no injustice to any stone/human being—and produce a beautiful, diversified wall. Offering another text from scripture to support his view that God owes us humans/stones nothing, Aquinas in article 5 of Question 23 (ad 3) takes a phrase from Christ's parable of the lord, the workers in his vineyard, and their wages: "Take what is yours and go: is it not licit for me to do what I will?" (Matt. 20:14, 15). It is worth reiterating what Aquinas chooses to omit from Jesus's parable: he neglects to mention that the lord rewarded *all* the workers with the *same* payment for their different labor. He did so even to those who grumbled at his payment (one denarius) as a figure for eternal life, as Aquinas's own *Catena Aurea* displays.[67] So while Aquinas began his *Summa Theologiae* with an account of scripture as the decisive source of Christian teaching, Jesus's parable actually works against Aquinas's attempt to appropriate it as a proof text for his tradition's teaching on reprobation.[68]

Bromyard probably had this article in front of him as he wrote his own work on predestination. Not only does he use the analogy of wall building, but he also includes Christ's parable of the lord, his workers in the vineyard, and their payment (*SP*, 251–52). However, Bromyard gives Aquinas's analogy and exegesis of the wall and the builder a subtly

different inflection. In doing so, he also offers a very different reading of the parable Aquinas had constrained to fit received Augustinian
teaching on predestination. Bromyard's aim is to illustrate how God's
gifts are varied. Just as good contemporary lords give different gifts to
different people, so God gives different gifts to different people. For
example, angels and humans receive different—and unequal—gifts. In
terms of the analogy of stones in a wall, various stones represent various gifts. Bromyard identifies this edifice with the church, an edifice
founded on Christ as the chief cornerstone, a dwelling place for God
and humanity (*SP*, 252; Bromyard cites Eph. 2:19–20). Thus Bromyard
envisages Christians as many members within one body (1 Cor. 12), as
living stones, and Christ himself as one of their kind. He follows this
very different treatment of the mason and wall with a discussion of
Jesus's parable of the workers in the vineyard. He quotes more of the
evangelical text than Aquinas had done, and he goes back to the workers who murmured against the lord after they received the covenanted
denarius. They grumble because they now think they deserve more for
working more hours and for working in the heat of the day. After all,
it now transpires that the lord is paying the same wage, the agreed
denarius, to those who only worked in the evening (Matt. 20:10–12).
Bromyard quotes the lord's response to the complaint. The lord denies
doing the workers any wrong and reminds them of their covenant.
Bromyard agrees with the lord that he has done no injury to those who
worked according to their agreement and were paid accordingly. They
are not injured by the fact that other workers were paid the same wage
for less, and for less demanding work (*SP*, 252). Unlike Aquinas, however, Bromyard does not have to transform Jesus's parable into a text
teaching doctrine quite alien to its concerns; he does not impose on it
the inclusions and exclusions of doctrines about hidden predestination
and reprobation in the eternal mind of God. Because of this, he does not
have to occlude the fact that *all* workers receive the precious and promised denarius (salvation). Bromyard does not draw attention to the difference between his teaching and that of his canonized Dominican prede-
cessor, nor does he engage in scholastic disputation with him (unlike
the way, for example, Ockham often does in his reading of the *Sentences*,
including his cautious teaching on predestination). The preachers for

whom Bromyard was writing might neither have needed such disputation nor have been much edified by it. They might have had enough of literate laypeople disputing their preaching: " 'Contra,' quod Y as a clerk, and comsed to despute ['Contra,' said I as a clerk, 'and began to dispute]" (*Piers Plowman* X.20).

Not that Bromyard ignores reprobation here, an issue some of his readers might understandably raise at this point. After all, he would have been aware that he was working in a paradigm of election that went against one that had recently been hegemonic. He knew that in this version of election it was believed, as we have seen in both Aquinas and Gerson, that most of us will be eternally damned by God, a confidence widely shared in the magisterial Reformation. We remember that Wille thought Scripture maintained such a position, as did Wille's surrogate Rechelesnesse, who claimed to have heard such stuff proclaimed by preachers. So Bromyard acknowledges that some might object that God foresaw many (*multos praesciunt*) who were not predestined to joy. This seems to be exactly what Rechelesnesse had picked up from preachers:

> For Clergie saith that he seyh in the seynt evaungelie
> That Y man ymaed was and my name y-entred
> In the legende of lyf long ar Y were.
> Predestinaet thei prechen, prechours that this sheweth,
> Or *prescit* inparfit, pult out of grace,
> Unwriten for som wickednesse, as holy writ scheweth:
> *Nemo ascendit ad celum nisi qui de celo descendit.*
> (XI.202–7)

———

> [For Clergy says he saw in the holy gospel
> That I was made man and my name entered
> In the book of life long before I was.
> They preach men are predestinate, preachers who declare this,
> Or beforehand known to be imperfect, thrust out of grace,
> Not written down because of some wickedness, as holy writ shows.
> *No man hath ascended into heaven but he that descended from*
> *heaven.*]

Bromyard's response is to reiterate an un-Augustinian and un-Thomist view: those foreknown as reprobates are foreknown purely because God foresaw their wicked actions. God foresaw that they would prove themselves to be unworthy of predestination (*non esse praedestinatos dignos*) (*SP*, 252). In the jargon of "scole," we could identify Bromyard's view here as belonging to a strand of Christian tradition that generated a model of predestination *post praeuisa merita* and of reprobation *post praevisa demerita*. This is actually distinct from the model of general election identified by Halverson, but whether Bromyard thought it to be so, I am not at all sure.[69] He is certainly challenging what Heiko Oberman describes as "absolute predestination *ante praevisa merita*," the position intrinsic to all varieties of double predestination, including that of Langland's older contemporary, Gregory of Rimini.[70] Bromyard's model and others like it always ran the risk of being dismissed as Pelagian. We find this dismissive response in both the fourteenth century and the seventeenth century.

If God does not save all human beings, as the church insisted (at least since its condemnation of Origen), does he want many people to act wickedly so that he can display his justice by reprobating them while he keeps his mercy for the elect minority? This is Bromyard's way of raising a standard question in medieval theology, one that will later be made even more pressing by the normalization of double predestination in Calvinism: in permitting sin, is God the author of sin?[71] Bromyard is emphatic that God never wills sin (*SP*, 252–53). He recalls a well-known declaration by the prophet Ezekiel: "As saith the Lord God, I desire not the death of the wicked, but that the wicked turn from his way to live. Turn ye, turn ye from your evil ways" (*SP*, 253; Ezek. 33:10; Bromyard links this to Ezek. 18:32). According to Bromyard, scripture copiously affirms that if the divine invitation in the covenant is rejected, it is rejected freely. Those rejecting it do so unilaterally and are responsible for the ensuing troubles (*SP*, 253). What then of apparently contradictory texts, such as that by the prophet Amos? Consider the following statement: "Shall there be evil in a city which the Lord hath not done?" (Amos 3:6). Or Isaiah hearing God say to him, "I form the light and create the darkness, I make peace and create evil [*Formans lucem et creans tenebras, faciens pacem et creans malum*]" (Isa. 45:7). Bromyard is not troubled by these famous texts. He sees both statements in the context of a divine covenant with its characteristic condition *"si* [if]*"* (*Piers Plowman* III.329). God's invitation is both the gift of the covenant offering eternal life and a demand issued to free persons. God does not *need* angels or humans or any of the secondary causes he deploys; he has created and conserved purely out of his immense goodness (*ex immesitate bonitatis*). He has chosen to communicate his likeness to foster love between human beings. As for human sin, this is caused by free will (*per motum liberae voluntatis*) (*SP*, 253). The reprobate freely rejects the covenant, resists divine grace. Bromyard's approach is, as we shall see in chapter 5, not far from one given eloquent expression by Milton's God in *Paradise Lost* (III.93–102).

Bromyard addresses another topic that is at the heart of Wille's troubles surrounding predestination in *Piers Plowman*. It is a subject that will go on to have a disturbing history in the Reformation: the quest for certainty concerning one's eternal state (*SP*, 253). Can we be certain of our salvation? Or reprobation? In the terms of Langland's Wille, can I know whether "Y were chose or nat chose" (XII.50–52)? Or in the language of his despairing surrogate, whether "my name" has been "y-entered / In the legend of lyf long ar Y were" (entered in the book of life before I was created)? Asking about one's entry or absence from "the legende of lyf" is a question about one's predestination or reprobation: am I "Predestinaet," or am I *"prescit"* (foreknown)? (XI.202–6).

Aquinas devotes a whole question to the "legende of lyf," or *Liber Vitae*, in the *Summa Theologiae*, and he does so immediately after the treatise on predestination (I.23–24). He affirms that the book of life is indeed predestination (I.24.1). Can somebody's name be written and then deleted? Psalm 68 seems to warrant such a view: "Let them be deleted from the book of the living" (*Deleantur de libro viventium*) (Ps. 68:29). Twice Aquinas quotes this verse in his treatment of the book of life. The explication he offers may not have provided much reassurance to Wille and Rechelesnesse. Those who are predestined to salvation, Aquinas says, are indeed written in the book of life eternally and are never deleted from it. This remains so even if they commit murder and adultery, as Rechelesnesse remarked (XI.262–65). For both Aquinas and Rechelesnesse, one's final destiny is not made legible in the moral

quality of one's actions (XI.205–21, 252–71). In trying to clarify the
difficulties inherent in the idea that one might be deleted from an eternal
text, Aquinas invents another distinction: some, he asserts, are *ordained*
to eternal life but not *predestined* to eternal life. Such people receive
grace that makes them worthy of eternal life; however, when they commit mortal sin, they are denied eternal life. Unlike mortal sinners such as
David and Paul, these mortal sinners are not given the grace of conversion and are finally damned. Yet, according to Aquinas, they could have
been written in the book of life. What sense can one make of these
claims? Aquinas says that such ordained (but not predestined) folk had
not been written in the book of life in an unequivocal manner. They can
thus, Aquinas declares, be deleted without God contradicting himself.
Nevertheless, he tells his students not to imagine that God foreknew
something and then did not foreknow it (*quas Deus aliquid praesciat
postea nesciat*) (*ST* I.24.3, resp.). Aquinas does not name this group of
ordained and graced people who fall into mortal sin and become cast-
aways from eternal life. Perhaps not surprisingly, since his church made
aural confession mandatory and taught about vices in such a way that all
Christians would be persuaded that they were mortal sinners desperately in need of sacerdotal absolution. Aquinas's invention of the distinction between those of us ordained to grace but not predestined to
salvation would do nothing to address the troubled questions of Christians such as Wille. After all, we know that we are all sinners prone to
sliding into habits of mortal sin and obligated to acknowledge this in
both the sacrament of penance and the sacrament of the altar. But are
we predestined or foreknown? Still written in the book of life or now
deleted—"Unwriten," in the language of *Piers Plowman*—from the
book (XI.207)? Or were we never inscribed in the first place? How
could anyone discern their destiny in a paradigm built upon and elaborated through such shifty language?

As I showed in chapter 1, Langland's *Piers Plowman* offers in its
poetic form and relentless theological questioning a dialectical and visionary process that liberates Wille and readers from captivity to such
a paradigm, to its pictures and language. Had Wille read Bromyard
on predestination, however, he might never have been trapped in these
theological chains in the first place. He might have realized that the

panic stirred up by his quest for certainty was grounded in a mistaken, impossible question. True enough, his question is one encouraged by Augustinian versions of original sin and election, especially given the propensity of such teachings to lead to forms of reasoning whose logical outcome is double predestination. But Bromyard coherently supports the medieval norm that followed Augustine in denying that the kind of certainty desired by Wille, or by John Bunyan three hundred years later, is possible. He quotes a passage from Ecclesiastes: "There are just men and wise men, and their works are in the hands of God: and yet man knoweth not whether he be worthy of love or hate" (Eccles. 9:1; 253). Bromyard stresses that this lack of certainty is the common teaching of scripture, and he turns to two of the terms that disturbed Wille: *pauci* and *multi* (*SP*, 253; see *Piers Plowman* XII.45–49). He observes that Jesus declares on more than one occasion that many are called, but few are chosen ("Multi enim sunt vocati, pauci vero electi") (Matt. 22:14; *Piers Plowman* XII.41–49). For Bromyard, such declarations should not encourage attempts to definitively discern one's final state of salvation or damnation in God's judgment. Rather, he sees these statements as exhortations to strive harder so that we can rejoice in the *hope* that we will be included in the kingdom, however many or few of us may finally reside there (*SP*, 253).

There is great emphasis on hope in Bromyard's writing. He tells his readers to travel in the ways that are certain, the covenanted ways of life taught in the church. Fare forward in hope, Bromyard encourages, not in epistemophilia. He emphasizes that hope is an essential constituent of a Christian life (*SP*, 253). Those who lack hope cannot truly seek: they are lost in despair. Among the texts he invokes on this subject is one from the book of Job: "For I know that my Redeemer liveth.... Whom I myself shall see, and my eyes shall behold, and not another: this my hope is laid up in my bosom" (Job 19:25–27). He also quotes often from the Psalms ("For thou, O Lord, singularly hast settled me in hope") (Ps. 4:10), and from a beautiful passage from the Book of Wisdom: "But the souls of the just are in the hands of God, and the torment of death shall not touch them.... And though in the sight of men they suffered torments, their hope is full of immortality" (Ws 3:1–4). Bromyard's teaching, through argument and through copious citation of scripture, centralizes the hope and trust that encourage people to hold to God's revealed precepts and, as Langland endlessly reiterates, Dowel. Bromyard invokes Peter's instructions: "Wherefore, bretheren, labour the more, that by good works you may make sure your calling and election [ut per bona opera certam vestram vocationem, opera certam vestram vocationem, et electionem faciatis]" (2 Pet. 1:10). Again and again Bromyard's treatment of predestination emphasizes practicing the virtues (*SP*, 253). Indeed, in his version predestination might be understood as good works shaped by divine precepts. Without such *practice*, Bromyard thinks, our hope in being predestined would be mere hypocrisy. He tells us that Job actually calls such hope (that is, hope divorced from proper works) "the hope of the hypocrite [*spes hypocritae*]" (Job 27:8–10).

When Bromyard returns once again to Paul he does not focus on the image upon which Augustine and ensuing predestinarian discourse had fixated, God's alleged hatred of Esau and love of Jacob (Rom. 9:13). He goes instead to the penultimate chapter of Paul's letter to the Romans: "Now the God of hope fill you with all joy and peace in believing: that you may abound in hope and in the power of the Holy Ghost" (Rom. 15:13). In this, we see that Bromyard's advice to Wille, to Rechelesnesse, or to anyone troubled by the legacy of Augustine's teaching on predestination and reprobation would be that Christians should trust in their works and dwell not on their anxious thoughts. Again he thinks of Paul, this time writing to the Ephesians: "That the God of our Lord Jesus Christ, the Father of glory, may give unto you the spirit of wisdom and of revelation, in the knowledge of him: The eyes of your heart enlightened, that you may know what the hope is of his calling, and what are the rules of the glory of his inheritance in the saints" (Eph. 1:17–18). Bromyard concentrates on the words "spes vocationis eius [the hope of his calling]." He trusts that Paul's hope is warranted, that the God who raised Jesus Christ from the dead will give to his people the spirit of wisdom and knowledge of this calling (*SP*, 253). However, Bromyard warns, if we find that we produce wicked works (*opera mala*), then we should fear that we may be *prescit*, foreknown (*Piers Plowman* XI.206). Yet this is emphatically not a suggestion that we have been deleted from the book of life or eternally decreed to damnation by a hidden God that wills us among the reprobate. For Bromyard, that is simply not what *prescit* means. It means instead that we ourselves are making disastrous choices, like Wille in "the lond of longyng." And like Wille, it means that we are likely to fall into despair as we come to understand that we have chosen against the ways of God and are wandering further astray (*SP*, 253). But this potentially catastrophic path does not mean we have to recite the limerick recorded by a later Dominican:

> There was a young man who said, "Damn,
> It is clear to me now that I am
> A being that moves in predestinate grooves:
> Not even a bus, but a tram."[72]

On the contrary, Bromyard sees the very recognition of our destructive choices as a moment of potential change. As soon as one makes such a recognition, such an acknowledgment, one may hope in a God who is *pro nobis*, a God who justifies the lapsed. Bromyard finally brings together doctrines of justification, sanctification, and predestination, now quoting Paul to show the source of this teaching in Christ (253): "Who was predestinated the Son of God in power, according to the spirit of sanctification, by the resurrection of our Lord Jesus Christ from the dead; By whom we have received grace" (Rom. 1:4–5).

Bromyard returns to some of these issues in his article on *Vocatio* (450–61). This includes a section on the many and the few, *multi* and *pauci* (459–60). He affirms that all mortal sin takes us away from the path of our calling and is a sign of ingratitude to God. He considers each of the traditional deadly sins to represent the varied motives people have for choosing to reject the Lord's invitation to his feast. Many people simply prefer other activities and dislike the inconveniences of the way to the banquet. Drawing on Jesus's version of the feast recorded in Luke 14, he notes that the lord of the feast invites many (*vocavit multos*), but they all begin to make excuses. Bromyard suspects that only those who have nothing to lose will accept the invitation. These, he says, are the poor: the homeless and the hungry (Luke 14:18–21; 459–60). Only a few (*pauci*) will accept the call. Once more Bromyard has composed a model of divine calling and human response in which God is

figured forth as inclusive. It is the many who exclude themselves—
who, that is, resist grace. The God Bromyard worships does not determine human responses to his offer.

If Bromyard develops a paradigm antithetical to the double predestination of Gregory of Rimini elaborated in the early 1340s, he also
continues to be far removed from Aquinas's Augustinianism. This was
true, too, of his fellow Dominican, Robert Holcot. Eclectic as he was,
Holcot's affinities seem to be toward some form of what Halverson describes as general election. Thus he, too, bears witness to the way that
"the Scholastic consensus" of the thirteenth century, articulated by
Aquinas's treatise on predestination in his *Summa Theologiae*, "was irrevocably shattered" in the fourteenth century.[73] Bromyard suggests
the existence of a refuge where Wille, had he returned to "scole," might
have been most likely to find theological and pastoral help for his troubles with some versions of Christian teaching on predestination and
reprobation. It seems to me that besides some important common
ground with his fellow Dominican, Holcot, Bromyard has also learned
something from the older English Franciscan, William of Ockham.
Despite the complexity of his critique of both Aquinas and Scotus on
election, Ockham's commentary on the relevant distinctions in the first
book of Lombard's *Sentences* represents a clear, unequivocal break with
the Augustinian and Thomist paradigm.[74] In Ockham's view, God has
committed himself to accepting our efforts to do well, even if we are at
the same time in a state of mortal sin. God certainly does not have to accept such works, but in his gracious covenant he accepts these efforts in
preparation for the grace that will lead the person toward a good end—
that is, an end in which God freely *accepts* the sinner. Ockham decisively rejects Aquinas's claims (examined above) that God reprobates
some and predestines others like a builder of walls placing stones in
different places as a demonstration of his goodness. He is convinced
Aquinas cannot escape the disastrous implication of such a model: God
intends sin. But, of course, God does not intend sin. It is the traditional
model, not God, that has problems. In Ockham's paradigm, God is
committed to the freedom of choice he has given humans, and he is *pro
nobis*. He could have created a different kind of order; he can make different worlds, and he can displace, as he has done, the old covenant

with the new covenant in Christ. But Ockham insists that we need to live in the current dispensation using our freedom to the best of our ability knowing that, in his own freedom, God will accept this. Such is predestination.

Here, too, we can take 1 Timothy 2:4 seriously: God wills *all* to be saved. But if we choose to live lives directed against right reason and against the precepts revealed by God, we will become reprobates, those whose will leads them to death in a state of sin. This is foreseen by God but as a future contingent. As Ockham writes in his little work on predestination, God's foreknowledge, and future contingents: "It is impossible to express clearly the way in which God knows future contingents. Nevertheless it must be held that he does so, but contingently." Why must we hold this? Because of "the pronouncements of the Saints, who say that God does not know things that are becoming in a way different from that in which he knows things that have already occurred." Here, too, we are directed against the preceding Augustinian/Thomistic paradigm's mode of representing knowledge of future contingents.[75] As Halverson has shown with such helpful specificity, by the time of Langland's *Piers Plowman*, let alone by the time of the Reformation,

> the Scholastic consensus concerning predestination had been replaced by multi-sided debate centering on the nature and extent of divine election. . . . While this debate did not occupy center-stage in the later Middle Ages, it was prominent; and once introduced into the polarized atmosphere of the Reformation, it became a leading point of conflict. (158)

Not only of conflict between Catholics and Protestants, not only between different churches in the Reformation, but also within the lives of individual Christians pursuing new models of conversion in a Calvinist paradigm. To that I now turn.

CHAPTER THREE

Crossing a Great Divide?

Calvinistic Revolution and the Ecclesia Anglicana

*We call predestination God's eternal decree, by which he
compacted with himself what he willed to become of each man. . . .
[E]ternal life is foreordained for some, eternal damnation for others.
Therefore, as any man has been created to one or the other of
these ends, we speak of him as predestined to life or death.*

. . .

*The reprobate are sometimes affected by almost
the same feeling as the elect, so that even in their own
judgment they do not in any way differ from the elect.*

—John Calvin, *Institutes of the Christian Religion*

As the previous chapter indicated, medieval theology bequeathed to the
Reformation a diverse discourse on predestination and reprobation. It
generated a plurality of paradigms for understanding predestination
that were acceptable to the Catholic Church, yet in none of these was
this doctrine made focal for Christian teaching. Furthermore, none
of these paradigms became politicized since none of them became sym-
bols adopted by those proposing different forms of ecclesial polity or

cultural politics. This was for at least two reasons: first, the medieval church did not anathematize any of the models her theologians generated in this field; and second, the medieval church was remarkably heterogeneous, fostering many quite different forms of Christian life and practice across very different social communities. The medieval church was not the fragmented subject of competing secular rulers contending for power with other rulers and with their own powerful elites; nor was it the unitary subject of secular rulers trying to make religion a social cement rather than (as in seventeenth-century England) one of the potential sources of civil war.

One of the paradigms encountered in chapter 2, Gregory of Rimini's version of double predestination, was committed to formalizing Augustine's later anti-Pelagian teachings on election and reprobation. This paradigm swept aside received constraints placed on Augustine's teaching on reprobation, constraints that sought to ward off any incipient suggestion that the God imagined in such teaching was a cruel and capricious one.[1] A version of this model of double predestination was developed by Calvin and became part of Christian orthodoxy in the late sixteenth- and seventeenth-century Church of England. Reflecting on the Augustinian sources of this model—sources that were deeply important to Calvin—I now return to James Wetzel's essay on free will and predestination in Augustine's work. Wetzel's sympathetic interpretation of Augustine's extraordinarily varied and copious writings concludes with an observation that Augustine's theology of reprobation takes a direction that undermines his own theology of love: "The doctrine of reprobation has mixed poison into Augustine's motives for affirming predestination." According to Wetzel, Augustine's doctrine of predestination was intended to affirm "God's priority as a lover acknowledging the inspiration behind all human love of God."[2] This is a just perception of the seed of Augustine's teaching on divine grace and human agency, one that seems to me especially illuminating in relation to the Reformation materials discussed in this and the following chapter. But, as Wetzel notes, as Augustine continued to elaborate his doctrine of reprobation in his long and often repetitive battles with the Pelagians, he made a hell out of the very desire that God had planted in his human creatures: "It would be hell to desire God and never have the desire requited." Furthermore, his teaching came to assume that, like the unborn Esau, "some who feel abandoned by God are, in fact, abandoned by God."[3] It thus seems to me that when Julian of Eclanum considered Augustine's later teaching on reprobation and infant mortality, he had good reason to tell Augustine, "Your God is a persecutor of the newborn. With bad will He hands over to eternal fire little children whom He knows could not have either a good or a bad will."[4]

Gregory of Rimini also encountered similar objections in response to his own Augustinian treatment of infants dying without baptism within the paradigm of double predestination. It is no wonder that a church proclaiming that God is love—*Deus caritas*, as Langland's Holy Churche declared (*Piers Plowman* I.82; 1 John 4:8, 16)—should seek to set up barriers against the full implication of Augustine's doctrine of double predestination. Still, as noted in chapter 2, Augustine's "poison" seemed veritable nectar to Gregory of Rimini. However, his enthusiasm for this model remained extremely rare in the late medieval church. The anxiety and panic that Langland explores through Wille's encounter with the doctrine of predestination and reprobation are therefore prophetic of a much later development in Christian tradition, one in which what had once been only peripheral became the mainstream. The *ecclesia anglicana*, part of the Catholic Church to which Langland belonged, would, for a time, be transformed into a church in which double predestination became a symbol of orthodoxy. There is, then, not a little irony in the fact that the Protestant editor of the first printed edition of *Piers Plowman*, Robert Crowley, was a defender of double predestination before the doctrine became dominant in the Church of England.[5] By the time Crowley's edition was published in 1550, a divide had been crossed. One telling indication of the magnitude of this crossing was the assimilation of Langland—the writer whose Wille so profoundly wrestled with questions of salvation and reprobation—to a Protestant ideology centered on the doctrine of double predestination.

Chapter 4 explores this ideology through close engagement with an immensely popular work first published in 1601, Arthur Dent's dialogue, *The Plaine Man's Path-way to Heaven*. Dent's text displays a distinctly Calvinist version of predestination and reprobation in his account of conversion, and resistances to conversion, in agrarian England.

The present chapter provides a transition between the medieval discourses I have been studying in chapters 1 and 2 and the Reformation discourses that inform Dent's classic work of Calvinist theology and pastoral ideals. In outlining this transition, I shall focus on one cluster of issues related to the dogma of double predestination, issues that seem unknown to medieval theologians, confessors, and vernacular writers—unknown, it should be said, even to the foremost theologian of double predestination, Gregory of Rimini. These issues emerge in relation to teachings on the assurance of faith ascribed to the elect in Reformation doctrine. In Calvin's words, faith "requires full and fixed certainty, such as men are wont to have from things experienced and proved[,] . . . full assurance that in the Scriptures is always attributed to faith."[6] Later in the same chapter he acknowledges that this demand is an ideal and not the norm, insisting that he does not mean the elect have assurance totally without doubt or anxiety. Nevertheless, Calvin states, "we teach that faith ought to be certain and assured" and that the elect *never* "fall away and depart from the certain assurance received from God's mercy" (III.2.17). This double mantra is one to which I return throughout this chapter. Calvin asserts that on the one hand, the predestinate must seek and find the certain and full assurance that proves they do indeed belong to the elect. In such assurance alone is the Christian conscience rendered calm and peaceful; without it, the conscience is torn with terror (III.2.16). On the other hand, the elect are in perpetual conflict with their own failures of assurance (III.2.17). Even in the elect, unbelief is always mixed with faith (III.2.4). So, while the confirmation of one's election is assurance, the elect can be taught that they will have no such full assurance in this life. Calvin acknowledges that he must "solve this difficulty" if his doctrine is to be sustained (III.2.17). Whether he has generated a "difficulty" that can be fruitfully "solved" or whether he has in fact generated a double bind, an unresolvable contradiction imposed on his followers, is a question to which I will return.[7]

Whatever the outcome of this exploration, it should already be clear that Calvin and Reformed theology made a decisive break with medieval Christianity and pastoral traditions, at least in this field. As Calvin and his successors are happy to emphasize, his teaching is incompatible with the common opinion of the medieval church. There,

Christians were taught to live by faith and hope in God's love and to be assured by Christ's Incarnation and the gifts flowing from his Passion, gifts mediated by the church (the mystical body of Christ). These gifts were manifest especially in the sacraments and consummated in the eucharist (the body of Christ).[8] Despite the presence of Christ in these gifts, there was in the medieval church no expectation that an individual Christian should require personal assurance that she or he is one of the predestinate. Such inquiry is alien to medieval understandings of faith, and of the forms of knowledge inspired by this theological virtue.[9] The medieval approach was formalized and confirmed in the Counter-Reformation Council of Trent.[10] As we will see, Calvinists habitually berated this tradition for destroying the certainty of faith in one's personal election and concomitantly praised themselves for enabling such essential assurance. Conjuring up assurance of one's predestination thus became one of the self-identifying markers of Calvinist ministers and laity.[11]

❖ ❖ ❖

Calvin's preface to the final edition of the *Institutes* (1559) presents the work as a *Summa Theologiae*. St. Thomas introduced his own *Summa Theologiae* by explaining how it was ordered to the educational needs of beginners (*incipientium*) in the study of catholic truth (*catholicae veritatis*). Calvin, too, states that the *Institutes* is a book designed "to prepare and instruct candidates in sacred theology" and that he has written "the sum of religion in all its parts" to benefit "the church" by maintaining "the pure doctrine of godliness."[12] Bearing this claim in mind, it seems right to offer an account of his much-discussed teaching on predestination and reprobation insofar as it pertains to the topics explored in the present chapter.

In the final version of the *Institutes,* Calvin situates his teaching on the doctrine of predestination and reprobation in the third book, which, as the book's subtitle suggests, discusses the "mode of obtaining the grace of Christ," the "benefits it confers, and the effects resulting from it." In earlier versions of the work, however, Calvin had placed his treatment of predestination within his teaching on providence or (as in the first edition of 1536) as part of his discussion of the church. More important to my present concerns than such shifts in location, however, is Calvin's expansion of his treatment of predestination and reprobation in each new version of the *Institutes* and his simultaneous proclamation of the importance of the doctrine in his other writings—tracts on predestination, sermons, catechisms, and commentaries on scripture.[13] François Wendel observes that Calvin accorded "a growing importance" to this doctrine as "the passages relating to reprobation" appear "in more amplified form, notably in 1559," the final version of the *Institutes* and the one that was first translated into English by Thomas Norton in 1561.[14] English Calvinists who made predestination one of the "focal points" of Christianity were not misinterpreting its importance to Calvin's theology, nor were the assorted anti-Calvinists (emerging in the Church of England from the mid-1580s) who centered their objections on this same doctrine.[15]

Calvin's own version of double predestination is affirmed unequivocally, as the epigraph to this chapter suggests. God's hidden "eternal election" orders our lives: some of us are eternally chosen to salvation, others of us—the vast majority in fact—are eternally chosen for damnation (III.21.1). God's grace, if given, is irresistible (III.3.6–14). Calvin stresses that "all are not created in equal condition: rather eternal life is foreordained for some, eternal damnation for others" (III.21.5). In his consideration of those views that suggest one's final destiny is not fixed but rather is responsive to acts that God permits humans to freely choose, Calvin dismisses such positions as "absurd" (III.21.5; with III.22.1). God's eternal decree determines that each individual person has been created for one of two ends: "predestined to life or death," heaven or hell. Double predestination fixes the destiny of individual persons from eternity and is not in any way a response to their faith and works (III.21.5; see too III.21.7). Calvin's view is lucidly and repeatedly summarized, and he seems to have had no doubts about the shape of God's "secret plan." The teaching is exemplified in his reading of a text that has accompanied my engagement with Augustinian Christianity, "Jacob I have loved, but Esau have I hated" (Rom. 9:13):

> He does not with indiscriminate grace effectually elect all. . . . As Scripture, then, clearly shows [Rom. 9.13; Mal. 1.2], we say that God once established by his eternal and unchangeable plan those whom

he long before determined once for all to receive into salvation, and those whom, on the other hand, he would devote to destruction. . . . [A]s the Lord seals his elect by call and justification, so, by shutting off the reprobate from knowledge of his name or from the sanctification of his name or from the sanctification of his Spirit, he, as it were, reveals by these marks what sort of judgement awaits them. Here I shall pass over many fictions which stupid men have invented to overthrow predestination. They need no refutation. (III.21.7)

Following this passage, Calvin pulls from scripture a selection of texts allegedly proving that the God revealed in scripture shares Calvin's version of election and reprobation (III.22). Inevitably, his selection includes those paradigmatic examples of predestination and reprobation, the unborn Jacob and his twin, Esau. Calvin reiterates that the divine choice of rejection exemplified in the unborn Esau has nothing to do with foreseen vices, just as the salvation of Jacob has nothing to do with foreseen virtues: "This is to prove that the foundation of divine predestination is not in works." As for those who might question the justice of Calvin's God in this double predestination, they are told to instead admire God's self-glorification in the eternal reprobation of the many represented by Esau (III.22.11). Furthermore, such questioners should silence their disputations in the knowledge that there can (according to Calvin) be no ethical criteria other than those Calvin himself gathers from his interpretation of God's will (III.23.2–4). He sponsors a form of divine command ethics coupled with an exaltation of an extraordinarily abstract version of divine will. This strand of his theology, it seems to me, has bracketed Christology and the revelation of God in Jesus of Nazareth, despite the concentration in Book II (devoted to "the knowledge of God the redeemer in Christ") on the role of Christ the Mediator. He has also bracketed those strands of his thinking that assume a theory of natural law that is congruent with its elaboration in St. Thomas's *Summa Theologiae* (I–II.100) and in Richard Hooker's *Of the Laws of Ecclesiastical Polity*.[16]

If these various strands do not form a coherent picture, Calvin would hardly be the first or last theologian to propound contradictory positions. Certainly his successors had no hesitation proclaiming enthusiastic versions of divine command ethics alongside a similarly abstract account of divine power. A typical example can be found in a sermon on predestination preached by Richard Crakanthorp at St. Mary's, Oxford, and published in 1620. Discussing the predestination and reprobation of the unborn Jacob and Esau, he declares, "How soever this may seem unjust to the eyes of man, yet it is in truth most righteous, because it is the will and the good pleasure of God so to doe." Crakanthorp emphasizes that God's "will" and "pleasure" in the decision to save the unborn Jacob and to damn the unborn Esau has "nothing" to do with any qualities in Jacob and Esau.[17] Similarly, in considering why "God's righteousness" would condemn so many to eternal damnation before they are even born, Calvin is content to reply that because "it so pleases God," it is therefore just. True enough, Calvin admits, this eternal decree is "dreadful [*horribile*]," but then God predestined Adam's fall with all its dreadful consequences for humanity (III.23.7–8). Here, Calvin treats with utter contempt the idea (later advanced by Milton) that God *permitted* Adam and Eve to sin but did not decree this fall. He would certainly have found the teaching propounded by Milton's God on the fall, divine permission, and human freedom quite absurd (*Paradise Lost* III.80–134).

Setting aside disputes surrounding Calvinist ideas of human agency in relation to divine will, I now return to an issue introduced earlier in this chapter: namely, the tension, or even double bind, into which Calvin draws his adherents through his teaching on assurance. As we saw, the elect are exhorted to discover the certainty of their salvation, to find signs that they are not reprobates. Yet the elect, Calvin confesses, will be nevertheless immersed in doubts, confusions, and terrors nearly indistinguishable from those experienced by the reprobate. The difficulty here turns out to be very complicated, and opens out onto some thoroughly disturbing insights. Let us consider these.

It becomes apparent that Calvin's God plays tricks with the perceptions and emotions of his worshippers. God bestows faith on both the elect and the reprobate, yet only those "predestined to salvation" will "truly feel the power of the gospel." The texture of one's feeling, one's affect, thus seems a decisive indication of one's election. Calvin maintains, however, that God sometimes gives to the reprobate "almost the same feeling as the elect." These feelings are indeed so similar that as reprobates "carefully and humbly" carry out the kind of introspection Calvin demands, they find that God has persuaded them "even in their own judgment they do not in any way differ from the elect." God himself gives these reprobates wondrous feelings: "a taste of heavenly gifts," a taste of Christ. These "gifts" are certainly authentically from God; they are not, that is, the delusive fantasies caused by Satanic meddling, which Milton's Eve experiences in her dream as she sleeps in Eden.[18] In Calvin's paradigm, inner searching of feelings, of affect, may very well elicit the same finding for both reprobate and elect. How tricky for the human subject. Not only does God elicit misleading feelings in the reprobate's inner life, but he does so "to render them more convicted and inexcusable." Calvin reaffirms that "there is a great likeness and affinity between God's elect" and these reprobates in terms of their perception of the gifts God has bestowed. Is there not any difference? Apparently not in the texture or intensity of feeling. There is, however, a difference in the duration of such feelings: while the elect persist in their experience of assurance, to the reprobate these feelings are given only "for a time" (III.2.11). How does the difference between real assurance and feeling assured "for a time" work? How is it to be discerned by either reprobate or elect?

Calvin describes the temporal difference as that between "a transitory faith" that lacks the gift of final adoption and a persistent one that endures "even to the end." Only the elect have the gift of final perseverance. Because of this, only their feelings warrant the name of true assurance, as only theirs grow from the "incorruptible seed" sown by God to seal their adoption as predestinate. The reprobate have only a divinely given simulacrum of this, a "lower working of the Spirit" (III.2.11). One can see how hard it would be for introspective Christians to discern whether their God-given feelings were the Spirit's "lower working"—a "transitory" or "temporary" faith on the eternally ordained path to everlasting damnation—or whether they were the Spirit's higher working, yielding adoption to everlasting felicity. This brings back the question posed at the end of the previous paragraph: What are the criteria by which we can discern the "temporary"? What are the criteria by which one can discern "transitory" feeling from that which warrants assurance?

After all, we can see quite clearly in the spiritual autobiographies written by Calvinists that those who find assurance also find abundant evidence of "transitory" and temporary feelings of joyful communion with the divine. Bunyan's *Grace Abounding* is an exceptionally powerful display of such agonizing tensions, but part of its greatness is its ability to dramatize shared experiences and their most longed for outcome—assurance of election.[19] It concentrates on what historians have identified as "anxieties in parishioners over the question of assurance," ones exacerbated by the hermeneutic stumbling blocks created by Calvin's teaching on temporary, transitory faith.[20] Both creating and dissolving such anxieties were among the pastoral skills required of Calvinist ministers. We will follow one self-representation of such skills in the next chapter.

Calvin himself does postulate methods of discernment between true and false faith even as he stresses the God-given closeness between the experience of the elect and the experience of the reprobate in matters of assurance and doubt. Reprobates, he asserts, "never receive anything but a confused awareness of grace, so that they grasp a shadow rather than the firm body" (III.2.11). Is this really a helpful solution for perplexed Calvinist Christians? Hardly, for it simply contradicts Calvin's own emphasis on the "great likeness" between the reprobate's taste of Christ and the elect's taste of Christ. Calvin does not focus on the distinction between "confused awareness" of divine grace and clear awareness. On the contrary, he suggests that God himself makes it impossible to distinguish the lower grace in the simulacrum from the higher grace that is the seed of adoption. Without apparently intending any such outcome, Calvin has drawn us into the kind of world so brilliantly invoked by Edmund Spenser in his "Legend of the Knight of the Red Crosse, or Of Holiness," the first book of *The Faerie Queene* (1590; 1596). There, even the most virtuous figure of truth and the one true church, Una, cannot distinguish the Red Crosse Knight who "ador'd" Jesus Christ from his counterfeit, the demonic Archimago, also named "Hypocrisie."[21] As for the Red Crosse Knight—named by Una as one "chosen" by God to share in "heavenly mercies"—his own feelings prove to be extremely unreliable guides. Introspection discloses the Knight's "deformed crimes," and he becomes sure that he is one of the reprobate. Convinced his God-given gifts are not true virtues but merely the simulacra given to reprobates, he thinks and feels his way into crushing despair and attempts suicide, "resolv'd to worke his finall smart" and take "a dagger sharp" (I.ix.48–53). How is this troubled member of the elect delivered from what he takes to be his experience of reprobation? What theological and pastoral resources does Spenser discover in his Protestant tradition? He in fact finds none because this tradition is, of course, deeply suspicious of the rule of habit in a Thomistic virtue ethics. The Red Crosse Knight is cut off from all memory of the divine virtues with which he has been graced. His faith can offer him no consolation or guidance because it might, after all, be the mere shadow of virtue that God gives to reprobates to make them, as Calvin insists, quite without excuse (*Institutes* III.2.11). Utterly bereft, the Knight gives in to despair. But the elect do not, of course, commit suicide—to do so would be proof of reprobation. Spenser thus figures the Red Crosse Knight's delivery from suicide as a totally extrinsic action: Una, symbol of the one true church, snatches "the cursed knife" from him (I.ix.52). This moment symbolizes the passivity of saving conversion and the irresistibility of divine grace. The model for such extrinsic conversions is that of Paul on the road to Damascus rather than the complex relations of divine and human agency explored in Augustine's *Confessions* or in the conversion of Adam and Eve in *Paradise Lost*.[22]

Una's action delivers the Knight from suicide but does not alleviate his despair. That requires a long process of training in holiness that will lead him from suicidal despair to a vision of the New Jerusalem. Here it is confirmed that he is indeed, as Una had told him, one of the elect "ordained a blessed end," life as "a Saint" among "those Saints" (I.x.53–61). Behind him is the cave of despair. There he leaves the "dreary corse" of Sir Terwin, a knight wallowing "in his own yet luke-warme blood." Terwin's suicide in despair was not prevented by irresistible divine grace acting through Una, and this is seemingly all that separates his fate from the Red Crosse Knight's (I.ix.27–37). Suicidal reprobate, suicidal elect: the same inner experiences and decisions but very different teleologies. This would hardly have surprised Calvin. But it might suggest to some readers that Spenser's narrative of the Red Crosse Knight assumes a version of the human person closer to Augustine's than to Calvin's, despite the emphasis on the Knight's total passivity in his delivery from suicide. For Calvin vehemently rejected the Catholic tradition that insisted that nobody can know their final destiny without a special revelation. Against this tradition, as we have seen, Calvin summoned Christians to an introspective quest for just such knowledge concerning election. But no introspection could give the sinful Red Crosse Knight any such knowledge. On the contrary, introspection and attention to inner experience convinced him he was reprobate, cast him into despair, and led him to attempt suicide. Una's knowledge of his elect status was not available to him. It is as though Spenser had been musing upon Stachniewski's account of Calvinism, despair, and suicide in *The Persecutory Imagination*, an account that never addresses Spenser's work.[23] Augustine, however, in the face of his own espousal of double predestination and sustained anti-Pelagian polemics, makes it quite clear that any such quest for certainty over one's everlasting life is seeking assurance where it cannot be found. He insists we can't even be certain about our will for our own selves, let alone about God's will for us.

> "But," someone says, "I am uncertain about God's will for me." What then? Are you certain about your own will for yourself? And do you not fear these words, *Let one who thinks he stands watch out that he does not fall* (1 Corinthians 10:12)? Since each of these, therefore, is uncertain, why does a human being not entrust his faith, hope, and love to the more firm [God's promise] rather than the less firm [human weakness].[24]

Earlier, Augustine in his *Confessions* composed many interlocking narratives that make evident the opacity of the fallen human person. There, Augustine's version of the human person, together with his accounts of the relations between divine and human agency, makes any kind of Calvinist epistemophilia seem grounded in a serious misunderstanding of what it is to be a human person.

Perhaps the roots of Calvinist epistemophilia and the intractable difficulties it generates are seeded in the distinctive form of reflexive faith that was a central component of Luther's theology and anthropology. This version of faith attacked and displaced medieval understandings of the virtues.[25] How it did so has been carefully identified and analyzed by Paul Hacker, who many years ago showed how in the very act of Lutheran faith "the ego bends back on itself" such that this sort of faith "may fittingly be called reflexive."

> [It is] comparable to a missile launched toward a target with contrivances devised to make it rebound and return to its starting point which is thus its ultimate aim. The act of reflexive faith is directed to the Divine Person of Christ, but is intended to recoil on the believer's ego in order to evoke in him a consciousness of his own relation with God, a consciousness of consolation and salvation.[26]

The aim is, as we see in Calvinism, "assurance" or "certitude." Luther affirms that if we lack assurance, if we doubt that our sins are forgiven, we are simply not Christians and we make God a liar. Nevertheless, he also says—in a self-contradiction that permeates Reformation teaching in this field—that while "we are certain that we believe in Christ," we are simultaneously "not certain."[27] Still, the faith that alone justifies yields assurance, and we recognize it by the assurance it yields. In 1523 Luther proclaimed that the content of faith is "that man be certain, each one for himself. . . . Therefore let everyone teach whatever he likes; you have to see what you believe, at your own ultimate peril or for your own profit." All comes back to the individual's assurance of their own salvation: through Christ, of course, but known assuredly through reflexive faith.[28]

Unlike Luther, Calvin does give considerable attention to ecclesiology in the *Institutes* (Book IV). Although the focus here is different from the quest for individual assurance we have been following in the third book, it does not explicitly qualify the latter, and it may even reproduce this matrix in an ecclesiological form. This pattern of thought may contribute to his representations of the church in which he himself had been baptized. The demand for certainty and assurance concerning one's election returns in Calvin's version of the "true" church as defined against the "false" church to which most contemporary Christians in Western Europe belonged, the Roman Catholic Church (*Institutes* IV.2). It is, he declaims, a church where Christian doctrine "has been entirely buried and driven out," a church designed "to snare us in idolatry, the ignorance of God, and other sort of evils" (IV.2.2). The Roman church is nothing but a cluster of "external masks" (IV.2.3). Indeed, it is the home of "Christ's chief adversaries" (IV.2.4). Yet it was also, of course, the church where Calvin himself had received his Christian formation. Using the language of "masks" to designate hypocrisy, and homogenizing this strikingly diversified church into the singular home of "Christ's chief adversaries," Calvin seems here to be reproducing precisely the structure and rhetoric displayed in his teaching on the Christian elect and the Christian reprobate. Here, too, there is an intense need to know with absolute certainty—that is, to be assured—that one is a member of the "true" church and not, like the majority of Christians, a part of the "false" church of Rome. The "false" church is one replete with "idolatry, superstition, and ungodly doctrine," the very "receptacle of idols," and "nothing but a wicked conspiracy against God" (IV.2.10). As for the earthly head of this church, the pope, he is the "standard bearer of that wicked and abominable kingdom" of Hell and "plainly declares himself to be Antichrist" (IV.2.12; IV.7.24–25). The central sacrament in this church, the eucharist, is simply Satan's attempt to ensnare the world (IV.17.1). Indeed, the Roman church persecutes the gospel that is proclaimed in "true" churches, such as Calvin's (IV.7.24). Just as some whose practices and experiences seem like those of the elect but are actually reprobates, so there may exist "churches" in the world to which "we categorically deny" the title "church" (IV.2.12). We must know with certainty how to discern God's church from this simulacrum of a church.

This nexus may make more intelligible the fierceness with which Calvinists in the Church of England in the period between 1590 and 1640 argued against those who had begun to deny that the pope is Antichrist. Indeed, one of the claims that Calvinists found so deplorable in Richard Montagu's A New Gagg (1624) was the suggestion that Rome is a *true* church and the pope is not Antichrist.[29] To Calvinists such arguments were unsettling signs that their own Church of England might, after all, not be a "true" church but instead one creeping toward union with the "false" church. Continue like this, and one would soon be accepting the traditional and Roman teaching that nobody in this life could be certain they are elect without a special revelation. In his great study of the Roman and Protestant churches in English Protestant thought from 1600 to 1640, Anthony Milton asks why the apocalyptic naming of the pope as Antichrist had become so important to Calvinist writers. Part of his answer seems strikingly relevant to the issues just raised in this chapter.

> The absolute, polarized vision of the churches engendered by the apocalyptic schema complemented and encouraged the more general dualistic world-view typical of puritan spirituality. Puritan practical divinity sought to make dynamic use of the division of the world into the elect and the reprobate. Puritan devotional writers called upon the individual believer to make his election sure, and to join the purified ranks of the community of the fellow-godly, in opposition to the wickedness of the ungodly mass outside.[30]

No wonder that Calvinists felt essential components of their theological and political identities were threatened by challenges exemplified in Montagu's *New Gagg* and its successor, *Appello Caesarem* (1625). No wonder that these works were debated and attacked in parliament during 1625 and 1626.[31]

But before leaving Calvin for some English Calvinists and anti-Calvinists I want to consider one further aspect of Calvin's version of predestination and reprobation. This emerges from a strand of his teaching discussed earlier in this chapter: namely, the way that God actually "illumines" the minds of reprobates so that they recognize the presence of his grace and persuades them "that they do not in any way differ from the elect" (III.2.11). Along with this doctrine Calvin introduces a strange charge against these Christian reprobates with their God-given experience, feeling, "taste of heavenly gifts," and faith in Christ. He claims that these Christians are actually hypocrites. Sharing holy communion, they remain reprobates diving under "a cloak of hypocrisy" (III.2.11). This charge, in this context, seems to me a revolution in language and conceptualization. It is another sign that we are crossing an important divide in the making of Christian traditions.

Let us recall the figure of the hypocrite in medieval culture. A hypocrite is somebody who chooses to dissemble their form of life and their predatory designs on other people. Langland follows medieval conventions when he writes that "to prechen and preve hit nat" (to preach and not practice what you preach) seems to be "ypocrisie" (*Piers Plowman* XVI.264). He thinks this is a vice to which "clerkes" are especially tempted. They become the proverbial wolf in sheep's clothing, the shepherd who so loves his flock that he kills and eats the sheep (XVI.265–71 [Matt. 7:15]). Ypocrasie presents a major threat to "holi church," undermining its teachers and their relations to Conscience (XXII.297–305). In the medieval tradition, hypocrites seek to deceive people for their own gains. The hypocrite is not, as in Calvin's usage, himself a deceived person.

Behind Langland's usage of the language of hypocrisy is a long and rich tradition exploring a range of social practices and the lust for dominion. This tradition's relationship to the latter is one reason Langland writes that "Ypocrisie is a braunche [species] of pruyde" (XVI.265). A dazzling example of the figure of hypocrisy is Jean de Meun's personification False Seeming (Faux Semblant) in his part of the thirteenth-century poem *Romance of the Rose*. The subjects of Jean's satire are the contemporary religious.[32] Aquinas treats this vice in his *Summa Theologiae* during his exploration of Justice and the vices that oppose it (*ST* II–II.111). For Aquinas, hypocrisy is the simulation of virtue with the aim of deceiving others. Although Aquinas's is a characteristically nuanced account of the vice's different forms, nothing he writes prepares us for Calvin's strange version.[33] In Calvin's rendering of the vice, the agent of hypocrisy is, astonishingly enough, God. Calvin's God infuses his grace in the minds of some eternally decreed to be reprobates. These people are inspired to feel as if they were among the elect and to practice Christianity like the elect. They do so under divine influence and hence act in good faith. They are not intentionally deceiving others. In fact, the only agent of deception in Calvin's rendering is God himself: it is he who creates delusions of election in those he (and he alone) knows to be reprobates. Moreover, he instills these deceptions through grace, which in Calvin's theology is *irresistible* (*Institutes* III.3.6–14).[34]

This Calvinist revolution in Christian understandings of hypocrisy became normative within the Calvinist tradition, and its disturbing psychological and pastoral consequences have been illustrated by

Stachniewski and others.[35] As a result of this change, Calvinist ministers were pushed to invent typologies of hypocrisy to account for the distinction between "gross" hypocrisy and "formal" hypocrisy, the latter being the peculiarly Calvinist version in which the alleged hypocrite is actually deceived by God's grace in "his owne heart."[36] This revolutionary model of the relationship between God and Christians provided great scope for Satan's assaults on the devout. Alec Ryrie gives an example from what he calls "a best-selling tract" written by Henry Greenwood in 1606: "'Shewe me God's seale' demands Satan: prove that you are saved!'" According to Ryrie, the author offers a "knock-down reply." What could be this balm from Gilead? "'I can weepe for sinne and hate sinne in my selfe and others . . . which are the Arms of Christe in his seale.'"[37] Greenwood apparently thinks this ability to weep for sin proves to the anxious person that they therefore are not a hypocrite reprobate. But it could mean otherwise for someone formed within a Calvinist paradigm. Any Calvinist would, after all, have learned that tears could just as well be signs of hypocrisy as of election. Ryrie himself gives an example of a minister warning that one's weeping could very well be hypocrisy.[38] How could one be assured, with the certainty Calvin encouraged his adherents to seek, that one's penitent tears were not part of a transitory, temporary faith in a finally ineffectual calling?[39] In such contexts we can see just why someone like Richard Baxter might be compelled to buy all the books he could that promised "Evidences and Marks of true Grace, and tended to discover the Difference bitwixt the true Christian and the Hypocrite or Unsound."[40] But no quantity of books on such "Evidences and Marks" could ever satiate the epistemophiliac's thirst; on the contrary, they could only stimulate it.

How can the introspective gaze of reflexive faith discern the "Evidences and Marks of true Grace" when God himself may counterfeit such signs among those who are in fact (as one English divine named them) "the rabble of reprobate hypocrites," those "subject to God's extraordinary hatred"?[41] In this cycle of doubt, we have been drawn into a world analogous to Othello's pursuit of the missing handkerchief. In Othello's mind the handkerchief is the privileged *evidence* and *mark* of Desdemona's love for him or of her rejection of him. If he can find the stolen object he will be certain she has chosen him faithfully. He will find assurance. But no recovery of the handkerchief or any other mark of Desdemona's faithful love can give Othello the assured certainty he craves. Such epistemophilia can never be satisfied; it can only be cured by the abandonment of the paradigm that generated it.[42] This is shown by Langland in his careful leading of Wille away from the sources that prompt his acute anxiety over his possible reprobation, a strand of *Piers Plowman* discussed in the first chapter of this book.

Perhaps the best balm a Calvinist minister could offer somebody caught up in a quest like Baxter's, or the one traced in Bunyan's *Grace Abounding*, was a familiar argument: whereas the elect should seek assurance of their election, they must also realize that nobody can be certain that they are one of the reprobate. Evoke epistemophilia over one's election; forbid it concerning one's reprobation. This is the line taken by a leading English Calvinist to whom I shall return, William Twisse, in *The Riches of God's Love unto the Vessells of Mercy, Consistent with His Absolute Hatred or Reprobation of the Vessells of Wrath*.[43] Such a solution, if it was one, did not mean abandoning the paradigms of double predestination and assurance. Another balm widely offered to console troubled souls among the godly was a schema developed by ministers for delineating different degrees of assurance among the elect. These ranged from tiny sparkles of faith within what might be an experience of unbelief to full assurance. Those troubled by their lack of assurance and fears of eternal reprobation could be assured that this was a perfectly normal aspect of life among the elect. As the Calvinist Lucy Hutchinson wrote in her record of "My owne faith and attainment," "Faith in the godly hath difference in degrees the lowest of which is resignation with adherence to god as the highest is full assurance through Christ."[44] Hutchinson devoted an entire work to the subject of assurance titled, "Concerning self examinations whither [sic] we have interest in Christ." She addresses the "doubting" godly who fear they are "not in the number of the elect" and will be damned as reprobates. She assures them that they may well have faith when they feel they have "none." How could this be so? She maintains that "a true sence of the want of faith is a low degree of faith" (142). Perhaps such casuistry could keep troubled Calvinists from despair even if it hollowed out the language of assurance. Perhaps it could even persuade them not to ask the obvious question of their theological paradigm: how is this "low degree," devoid of confirming feelings of faith, distinguishable from a reprobate's feelings of confusion and ineffectual faith? Perhaps this circular logic was received by Hutchinson's readers and other Calvinist believers as a comforting balm from Gilead. But did it also register anomalies in the paradigm that might be the signs, evidences, and marks of an unsustainable incoherence?

* * *

I continue this chapter by considering two English Calvinist works and one explicitly anti-Calvinist work, all particularly concerned with the versions of predestination and reprobation explored thus far. These works, like the text I will turn to in chapter 4, were written in the Church of England before the civil war.

I begin with a text by the eminent Calvinist clergyman Robert Bolton, *The Last Conflicts and Death of Mr. Thomas Peacock, Batchelour of Divinity, and fellow of Brasen-nose Colledge in Oxford.*[45] The titular Mr. Peacock, a distinguished Calvinist teacher, died in 1611. An account of his death was written by his former student, "that famous Divine, Mr Robert Bolton," in the same year but not published until after Bolton's death. In 1646 Edward Bagshaw edited the text, and it was licensed by that "eminent Divine of the Assembly [of Westminster]," the Presbyterian Edmund Calamy (who, once upon a time, enjoyed the support of one John Milton). I mention these facts because they provide a picture of the contexts of making and distribution that shape the work: *The Last Conflicts* is the product of several Calvinist teachers of distinction working within their community.

The Last Conflicts belongs to a genre of Calvinist writing about dying well that teach, as Henry Valentine argues in his *Private Devotions* (1635), that "to dye well is a point of the greatest consequence in the world, because eternity depends upon it." Alec Ryrie, Leif Dixon, and others have noted that it is somewhat surprising that Calvinists should have produced such a genre since, as Ryrie observes in relation to Valentine's comments, "doctrines of assurance and the perseverance of the saints ought to have quenched the deathbed's supposed spiritual dangers."[46] Both Ryrie and Dixon find the sources for the peculiarities of these texts in the juxtaposition of what they call "medieval patterns" (i.e., modes of instruction drawn from the medieval tradition of *ars moriendi*) combined quite incoherently with "Reformed theological justifications" drawn from Calvinist theology.[47] I am less persuaded than Ryrie and Dixon that the agonies of Mr. Peacock on his deathbed were caused by "medieval patterns" of instruction displacing the putative consolations of Calvinist doctrines of election and reprobation. But rather than pursue this comparison, I want to focus on the dominant and explicit Calvinist paradigm that shapes the work's narrative, and on Bolton's representation of the particular deathbed terrors encompassing Mr. Thomas Peacock.

The ideological scheme of Bolton's narrative is clear and would have been very familiar to Calvinists, those "connoisseurs of despair," as Ryrie describes them.[48] They were adept at "judging its varieties," and interpreting its import.[49] This is hardly surprising, for these "connoisseurs" had of course invented the very schemes that provoked forms of despair quite distinctive to their own theology and preaching. At the heart of the "conflicts" Robert Bolton relates during the final days of Mr. Peacock's life are two closely related strands central to the Calvinist paradigm on which this chapter has concentrated: the twin doctrines of double predestination and assurance, manifest in the consuming desire for certainty of one's predestination to salvation. Progression through increasing degrees of assurance was at the heart of models of conversion in this tradition of Christianity. As we will see in Arthur Dent's account of conversion in the next chapter, the Calvinist minister's role is to stimulate in his flock an internal struggle through which the Christian would come to discern how their feelings and experiences distinguished them from the reprobates who constituted the vast majority of human beings. Of course, as I have observed, in this struggle a Calvinist might well agonize over their own identity: am I graced with the persevering grace of the adopted or graced with the transient faith given to reprobates and hypocrites? Conventionally this struggle involved a journey into overwhelming terror and an encounter with God's wrath. The experience of being abandoned by God and subjected to his wrath compelled the subject to acknowledge the truth of the Protestant version of justification by faith *alone*. Only by experiencing oneself as Esau can one gradually come to recognize that one's agony is not the despair of the reprobates (like Judas or Francis Spira) but a *holy despair*.[50] Whatever the ambiguities of experience and feeling for the elect, gradually these emotions and feelings become "a form of revelation."[51] The Calvinist doctor of theology, William Twisse, emphasizes in his *Riches of God's Love* that it is "a hard matter to distinguish" those he calls "sincere professors" from those he calls "hypocrites," but as a minister he is confident that the path to consolation is through terror: "I would think fit to use all meanes and motives to make them [the troubled Calvinists] feare."[52] We will see how Dent's work of conversion shares this strategy recommended by Twisse. After a terrible immersion in the depths of reprobate-like conviction, divine grace brings the soul out of this encounter with hell and into a new assurance of salvation.

Robert Bolton's account of Mr. Peacock's death deploys a version of this scheme, tracing Mr. Peacock's last few days on earth from the horror of discovering himself to be a hypocrite and reprobate to final assurance of election. The subject of this narrative is a man whose life was that of a devout Calvinist teacher, revered by colleagues and students. In the preface to the work, the editor, Edward Bagshaw, writes that Mr. Peacock was "a man whom I well knew, and bless God that ever I knew him." He tells us to observe three things in the account he publishes. First, the reader should note that "the sorest and sharpest afflictions doe very often befall the dearest and choicest servants of God: I mean, not outward and temporall afflictions, common to good and bad: but inward and spirituall desertions, whereby God withdraws his glorious countenance from his children: and Satan in liew thereof, shows them his ugly visage." This struggle teaches the elect that "the safest and surest way" to Heaven "is to sayl by the gates of Hell." Second, he reminds readers that the "highest consolations" come after "the deepest humiliations." Third, Bagshaw insists that though "a spirituall desertion be the highest affliction that befalls God's childe; yet it discovers in him the greatest sincerity of an upright heart." Bagshaw acknowledges that the elect person confronts "the terrour of sinne" in "hellish agony," suffers "bitter-convulsion-fits in the soul," and endures "the absence of God and his consolations." It is only by passing through these agonies that the person discovers their own "sincerity"—that is, that they are not a hypocrite. The very desolation of Mr. Peacock is itself "a true touch of grace" and soon followed (not at all soon in John Bunyan's case) by "the comforts of grace [and] . . . leapings for joy." This, Bagshaw relates, "was the case of Mr Peacock" whose end was "peace" (A5r–A6v). Such is the way of assurance. Thus Bagshaw guides us to read the narrative of Mr. Peacock's death within a paradigm familiar to all Calvinists and to none more than the distinguished divine, Mr. Peacock himself.

In the first stages of his sickness Mr. Peacock displays full assurance, blessing a lifetime of laboring in the Lord's vineyard. He thanks God that "he had no trouble of conscience," but some of the attendants gathered around his bedside fear that such assurance might be fragile (2). Sure enough, his assurance soon begins to waver: his conscience starts to make trouble and uncover his hidden sins. What were these sins? He confesses that he now thinks he fed his students too much food. Wicked generosity, "letting them eat their fill of meat when they mealed with me." He judges this to be educating them in "Gluttony" (3). What else has his conscience unearthed? His table talk: he laments that he provided inadequate exegesis of scripture. For this, "I feel a Hell in my conscience." So he begins to be sure he is a reprobate. After all, he also "did eat too much of such meat to breakfast such a morning" (4). "*Sinne, Sinne, Sinne.*" He describes himself as "*A damnable wretched & c*" (5). Any Calvinist would be able to fill in "& c" with the familiar typologies of reprobates' confessions.

Among Mr. Peacock's friends and companions is the distinguished theologian John Dod, who himself wrote about the centrality of being terrified by God and one's conscience in any proven experience of genuine conversion.[53] Bolton relates how Dod reminds his friend Mr. Peacock of "God's kindness" and explains how his present spiritual dereliction is but a transition to the new life of holy happiness. Dod acknowledges that this process is only for "the good," the elect (6–7). This, of course, was a teaching as well known to Mr. Peacock as to John Dod; the trouble is that Mr. Peacock has lost all assurance that he is "good." All he can now see is God as "a most severe Judge displeased, angry and chiding with him; yea yeelding him [Mr. Peacock] up into his clawes" (8–9). Such a God displaying "his clawes" seems identical to traditional representations of the adversary, Satan, who "as a roaring lion, walketh about, seeking whom he may devour" (1 Pet. 5:8). No wonder, then, that Mr. Peacock is "dashed upon the rocks of despaire" (10). Bolton comments that God "trieth his metal" to test whether Mr. Peacock be "good or reprobate" (14). This is a rather odd locution since presumably Bolton's God knew from eternity whether Mr. Peacock was "good or reprobate," and nothing in the text suggests that God has lapses of memory. The intended meaning here must of course be that God "trieth his metall" for Mr. Peacock's benefit (see James 1:2–6, 12–14). Yet this is not quite the commonplace Bolton has written.

Beginning to see himself as a reprobate, Mr. Peacock judges all his devout life to have been that of "*a foolish glorious Hypocrite*" (16). This lament reinforces how thoroughly Calvin transformed the concept of hypocrisy into one unknown in the Middle Ages. Nothing done during his life now seems to Mr. Peacock to have been done "sincerely." Bolton comments on the "secret mixture of pride and hypocrisy" present even in "the best" Christians (16). Mr. Peacock, however, now feels that God's eternal "*decree*" stands against him, revealing him to be one of the reprobate (17–18). He exhorts the "younger sort" around his bed not to pray for him as "*praying for a Reprobate*" breaks the third commandment. That is, "Thou shalt not take the name of the Lord thy God in vain" (Exod. 20:7). Is Mr. Peacock's scrupulous prohibition a sign of inspired and reaffirmed obedience to God or a sign of reprobate despair? Reminded of his virtuous life, Mr. Peacock dismisses this as yet more deception: "*I did good outwardly, all hypocritically*" (20). Presumably, he feels he has been misled by those divine gifts that are of the transitory sort given to the reprobates. He declares that his orthodox teaching has been worse than useless: "*I have destroyed a thousand souls*" (23). All his teaching was "hypocritically" done.[54] As we saw earlier in this chapter and as Mr. Peacock himself would have taught, *hypocrite* and *reprobate* are bound together in Calvinist vocabulary.

It takes more than one interjection from John Dod to shift Mr. Peacock's perceptions and to allow Bolton's narrative to turn toward a renewed sense of Mr. Peacock's life and present suffering as signs of his election, and *not* those of the hypocrite reprobate. Deploying familiar distinctions, John Dod tells Mr. Peacock to stop searching "the secrets of God." Nobody, after all, can truly know that they are among the reprobate. Dod advises the dying man to stop "digging in at your sinnes" (39). And he reminds him of "the calling of the good thief upon the crosse" and how "Christ rising again, did first appear to *Mary Magdalen* that sinner" (37–38). We must "distinguish between unperfect desire and hypocriticall," and Dod insists that Mr. Peacock can indeed know by "signes" that his desire is the "true" desire of the elect (40). What are these clear "signes"? Constancy and "a conscionable using of the means" given by God (40). But Mr. Peacock still insists he cannot "*truly desire.*" In response, John Dod tells him that there is no logic in the argument that because one does not feel something one does not have it. Indeed, he reminds Mr. Peacock that he himself had once denied such an argument. The example Dod gives to illustrate the unreliability of feeling is striking: a reprobate feels "no sense of the wrath of God," but it does not follow that "he is not under it." (40). This emphasis on the unreliability of feeling is congruent with Julian of Norwich's teaching on prayer, but it seems to clash with the immense emphasis on feeling and emotion in the Calvinists' pursuit of assurance. As Ryrie observes, "The primary reason why early modern British Protestants paid such close attention to their emotions was that they expected to meet God in them. Emotion was a form of revelation."[55] Indeed, "feelings might provide testimony on a whole range of subjects, but in particular they could provide unparalleled evidence—perhaps the only true evidence—of election and of salvation."[56] But ministers had to address the godly even when their feelings were delivering evidence that presented a disastrous impediment to assurance and peace. In his responses to Mr. Peacock's distress here, John Dod exemplifies sensitivity to the way that Mr. Peacock's Christian formation is itself now causing trouble that alienates him from God: "digging in at your sinnes" and attention to feelings were, after all, habitually encouraged. Dod's pastoral skills enable him to set these habits aside, to displace the contemporary Protestant "truism" that "affections and passions" were vital sources of data about God's work in their lives.[57]

Gradually Dod's ministry elicits a conversion: "*I thank God* (saith he) *he hath begun to ease me*" (46). Mr. Peacock now understands the exemplary role of his suffering and torment: God has made him "*a spectacle*" for Christians. As such, he will finally serve as a model of how God works through Calvinist doctrine and pastoral practice (46). True enough, Mr. Peacock again relapses from this assurance (48–49), but we are shown that divine grace and consolations are made accessible to him even in this relapse. As an exemplary sufferer, Mr. Peacock is able to reinhabit his own vocation as a teacher to the students who visit him (50–54). He himself begins to identify the processes he has endured as "temtations" to misidentify himself as a "*Reprobate.*" "*I thank God,*" he prays, "*they are eased in good measure*" (53). He now recognizes that he has misread the signs, mistaken the meaning of his feelings. Attended at his deathbed by his friends, these companions are God's means to help him overcome the fear that in these temptations he had been "*an Apostate.*" They remind him, "Man is not the Judge" (55). Finally, the dying man becomes convinced of the sincerity with which he has practiced his calling as a teacher: "I have not dealt hypocritically in it" (55–56). His friends rejoice, recognizing that Mr. Peacock no longer relies at all upon "inherent righteousness" (against all his teaching) but now trusts only in Christ (56–57, 61). At last he can utter the talismanic confession and does so, perhaps surprisingly, in Latin: "*ideo me in coelos transiturum pro certo habeo. . . .* I am assured I shall goe to Heaven." He longs to complete his time on earth: "*Tollite, Tollite, Eripite, Eripite, ut coelum adeam . . .* Take me up, take me up, carry me hence, carry me hence, that I may go to Heaven" (62–63). In this, Mr. Peacock says, "*I doe (God be praised) feel such comfort*" (63). Retrospectively recognizing his agonies as mercies, his feelings can, once again, be trusted as evidence of election. Commending his soul into Christ's hands, he prays the Lord's prayer and the Creed, and, Bolton concludes, "so he slept in the Lord" (65–66).

Bolton's work is a dramatic performance of many of the distinctly Calvinist doctrines considered in this chapter. It demonstrates how Calvinists found ways of living and dying with the ambiguities and contradictions apparently woven by the God they worshipped and his interpreter John Calvin. The narrative displays how productive were central antinomies in the spiritual life of such Protestants. In Mr. Peacock's "last conflict," we see clearly how the dynamics of reflexive faith, double predestination, and the conviction of pervasive iniquity interact at the heart of the pursuit of assurance. The Calvinist demand to seek assurance and certainty of election when God was known to give the same signs and feelings to elect and reprobate alike aligned with the traditional teaching that nobody is righteous, "all have sinned and come short of the glory of God" (Rom. 3:10, 12, 23). This paradigm could make a saving virtue of the acute terror and despair it generated. The model's double binds and contradictions became part of its power and persuasiveness.

It seems appropriate to conclude this account of *The Last Conflicts and Death of Mr Thomas Peacock* by returning to Calvin himself. In the light of Mr. Peacock's spiritual torment on his deathbed and its final resolution, I will consider a part of the *Institutes* not addressed so far: Christ's descent into hell. Calvin decides that this event took place on Good Friday, on the cross (II.16). This inventive decision is another example of a revolutionary break from Christian tradition. It is, in fact, a remarkable rejection of a tradition that understood the descent into hell (affirmed in the Apostles' Creed) as a profoundly significant moment of soteriological reflection in the liturgy of Holy Week. In this tradition, on Holy Saturday Christ's soul continued the salvific work of Christ's Incarnation, now illuminating and liberating the souls of the just who had already died. In chapter 1, I touched on the importance and power of Langland's version of Christ's descent into hell in *Piers Plowman* (Passus XX). Calvin, however, claims that the traditional way of understanding the creedal confession ("He descended into hell") and its biblical source (1 Pet. 3:18–20) is nothing but a "childish" fable (II.16.9). Unlike Langland and medieval tradition, he does not recognize that the mystery of Christ's descent into hell has strong symbolic resonance for the life of all, nor does he acknowledge its power as a meditation on the scope of God's mercy. For Calvin it can have no place in the "last conflicts and death of Mr. Peacock," and it can no longer carry the soteriological meanings explored by Langland. Instead, Calvin understands Christ's descent into hell, in the crucifixion, as a means of illumining the souls of the dead while making the reprobates more clearly convinced than before that they are completely excluded from all salvation (II.16.9).

The truly revolutionary dimension of Calvin's relocation of Christ's descent into hell, however, is his use of this event as a lens through which to view the crucifixion. This lens allows him to see some surprising things. Most strikingly, Calvin discerns in the crucifixion a view of the relations between the Father and the Son that was unknown to medieval Christianity but found in Luther. This transformed version of the relationship is intrinsic to the Reformation's invention of a new theology of the atonement, one based on ideas of penal satisfaction and substitution.[58] In Calvin's version, the descent into hell happens on the cross as the wrathful Father inflicts punishment on the Son who substitutes for sinful humankind. The violent torture the Father himself imposes on the Son is spiritual as well as bodily, and it is presented as an act of justice. Calvin asserts that Jesus descended into hell on the cross to appease "the severity of God's vengeance, to appease his wrath and satisfy just judgement" (II.16.10). No wonder, says Calvin, "if he is said to have descended into hell, for he suffered the death that God in his wrath inflicted upon the wicked." Jesus becomes the cursed sinner "in suffering in his soul the terrible torments of a condemned and forsaken man" (II.16.10). With some bizarre exegesis of Acts 2:24, Calvin forces this text to support his assertion that Jesus Christ endured "the curse and wrath" of his Father (II.16.11). Christ becomes the condemned sinner cast into the "terrible abyss," abandoned by God and "estranged" from him. The Father wrings from his Son "anguish deep within his heart" and imposes on him the weight of divine anger "so that he experienced all the signs of a wrathful and avenging God" (II.16.11). Calvin is confident that Christ "knew that he stood accursed before God's judgement seat" and that in experiencing the despair of subjection to the "curse and wrath" of God, Christ entered the state of reprobates. In this way, Calvin rejects medieval accounts of the descent into hell and traditional accounts of the crucifixion.

Calvin goes on to rebuke those "untutored wretches" who object that he ascribes to the Son of God "a despair contrary to faith" (II.16.12). In traditional theology, despair was a mortal sin that alienated one from God: its subject needed repentance, conversion, and divine forgiveness.[59] Calvin does not deny that he ascribes the sin of despair to the Son of God. He continues to emphasize the distinctiveness of his theology against the tradition of "untutored wretches" such as Augustine and Aquinas, Dante and Langland. He insists again that the Father's punishment of the Son included punishment inflicted on his soul (II.16.12). He attacks the traditions of those "unlearned" people who teach that Jesus Christ neither endured nor feared "God's curse and wrath" (II.16.12). These "quibblers," says Calvin, "boldly chatter about things they know nothing of," whereas Calvin (he implies) knows confidently that their tradition has misunderstood the implications of the Chalcedonian Christology he also follows. One person, two natures: so taught Chalcedonian orthodoxy and so taught John Calvin (I.13.6–13; I.13.23–27). For Calvin, however, the divinity of Christ was "hidden" on the cross as he substituted for humanity: in the crucifixion, "the divine power of his Spirit remained hidden for a moment," a moment which encompasses the whole process of the Passion (II.16.12).

Earlier in the second book, Calvin again (as he does in I.13) asserts his traditional Christology, affirming that Jesus Christ fulfilled the office of Mediator "clothed with our flesh" (II.13.1), a traditional way of emphasizing the complete distinctness of the divine and human natures in Christ. Calvin maintains that in the Incarnation the divine person was *not* "confined within the narrow prison of an earthly body": "The Son of God descended from heaven in such a way that, without leaving heaven, he willed to be borne in the virgin's womb, to go about on earth, and to hang upon the cross; yet he continually filled the world even as he had done from the beginning" (II.13.4). Calvin reiterates this position when discussing the eucharist in Book IV. Jesus Christ is "one person" consisting of "two natures," and in the Passion this person did *not* suffer anything "in his divinity." All the time Jesus Christ lived on earth he was simultaneously "God in heaven." The Incarnation does not mean that Christ's "divinity left heaven to hide itself in the prison house of the body." No, "it filled all things" even as "in Christ's very humanity it dwelt bodily" (IV.17.30). The images of the body of Jesus of Nazareth as clothing and "prison house" emphasize the complete separation between the impassible Word and the human nature. This position is known in Protestant literatures as the *extra Calvinisticum*, but in it Calvin is actually affirming Catholic and medieval tradition.[60] No revolution here, as Calvin sustains a traditional high Christology of the kind we find in the Catholic liturgy, in Augustine, in Lombard, and in

Aquinas. This Christology did, however, raise some profound difficulties around Christ's passions, difficulties with which Aquinas explicitly engaged.[61] Yet in the *Institutes* Calvin simply combines this tradition with his revolutionary account of Christ's crucifixion, descent into hell, and despair that I have outlined. This, as noted above, produces an innovative version of the role of God the Father as punisher together with a model of the atonement as penal substitution equally unknown to medieval and patristic Christianity.

Calvin was not the first theologian to have thought hard about one of the sayings of Christ on the cross: "My God, my God, why hast thou forsaken me [*ut quid derelequisti me*]?" (Mark 15:34). No late medieval theologian or devotional writer with whom I am familiar denied that in his love for sinful humanity the Son of God subjected himself to the terrible consequences of human evil. The cry in the Gospels of Mark and Matthew concentrates on this dereliction. But simultaneously the Gospels offer other sayings of Christ on the cross. Let us recall them: "Father, forgive them; for they know not what they do" and "Today shalt thou be with me in paradise" (Luke 23:34, 43); and to his mother, "Woman, behold thy son!"; and to his disciple standing by the cross, "Behold thy mother!" (John 19:26–27); and finally, "Father, into thy hands I commend my spirit" (Luke 23:46). The pre-Reformation tradition saw no signs of God the Father torturing his Son in body and soul with punitive wrath. Nor was any such version of the Father represented in any depictions of the crucifixion I have yet seen. On the contrary, medieval depictions of the Father in scenes of the crucifixion are images of compassion and love. As for the accounts of Christ's crucifixion in the Gospels, we read in medieval texts of both the cry of dereliction and the other utterances just recalled. Any remotely adequate discussion of the crucifixion will have to hold onto all the sayings in all the accounts. A dialectical and inclusive reading is needed. Late medieval texts vary widely in their versions of this, but they tend to hold together the scope of the gospel sayings. Many devotional texts offered powerful representations of the immense suffering of Christ in the redemption of humanity as he confronted and bore the force of human sin, violence, and alienation from the God who is Love. Some, like Langland's *Piers Plowman* and (in a very different mode) Julian of Norwich's *Book of Showings*, resisted the abstraction of the cross from Christ's victory over sin and death. But none of the writings with which I am familiar, however diverse, offered a picture of God the Father inflicting his punitive wrath on the Son who was substituting for fallen humanity to satisfy the Father's punishments. With such teachings, intrinsic to Reformed Christianity, we have again crossed a great divide between medieval and Protestant traditions. To even begin to grasp such revolutionary transformations, we need to attempt some form of diachronic historiography.

Some readers may perhaps wonder why I have not mentioned St. Anselm's *Cur Deus Homo* as at least a precursor to the Calvinist traditions I have been addressing. The answer is quite simple: Anselm's model of the atonement is very different. The language of satisfaction in some Protestant writers might seem Anselmian at first glance (as in, perhaps, *Paradise Lost* III.210–12), but it is actually nothing of the sort. In *Cur Deus Homo,* Christ's satisfaction for humanity's dishonoring of God involves no wrathful Father justly punishing his Son as substitute for fallen humanity. Instead, Anselm carefully distinguishes Christ's satisfaction from his punishment. He is quite clear that Christ's Passion was in no sense a just punishment inflicted by the Father on the body and mind of the substitute for sinners, Jesus Christ. On the contrary, the crucifixion is understood as an act of gross *injustice* through which the Son makes satisfaction for the human sins that have alienated us from God. How so? The totally innocent Christ lives a life of perfect love and obedience to God, a life culminating in his knowing submission to enduring the most wicked act of the crucifixion. In love, obedience, and death, so *Cur Deus Homo* argues, the Son of God makes satisfaction for human sins, sins that have estranged humanity from God and introduced disorder into the world God has created. But because he is himself God, the Son's satisfaction is infinitely in excess of the demands of reparation. As a consequence, his act reconciles fallen humanity with God and liberates humans from sin and the tyranny of the one who unjustly deceived and lured humankind to reject God and God's ordering of the world. Anselm knows absolutely nothing of Calvin's doctrine of penal satisfaction under the vengeful wrath of a Father who tortures his Son in soul and body, nothing of Calvin's version of the descent into hell.[62] Nor, of course, did Aquinas (see *ST* III.46–48).

I have returned to Calvin and addressed these issues, including briefly invoking a diachronic perspective that highlights the revolutionary nature of Calvinist dogmatics in this area, because they shed further light on Mr. Peacock's deathbed dialogues and the culture to which they belonged. If the Son of God, the beloved, had been tortured into the despair of the reprobates by his own loving Father, what might the Calvinist God—he who infused temporary faith and joy in those decreed to everlasting torment—do to sinful human beings? Some might respond that although the Father unleashed his punitive wrath on his Son in the way Calvin describes, this act meant that Christ now stood as a shield between such wrath and humanity, forever protecting humanity from such divine punishment. Christ, so the answer might continue, died for *all*; thus every human can be certain that the infinite wrath and punitive vengeance that is allegedly our just due has been absorbed by him. But such an answer will not do for Calvin. Humans could *not* be certain that Christ died for all. If Calvinists had assurance they were one of the elect, certainty was appropriate. But if they had lost assurance— as Mr. Peacock did on his deathbed, or as John Bunyan relates in *Grace Abounding*—then they could not be certain that Christ died for them, that justice had been paid on their behalf. Indeed, many Calvinists explicitly and vehemently denied that Jesus Christ died for all humans, maintaining that he made only a limited atonement. Some were prepared to concede "hypothetical universalism" in which it was accepted that while in principle Christ's death was sufficient for all, in effect it was *not* for all. This of course did nothing to qualify the Calvinist paradigm of double predestination, and the English delegation at Dort signed the final position: God only applies Christ's death to the elect. Here, too, Calvinist teaching rejected the way medieval Christianity affirmed that Christ's atonement reconciled humankind with God (2 Cor. 5:19). In the medieval tradition, Christ came among us to redeem humanity by love, love of God and love of the "kynde" he assumed in the Incarnation. *Kynde* is the Middle English word that encompasses nature, kindness, and God. The play among all these meanings is central to Christ's oration during his descent into hell in Langland's *Piers Plowman*. Christ proclaims his redemptive love for humankind and deploys the full range of meanings in the word *kynde*.

Ac to be merciable to man thenne my kynde asketh,
For we beth brethren of o bloed, ac nat in baptisme alle.
Ac alle that beth myn hole brethrene, in bloed and in baptisme,
Shal neuere in hell eft come, be he ones out.

. . . .

And yut my kynde in my kene ire shal constrayne my will—
Domine, ne in furore tuo arguas me, &c.—
To be merciable to monye of my halue-brethrene.
For bloed may suffre bloed bothe aufurst and acale
Ac bloed may nat se bloed blede bote hym rewe.
(*Audivi arcana verba, que non licet homini loqui.*)
Ac my rihtwysnesse and rihte shal regnen in helle
And mercy al mankynde bifore me in heuene.
For Y were an unkynde king bote Y my kyn helpe
And namliche at such a nede that nedes helpe asketh
                              (XX.417–20, 435–42)

———

[But to be merciful to man then my nature demands,
For we are brothers of one blood, but not all in baptism.
But all that are my full brothers in blood and in baptism
Shall never come to hell again, once they are out.

. . . .

And yet my kind nature in my keen anger shall constrain my will—
Rebuke me not, O Lord, in thy indignation—
To be merciful to many of my half-brothers.
For blood may see blood both thirsty and cold
But blood may not see blood bleed without taking pity.
I heard secret words, which is not granted to man to utter.
But my righteousness and right shall reign in hell,
And mercy over all mankind before me in heaven.
For I'd be an unkind king unless I help my kin,
And namely in such need that needs to ask for help.]

Sublime poetry, sublime theology (both addressed in the first chapter of this study where I follow the way Langland frees Wille from the false picture of election and reprobation that held him captive). Yet howevur sublime the modes of Langland's writing, his meditation on the scope and nature of Christ's redeeming love is a manifestation of entirely orthodox medieval traditions of Christology and soteriology. It is, for example, perfectly congruent with Aquinas's commentary on the efficacy of Christ's Passion in the third part of the *Summa Theologiae* (III.48–49). During this exploration, Aquinas asks whether Christ's passion caused our salvation through the mode of satisfaction (*per modum satisfactions*).

> Christ, suffering in a loving and obedient spirit, offered more to God than was demanded in recompense for all the sins of mankind, because first, the love which led him to suffer was a great love; secondly the life he laid down was of great dignity, since it was the life of God and man; and thirdly his suffering was all-embracing. . . . Christ's passion, then, was not only sufficient but superabundant satisfaction for the sins of humankind; as John says, *he is a propitiation for our sins, not only for ours but also for those of the whole world* (1 John 2:2). (*ST* III.48.2, resp.)

This passage cites the first epistle of John, but it could just as well have quoted passages from other New Testament texts such as John 3:16–17 ("God so loved the world, that he gave his only begotten Son that whosoever believeth in him should not perish, but have everlasting life. For God sent not his Son into the world to condemn the world; but that the world through him might be saved") or 2 Corinthians 5:15 ("And that he died for all, that they which live should not henceforth live unto themselves, but unto him who died for them, and rose again").

In light of this tradition, we need to consider the theology of *limited atonement* forwarded in the Calvinist revolution a little further since this doctrine constitutes an extremely important part of the context of Mr. Peacock's agonized attempts to rediscover his eternal identity as one of the elect few. I have observed that Calvinists commonly taught that Christ died only for the elect. How then did they handle scriptural locutions (such as those just quoted) that insist "he died for all"? Predictably enough, a favored strategy among Calvinists was to apply the form of exegesis we found the Augustinian tradition using on 1 Timothy 2:4 (God "will have all men to be saved"). For example, preaching at Paul's Cross in 1617 the Calvinist Charles Richardson insisted that Christ's atonement was limited to "the elect alone." Richardson argues that when

> it is saide that our Saviour Christ died for all we may safely understand it that he died for men of all sorts and conditions, whether they be high or low, rich or pore, bond or free. . . . For them [the elect] Christ was given. And there is a world of them that shall be damned. For them Christ doth not pray. I doe not deny but that the death of Christ is sufficient to save al men, for his blood . . . is of infinite value. But it is not effectuall to save all.[63]

Here Richardson displays a conventional Calvinist distinction between the *sufficiency* of Christ's death (for all) and its *efficacy* (for a few). Richardson then reminds his listeners that "there are vessels of wrath prepared for destruction, as well as vessels of mercy prepared unto glory." He thinks of Esau and declares that some "were appointed to bee damned before ever they were borne."[64] For these reprobates Christ certainly did not die; many, indeed, were excluded from his love. Similarly, in a debate on "the rise of Arminianism" in the Church of England, Nicholas Tyacke quotes from a Calvinist treatise titled *Of the Redemption of Mankind* (1598). This was an English translation of a massive work by Jacobus Kimendoncius in which the theologian maintains that election and reprobation have no human sources whatsoever. They both depend entirely on the will of God, and we must know that "Christ effectually died for the elect and faithful onely."[65] Mr. Peacock, of course, knew this teaching intimately. We can see in these examples exactly why Mr. Peacock urged his students and friends not to pray for him: Christ himself did not pray for those who were not elect, and Mr. Peacock felt himself to be a reprobate.

Calvinists, of course, were not unaware of the traditional teachings that their doctrine of limited atonement opposed. In a 1571 sermon at Paul's Cross, John Bridges addressed one of the scriptural texts quoted above: "God so loved the world, that he gave his only begotten Son, that whosoever believeth in him should not perish but have eternal life" (John 3:16). Bridges claims that to read this text as an affirmation that

Christ died for the world, for all humanity, is a Roman Catholic error. How, then, should we read it? We need, Bridges insists, to gloss it according to Calvinist doctrine. The "world," which God so loved that he gave his son to save, designates only the elect few: "To say therefore it is God's will that all men should be saved is a false principle. But thus say the papists and wrest the words of God to deny his eternal purpose of election and reprobation, the papists therefore make an evident liar of God. For if God would, who could resist the will of God?"[66]

I observed above that some Calvinists acknowledged that in principle it could be said that Christ died for all: "hypothetical universalism." But hypothetical universalists also acknowledged that in dying for all Christ could give "genuine spiritual gifts" to those already reprobated. As Peter Lake writes, "The whole point about hypothetical universalism was that it was hypothetical." He quotes one of its proponents: "Christ died for all men sufficiently but God accepted not the price of redemption but only for the elect. Remission, redemption, reconciliation etc. in no way belong to the reprobate for if the benefit of these belong to all then should the gospel be preached to all and Christ intercede for all, both of which are false."[67] Hypothetical universalism, then, is a distinction within Calvinist theology—but one without a difference relevant to the concerns of the present book. Nothing in this distinction could have consoled Mr. Peacock until he regained confidence that he was one of the elect whom Christ's suffering had bought. Nothing in the orthodox Calvinist doctrine of the atonement could offer resources to ease the urgent need for the kind of assurance Mr. Peacock lost and found on his deathbed.

✤ ✤ ✤

Mr. Peacock's own church, of course, increasingly included powerful and articulate opponents of Calvinist dogmatics, ecclesiology, and liturgical convictions. This has been copiously exemplified by Nicholas Tyacke, Kenneth Fincham, Anthony Milton, and others, to whom I shall return. I now consider an explicitly anti-Calvinist work by Samuel Hoard (with Henry Mason) published in 1633 before turning finally to one of the replies this work elicited from Calvinist defenders.

Samuel Hoard's work, *Gods Love To Mankind Manifested, By Dis-Prooving his Absolute Decree for their Damnation,* concentrates on the Calvinist doctrine of reprobation.[68] As Hoard explains, Calvinists maintain that by his absolute decree of reprobation God "casteth men off from grace and glory, and shutteth up the farre greater part (even of those that are called by the preaching of the Gospell to repentance and salvation) under invincible and unavoyable sinne and damnation" (1). Hoard makes his sympathies with the Remonstrants at Dort (1618–19) explicit: God foresees people's choice of sin, but he also offers them the grace that would allow them to choose virtuously (1–2). This seems congruent with the position of those late medieval theologians who developed a theology of general election (see ch. 2). It also seems congruent with positions espoused later in the century by John Milton (see ch. 5). Hoard acknowledges the difference between Calvinists who take the "supralapsarian way" and those who take the "infralapsarian" way: the latter seek to avoid "the great inconveniences" of the former by locating "the decree of Reprobation" after the fall of humankind, "under the guilt of original sinne." Here, God decrees that "the greatest number" of humans are to end in everlasting "torments" in hell, "without all remedy." Hoard remarks that these Calvinists see the decree as a manifestation of God's "justice" (2). The supralapsarians, on the other hand, locate the decree antecedent to the fall, a position Hoard points to in Calvin, Beza, Zanchius, Gomarus, and others. The infralapsarians place it "a little lower" (2). However, Hoard derisively points out that when considering Calvinist versions of God, the difference between these two conceptions of the temporality of God's decree is "petty." He illustrates this judgment by noting that the final agreement between different Calvinist factions at the Synod of Dort included the settlement to allow either way as orthodox (2–4).[69] Hoard, in contrast, rejects both ways. His text is devoted to first combating the supralapsarian position (14–44), then the infralapsarian (44–110).

Hoard argues that supralapsarian Calvinism is contrary to the versions of God given in scripture and that it misrepresents God as damning millions of people without any cause in themselves (14–15). He rejects the widespread defense of this Calvinist position that relies upon an analogy between God's treatment of the reprobate and humans kill ing animals. Reflecting on this, Hoard argues that nowhere does scripture institute human sacrifice and instead actually forbids the shedding of human blood in the covenant recounted in Genesis 9:6: "for in the image of God made he man." As for animals, Hoard insists that the torture of animals by humans has no divine warrant. There is absolutely no scriptural justification for keeping animals alive only to torture them, so even this Calvinist analogy (used in the work of Twisse, discussed below) would not justify God torturing humans through an eternal decree. Such a God, Hoard maintains, would manifest "the greatest injustice and cruelty" (18–23; see, too, 38). Indeed, the Calvinist version of election and reprobation irrespective of human vices produces a God "worse than the Divell" (25). This is a view later shared by Archbishop Laud in an attack on the "Brownists" who espoused Calvinism, among whom he includes Prynne (then a Presbyterian). Laud says that this version of God "makes God, the God of all mercies, to be the most fierce and unreasonable tyrant in the world."[70] At least, Hoard reasons, the Devil only tempts us in ways we can resist, whereas we cannot resist God's eternal decree condemning us as sinful reprobates (25–26). Hoard alludes to the passage in Calvin's *Institutes* where reprobates are said to be *"raised up by the unsearchable judgment of God to illustrate his glory by their damnation"* (26; Hoard cites *Institutes* III.24, and the question is from III.24.14, which should be read with III.24.12). He goes on to note that many Calvinists reject the argument that God only *permits* sin (31–34).

To Hoard, the infralapsarian position seems as contrary to the direction of scripture as the supralapsarian one (45–50). His approach is shaped by Christ's declaration that "God so loved the world, that he gave his only begotten Son" (John 3:16), and by his own overwhelming conviction that God is, indeed, love. His vision is thus quite compatible with that expressed by Langland's Holy Churche: *"Deus caritas* [God is love]" (*Piers Plowman* I.82; 1 John 4:8, 16). Having been nurtured in the Church of England when Calvinism was dominant, Hoard is very familiar with Calvinist exegesis of scripture and of the passages he himself has taken to heart, for example, 1 Timothy 2:4: God "will have all men to be saved, and to come unto the knowledge of the truth." For Hoard, this and similar texts declare "God's will that men should enjoy a happy end, and be saved," while affirming God's will to offer humanity the means to that end. Such texts reject any theology asserting God's "absolute will, that many thousand men shall dye in unbeleefe and be damned" (41). He then rehearses all the forms of Augustinian-Calvinist exegesis of 1 Timothy 2:4—ones with which we are by now familiar—and he contests each of them (47–50; contrast Calvin, *Institutes* III.24.16 on this text). Hoard links his reading of Paul's statement with his sense that scripture includes testimony of God's patience and God's love to all (49–50, 85–86). He observes that some places in scripture are "darke and obscure"; 1 Timothy 2:4, however, is not one of these (50).

Hoard worries that Calvinist versions of election and reprobation subject God to a thoroughly abstract model of power: "Power is no vertue; But Holiness, Mercy, Iustice, and Truth are: acts of power are not morally good in themselves, but are made good or evil by their concomitants" (51). Furthermore, Hoard asserts that God created humankind in God's image and regenerates humanity to participate in divine life. Behind this assertion is a classic Athanasian account of the atonement.[71] Hoard contrasts Calvin's version of God by recalling *Institutes* III.23.7. There, Calvin maintained that God prepared many peoples with their infants for eternal death without remedy. This passage is from the famous section in which Calvin acknowledges that the decree is indeed dreadful ("horribile"). Calvin insists it is also, however, a sign of "the wonderful plan of God" who not only foresaw the ruin of humanity, but "at his own pleasure arranged it" (III.23.7).

Hoard also discusses how the English delegation at Dort confirmed one of the aspects of the *Institutes* considered earlier in this chapter: namely, that reprobates "receive many of God's graces" and yet are simultaneously "under the necessity of final sinne and impenitency." He illustrates this position with examples from Dort and from other Calvinists (56–59). He argues that the version of divine agency this assumes is incompatible with the teaching of God's mercy in scripture and in Christian tradition (55–65). Once again, he discerns in the God of Calvinists more of Satan, our adversary and destroyer, than the redeeming love of the Triune God worshipped in Christian tradition (62). He develops such claims by arguing that Calvin's God puts reprobates in a double bind: he demands from them performances he knows they cannot accomplish because he has denied them the resources they need to do so. Hoard finds this God unjust and incoherent (67–68). He offers an analogy: Think of a master commanding a servant to eat or be punished. This same master makes adherence to his own command impossible by ensuring the servant has no meat he can eat. Such a cruel master, Hoard argues, is the Calvinist God (68). Here and elsewhere Hoard attacks the divine command ethics that seem a constitutive part of Calvinist theology. I noted earlier that this strand of Calvin's theology coexists with different teaching that belongs to a recognizable tradition of natural law. Hoard himself draws on the latter to insist that "the light of nature" is God's gift to humanity, showing us how to live well. God and humanity thus *share* criteria for justice: "vertues in men being but the image of those perfections that dwell in God" (69). The mysteries of faith, such as the Incarnation of the Son of God and the resurrection of the body, are supernatural. But that which transcends nature is never in contradiction to the God-given natural virtues known to the image of God (70–74).

Hoard agrees with Calvinists and with earlier Christian traditions in seeing hypocrisy as a vice that the God who is Truth condemns. But he thinks that Calvinist theology actually makes God the hypocrite. God is a hypocrite, for example, when he commands repentance and belief in the gospel to those "whom he secretly purposeth shall not believe"— that is, to reprobates (74). Not only does the Calvinist God delude reprobates (76–80), but he also apparently persuades all people that faith, repentance, and grace "may be counterfeited" (109–10). He acknowledges that many Calvinists are "godly" people living virtuous lives. However, they are doing so in spite of their distinctive doctrines, not because of them. Many Epicureans, ruminates Hoard, lived virtuous lives despite espousing utterly false teaching about God (97–98).

Like Stachniewski in *The Persecutory Imagination*, Hoard argues that Calvinist theology tends to encourage desperation, despair, and even suicide. Yet the Christian gospel is good news and brings sweet consolation. Whereas Calvinists teach that there are one hundred reprobates to every one elect (100–101, 104–6), time and again Hoard returns to his central conviction: God loves all humankind, and Christ's death was therefore "for all men, the calling of poor sinners, without exception, to repentance and salvation with all other grounds of consolation" (102).

He thus rejects the Calvinist doctrine of limited atonement. God's love
in Christ is for *all* and Christ died for *all*—actually so, not just hypo-
thetically (107–8).

I will conclude this brief account of Samuel Hoard's work by turning to a passage that will be taken up by one of his Calvinist critics in a
way I have found fascinating and illuminating, hence the cover of the
present book. The passage concerns the nature of hens. It belongs to
Hoard's commentary on the differences between the versions of God's
love in traditional Christianity and those found in Calvinist versions.
In a section on God's mercy, Hoard considers many texts from scripture
(59–65). Unlike Calvinists, he says, scripture highlights divine mercy.
The model for divine mercy is the love of parents for children. Hoard
offers a striking contrast to the versions of the Father in Calvin's teaching on the crucifixion. There, we recall, the punitive, wrathful, vengeful
Father tortures his Son into despair as he substitutes for condemned humanity. Hoard instead foregrounds how Jesus taught his disciples that
in their own lives they should suspend judgment and model their actions
on divine generosity: "If ye then, being evil, know how to give good
gifts unto your children, how much more shall your Father in heaven
give good things to them that ask him?" (Matt. 7:11). Following these
reflections on God the Father, Hoard quotes the image of God that
Isaiah was given by the Lord: "Can a woman forget her sucking child,
that she should not have compassion on the son of her womb? Yea, they
may forget, yet will I not forget thee" (Isa. 49:15). On this text Hoard
writes, "Women are compassionate toward their children, because they
are the fruit of their wombes, and a part of themselves." Nevertheless,
"mothers may forget even theyr sucking children: but for God, he can
never forget his children" (61).

From this version of God as mother, one that had been profoundly
developed by Julian of Norwich in her *Book of Showings*, Hoard turns
to Jesus's self-representation in Matthew's gospel: "O Jerusalem, Jerusalem, thou that killest the prophets, and stonest them which are sent
unto thee, how often would I have gathered thy children together, even
as a hen gathereth her chickens under her wings, and ye would not!"
(Matt. 23:37).[72] Reflecting on Christ's comparison of himself to a hen,
Hoard remarks that Christ does so in order to liken his love for humanity to the hen's "singular expressions of love to her young ones, even

when they are out of sight" (62). He assimilates this observation to his argument that scripture puts immense emphasis on God's mercy and love to humankind. He maintains that the Son of God's self-representation is incompatible with Calvinist versions of God and the absolute decree that makes God "a Father of cruelties" (62).

Hoard's reading of Christ's language is thoroughly traditional. He draws explicitly on Augustine, but he could as easily have drawn on the *Glossa Ordinaria*. There the marginal gloss on the hen ("gallina") tells readers that the hen is an animal with great affection for her children in their weakness, protecting them under her wings against birds of prey. In the same manner, the incarnate wisdom of God protects us and defends us from the devil. In his literal commentary on the verse, Nicholas of Lyra (whose continuing relevance is evident in that he is still being consulted by John Donne in the seventeenth century) similarly says that Christ chose the example of the hen to show his affection for the Jewish people. According to Lyra, the hen displays greater love and greater commitment to protecting and nurturing her chicks than any other bird.[73] The fifteenth-century theologian and contemplative Denis the Carthusian compares the hen to other "winged animals" and finds her the most affectionate, caring, nurturing, and protecting of her chicks. Christ also chose this simile because the hen is a fruitful, peaceful, and domestic bird. Christ himself was most fruitful, peaceful, and sociable when he was on this earth and conversing with humans.[74]

At one point in the *Institutes* (III.20.36), Calvin himself brings together Matthew 7:11 and Isaiah 49:15 but does not mention Christ's invocation of the hen in Matthew 23:37. His context is a discussion of prayer, specifically, the opening words of the Lord's Prayer, "Our Father." Here there is no trace, let alone any explicit mention, of the Father he depicts so graphically in the crucifixion of the Son. On the contrary, Calvin insists that when we call God "our Father" we must only do so through the name of the Son of God, Christ. The images of the vengeful Father found in the previous book of the *Institutes* that I discussed earlier have now disappeared as though they had never been given such force and prominence. This seals off Calvin's conflicting versions of God into separate compartments. As such, it avoids the kind of dialectical thinking that might force a critical return to his earlier account of the Father in the crucifixion. One can perhaps understand

Calvin's motives for avoiding such dialectical exploration, but this evasion did not enrich the resources with which his followers could respond to the anti-Calvinists emerging within the Reformed tradition itself, whether Arminians like Hoard or Antinomians like Eaton.[75] Later in Book III, Calvin notes that those who oppose his version of election like to cite Christ's likening of himself to a hen in Matthew 23 (*Institutes* III.24.17). But Calvin dismisses these adversaries, telling them that Christ's analogy "gives them no support." He claims that Christ's words simply reproach the people of Israel who rebelled against God in Christ, a rebellion that was, of course, a determinate part of God's eternal plan. Apparently Calvin thinks this retort proves that his opponents' reading of Jesus's image of the hen and her chicks is merely "frivolous." He simply refuses to engage substantively with the figuration and its traditional exegesis, if he was even aware of it.

Of course, most Calvinists did not think that Arminians posed serious and troubling challenges to their version of God and Christian doctrine. On the contrary, those classified as Arminians were seen as undermining the foundations of the Reformation's recovery of true religion, orthodox Christianity. William Twisse's attack on Hoard is a good example of Calvinist responses to Arminian criticism. Its vehement defense of double predestination is nicely signposted in its title: *The Riches of God's Love unto the Vessells of Mercy, Consistent with His Absolute Hatred or Reprobation of the Vessells of Wrath* (1653). Twisse's editor prints a preface by John Owen attacking Hoard and the "applause" his work received and praising Twisse, who (Owen argues) has been raised up by God "to stop the mouthes of . . . enemies of Gods Sovereignty and Grace."[76] The work, according to Twisse, was written in 1632 and displays the central convictions of supralapsarian Calvinism (258). It carefully rehearses the symmetry between "absolute" predestination to glory and "absolute" reprobation to everlasting hell: "God from everlasting did will to damne many thousands" (112). Not surprisingly, he deals with Paul's statement that God "will have all men to be saved" (1 Tim. 2·4). He does so in the familiar Augustinian mode that was explicitly criticized by Hoard (111–13). Here and elsewhere Twisse's arguments adhere to the orthodoxies of what Anthony Milton calls "high" Calvinism, "hyper-Calvinism," or "extreme" Calvinism.[77]

I will first look at Twisse's response to Hoard's celebration of God's mercy (128–45). In this response Twisse takes up Hoard's discussion of Christ likening himself to a hen. Twisse agrees that God is merciful; God's mercy, however, is *only* extended to the elect (130–31). These, Twisse is confident, are very few: "most of men" are reprobates (140). He reiterates this news on numerous occasions: "God saves but a very few" (269). True enough, as Hoard claims, God wills all to hear the gospel, repent, and believe; but God does *not* actually give to all who hear the gospel the grace to hear it to their benefit (271). Of course not, Twisse observes, for they do not belong to the "few" elect but rather to the reprobates who constitute "most" of us. This is the paradigm within which Twisse discusses the language concerning God's love and mercy that is so central to Hoard's work and to Christian tradition. And it is within this paradigm that he responds to Hoard's discussion of Christ's choice of the hen to represent his own manifestation of divine love for humanity.

Twisse is as unimpressed with Hoard as the puritan Malvolio was with Sir Toby Belch, Maria, and Feste in *Twelfth Night*. He sneers at the way we find in Hoard's book "much matter made of the Hen" (134). Oddly enough, Twisse's contempt for his Arminian adversary at first occludes the fact that it was Jesus Christ, not Hoard, who made "much matter" of the hen (Matt. 23:37). Twisse would rather ascribe this "matter" to the "loose dissolute discourse" of anti-Calvinism, the moral dissoluteness of those who reject Calvinist versions of God. Still, Hoard is in good company under such a charge: "The Son of man came eating and drinking, and they say, Behold a man gluttonous, and a winebidder, a friend of publicans and sinners" (Matt. 11:19). Be that as it may, Twisse seeks to debunk the image of the hen we find in Hoard and in the traditional exegesis of Christ's simile discussed above. Twisse gives us a Calvinist hen: a violent creature quite lacking in care for her offspring. Twisse asserts that hens are certainly not as selfless as the stork he has read about, who "when her nest was on fire . . . hath not forsaken her young ones till shee was burnt her selfe." In contrast, he declares, "we have seen also how a Hen hath sometimes peckt her young ones, and driven them from her, when they would have roosted under her" (134). So why did Jesus liken himself to such a violent, unloving creature?

Before we try to answer this question let us again recall the evangelical text: "O Jerusalem, Jerusalem, thou that killest the prophets, and stonest them which are sent unto thee, how often would I have gathered thy children together, even as a hen gathereth her chickens under her wings, and ye would not!" (Matt. 23:37). This offers an unequivocal contradiction to Twisse's account of the image. But Protestant advocacy of the authority of scripture alone, with its contempt of medieval scriptural hermeneutics, did not mean that scripture should ever be allowed to undermine the exegete's version of Protestant dogmatics. So Twisse simply asserts that Christ "doth not represent his tender affection to the Jews, by the general affection of an Hen to hers, but to that particular carriage of hers in desiring to gather her chickens under her wings." Once more he *denies* that Christ's own simile of the hen could represent "his singularity of affection toward them [the Jewish people he is literally addressing]" (134). Twisse can think of no reason God should be merciful to any humans other than "the good pleasure of his will." He can think of no reason God should not "restraine his saving mercy to some few." And he is sure that it is the pleasure of God's will not to offer mercy to those he has eternally chosen to be "vessels of wrath," the reprobate (135; recalling the work's title). Not surprisingly, Twisse invokes God's alleged eternal reprobation and hatred of the unborn Esau and his love of the unborn Jacob, a Pauline text encountered often in medieval and Reformation discussions of election and reprobation (135). Does God's eternal hatred of Esau, Twisse asks, "in any way hinder his love of *Jacob*?"

Twisse is outraged by Hoard's charge that Calvinists make God a "father of cruelty," a veritable devil. He apparently has no sense that his substitution of a hen who attacks and rejects her offspring for Jesus's own version of God as a hen who would have gathered them under his wing might vindicate Hoard's account of Calvinist ideology. For the substitution suggests that Twisse may find it easier to imagine the Son of God as a being who attacks and rejects his creatures than as the one Jesus himself represents in the passage. This seems to me at least part of Twisse's answer to the question of why Jesus likened himself to a hen. The suggestion is supported by the way Twisse rejects the charge that Calvinists make God "the father of cruelty." He asks, "If many thousands, even all the Infants of the Turkes and Sarazens dying in originall sinne, are tormented by him in Hell fire, is he to be accounted the father of cruelties for this?" (135). No wonder, then, that Twisse dislikes Hoard's invocation of the image chosen by the Son of God to illustrate divine love. Conventionally enough in Calvinist discourse, Twisse does not think that the everlasting torment of those eternally decreed to be reprobates poses any ethical problems. Being the decree of God, it simply cannot be described as cruelty. He is content to acknowledge that the everlasting torture of those who die as infants looks cruel and unjust to some, but he thinks the real problem is in Hoard's "petty dogge-tricke" of implying that God wills mercy to *all*. We are back in the field of 1 Timothy 2:4 and its claim that God does indeed will *all* humans to be saved. Twisse reiterates that God's love and mercy is willed only to the few elect, but he denies that there is any trace of cruelty in the God Calvinists worship (135–36). In fact, Twisse continually exalts in God's restriction of mercy to the predestined few. Such is the confidence of the kind of Calvinist assurance that Mr. Peacock had, lost, and found.

I suspect that there is another aspect of Christ-as-hen that troubles Twisse. What the image of the hen does (in Jesus's version rather than Twisse's) is hint at an implication that is anathema to Calvinists— namely, that divine love and grace is *not irresistible*. How often, says the Son of God, I would have gathered you together and you refused. But Calvinists were convinced that the idea that grace could be refused was an Arminian heresy. Certainly, Arminius himself had opposed Calvinist teaching on the irresistibility of grace, arguing that "God truly wills the salvation of all men, on the condition that they believe."[78] As with the late medieval account of general election, in Arminian thought grace is offered to all, but humans are free to resist and reject the offer. Similarly, preaching in the 1630s, John Gore maintained that God in Christ offered grace to everyone but refused to coerce anyone, leaving them free to resist grace and "goe to Hell without it."[79] For Calvinists, this model of the relations between divine and human agency was an offense against divine sovereignty and omnipotence, mere Pelagianism. It was no coincidence that the medieval theologian Thomas Bradwardine's anti-Pelagian *De Causa Dei* was printed in 1618 as a Calvinist preparation for the forthcoming Synod of Dort. As Nicholas Tyacke notes, published "by order of Archbishop Abbot, and dedicated to King James, the book was clearly intended as English Calvinist propaganda—Bradwardine's cause being that of the irresistible grace of God. From an Arminian point of view, however, Bradwardine was an 'enemy of God,' as Matthew Wren called him."[80] Both Bradwardine in the fourteenth century and Calvinists in the seventeenth century saw themselves in a holy war against contemporary Pelagians.[81] The centrality of issues of grace and human freedom to these ongoing disputes persuades me that Twisse, who was to be a leading divine in the Westminster Assembly, would have reason to be anxious at the way Christ's invocation of his chicks' refusal to be gathered under his wing seems to know nothing of the irresistibility of divine grace, and nothing of double predestination.

As for Hoard's invocation of God as mother (Isa. 49:15) alongside Christ as hen, Twisse continues to be scathing. Whatever Isaiah or Jesus says in the texts quoted by Hoard, Twisse knows that his God is the God content to kill infants in the Flood and in the destruction of Sodom (136). God is nothing like a loving mother or father to reprobates. After all, he muses:

> What Father or Mother would be content to execute a Child of theirs upon the Gallowes, when by some capitall crime he hath deserved it? How much lesse hold them upon the rack of continuall tortures; what then? Must God not be allowed to inflict eternall death upon his creatures? (137)

As I have noted, Twisse, like other Calvinists, is confident that this is how God treats most humans. God reserves love and mercy for the elect few: "Doth man or any creature shew more love to their Children, than God doth towards his Elect?" (138–39). Christ himself only came for the elect, and he only offers the benefits of his death to these few (139). Twisse finds it preposterous that Hoard accuses Calvinists of making God "unmercifull to all men": "this doctrine of ours," Twisse insists, simply describes the reality of God (139–40). We Calvinists, he goes on, know that "the number of Reprobates is farre greater then the number of the Elect," and we likewise know that God "foresaw what the condition of most men would be, if they were brought forth into the World." So, Twisse expostulates, "where was his mercy in this?" (140). He continues, "By being borne, was it not infallible that their condition would be a thousand times worse than the conditions of beasts?" (140). Not surprisingly, he can make no sense of Isaiah's language (God as mother) or Jesus's language (the Son of God as hen whose agency is resisted).

Twisse emphasizes that the Creator knew that most humans would not repent and believe. God certainly has the means to give *effectual* faith to all humans "were he pleased to use them." But he is not pleased to use them. He prefers to play tricks on his creatures, as we saw in Calvin's account of the grace and faith God gives to reprobates: *ineffectual* gifts but nonetheless gifts from God. Twisse follows Calvin: only the elect receive effectual grace, while the reprobates receive temporary faith. This is, Twisse argues, congruent with "God's absolute decree . . . to make them [most humans] vessells of wrath," subjects of divinely inspired delusions (141). Twisse is convinced that the eternal punishments of those eternally reprobate displays God's "vindicative justice" (141). He is also convinced, like other Calvinists, that the elect should seek "evidence" of their election (293).

As for God's reprobates, they will "curse the day of their birth, and wish they had been made Toads or Snakes" (141). However, they should meditate on Paul's famous image of God as the potter, humans as the clay (Rom. 9:20–23). After all, the potter makes some vessels to be "a close-stoole or chamberpot." Twisse also imagines Nebuchadnezzar's bones being the pitch for "some common jakes" (141). Perhaps Twisse is conflating Paul's image of the potter and his various products with Shakespeare's Hamlet ruminating on the fate of the body after death as he considers the skull of Yorick dug up from the earth where Ophelia is about to be buried (*Hamlet* V.75–216). Twisse comments that no complaints by Nebuchadnezzar for being born to such an ending can derogate from divine power (141). After all, God did not just *permit* and *foresee* Judas's betrayal of Christ; Judas in fact acted subject to "the absolute decree of God for his damnation" (141). As for the death of non-Christian infants, they are simply "borne children of wrath"— just like Esau (142; see also 268).

Does the Calvinist paradigm lead to despair, as Hoard claims?[82] According to Twisse, certainly not (255–95). Indeed, he sets out to prove that the devil has an easier task persuading an Arminian that he is a reprobate than persuading a Calvinist (258–59). For Calvinists know that God keeps secret who is a reprobate, and they know that sins do not make one a castaway (267). Twisse asserts that Arminians offer consolation only to those who do good works, whereas the Calvinist minister will candidly acknowledge that God simply has not ordained *all* to salvation (268). The minister will recall that God loved Jacob but hated Esau, before they were born. Here Twisse approvingly cites Aquinas's treatment of predestination in the *Summa Theologiae* because Aquinas acknowledges that God did not will good to all, taking good as eternal life (*ST* I.23.3, ad 1). This passage comes from Aquinas's article on reprobation (considered in ch. 2) in which he quotes the mantra, "Jacob dilexi, Esau autem odio habui" (I have loved Jacob, but I have hated Esau) (*ST* I.23.3, sed contra). Surely, Twisse says, no Arminian will deny that "God saves but a very few" (269). God, after all, "gives faith and repentance to a very few, which no Arminian denyes" (274). But Calvinist ministers reassure their flocks by reminding them that nobody who has not sinned against the Holy Spirit should despair that he is a reprobate. Of course, "we doe not say there is no cause of feare. In as much as he hath no evidence of his election, there is just cause to feare," but there is also cause for hope in knowing that he concomitantly cannot have "evidence" that he is a reprobate—unless, of course, he sins against the Holy Spirit. Twisse acknowledges that his pastoral strategies for consoling troubled souls are different from Hoard's: "I would think it fit to use all meanes and motives to make them feare," for such fear is "good comfort" and the prelude to discerning the spirit of adoption (293–94; Rom. 8:15). True enough, the elect may continue to have "feares and terrours" after their calling. Indeed, they may well think they are reprobates—given the tricks we have seen Calvin's God playing on his creatures, this is not surprising—but the elect are again reassured that nobody (not even a reprobate) can have evidence of reprobation unless they commit the sin against the Holy Spirit (295). Twisse claims that it is only Calvinists who can give and receive comfort, whereas Arminians lack the "grounds of comfort" because they have no resources for reading the signs of election and reprobation (295). All Arminians can do is talk about the love of God and mistakenly claim that Christ died for all.

Twisse thinks Arminians dissolve the decisive differences between Christians, Turks, Saracens, and reprobates in their false "universalities" (295). No Arminian minister can give "comfortable assurance that I am no reprobate" unless there is "no reprobate at all in the world" (295). Not Calvinists but Arminians lack the "balme of Gilead to administer to a sick soule" (296). Once again Twisse attacks Hoard for teaching that Christ died for all: such a false doctrine cannot give consolation or assurance (296). He continues to insist that outside the Calvinist paradigm of election and reprobation the Arminian minister "can give no assurance of election, no not to a believer no certainty of salvation; and yet he pretends to be a comforter, when he leaves him in doubt whether he shall be saved or damned; yet upon this pillow Arminians sleepe sweetly, and presume that others may sleepe sweetly also, that they are not absolute reprobates" (297). There is something puzzling in this charge since Twisse has written that converted, called Calvinists may continue to suffer the terrors of reprobation and to doubt their election. But the key for Twisse, despite this, remains the Calvinist doctrine of assurance. Yet once more he charges that "their [Arminians'] doctrine can administer no assurance either of election or salvation." Whereas "our doctrine gives assurance of perseverance in the state of grace, to them that are once in the state of grace; the Arminian doth not" (297).

Earlier in this chapter I discussed the peculiar and innovative account of hypocrisy developed by Calvinists. Twisse thinks that although Calvinists can discern wolves in sheep's clothing, "we may be deceived; but most commonly it comes to passe that hypocrites are the greatest deceivers and coseners of themselves" (297). As in Calvin, the hypocrite may be a convinced Christian who is not seeking to dissemble and exploit others. Such a person is self-deceived. We saw the suffering this doctrine could catalyze in Bolton's account of Mr. Peacock's "last conflicts and death." Nevertheless, Twisse, like those gathered around Mr. Peacock as he confessed his alleged hypocrisy, can discern the "sparkles of grace" and divine forgiveness in the hypocrite's confession (297). This, he says, is consolation. And this is the cure against despair that Calvinists, unlike Arminians like Hoard, can offer.

❊ ❊ ❊

The paradigm within which Twisse teaches had been cultivated for well over fifty years in the Church of England. It had already received a powerful and popular articulation in William Perkins's *A Golden Chaine: Or,*

The description of theologie: containing the order of the causes of salvation and damnation.[83] Here the discussion of the decree of reprobation (chs. 52–54) offers a classic treatment of the calling and grace received by reprobates (esp. ch. 53). Throughout his prolific career, Perkins returns time and again to the issues of assurance in works that foreground the question, "how a man may know whether he be the childe of God or no."[84] The work to which the next chapter is devoted, published in 1601, includes in its title the promise that it discloses how "every man may clearly see whether he shall be saved or damned."[85] In doing so, it relies on the distinctive processes of conversion and assurance at the heart of Calvinist Christianity, together with Calvinism's particular version of God. Twisse, Perkins, and Dent represent what Ryrie describes as "the Calvinist doctrine of predestination which had become the orthodox consensus [in the Church of England] by the later sixteenth century."[86] This "orthodox consensus" has been richly documented and debated over the past four decades. As Tyacke writes in his *Anti-Calvinists*, "The characteristic theology of English Protestant sainthood was Calvinism, centering on a belief in divine predestination, both double and absolute." Writing in 1987, he comments, "That Calvinism was the *de facto* religion of the Church of England under Queen Elizabeth and King James may surprise those brought up to regard Calvinists and Puritans as one and the same."[87] None of the statements by Tyacke or Ryrie make claims that the "consensus" was one in which there was no opposition to the dominant ideology and ecclesiology. In *Anti-Calvinists*, Tyacke himself takes note of Samuel Harsnett's "complete rebuttal of Calvinist teaching" in a sermon preached at Paul's Cross on 27 October 1584.[88] Because Harsnett anticipates and addresses many issues considered in this chapter I will conclude with a consideration of this lucid and eloquent sermon.[89]

Harsnett preaches on Ezekiel 33:11: "As I live (saith the Lord) I delight not in the death of the wicked." He reads the text as "a solemn *Protestation* made by Almighty God in his own cause to clear himself of *Infidelitie* and *Injustice*" (122). The passage serves as a gateway to a sustained critique of central strands in Calvinist teaching about God, election, and reprobation. The version of God Harsnett presents is a God who loves his human creatures and is committed to their flourishing, a flourishing that involves their freedom to cooperate with God's grace or to resist this grace together with its conditions. His sermon is replete with sources in scripture that seem to demand such a view, but he acknowledges that in this he goes against the grain of the teaching currently dominant in the English church, teaching shaped by what he calls "the Genevian conceit." This conceit, he says, subverts the "gracious bounty of God" and his will that all humans be saved (153; 133–34).

Against the Calvinist doctrine of double predestination, with its view that God designed most of us for Hell before we existed, Harsnett takes up one of the texts that has been particularly prominent in the debates followed in the present book: 1 Timothy 2:4. Harsnett quotes the statement that "the Holy *Ghost* hath taught us by the mouth of holy *Paul . . . Deus vult omnes salvos esse*, God would have every man living saved, and none to die *eternall* Death" (153). Harsnett would have known that the Calvinist exegesis of this text ("the Genevian conceit") was as Augustinian and Thomist as it was Calvinist, but he chooses to focus his critique on the baleful tradition's most recent inflection. He describes Calvinist readings as curtailing the grace of God to fit an alien ideology when they say of 1 Timothy 2:4:

> It must not bee meant, that God would have every living soule to come to *Heaven*; but one or two out of every *Order* and *Occupation* to come unto *heaven*. As if our gracious God were fallen out of liking with *Christian souls*, and suddenly fallen in love with *Orders* and *Occupations*. And yet I feare me, beloved, it were as easie to bring up all *Christian souls* unto heaven, as it is to bring all *Orders* and *Occupations* thither. But the spirit of *Peter* (a great deale wiser than that of *Geneva*) saith plainely, *2 Ep. 3.9* [2 Pet. 3:9]. . . . God would not have any one to perish. (153)

Harsnett hopes that we have the grace to believe God as he reveals his will and love in scriptural texts like Ezekiel 33:11, 1 Timothy 2:4, and 2 Peter 3:9. For God "himselfe can better tell what himselfe would have, then the men of Geneva can" (154). As for the old question that asks why people are damned if God wills their felicity, Harsnett says the answer is "easily" given. It is the answer we find among fourteenth-century theologians who advocate some form of general election and covenant theology: God's will and his grace to all is conditional, covenantal. Furthermore, it has been manifested in Christ's life and death.[90] Here, too, Harsnett attacks the Calvinist teaching that Christ did *not* die for all but for "a few of the Elect only." He finds such teaching goes against explicit accounts in scripture that emphasize that the Son of God came to save the lost, the sinners, and the world from the consequences of human sin (155–57). Returning to Calvinist exegesis of the "all" in 1 Timothy 2:4 and other texts of the New Testament, Harsnett derisively mimics the "Genevian" mode of exegesis and its outcome: "God would have all to be *saved*, that is, God would have a few to be *saved*; God would not have any to *perish*, that is, God would that almost *all* should perish" (156).

Harsnett rejects any interpretation that makes God invite all to salvation but eternally intend it for only a few: "Is God as a man, that he should dissemble?" (158). As we have seen, the tradition Harsnett opposes did indeed think God dissembled in his bestowal of faith and spiritual joy among the reprobate. These reflections lead Harsnett to consider one of the sayings of Jesus discussed by both Hoard and Twisse many years later. Harsnett argues (again against "the *Genevian* supposition") that God in Christ "quits himselfe of our destruction." He quotes Matthew 23:37, in which Jesus likens himself to a hen that "doth gather her chickens under her wings," but those Christ would gather together resist and reject his will: "ye would not." Harsnett focuses on the grammar of this passage, contrasting *"Ego volui*, I would, *salus ex me*, thy salvation is wrought by me," with *"tu noluisti*, thou wouldest not; *perditio ex te*, destruction is willed by thy selfe" (163). The passage in Matthew's gospel opens with Jesus weeping over Jerusalem and its rejection of divine love, but Harsnett argues that Calvinists dislike the plain meaning of this text because it is incompatible with their models of divine and human agency, of election and reprobation. Calvinists have to assume that God in Christ has eternally decreed the destruction of those Jesus addresses (163–64). Harsnett objects that "this is a very bad and profane device." Why? Because, Harsnett asserts, "it would make our *Saviour Christ* to shed Crocodiles teares, to laugh and lament both at once" (164). Shedding further light on this text's place of prominence in the works of Hoard and Twisse nearly fifty years later, Hars nett's remarkably sharp commentary makes clear the hermeneutical and theological problems the image of Christ as loving mother hen posed for Calvinists.

In 1624, while Harsnett was bishop of Norwich, the House of Commons complained to the Lords about his theology. Harsnett replied that he could not see why he should be thought "a Papist" but wondered if it was because of the sermon preached forty years before but not yet published. He recalled that in it he had discussed reprobation and had been "checked by the Lord Archbishop Whitguifte and commanded to preach no more of it," a command he claims to have obeyed.[91] Such was the form of Calvinist domination in the Church of England.

As I observed earlier in this section of the chapter, however, Tyacke and many other historians have now shown that from the early 1620s there emerged an increasingly public and confident opposition to Calvinist paradigms of theology and ecclesiology. By the time of the debate around Samuel Hoard's *Gods Love to Mankind* (1633), it is clear that Calvinism within the Church of England had generated divisions, doctrinal shifts, and pluralism surrounding a wide range of topics, including election and reprobation. This was the very last outcome desired by Calvinists. Indeed, so pronounced was the fragmentation in the pre–civil war Church of England that there began to develop a profound challenge to historiography of the "true church" as elaborated by John Foxe, a genealogy that had by the late sixteenth century achieved the status of orthodoxy in the Church of England. In this ideology, the medieval church was understood as "the false church of Antichrist." The "true" church, in contrast, was the one sustained and nurtured among those groups judged heretical in the Middle Ages (such as Waldensians and Lollards), as well as by some of the elect hidden in the folds of Antichrist's church but not perceiving the mystery of iniquity in which they dwelled. As Anthony Milton has shown in fascinating detail, in the early seventeenth-century Church of England a new version of the historiography of Protestant succession and the medieval church was on offer. This elucidation was worked out by Richard Field and "rapidly gained acceptance in the Jacobean Church." In it, the medieval church was rehabilitated: despite the tyranny of Rome, it was "the true Church of God." This proposition necessarily entailed a defense of the Mass, which Field provided. Indeed, Milton discusses how "even the medieval Schoolmen could be shown to have preserved the elements of right doctrine." He shows that the scholastics also gained "a certain theological respectability" in the English universities, a development explicitly deplored by Calvinist divines such as John Prideaux (professor of divinity at Oxford and vice-chancellor on numerous occasions). Milton describes how under Laud's leadership the rehabilitation of the medieval church moved "towards a celebration of the high standards of piety and the elaborate patterns of worship it had sustained." Indeed, in Laudian times, "forms of medieval piety were more likely to be held up for unqualified emulation." This story has been brilliantly elaborated and particularized since Milton's work by Kenneth Fincham and Nicholas Tyacke in *Altars Restored.*[92] The Calvinist revolution had become internally fragmented and had generated a range of adversaries *within* the Reformed Church of England, some of whom were looking at medieval theology, sacramentality, and ecclesiology with considerable sympathy.

There may be some instructive ironies in this history. Christian tradition, whether medieval or Reformation, is many-stranded, replete with contradictions and as unstable as it is dynamic. Just as the late medieval church generated a number of paradigms for understanding election and reprobation, so had the Reformed Church of England by the time of the civil war. The same could be said of the plurality of models addressing ecclesiology in the later Middle Ages and in the English Reformation from 1558 to 1660. It also seems clear from the complex trajectory I have been examining that ideas once rejected and apparently forgotten often survive and return with new inflections as the tradition encounters different contexts. We glimpse something like this in the return of late medieval ideas of general election in Samuel Harsnett and Samuel Hoard. We also see this in John Milton, as I will discuss in chapter 5. Perhaps it is only by centralization and violence that Christian tradition and its churches can be held in a unity of doctrine and practice, and then only for a very brief time. The view I suggest here may have some continuities with aspects of John Henry Newman's famous account of Christian tradition, but the materials I have been discussing also demand some sharp differences.[93]

CHAPTER FOUR

_____

Conversion in Arthur Dent's
The Plaine Man's Path-way to Heaven

Christ by the Preaching of his word, doth dissever his elect and reprobate.
—Robert Cawdrey, *A Treasurie or Store-House of Similes*

In 1601, the Essex minister Arthur Dent published *The Plaine Man's Path-way to Heaven. Wherein every man may clearly see, whether he shall be saved or damned. Set forth Dialogue wise, for the better understanding of the simple.*[1] This was an immensely popular text, "one of the best sellers of the early seventeenth century."[2] Christopher Haigh describes Dent's dialogue as "a real, often acrimonious debate," one in which "the things Dent's characters say were said by real people in a real England." This, he continues, "makes Dent's text useful to a historian."[3] Certainly many historians have shared Haigh's opinion and, despite the rather obvious hermeneutical problems embedded in their assumptions, have employed Dent's work as a window onto early modern popular culture and its resistances to Calvinist ministers in the Church of England. My own interest in this work, however, centers on the particular model of Calvinist conversion that Dent develops through his text. Dent names himself on the title page as "Preacher of the word of God

163

at South-Shoobery in Essex" and characterizes his work as a dialogue "for the better understanding of the simple." His Calvinist representative in the text is "a Divine" named Theologus. This divine is accompanied and supported by his lay admirer, the "honest man" Philagathus. Those who oppose the minister are two countrymen who have come from a neighboring parish to buy a cow: one is "an ignorant man" (Asunetus), the other "a caviller" who denies the minister's teaching (Antilegon). Although the latter offers distinctly Christian opposition to the minister's position and is a fellow member of the Church of England, he is nontheless called "a notable Atheist, a caviller against all goodnesse" (2). Such language was commonplace in Calvinist proclamation.

In this chapter I will concentrate on some of Dent's most prominent theological commitments as he seeks to show how "a true conversion unto God" may be initiated within a Calvinist paradigm and to articulate the forms of pastoral care that might sponsor such a conversion (429). As I do so, it will become obvious why, as Haigh observed, the work has enthralled cultural historians. For Dent situates the minister's doctrine and ethics as pervasively hostile to what he represents as the traditional rural Christianity popular among agriculturalists—among, that is, those who might be going to buy a cow at a time of year when "we shall find dear ware of her" (May; 2–4). Dent's work is thus a salutary reminder of the ways in which theological discourses, including accounts of election and conversion, may be bound up with determinate political cultures and their conflicts.[4] As the learned minister Theologus condescendingly engages with his rural neighbors, we may also discern in Dent's dialogue one of the consequences of the English Reformation observed by Keith Wrightson—namely, the emergence in rural England of resident clergy educated at Oxford and Cambridge, "drawn from the upper and middling ranks of society" and hence "distanced from their charges in an altogether novel way."[5] These "new clergy" were "less attuned to local customary standards of devotion and behaviour which they were charged with transforming."[6] In such a context, the conversion of Christians within the reformed Church of England would inevitably include both personal and collective dimensions, inextricably bound together. It could not help but be politically charged.

And yet Dent is a minister of the national Protestant church addressing his fellow members grafted into the body of Christ's church, all of whom are partakers in the death and resurrection of Christ according to the "Public Baptism of Infants" in the Church of England's *Book of Common Prayer*. As such, Dent's readers will have received Christian instruction from a range of lay and clerical sources, formal and informal. They might therefore assume that they have already been placed on the "path-way to Heaven" founded by the one who declared that he had "not come to call the righteous but sinners to repentance" (Luke 5:30–32), one who "came into the world to save sinners" (1 Tim. 1:15). The latter saying was rehearsed in the communion service of their parish church among the "comfortable words our Saviour Christ saith" after the minister pronounced "absolution" in response to the people's confession. These early readers of Dent might well find their own thinking reflected on the page when one of the speakers in Dent's dialogue maintains:

> If a man say his Lords prayer, his tenne Commaundements, and his beleefe, and keepe them, and say no bodie no harme, and doo as hee would bee done too, have a good faith to Godward, and be a man of Gods beliefe, no doubt he shall be saved, without all this running to Sermons and prattling of the scriptures. . . . As long as I serve God, and say my prayers duly, and truly, morning and evening, and have a good faith in God, and put my whole trust in him, and do my true intent, and have a good mind to Godward, and a good meaning: although I am not learned, yet I hope it will serve the turn for my soules health: for that God which made me, must save me. (27–28)

The speaker here is Asunetus (the "ignorant" person, the witless one). He acknowledges that he is "not learned"—not, like Theologus, a person educated at university—but a "simple" agrarian laborer. Nevertheless, he displays Christian insights and convictions far more developed than those William Langland represents as belonging to the penitent, confessed, and absolved Christians in *Piers Plowman*, a poem embraced by Protestants from Robert Crowley's printing in 1550.[7]

Arthur Dent, however, does not accept that Asunetus is a fellow traveler on the Christian way. Dent's persona in the text, Theologus, judges Asunetus to be "a very ignorant man in Gods matters," one whose statements about Christian practice actually "despise Gods word" and represent no more than a "fantasticall serving [of] God" (2, 28). A clear mark of Asunetus's ignorance and contempt for God's word, in the minister's judgment, is his dismissive reference to "all this running to Sermons." Asunetus considers a commitment to hearing many sermons something frivolous and extrinsic to the love of God and neighbor that forms the core of his theology. For Dent/Theologus, on the other hand, obedient service to God demands frequent attendance at the sermons of (Calvinist) ministers in the church. Refusal to attend sermons frequently is to "stop your eares against God" (33).[8] After all, ministers in Dent's Calvinist tradition were certain that God's favored way of saving his people was through the sermons of Calvinist ministers. Asunetus is not at all persuaded by such a view of divine means and priorities: "but this I am sure of, that God is a good man, he is merciful, and that we must be saved by our good prayers, and good serving of God" (30). To Theologus, this is simply more folly and ignorance. His task, then, is to *convert* the ignorant, foolish Asunetus to the correct (Calvinist) form of Christianity.

In the course of his attempt to do so, he tellingly declares that true regeneration is so inward, so "secret, and altogether hid from the world," that "no man" knows if it is real but only God (27; see also 32). This profoundly un-Langlandian move might have made even George Gifford, whose *The Country Divinity* was a model for Dent's dialogue, uneasy.[9] But its role in Dent's order of conversion is clear: the hiddenness of true regeneration undermines the assurance of "plaine" and "simple" people, traditional agrarian Christians, that God's final judgments will be inseparable from their daily practices and benevolent intentions. Of course, what Theologus calls "ignorant" and "fantastical" Christianity actually seems to reflect the form of Christianity encouraged by Jesus's teaching in Matthew 25:31–46, teaching grippingly affirmed in the representation of the Last Judgment in the York Corpus Christi play. In this evangelical teaching, the saved are those who feed the hungry, welcome the stranger, clothe the naked, visit the sick, visit prisoners, give drink to the thirsty: "inasmuch as ye have done it unto one of the least of these my brethren, ye have done it unto me" (Matt. 25:40; cf. 25:46). This merciful work is not a component of Dent's vision of the "path-way to Heaven," so his model of conversion will not focus on such doctrine and practice. Though Dent would not deny that such good works would be the fruit of conversion, the fruit of divine justification for the elect, these are not the stones with which his pathway is built.

Dent's own model of conversion foregrounds the doctrine of election and reprobation by which God eternally predestines some to salvation and others (most people, it will emerge) to reprobation. It thus belongs to the Calvinist paradigm of Christianity dominant in the early seventeenth-century Church of England and discussed at length in chapter 3. The title of Dent's work makes clear that it aims to offer a guide whereby one "may clearly see, whether he shall be saved or damned." In this process of discernment, this attempt to "clearly see" one's eternal fate, conversion turns out to be the decisive factor. But how can one's status be discerned if, as Dent asserts, regeneration is hidden from all but God? How can Dent possibly make good on the promise of his title? After all, as we saw in the discussion of William Twisse in chapter 3, Calvinist orthodoxy insisted that while the saved can be assured of their election, the damned can never know for sure that they are reprobates—nor, for that matter, can anybody else.

Dent's answer to this conundrum is that conversion itself bestows upon the elect hermeneutic powers and methods of discernment that the unconverted resist and, by this very resistance, display their unregenerate state to the converted. It is thus only the elect who will be able to read actions and who will do so legitimately. For example, Theologus offers "whoredom" as a sign of damnation. His incorrigible opponent Antilegon thinks this very silly: "Tush whoredom is but a trick of youth, and we see all men have their imperfections." The minister is outraged, declaring, "You speak prophanely and wickedly." He informs his interlocutor that for this trick of youth God himself "smote three and twentie thousand of his own people in one day" (63; Num. 25:1–2, 7–9; 1 Cor. 10:8). The assumption behind Theologus's outburst is that such smiting was a sign of God enacting the eternal decree of reprobation, a sign illegible to the unconverted Antilegon but transparent to the elect Theologus. Later, Theologus offers swearing as another sign of reprobation (154–81). Indeed, this is apparently "more than a signe. It is indeed an evident demonstration of a reprobate" (154). Yet

another sign of reprobation perfectly legible to the preacher is drunkenness (181–89). His adversary objects to this interpretation, invoking
the role of drink and the alehouse in traditional forms of neighborliness
and community: "If neighbours meete together now and then at the
Alehouse . . . meaning no hurt: I take it to be good fellowship, and a
good meanes to increase love amongst neighbours, and not so hainous
as you make it" (186).[10] Shakespeare, too, takes up this arena of cultural
conflict when in *Twelfth Night* he dramatizes the antagonisms between
the puritan Malvolio and the revelers in Sir Toby Belch's circle (Fabian,
Feste, Sir Andrew Auguecheek, and Maria).[11] Likewise, William Blake's
"Little Vagabond" might find a kindred spirit in Antilegon as he tells
his mother that in contrast to the church, "the Ale-house is healthy and
pleasant & warm."[12]

Of course, the competition between church and alehouse, minister
and publican preceded the Reformation. In *Piers Plowman*, Langland
represents the alehouse as an impediment to Glutton's conversion. On
his way to hear mass, confess, see Christ in the eucharist, and sin no
more, Glutton goes by the house of Betene "the brewstere [brewer-
ess]." He declares his intention ("To go to holy churche"), but she asks
him if he would taste the "good ale" she has, together with an array of
spices. He goes into the alehouse and meets a host of neighbors.[13] But
while Langland's long passage on Glutton graphically displays a col-
lapse into drunkenness and a vomiting waste of resources in which the
alehouse stands explicitly as a substitute for church and mass, the writer
does not present either the drunkard or the company in the alehouse
as souls irrevocably marked by eternal reprobation. For, although he
is still the figure of a mortal sinner ("Y, Glotoun"), at the end of the
passage Glutton repents in shame, begs for forgiveness, and promises
to amend his life.[14] Dent, by contrast, has Theologus confidently declare, against Antilegon and his account of neighborly solidarities being
sealed at the alehouse, "All drunkards are notorious reprobates and
hell-hounds, brandes of Sathan: and devoted to perpetuall destruction
and damnation" (186–87).

The aim of such doctrine is twofold: both to reform rural, plebian
culture in accord with the demands of agrarian employers and to prepare the way for the form of conversion advocated by Dent, "Preacher

of the word of God" in the Church of England. If he can persuade readers or listeners to discern the signs as *he* does and to interpret them as
he does, then he will have turned "simple" adversaries such as Asunetus and Antilegon from ordinary sinners in traditional paradigms of
Christian ethics and community formation, like Langland's, into figures belonging to distinctly Calvinist narratives. Looking at their own
moral and spiritual failings, they would no longer be able to say that
"all men have their imperfections" and that God is mercifully committed to saving all whose "intent" to God and neighbor is "good," even if
flawed and failing (63, 28). Instead, they would have to see that every
failing, however pardonable in traditional paradigms, might well be an
"infallible" sign of reprobation. Concomitantly, whatever the Calvinist
minister discerns as "good providence" should be taken as an "infallible"
sign of election (33–36).[15] If the Calvinist's approach takes effect, then a
Christian will experience increasing anxiety as they seek to decipher the
signs that identify their state as one of either eternal election or reprobation. Only by confronting this dichotomy and its anxiety could one
hope to reach assurance. Dent's approach does not contradict the pastoral resources that Calvinists developed to reassure their flock's anxieties concerning their own election. Chief among these resources was a
strategy of hollowing out the demands of assurance so that the conviction that one *lacked* assurance could be seen, as Lucy Hutchinson maintained, as itself a low degree of assurance.[16] These pastoral resources
were to be applied only to the followers of Calvinist ministers—not to
their adversaries in the Church of England, and certainly not to adherents of the Church of Rome.

   The last seventy pages of Dent's book are devoted to instructing
readers in the interpretation of those signs by which Christians can discover their eternal state and to an articulation of the final stages of resistance and, if one is elect, conversion. When Theologus offers nine
"certaine signes and tokens" by which one can distinguish the elect
from the reprobate (such as industry, chastity, and strict observation
of the Sabbath), his admirer, the "honest man" and lay Calvinist Philagathus (lover of the good), expresses a worry: could not such "good
signes" be seen in "the reprobates" as well as in the elect (258)? Such familiar ambiguity seems to undermine the kind of clarity and certainty

that Theologus has promised. So the ever resourceful teacher adds another eight signs to the previous nine in an effort to alleviate the hermeneutic and spiritual worries voiced by Philagathus. What are these putatively even *more* decisive signs? They are identified as follows: Faith; Virtue; Knowledge; Temperance; Patience; Godliness; Brotherly Kindness; Love (258). Were these to be fleshed out as fully as one finds in Langland's *Piers Plowman* or Calvin's *Institutes* (e.g., III.6–10), then perhaps Philagathus would be able to find his way out of the hermeneutic labyrinth into which he is being drawn.[17] But Theologus does not elaborate on his list, and Philagathus is left to reiterate the same anxieties, the same fears that we have already encountered concerning the possibility of assurance. We seem at this point in Dent's text in danger (with Philagathus) of sliding into a truly wretched infinite regress. With this would come an irresolvable panic as the teacher seems unable to do more than pile ambiguous sign upon ambiguous sign in a quest for certainty beyond equivocation. Here, the specter of a much-abused "Papist" failure in doctrine and pastoral care seems to be emerging. Protestants habitually attacked Papists for denying Christians the joys of assurance, of certainty about their state of election. Here is Perkins on this endlessly reiterated Calvinist complaint:

> This [Catholic] religion teacheth, that a man must doubt of his salvation as long as hee is in this life: beholde a Racke or Gibbet erected by the church of Rome, for the tormenting of tender consciences, for when a man doubteth of his salvation, he also doubteth of Gods love and mercie to him: and hee which doubteth of Gods love, cannot love God againe: for how can any man love him of whose good will he doubteth: and when a man hath not the love of God in him, hee hath no grace in him.[18]

So, Perkins urges, any Calvinist teacher must avoid "tormenting" Protestants with the "Racke or Gibbet" of uncertainty intrinsic to the traditional Augustinian teaching on the hiddenness (without special revelation) of God's final judgment of individuals. Yet Dent himself seems to be composing precisely the kind of uncertainty anathematized within Reformed dogmatics and its pastoral commitments, even as he assumes the possibility of Calvinist assurance. It is not surprising that the good disciple Philagathus begs for "infallible evidences" of election, ones that will secure the identity of the elect that "no Lawier can find fault with" (258–59). Not surprising but a remarkable break with medieval Christianity. Far from objecting to such a demand, or balking at the assimilation of theological persuasion to "infallible" proofs among lawyers, the minister welcomes it. He now offers what he claims are (apparently in contrast to his previous lists) "sound and infallible" signs by which to distinguish evidence of election and reprobation in oneself and among one's fellow Christians. Philagathus delightedly accepts this new list, agreeing with Theologus that surely none of *these* signs could be found in reprobates and so provoke hermeneutic perturbation (260).

What are these decisive signs of one's effectual calling in conversion, one's predestination to eternal life? They are as follows: (1) assured faith in God's promises; (2) sincerity of heart; (3) the spirit of adoption; (4) sound regeneration and sanctification; (5) inward penance; (6) groundedness in truth; and (7) perseverance (259). Here Theologus embraces Philagathus's remarkable analogy between divine and lawyer as he declares that these seven signs are certain evidences of election, "sound and infallible" (259). He presents himself as a lawyer examining a document establishing tenure.

> No I assure you, no more than a Lawier can finde fault with the Tenure of men[s] lands and fee simples, when as bothe Title is good and strong by the Lawe, and the evidences thereof are sealed, subscribed, delivered, conveyed, and sufficient witnesse upon the same, and all other signs and ceremonies in the delivering, and taking possession thereof according to strict Law observed. For if a man have these forenamed evidences of his salvation, sure it is, his Title and interest to Heaven, is good by the Law of Moises and the Prophets. I mean the word of God. God himself subscribed to them: Jesus Christ delivered them as his own deed: the holy Ghost sealeth unto them: yea the three great witnesses which beare record in the earth: that is, water, blood, and the spirit, do all witnesse the same. (260)

Such is the model of assurance and certainty that conversion to Calvinist Christianity will allegedly yield, the assurance of the most secure legal contracts in the contemporary market in land. This legalistic metaphor enables us to avoid the putative uncertainties, the "Racke or Gibbet," of Romanism.

But where exactly does one find this legal document? Dent's answer to this question has two parts. First, one finds it in Scripture, the word of God including both the law of Moses and the "deed" delivered by Christ, sealed by the Holy Ghost. Dent's legalistic language is meant to assure his reader that certainty is to hand. Second, one finds the document written within one's inner life. There introspection will deliver the "evidences" that constitute the true "Title" to salvation. We are lured here by a thoroughly un-Augustinian version of the human person as transparent to the inward gaze. One strand of Protestant doctrine maintained that scripture was perspicuous and self-interpreting, although Calvinists also argued that the true meaning of scripture was revealed through the agency of the Holy Spirit. Only if the same Spirit who spoke through the prophets works in our own hearts can we grasp the authority and teaching of Scripture (Calvin, *Institutes* I.7). But if the Reformation had generated some versions of *sola scriptura* (however qualified they were in practice), it was surely a harder task to find in the murky text of an individual Christian life clear "evidences" and sure signs analogous to the unambiguous language of legal documents and land titles. Dent's *Theologus* seems, then, to be reintroducing the complex burden of interpretation from which he had promised to deliver Philagathus. Take, for example, his declaration that among the "infallible evidences" available in the Christian inner life are "assurance" in the promises of salvation found in scripture and "sincerity." It is not at all clear why the minister thinks a feeling of "assurance" is warranted and why the feeling of "sincerity" is not actually its shadow, one that so troubled Protestants in the Reformed tradition and that received attention in the previous chapter: hypocrisy. How could Theologus know if someone's "regeneration" is "sound"? Think of Mr. Peacock (see chapter 3): How is Philagathus to be confident that what he finds within is actually "perseverance" and not a temporary and fading faith? After all, as we have seen, Calvin taught that God himself often instills such counterfeit perseverance in reprobates (*Institutes* III.2.11–12 and III.24.8).[19] This was precisely Mr. Peacock's terror on his deathbed.

Dent alludes to such struggles concerning assurance by having Philagathus observe that many Protestants seem to doubt even the possibility of the kind of assurance his teacher has invoked as an "infallible evidence" of election. As for Papists, he rightly recalls, they simply "deny it" (260–61). It is significant that Dent assumes that these difficulties must be addressed in a work directed to "the simple" and set in rural England. His own ministry has shown him this. And it is interesting that John Bunyan, author of *Grace Abounding*, read Dent's *Plaine Man's Path-way* at the beginning of his long, tortured process of conversion because it was one of the two books his impoverished wife brought to their marriage.

Theologus confirms his teaching on assurance by applying to six texts from scripture his powers of "evident reason" (261–63). While this apparently helps Philagathus, it does not convince Asunetus. Dent's figure of ignorance denies that anybody "can certainly know in this worlde whether he shall be saved, or damned: but all men must hope well, and be of good beleefe" (263). As we have observed, this is traditional Catholic and Augustinian teaching, what Perkins called the papists' "Racke or Gibbet." But it was also, according to Thomas Brook's treatment of Christian assurance in *Heaven on Earth*, Arminian teaching.[20] It is not surprising that Dent should be unimpressed by theologians from traditions that oppose his own, but the direction of his objections is very striking. Theologus tells Asunetus that the latter's advocacy of "hope" is a bad mistake. How could this retort of Theologus be plausible? Did not Paul declare that "we are saved by hope: but hope that is seen is not hope" (Rom. 8:24) and that "we desire that every one of you do show the same diligence to the full assurance of hope" (Heb. 6:11)? Perhaps so, but Theologus's (and, through him, Dent's) dismissal of hope as a motivation for Christians makes no concessions to Asunetus or Paul.

> We may not venture our salvation upon uncertaine hopes, as if a man should hope it would be a faire day to morrow, but he cannot certainly tell. No, no, we must in this case being of such infinite importance as it is, growe to some certaintie, and full resolution. We see worldly men will be loath to hold their Lands and Leases uncertainely, having nothing to show for them. They will not stand to the curtesie of their Land-lords, nor rest upon their own good willes. They will not stay upon uncertaine hope. No, they are

wiser then so: for the children of this world are wiser . . . [Luke 16:8]. They will be sure to have something to shewe. They will have it under Seale. They will not stay upon the words and promises of the most honest men, and best Landlords. They cannot be quiet till they have it in white and blacke, with sound counsell upon their Title, and every way made as sure unto them, as any Law of the Land can make it. (264)[21]

This passage gives us a vivid sense of increasing anxiety and insecurity in tenure and leasehold in the transition to agrarian capitalism. What kind of landlord is the God worshipped in Dent's church? From what social formation is he projected? And what kind of "tenure" and "title" do his tenants, justified by Christ, hold?[22] It is hard to see how this gripping passage is congruent with Paul's insistence that we are saved by hope and that hope that is seen (let alone envisaged as a transparent tenurial contract) is simply *not* hope. Dent's dismissal of the hope by which Asunetus lives is an equally striking contrast to the beautiful treatment of hope in Aquinas's *Summa Theologiae*, where it is understood as one of the three theological virtues (*ST* II-II.17–22). In my view, Dent's Calvinist concepts are being shaped by the social and economic transformations I have just mentioned. Naturalizing these contingent processes, Dent is sure that hope, even in the God revealed in Christ and trusted by Asunetus, is simply an inadequate motivation for contemporary Christians (263–64). But even though he, too, lives in rural Essex, Asunetus is unpersuaded: "Yet for all that, a man cannot be certaine." Ironically, sounding more like Paul here than Theologus, Asunetus the witless is prepared to hope and trust in God's faithful benevolence (265).

Theologus, however, insists that we *can* be certain—or, at least, the *elect* can know, and know beyond hope: "he that shall be saved, knoweth he shall be saved" (265). *Knoweth.* By confessing his "hope" and being happy to trust this to God, Asunetus is giving indications that he is probably not one of the elect. Theologus again insists that the "knowledge" of election is "within us," "in himself," and "infallible" (266). If the Christian peers "within," she will *see* the work of God's grace and be "certainly resolved one way or the other" (266). True to the promise of Dent's title, Theologus here shows how "every man may clearly see, whether he shall be saved or damned." Thus will the reader be "certainly resolved *one way or the other*" (266; my emphasis). If they belong to the elect, they know certainly by the motions and stirrings of the Holy Ghost within them that they have conceived Christ, and shall undoubtedly be saved (266–67). Including himself in the elect, Theologus observes that "the ground-worke of our salvation is laid in Gods eternall election," in God's "eternall, and immutable decree" (267). The convert will be able to exult in being Jacob, not Esau (266–67; Rom. 9:13). Such is the joy of knowledge beyond hope, and such is the increasing pressure on Asunetus and Antilegon, challenged to "make a due triall" of their eternal state (265).

The rhetorical drive to the "triall" whose outcome is a certain resolution, "one way or the other," is a crucial moment in Dent's model of conversion. But Theologus now makes a new acknowledgment. It is one we followed in Calvin and his adherents in the previous chapter. The converted elect will experience "doubtings and waverings." Indeed, as Theologus pithily quips, "he that never doubted, never beleeved" (268–69). The struggle between "faith and infidelitie" continues in the converted elect, and they "may fall into fits, and pangs of despaire" (270). In combining claims of unambiguous, completely certain knowledge with a simultaneous affirmation of the continuation of doubt, infidelity, and despair, Dent's "path-way" follows in the footsteps of his leader, John Calvin.[23] So, too, of course, will William Perkins and many other future Calvinists.

Is this a slide back to the papal or Arminian (that is, traditionally Christian) denial of the possibility of unequivocal certainty affirmed by Asunetus and attacked by Theologus? Not according to the latter, or according to Calvin. Dent's minister asserts that the "doubtings and waverings" of the converted elect "no whit impeach the certaintie of their salvation." Indeed, he even asserts that the elect "easily" overcome these doubts and pangs of despair (269–70). This is a surprising claim, not least because of its pastoral implications for the individual Christian believer, implications that Bunyan explores with intensity in *Grace Abounding*. There, Bunyan confesses that he has experienced a "reprobate mind" and fallen "deeply into despair" for "some years together."[24]

His agonized pathway is conspicuously lacking in the easy supersession of despair asserted by Dent. Such a subject might indeed feel confirmed in his sense that he must have a "reprobate" identity. Here, too, we are reminded of Mr. Peacock, dying ten years after Dent published his *Path-way*.

In fact, Theologus does turn back to the issue of reprobation at just this moment. He claims that far from emerging "easily" from their doubts, waverings, and pangs of despair and into the peace of Christ, reprobates fail to find assurance or "inward peace." Their faith in the promises is not "steadfast." They lack the conviction given by the spirit of adoption to the elect (272). Yet once more Christians seem to be thrown back into the hermeneutic issues by which even Philagathus has been troubled. How are they to determine whether their "fits, and pangs of dispaire," their lack of peace, is the experience of the elect or the sign of a reprobate's temporary and fading faith, with its lack of steadfast assurance?[25] The convert seems, once again, left alone to work out whether the "infallible" evidence promised by Theologus is true evidence of election or merely the reprobate's simulacrum.

Dent finally identifies the model of reprobation in his text as Antilegon and not, as one might have assumed, the "ignorant" Asunetus. The latter, as we will see, becomes a disciple of Theologus in a tormented conversion. But Antilegon maintains positions his friend will ultimately abandon: Antilegon continues to affirm God's kindness and his own hope in this. Theologus rightly identifies this trust in God's faithful love and mercy as a rival version of assurance, an assurance outside a Calvinist paradigm and its model of conversion. He therefore insists to Antilegon that the latter's assurance lacks any "ground," that it is a mere simulacrum of assurance as understood by the minister. Likewise, Antilegon's hope in God, like his friend Asunetus's, is unfounded (273–74). In support of this charge, the preacher offers what he and his author seem to consider infallible evidence. What might this be? "There is no true feare of God in your selfe, nor in your houshold. You seldome heare the word preached. You content yourself with an ignorant Minister. You have no praiers in your family: No reading, no singing of Psalmes, no instructions, exhortations, or admonitions" (274). Here, of course, the Calvinist minster is not attempting to search the labyrinths of another's inner life, the complexity of the human will. He is instead quite sure that these mysteries are legible through ecclesial and social practices, practices that indicate the eternal identity of Antilegon. The very refusal to search out a properly Calvinist minister in place of his "ignorant" parish minister in itself displays what Theologus confidently judges to be "Atheisme" (275; a judgment already made on p. 2). Yet despite Theologus's admonitions, Antilegon is clearly neither a Pelagian nor a non-Christian, since he affirms without equivocation that "we must be saved by mercy, and not by merit," saved by Christ's mercy (276). Theologus is appalled at the unconverted Antilegon's pronouncement, as it expresses a form of Christian faith and hope with profound roots in the New Testament and in traditional Christian teaching but quite alien to Calvinist dogmatics.

The Calvinist's attack on Antilegon reiterates central strands of his attack on the hope of Asunetus but now concentrated specifically on the Christocentric dimension of Antilegon's hope. He asks Antilegon how he knows Christ died for him: "How do you knowe that Christ dyed for you particularly, and by name?" In response to this strikingly unscriptural locution, Antilegon implicitly draws on 1 Timothy 2:4 and Titus 2:11, reminding the preacher that "Christ died for all men, and therefore for me" (279). Dent is of course seeking to lure Antilegon into an area of soteriology in which doctrinal divisions were sharp. As I demonstrated in the last part of chapter 3, many Calvinists denied that Christ died for all. They insisted that in effect he only died for the elect. This position is unambiguously affirmed by Dent through Theologus. Antilegon, however, gives a shrewd response: he accuses Theologus of trying to destroy his faith and drive him away from Christ (280). And he is right. For the Calvinist strategy of conversion must necessarily destroy the form of faith Antilegon possesses. Theologus insists that Christ's mercy does not extend to all, reiterating that most of us are destined to "perish" (292).[26] As for driving his pupil away from Jesus Christ, Theologus retorts that Antilegon has never been with Christ. The minister claims he is now trying to drive him toward Christ, but it quickly emerges that he is doing this without any faith or hope in the success of Antilegon's journey.

Theologus reiterates that most people are actually reprobates from eternity and on the road to hell: "it is most certaine that fewe shall be saved" (283); "The greatest part shall perish" (292; see, too, 324–25).

In support of his confident pronoucements, he abstracts the text from scripture that so troubled Langland's Wille in *Piers Plowman* (XII.41–52: discussed in ch. 1): "many be called, but few chosen" (Matt. 20:16; see, too, Matt. 22:14). The minister is happy to dissolve the full context of the sentence and instead muses on the "fewe" who shall be chosen, expressing his own "wonder that any shall be saved" (285). After all, he proclaims, "the greatest part shall perish," "there be fewe in heaven, and many in hell" (292, 294). Dent is so emphatic about this, so repetitive, because it is utterly central to the model of conversion and salvation he assumes. He is acutely aware of traditional objections to the version of God and Christology he affirms, an awareness evident in Dent's critical placement of the articulation of these objections in the mouth of Antilegon, the figure who resists Calvinist theology and conversion, the figure of the reprobate.

It is Antilegon who, like Samuel Hoard later in the century, identifies Calvinism as a doctrine "to drive a man to dispaire" (307). A Calvinist minister could comfortably agree with this, adding that this passage through despair is only part of a process of conversion. We recall William Twisse affirming, a few years after Dent, that as a Calvinist minister seeking to lead troubled Christians to conversion, "I would think it fit to use all meanes and motives to make them feare."[27] But Antilegon is utterly disgusted by the idea that God would create us only to damn us, incredulous "that sentence of death should be passed upon men before they be borne" (307–9). Antilegon is confronting a supralapsarian Calvinist happy to acknowledge that in terms of the decree, Adam "sinned necessarily" because God decreed he "should fall of himselfe" (310–13). The more Antilegon objects to the minister's theology, the further he strays from the path to conversion and the more fully he confirms his status as a reprobate.

As such, Antilegon elicits from Theologus a sermon on eternal damnation and the sufferings of endless "torture" (402; see 386–407). This conventional preaching of hell will not convert the reprobate Antilegon, but it is the means for converting Asunetus. In his terror at the prospect of the tortures of hell, the laborer finally abandons all his objections and resistance to the theology of Theologus. He subjects himself to Dent's model of election and reprobation. He thus becomes converted. He joins the preacher's elect. We should note that this conversion is accomplished not through a dialectic woven from scripture and a will responding to God displayed in Christ. Dent shows the source of this conversion to be Asunetus's unqualified terror in response to the preacher's vivid account of hell's eternal torments (386–407).

Antilegon is appalled at this conversion. He tells Asunetus, his neighbor and friend, that he need not be terrified by the preacher, or by his model of God, salvation, and "eternal torture." Why not? Because Antilegon knows Asunetus to be "an honest man, a quiet liver, a good neighbor" (407). Fascinatingly, Antilegon sees his friend's conversion not as the manifestation of divine grace working through the minister's theology and his sermon on hell but as the product of "melancholike humour" stirred up and manipulated by the preacher (408). Far from having found the way, the truth, and the life that is the merciful Christ, Asunetus, according to his neighbor, has been made a sick man in need of *medical* remedies (408).[28] For Dent, Antilegon's concern for his friend represents not loving kindness but rather the way a reprobate mind seeks to undermine the power of the minister's converting word. He also associates Antilegon with a rival tradition of texts as he shows the reprobate advising Asunetus to turn away from sermons and toward old romances and fictions such as *Bevis of Southampton*, *The mery jest of the friar and the boy*, or the *Court of Venus* (408). Antilegon, it turns out, is not only a reprobate, but a medievalizing, fiction-reading reprobate.

Dent, however, has set out to represent what he sees as a successful conversion, so the converted Asunetus must now reject his neighbor's cultures of discourse. He does so in language that has converged with his teacher's, condemning "your vaine and frivolous bookes and Tales, Iestes and lies" (408–9). The already converted Philagathus joins in this attack, calling Antilegon's books mere "trashe" (409). Here the preacher steps in and counsels his disciples to leave the reprobate alone, "for you see what he is" (410). Their attention should instead be on the new convert, liberated from a doomed culture bound for hell.

Has conversion brought Asunetus the joy and cheerfulness that St. Paul saw as intrinsic to Christian life?[29] Not quite yet. So far conversion has apparently made him "very sadde" (410). But it has also made him very grateful to Theologus, the preacher responsible for his conversion, the one who has freed him from being an "ignorant" person and transformed him into one convinced of his total depravity and now able to repent in a manner that the Calvinist ministry can recognize as true penance (410–11).[30] Now Theologus can exult in the way God has opened the eyes of this man through the means of the preacher, and he welcomes Asunetus as one of God's elect (411). Whereas Antilegon had perceived the conversion of his neighbor as a psychosomatic disorder in need of carnal medicines, the "honest man" Philagathus identifies the converting minister as the "spirituall Phisitian" he himself needs, a doctor for the tiny minority of the eternally elect (411).[31] As Theologus celebrates the new conversion, he tells the "very sadde" Asunetus that he should "be no more heavy and sad" (410, 418). Convinced by the minister's theological paradigm and his newly revealed identity as one of the elect, Asunetus is thus "greatly comforted and cheared up" (428). He celebrates this day, "the first day of my repentance and true conversion into God" (429). Such is the "path-way to Heaven" and the way "every man may clearly see, whether he shall be saved or damned," elect or reprobate.

Once again we seem to have crossed a great divide between Langland's *Piers Plowman* or Julian of Norwich's *Book of Showings* and the culture of Calvinist Christianity in the areas that concern the present study. In attempting to describe the nature of the crossing, the modern language of revolution may seem the best available. Such language has been deployed explicitly in James Simpson's monumental work, *Reform and Cultural Revolution (1350–1547)*, and is implicit in Eamon Duffy's *Stripping of the Altars*.[32] This language seeks to identify a profound break from traditional formations of culture and society, including the systems within which people understood their relations with God and with each other. The materials I have been addressing in this and the previous chapter often manifest the kinds of transformations that indicate a revolution in the paradigms constituting what Duffy calls "traditional religion." Dent's work gives us some hints of how discourses that are metaphysical and theological may assimilate contemporary transformations in the social relations that surround agrarian production and its concomitant forms of property and dominion. But it also gives us hints of resistance to Calvinist Christianity and Dent's suspicion, through the figure of Antilegon, that such resistance may be inassimilable to the Calvinist project within the Church of England to which Theologus and Antilegon both, in 1601, belong. Of course, Dent represents such resistance as coming from an uneducated agricultural-ist with a gaudy taste for medieval romances and an aversion to godly (Calvinist) sermons. Writing before major theological challenges to Calvinism became public, supported by those in power, and given liturgical dimensions, this containment of resistance to the unlearned might have seemed plausible. But what Dent's work occludes, from himself and his fellow Calvinists, are the contradictions, tensions, and anomalies within Calvinist paradigms.

In the final section of chapter 3 I considered an anti-Calvinist work published in 1633 that became well known and elicited Calvinist attacks and concluded the chapter with some reflections on the fragmentations and instability within the reformed Church of England and the Calvinist projects it had centralized. I suggested that whatever the drive for unity, hegemony, and monopoly pursued by Calvinists within the church (distinguishing them from Calvinists who had separated from the magisterial Reformation's national church), such ambitions went against the very grain of the Christian tradition to which these revolutionaries belonged even as they sought to purge it of centuries of error and apostasy. The history in which they were immersed would in time bring out the contradictions and fragilities so vehemently denied by its adherents. It would also bring to the forefront aspects of Christian tradition in theology, ecclesiology, and liturgy that the Calvinist revolution had sought to liquidate. I touched briefly on this toward the end of chapter 3 in my reflections on the extraordinary rehabilitation of the medieval church and its theologians within the ascendant Laudian church. I return now to reflect on the implications of the history I am following for our understanding of the makings of Christian tradition. For, as extraordinary as the restoration of the altars and the rise of sacramental theology against the dominant Calvinism in the 1620s and 1630s was, equally surprising was the return to prominence of models of election and reprobation articulated by the early fourteenth-century theologians discussed in chapter 2. The fact that many of those who catalyzed the return of these models may never have read Aureol, Holcot, Ockham, or Bromyard seems to me an illustration of the complex ways in which Christian tradition is woven: continually breaking, continually forgetting, continually remaking and recalling.

CHAPTER FIVE

John Milton

Versions of Divine Election, Predestination,
and Reprobation

This very thing the whole of Scripture most distinctly declares,
while it sets forth for all equally salvation and eternal life,
subject to obedience in the Old Testament, and of faith in the New.

[Hoc ipsum tota Scriptura dissertissime declarat, dum salutem
atque vitam aeternam sub conditione obedientiae in veteri
testament, fidei in novo aeque omnibus proponit.]

—John Milton, *De Doctrina Christiana*, I.4

In this final chapter, I consider John Milton's reflections on the topics
and traditions I have been exploring throughout. Yet once more I cross
the divide, still firmly entrenched in our universities, between the study
of medieval and early modern cultures. I concentrate on Milton's *De
Doctrina Christiana* (*On Christian Doctrine*), his ambitious attempt to
articulate his own theology in its entirety.[1] According to Milton's most
recent editors, he ceased writing this work around 1660. He stopped
working, that is, at the moment of the Restoration of the monarchy,
of the Church of England, and of the House of Lords (including the

bishops who sat as Lords Spiritual), a restoration that involved the defeat of the English revolution in both government and ecclesiastic order that Milton, in 1660, fondly referred to as "the good old cause."[2] The editors also maintain that the theology expounded in *De Doctrina Christiana* sits "in the theological mainstream" of Reformation thought.[3] Although Milton does habitually present himself as a Protestant, I rather doubt that he would have seen "the theological mainstream" as producing work in any way congruent to his own. Even if one sets aside Milton's most well known heresies, one still must take seriously the contempt for Christian traditions and customs that he frequently gives voice to, whether he is writing about divorce or politics, ecclesiology or polygamy. While such expressions of contempt are not the most thoughtful aspects of Milton's work—and though they encouraged some unexamined contradictions in his work, as we shall see—they were nevertheless recurrent and vehemently expressed.

Given this book's attempt to work across the medieval/early modern divide—a divide replete with complex endings and continuities so often occluded as much by early modern ideology as by disciplinary structures in modern universities—I have thought it worth beginning my discussion of Milton's *De Doctrina Christiana* with some considerations of its version of authority, of the sources of Christian doctrine. In my view, Milton's "best and most precious possession" (6–7) manifests a rather incoherent hermeneutics but one that is, ironically, the product of distinctively Reformation traditions. I say "ironically" because of Milton's habitual voicing of his own derision toward tradition and custom. Such generalizing contempt may have been an impediment to self-critical reflection on his own sources of authority, but it certainly freed him, especially in his treatment of election, predestination, and reprobation, to set aside some core teachings of the Reformation tradition to which he belonged. From my own perspective, setting out from medieval cultures of discourse, Milton's hermeneutic troubles (however unacknowledged by him) are inextricably bound up with his inheritance of a fragmentation specific to his Protestant tradition—namely, the Reformation's rejection of medieval understandings of the intimate relations between scripture, tradition, church, and reason, each an essential and interrelated vector through which the Holy Spirit guided humanity. This interrelation is quite alien to the large and small dichotomies that feature so prominently in *De Doctrina Christiana*, and that encourage a form of thought favoring an either/or rather than a both-and mentality.[4]

In his prefatory epistle to *De Doctrina Christiana* (hereafter referred to as *DDC*), Milton voices his ambition for the work in illuminating terms. Addressing "all the churches of Christ," he asserts that before the sixteenth-century Reformation, Christianity had been subject to "continual corruption" for over thirteen hundred years. He thus dates the onset of this corruption to a hundred years before the start of those processes whose legacy would be the making of Nicene Christianity, the orthodox tradition of the Middle Ages and the magisterial Reformation.[5] A long time indeed for "continual corruption" to have persisted, and a very clear indication of how Milton perceives Christian traditions. We will meet this charge of "continual corruption" again when addressing Milton's treatment of scripture and textuality later in *DDC*. But in the prefatory epistle he asserts that since the beginning of the past century, "Religion [*Religio*] began to be recalled in some measure to the purity of its origin" (3). This originary "purity" apparently lasted only very briefly: according to the archangel Michael in *Paradise Lost*, educating Adam to face the history of humanity, as soon as Jesus's own disciples die, "wolves shall succeed for teachers, grievous wolves" who will overwhelm Christianity with "superstitions and traditions."[6] However, during the Reformation, Milton says in *DDC*, quite suddenly "many books of instruction of purer Theology came forth." Unsatisfied with these "purer" publications, Milton states that having devoted himself "to the study of this doctrine above all else," he now seeks to remedy the inadequacies of contemporary Protestant theology. He declares that since "nothing can eject and expel slavery and fear, those two loathsome pests, from human life and mind so well as the Christian religion can," he has been led "by concerns for life's greatest benefits" to compose his own theological work (3–5). He laments the inadequacies informing the existing theological books of the Reformation and their "purer" but still deficient theology. Replete with "wretched shifts," frivolous arguments, "grammarians' empty jargon," and "logic-chopping formulas" that he finds "disgusting," the authors of these other theological books defend arguments "by misunderstanding biblical passages or snatching at fallacious inferences from them." In these works he consequently finds "truth at times fiercely attacked as error and heresy taken for truth."

Indeed, these volumes of Reformation theology are, according to Milton, "valued more from habit and partisan zeal than from the authority of scriptures" (5). So much for what the editors, John Hale and Donald Cullington, call "the theological mainstream" to which Milton allegedly belongs (lvii). As for "the authority of scriptures," so zealously affirmed in this epistle, this will turn out to be an issue more complicated than these confident locutions suggest. I return to this below.

Milton tells "all the churches of Christ" that he has thus been compelled to compose his own account of Christian doctrine, one more adequate to his current faith. It must, presumably, be freed from the grim legacy of "superstitions and traditions" produced by all those "wolves" foreseen by the archangel, "traditions" that have turned out to be part of the allegedly "purer" Reformation as well as of the postapostolic and medieval church. Not surprisingly, then, he claims to have built his own version of Christian doctrine from the ground up, "from the beginning [*apprime*]" (5). Only by razing tradition to the ground can he be sure he is unpolluted by custom. In this, Milton is obeying what he takes to be God's command to each person: "whoever wants to be saved must have a personal faith of their own," one that depends on "the faith or judgement of no one else"—on no person, on no church, and on no tradition (5). Fulfilling this command, he claims to have grounded his faith "exclusively on divine revelation." Exploring scripture "with the utmost diligence," he has allegedly investigated every "single point" by himself, "by my very own care" (5). He has thus written a work of theology free from "supine credulity," sure that God rewards such committed pursuit of the truth (7). Milton declares the resulting work is his "best and most precious possession." As such, he wants to share it as widely as possible in a "brotherly and friendly" disposition (7).

Milton then reiterates his confidence that *DDC*, unlike previous theology, is truly and exclusively scriptural. This is how he wants us to discern the difference between *DDC* and its precursors:

> And since the majority of those who have written at greatest length on these subjects have been accustomed to fill up almost the whole of their pages with explaining their own opinions, while thrusting into the margin the scriptural passages by which all their teaching

is most confirmed, with the numbers of the chapters and the verses
only summarily noted, I have preferred that my pages' space should
overflow with scriptural authorities assembled from all parts of the
Bible, even when they repeat one another, and that as little room
as possible be left for my own words, though they arise from the
weaving together of the passages. (9)

This is a clear example of the Protestant fantasy of tradition-free exegesis, tradition-free hermeneutics, tradition-free theology, and tradition-
free rationality. Let each tradition-free Christian start from the ground
that is scripture. Let him (and it is certainly "him," for Milton never acknowledges the female prophets and theologians teaching in his own
London, that mansion house of liberty, in the Revolution), let him admit
no dependence on any community but only on the Holy Spirit guiding
his reading. He declares, "I cleave to the holy writings alone [*libris tan-
tummodo sacris adhaeresco*]" (8–9). His chapter devoted to holy scripture (I.30) may seem to repeat this claim, for there he teaches us that
the holy scriptures are "perspicuous, both in themselves and through
God's illumination, in the matters which most pertain to salvation."
Scripture is, according to Milton, "self-sufficient, especially for faith,"
its texts the "utterly lucid" bearers of "divine truths" (801). The sense
of every text of scripture is single, except for those in the Old Testament that often give "a composite sense of the history and its type"
(803). Every Christian must interpret scripture for himself since "he
has the spirit, the guide into truth; he has the mind of Christ" (805).
Except, it is assumed, those who don't: Roman Catholics, adversaries
within the Church of England, as well as those diverse opponents of
the Cromwellian regimes Milton served who read the Restoration as
divinely warranted even as they searched the same scriptures as Milton.[7] But then, such Christians are, presumably, not truly believers:
they lack the Spirit who guides Milton.

Nevertheless, at one point in his discussion of scripture Milton
observes that "expertise in language" is a necessary part of the correct
interpretation of Scripture (*ratio recte interpretandi scriptoris*). This
proficiency in language should be combined with expertise in rhetoric,
grammar, and the knowledge of all the varied texts that constitute the

Bible (I.30, 802–5). Plainly enough, the skills Milton now demands as prerequisites to scriptural interpretation are the product of human traditions flourishing at universities, such as Milton's Cambridge, and available only to those who had a father rich enough and interested enough to sustain their apprenticeship in such elite cultural traditions.[8] This kind of insistence on advanced education was a familiar aspect of the magisterial Reformation, with its commitment to doctrinal systems allegedly rising from scripture correctly read and understood, unlike the church and traditions of the Roman adversary.[9] Yet Milton simultaneously claims that every Christian was competent to interpret scripture independently, regardless of their access to those educational resources advocated above. All those whom Milton recognized as Christians had access to the Spirit who wrote scripture to guide them. Neither the Spirit nor the mind of Christ in the believer needed the human traditions of education. This seeming incompatibility between the alleged perspicuity of scripture, on the one hand, and the not-insignificant education apparently necessary to rightly interpret it, on the other, was a familiar enough tension within Protestantism, one that Milton simply inherited.

But Protestant *sola scriptura* presented another, perhaps sharper challenge to Milton's hermeneutics. Unlike many of the fathers of the Reformation, Milton was seriously concerned about what he called the "corruption" of the received texts of scripture, especially the New Testament. He continued to maintain that the rule and canon of faith is scripture alone. But if the textual history of the Bible is truly the kind of corrupted and unreliable mess Milton describes it as, where does one find the authoritative text that provides the infallible source to which Milton habitually appeals? His much-discussed answer is as follows: We have been given an external scripture, the text edited by people such as Erasmus, Beza, Tremellius, and Junius. And we have also been given an internal scripture—at least we have if we are believers. This is the text written in the heart (I.30, 806–7, 810–11). Milton says that this means we have an "external authority for our faith" that is often thoroughly "corrupt." This seems somewhat contradictory, but Milton had to live with the contradiction if he was to maintain the Protestant version of *sola scriptura*. In addition to this external and unreliable human authority, every believer has in addition the internal text and the authority of the spirit.[10] This is "supreme and preeminent" (I.30, 810–11). Indeed, Milton suggests, how could it be otherwise when both the Christians handing on the texts and the texts they pass down are corrupted? The former Milton judges to be "untrustworthy custodians" who produce "corrupted" texts "from diverse and discrepant manuscripts" that are "transcribed and printed diversely too." Especially in the New Testament, instances of "a corrupt text are also found in almost all codices" (I.30, 810–13). This process has gone on "for many centuries" with "no exemplar in the author's own handwriting which, in preference to the others, we could claim as genuine" (I.30, 813). Scholars such as Erasmus, Beza, and others do the best they can to edit this mess, but they cannot remedy the dire situation.

What good, then, is Milton's piling up of putative proof texts from the external scripture, an amassing that Milton claims is unprecedented? By his own eloquent account these proofs are slippery, unreliable, and corrupt—hardly the stuff from which to build the foundation Milton wants for his dogmatics. It is not surprising then that along with this piling up of scriptural proofs, we also learn that the internal, unwritten word given to each Christian trumps the written scripture, the external word. In this, we encounter one of the possible consequences of the way the Reformation churches split apart the configuration of scripture, church, and tradition that persisted throughout the Middle Ages. There the Holy Spirit was active in all these dimensions, as well as in the individual Christian who participated in the sacraments and liturgy of her or his local church.[11] Milton's foregrounding of the corruptibility of the external word goes beyond even the Reformation's rejection of the medieval configuration and begins unraveling the foundational Protestant dogma of *sola scriptura* itself. Yet this is not something he is able to confront directly or even acknowledge, unlike contemporary Quakers. Instead, he ruminates on God's motives in allowing such "corruption" of his revealed word in the external scripture.

> I am totally ignorant as to why by God's providence it came about that the New Testament scripture was committed to such unsure and such slippery custodians, unless this very fact was meant to prove that the spirit, rather than scripture, has been offered to us as the surer guide whom we ought to follow.

[Quod nescio sane cur factum providentia Dei sit, ut novi testament scriptura custodibus tam incertis tamque lubricis commissa fuerit, nisi ut hoc ipsum argumento esset, certiorem nobis propositum ducem spiritum quam scripturam, quem sequi debeamus.] (I.30, 812–13)

This is a fascinating confession and one might expect it to become a major topic of critical reflection. If one is, like Milton, convinced that God's cunning plot is to give us the external and often "corrupt" scripture only as a means to drive us to the *certiorem ducem*, the more certain or reliable guide of the Spirit within, why would one stuff one's theology with the less reliable external scripture? Indeed, why would one continue to insist that this external scripture is "the authority," the norm or "criterion" for Christian doctrine (6–8)? God's ploy, as Milton describes it, would seem to be leading us toward a scriptural iconoclasm that would echo the Reformation's campaign against the traditional role of images in Catholic Christianity. That role had been partially revived in the Church of England in the 1620s and 1630s but smashed by the adherents of the new regime for which the author of *Eikonoklastes* worked.[12] In the passage I have just quoted, as in its immediate context, Milton's logic seems analogous with that through which he earlier described God's imposition of the law on Israel: in both cases, Milton sees God first bestowing a pedagogic tool and subsequently utterly abolishing its use for Christians. As Milton states in an earlier chapter, "With the introduction of the gospel through faith in Christ—the new covenant—the entire old covenant, that is, the whole Mosaic law, is abolished [*aboletur*]" (I.27, 698–99). Similarly, Milton's understanding is that God is driving us away from the external, written scripture and toward "the unwritten word [*verbum non scriptum*]," the spirit of God acting in individual behavior (I.30, 814–15). Were Milton to follow through with the logic of this position, he would make a fitting companion for the Quaker George Fox. To follow this logic to its conclusion would be to abandon his determination that his pages "should overflow with scriptural authorities assembled from all parts of the Bible, even when they repeat one another"—overflow, that is, with the external scripture

handed to him by "corrupt custodians," "such unsure and such slippery custodians" (I.30, 813). But Milton does not, perhaps could not,
exhaustively pursue the logic of his own theological hermeneutics and
textual scholarship. Despite the force of Milton's intense convictions,
he cannot acknowledge their Quaker teleology.[13] To do so would be
to erode the very premise of his theological project: No longer could
there be plausible reasons for composing a systematic theology like
DDC, one that I have noted on more than one occasion was committed to stuffing its pages with quotations from scripture. It would no
longer make much sense for Milton to go on reiterating the Reformation mantra that the only shared rule of Christian doctrine is scripture.
No longer could Milton treat theological topic after topic and controversy after controversy as though the external scripture could give a
correct and unambiguous resolution. All the often lengthy, fascinating,
and passionate arguments over the interpretation of scripture, all the
challenges to traditional readings that had sustained both Catholic and
magisterial Reformation doctrines of God, these would have to be abandoned as superfluous.

Since he cannot allow himself to, like the Quakers, relinquish his
recourse to the authority of scripture, Milton is left to build his systematic theology from corrupt texts handed down to us by "untrustworthy custodians" (I.30, 811). But what kind of foundation is this? Good
enough to disprove the Nicene doctrine of the Trinity, apparently; in
this project, Milton is quite happy to assert the sanctity and determinate
authority of the external scripture (I.5, 126). Indeed, in his extensive
refutations of Christian traditions in *DDC*, Milton constantly appeals
to this admittedly "corrupted" scripture. Take, for example, Milton's
discussion of the generation of the Son: against the teaching and liturgy
of the medieval church and the churches of the magisterial Reformation,
Milton confidently insists that scripture, the external scripture that is,
will easily (*facile*) disclose doctrinal falsity (I.5, 134–35). Characteristic
of *DDC*, we are given two texts to show Milton's correctness: Colos-
sians 1:15 and Apocalypse 3:11. These call the Son "first-begotten" and
"beginning of God's creation." Milton comments, "what else can more
plainly be understood" from this sacrosanct external scripture than
that the Son is a *creature* made by the Father (I.5, 134–35). This pattern

of appealing to scriptural proofs pervades not only his teaching about the Son of God and the Holy Spirit (*DDC* I.v–vi), but the whole treatise. Every chapter yields examples, but here is one on a much simpler topic. Discussing the "power of the keys" appropriated by the papacy, Milton marshals a veritable battalion of texts from scripture (external scripture of course) to show that the administration of discipline was never entrusted to Peter alone and therefore could not be so entrusted to any future pastor in any church (I.32, 858–59). Similarly, silencing the women prophets and teachers of the English civil war and the 1650s, as well as those admirable earlier ones in the Middle Ages from Julian of Norwich to the East Anglian Lollards, Margery Baxter, and Hawisia Mone, Milton asserts, "Women, though, are commanded to say nothing in church." Why? How do we know that in this case we should obey this commandment of external scripture, so often "corrupt"? Why not support the many contemporary Baptist and Quaker women who claim to have an inner scripture teaching them that they are in contrast commanded by the spirit of God to speak not only in church but also in the streets of London, at home, and across the seas?[14] All that Milton does here to address such objections is to throw forth another *catena* of texts from the sacred but external scripture (I.32, 856–59).

If Milton's confidence in the "perspicuous and complete" authority of scripture (I.30, 801) were set aside, or even seriously qualified by his own comments on its textual unreliability, then his confidence about his own dogmatics would dissolve. The endless *catena* of proof texts he relies on would have to be acknowledged as eliciting something other than proof of the positions he espouses. No wonder, then, that he does not discern the implications and teleology of his own hermeneutics and acerbic commentary on the reliability of external scripture, nor does he fully commit to his own explicit prioritization of the *unwritten* word of the Spirit working in each believer's heart. Whether *DDC* belongs to "the theological mainstream" of Reformed theology as its most recent editors assert or whether it is an eclectic work composed out of the vestiges of diverse Christian traditions, including ones utterly *anathematized* by the "mainstream," it seems clear that what Milton claims to be a work founded on the rock of sacred scripture, safe against all assault from his adversaries, is in fact a house built precariously on sand. He himself, of course, did not see his "best and most precious possession" in this way. On the contrary, he tells all the churches of Christ (*universis Christi ecclesiis*) (Epistle, 2–3) to read *DDC* with the spirit of God going before and leading them to a state of faith in which "every doubt has been removed by the clarity of Scripture" [de his, prout Dei spiritus vobis praeiverit, ita iudicate: his mecum utimini, vel ne utimini quidem, nisi fide non dubia scripturarumque claritate persuasi]" (Epistle, 10). So as far as he is concerned, *DDC* is a version of Christian doctrine guided by the spirit of God and grounded in the clarity of scripture. He has at last delivered scripture from centuries of metaphysical obfuscation (a pervasive theme, but see, e.g., I.30, 801). Apparently, Milton is convinced that this divine clarity, this perspicuity, remains unaffected by the "corruption" of texts, the traditions of transmission, and the custodians of scripture, even though God's mysterious ways here do, he acknowledges, rather puzzle him.

Puzzled or not, to the end of his life Milton claimed to envisage the scriptures (the external ones) as the perspicuous authority around which all Protestants could unite, even those who had so recently been anathematizing and killing each other in England's green and pleasant land.[15] As discussed briefly above, in *Paradise Lost* (1667, 1674), Milton has the archangel Michael teach Adam that after the death of the first generation of Christ's disciples "grievous wolves" will "succeed for teachers" and overturn divine truth, substituting instead "superstitions and traditions." Truth will survive but "only in those written records pure" (*PL* XII.502–13). Did the "grievous wolves," apparently controlling the church from the first century, transmit the written scriptures in a "pure" form? Did they not, as *DDC* tells us, "corrupt" them? Of course, Michael is giving Adam and Milton's readers a very compressed history of the church, in a very different mode from *DDC*. Nevertheless, we can discern here the same tension that is so marked in *DDC*. Although Michael does not convey the history of textual "corruption" as Milton did in *DDC* I.30, he does anticipate that text's emphasis on the inner and unwritten scripture. For the "written records," whether "pure" or corrupted, can only be read correctly by individual believers who are illuminated by the spirit of God: "Though not but by the Spirit understood" (*PL* XII.513–14). Here in a nutshell but elaborately in *DDC*,

Milton has generated a fascinating aporia. But, as I have suggested, Milton seems not to have discerned this unresolved contradiction in a central area of his dogmatics. He continues to happily do what he says, filling his pages so that they "overflow with scriptural authorities," as though by doing so he could produce an irrefutable claim to truth. Contradiction and incoherence? Indeed. This aporia is his own, certainly; but it is one that Reformation theology cannot avoid. Here Milton remained, indeed, at the heart of the tradition constituting Reformed dogmatics. Like all Christians, Milton is a *participant* in a Christian tradition of great complexity, one that enables his critical and creative work. This he could not himself recognize, let alone acknowledge with gratitude.

* * *

I will now leave these preliminary reflections on the sources of Christian doctrine and hermeneutics in *DDC* as I turn to address Milton's teaching on election, predestination, and reprobation. He begins his attack on the theology of double predestination in the third chapter of *DDC*, after chapters defining Christian doctrine (I.1) and the nature of God (I.2). The third chapter is on the divine decree (*De Divino decreto*). Milton opens his arguments by rejecting the Calvinist version of the absolute divine decree, as Samuel Hoard had done many years before in *Gods Love To Mankind, Manifested by Dis-Prooving his Absolute Decree for their Damnation* (1633; discussed in chapter 3). This is a crucial move in Milton's refutation of traditions that taught double predestination. Milton declares, "God did not decree anything absolutely which he left in the power of free agents" (I.5, 55). This is a position reiterated throughout chapter 3. The context of the argument has affinities with the teaching of Langland's Conscience in *Piers Plowman* (treated in chapters 1 and 2). Conscience insists that all God's gifts are given conditionally, given with a "*si* [*if*]." God gives humans the resources necessary to lead a virtuous life pleasing to him and finally rewards them with eternal life. Langland's Conscience envisages a covenant between God and humanity in which divine agency neither coerces nor rivals human agency. The latter remains free to resist and reject God's grace. He remarks that "god gyveth nothing that *si ne* is in the glose [God gives nothing without an *if* in the margin]" (*Piers Plow-man* III.329; see 315–22).[16] We saw similar models of divine and human agency in Bromyard's *Summa Praedicantium* and in other fourteenth-century theologians (chapter 2). I am aware that Milton and Miltonists might not delight in my drawing attention to such affinities with me-dieval theologians, but we will encounter even more affiliations below. It should be clear that to observe an affinity is not to claim anything re-motely like direct influence. It is merely part of the effort to perceive the many strange permutations of rupture, ending, and continuity that constitute living traditions.

Famously enough, and often celebrated among modern Miltonists, Milton's God has an unwavering commitment to human freedom, some-thing he has gifted and decreed.[17] God allows no shadow of extrinsic ne-cessity to impose on angels and humans. Why is Milton so sure of this? Because scripture knows nothing of double predestination or an ab-solute decree of the kind taught by Calvinists. On the contrary, its narra-tives display a model of divine and human agency that is thoroughly committed to human freedom and human responsibility (I.3, 55–57). Milton, as usual, gives copious examples from scripture in I.3 and com-ments that "to judge by these passages of scripture, then, and very many others of the same kind, to whose authority we must above all assent, it is beyond dispute that not everything is decided absolutely by the supreme God" (57). In a similar vein, Langland's Conscience takes up the story of Solomon's "grace," his later rejection of God, and God's consequent reprobation of him (*Piers Plowman* III.324–38; 3 Kings [1 Kings, in A.V.]). Milton also argues that Calvinist theologies of double predestina-tion not only deny God's commitment to the human freedom he himself decreed; they also imagine that God's foreknowledge of all historical events destroys this human freedom (59–65). The unintended outcome is the blasphemous invention of God as the author of sin (65–67).

> Such men [Calvinists], if I did not think they spake like this from error rather than wickedness, I would consider the most abandoned of all blasphemers; and if I should try to refute them, I should be doing the same as if I argued at great length that God is not the devil. (I.3, 67)

From this engaging discussion of the "general decree of God," Milton moves to a much longer chapter devoted to the exploration of predestination. This chapter not only elaborates on themes emerging in his treatment of the decree but also takes up many themes and texts that I have discussed throughout this book in both medieval and Reformation theologies of predestination and reprobation. Milton sets out by attacking a common error he finds in the schools (*in scholis*). This error is to think that predestination means both election and reprobation. He is thus addressing distinctively Calvinist schools of thought. Milton charges such teaching with being both rash and contrary to scripture (I.4, 70–71). How then does he understand predestination? Like most pre-Reformation theologians, Milton teaches that predestination means God's election to salvation. It should always be taken only in this sense (I.4, 73). But unlike most theologians, medieval and Reformation, he sets aside the doctrines of Augustine that, as James Wetzel observed, had poured poison into the church's teaching on predestination and reprobation.[18] Milton affirms, time and again, that the compassionate God gave humans the resources that each person needs for her or his life to culminate in eternal blessedness. Nobody is reprobate who does not, as it were, freely reprobate themselves by rejecting God's grace and his generous covenant with humanity (I.4, 110, 116).

In the previous paragraph I said that Milton's teaching here is "unlike most theologians, medieval and Reformation." But as we saw in chapter 2, some fourteenth-century theologians introduced new paradigms of predestination and reprobation. The one that concerns us in this chapter is the one I follow James Halverson in designating GE, general election. I noted previously that while there are variations within the new paradigm of GE, those who developed its various strands all had to displace the hitherto dominant Augustinian model. In models based on the concept of GE God so loved his human creation that he elected all of humanity to eternal life. When humans fell into sin, he gave them the resources to fulfill the covenants he made with them and so find life. In chapter 2 I focused on Ockham, Holcot, and Bromyard to show how this paradigm of GE might work; Halverson sees Peter Aureol as the inventor of this paradigm and has offered an extensive reading of his work.[19] GE should not, of course, be confused with uni-

versal salvation. In GE the gifts of God to humans include the freedom
to resist offered grace, the freedom to choose against God. In Ockham's
version of this, a human would be free to reject the beatific vision of
God as, presumably, some angels chose to do. Milton might have had
some sympathy with such an emphasis on human freedom.[20]

The chapter on predestination in *De Doctrina Christiana* teaches
a version of GE. Early in the chapter Milton invokes one of the texts
frequently encountered in this book: Paul's statement that God "will
have all men to be saved, and to come unto the knowledge of the truth"
(1 Tim. 2:4). We have seen how Augustinian traditions across the centuries read this text to make it mean the opposite of what it says, a classic
example of scripture's wax nose. We have also seen how those opposing
this dominant tradition, whether in the fourteenth or the seventeenth
century, understood quite differently the importance of Paul's statement
and the exegetical tradition that mastered the text. Milton first quotes
the text to illustrate his contention that in predestination there is no
reprobation. He joins it with 2 Peter 3:9: "he is patiently disposed to us,
not wanting any to perish, but all to progress to repentance [*nolens ullos
perire, sed omnes ad resipiscentiam tendere*]."[21] Both these texts include
the crucial word *omnes—all*. Against traditional exegesis Milton insists
that this *all* means "all humankind: not only the chosen [*electos*], as
quite a few claim" (I.4, 74–75). Unusually for the habitually hyperbolic
Milton, this is quite an understatement. He goes on to emphasize his
challenge to this tradition: all means all, "including the wicked" (74–75).
God has actually elected *all* people. A little later in the chapter, he ven-
triloquizes Paul's teaching in the first letter to Timothy without citing
the apostle and in his own words: "God has clearly—and frequently at
that—testified that he wants the salvation of all [*plane idque saepe testa-
tus est Deus, velle se omnium salutem*] and the death of none" (I.4,
76–77). God truly "hates nothing that he has made and has left out
nothing that might suffice for the salvation of all" (76–77). This is GE.

Milton emphasizes that not just 1 Timothy 2:4 and 2 Peter 3:9, but
"the whole of Scripture" affirms this "most distinctly." God has elected
all humans equally to salvation, "subject to the condition of obedience
in the Old Testament, and faith in the New." Only by acknowledging
this teaching of scripture as a truly general election can we avoid "falsely

imputing wickedness to God" (81). This seems a just comment. Like Langland's "*si* [if]," Milton makes clear that God's election is *conditional* throughout scripture (80–81). He invites us to think of Genesis 2:17: "do not eat of that tree, for on the day you eat, you will surely die." This is, says Milton, as though God had said, "I do not want you to eat of it, so indeed I have not decreed that you will eat, for if you eat [*nam si comederis*], you will die, but if you do not eat [*si non comederis*] you will live. The decree itself was conditional [*conditionale igitur decretum ipsum*]." After the fall, the same conditionality informs God's decree, a claim "proved from countless other passages" (80–81).

What I have been calling, following Halverson, GE, Milton calls *Praedestinatio Generalis* (which I shall abbreviate as PG). He writes, "Praedestinatio itaque et electio videtur nulla essi singularis, sed duntaxat generalis [There seems, then, to be no particular—but only general— predestination and election]" (I.4, 78–79). Whether named GE or PG, this version is one involving a God who does not eternally elect certain people in preference to others (say, Peter in preference to Judas), unlike the models invented by Augustine and Calvin. The "general decree of election [*generale electionis decretum*]" is finally applied to individuals who believe in God's covenant and persevere in following it (I.4, 78–79). God thus elects all and rejects none but those who persist in disobedience and unbelief (84–91). Milton is confident that "God, out of his mercy and his supreme grace in Christ, predestined to salvation all who would believe" (91).

Furthermore, just as Milton stresses in *Paradise Lost*, God imparts *sufficient*, if not equal, grace to all (*PL* III.183–202): "gratiam etsi non parem attamen sufficientem omnibus impertit" (*DDC* I.4, 100–101). Through this grace in Christ all can arrive at the recognition of the truth of salvation, all can find appropriate faith, and all can follow the way to salvation (100–101). Again and again, Milton reiterates that God wants sinners to turn back from their self-destructive choices, and wills a sufficiency of grace to all (104–5). Milton observes that if this were not so, God simply could not justify his ways to humanity (104–5). And Milton himself could not have framed *Paradise Lost*'s purpose as to "justify the ways of God to men" (I.26). Let us then be (as Milton is) quite clear: "God excludes no one from access to penitence and eternal salvation

cept after grace—and that sufficient—has been spurned and scorned."
God always shows great patience before rejecting anyone (104–5).

What then are we to make of the traditional language of reprobation and the terrors it could generate? Working within the paradigm of
GE/PG Milton has little difficulty answering this question in *DDC* I.4.
Perhaps the briefest way to illustrate his response is by quoting the statement he makes twice in the closing pages of the chapter: "Humans reprobate themselves before God reprobates them [*ante igitur reprobantes
hi quidem, quam reprobati, erant*]" (I.4, 110–11); and again, "themselves
reprobating before being reprobated [*reprobantes ipsi priusquam reprobati*]" (116–17).[22] This striking formulation encapsulates Milton's teaching on reprobation. If it needs elaboration, he provides it copiously. In
any consistent version of GE there can be no reprobation from eternity,
no reprobation of unborn individuals (like Esau or Judas). As Milton has
reiterated, God predestines all to salvation on the condition that they follow the ways of the covenant. Those who do not reach the divine end fail
to do so by their own choices (98–99). So if there is anything like a "decree of reprobation," scripture teaches us that it is contingent: "just as
election is grounded and established in faith, so reprobation is revoked
by repentance [*ita reprobationem resipiscentia rescindi scriptura passim
declarat*]" (100–101). Milton is thus sure that there is no support in
scripture for a Calvinist account of reprobation (98–101). We had better
take seriously, without Calvinist gloss, Ezekiel's teaching from God:

> When the wicked man, turning back from his wickedness which he
> was committing, practices justness and righteousness, this man
> preserves his soul. . . . [W]hen I have said to the wicked man, you
> shall surely die, if, having turned from his sin, he practices judge-
> ment and righteousness, etc., he shall surely live and not die. (100–
> 101; Ezek. 18:25–27 and 33:14–15)

Nor does taking God's teaching seriously in this and similar biblical
texts make one a Pelagian. For Milton emphasizes (here and in *Paradise Lost*) that we can only turn from our sins through God's grace,
grace offered sufficiently to all. Milton has thus utterly transformed the
Augustinian and Calvinist discourse on reprobation.

In this context it is not surprising that Milton should pay close attention to another text that I have often discussed in this book: Paul's brief invocation of Jacob and Esau from Malachi 1:2–3 during his highly wrought reflections on God's election of Israel and Israel's rejection and crucifixion of the Son of God (Rom. 9:10–13). As we have seen, this text was a major authority in Augustinian and Calvinist doctrines of predestination and reprobation. Familiar as it is by this stage of the present book, I shall quote the text as John Hale and Donald Cullington translate Milton's version of it:

> For when her [Rebecca's] boys were not yet born, when they had done nothing good or bad, so that God's purpose which accords with election might remain—arising not from works but from him calling—it was said to her, The elder shall serve the younger. . . . Jacob I loved, but Esau I hated. (I.4, 108–9)

Milton foregrounds the bizarre role this text continued to play in Christian dogmatics, recalling how it had come to seem to very many people "the hinge [*cardo*] of the question" about predestination and reprobation (106–7). Unlike most medieval and Reformation theologians who quote this text, Milton insists that it must be read in its full context (Rom. 9–11). If one does this, it will be clear that Paul's issue is not (as it is for Augustinian and Calvinist theorists) concerned with predestination and reprobation but rather with the undeserved calling of the Gentiles and the rebellions of Israel (106–7). Milton goes over Paul's treatment of God's promise to Abraham, a promise made not to Abraham's "fleshly sons" but to the sons of God. Like Satan in *Paradise Regained*, we might ask, who are these sons of God (*PR* IV.514–21)? They are, Milton asserts, people who accept Christ; such is the faith that makes humans "the sons of God" (*DDC* I.4, 108–9). As for the text so often abstracted from Paul's concerns and made to become the "hinge" of a very different inquiry, Milton asks exactly what "election" is referred to in Romans 9:11–12 (I.4, 109). The answer is the election of the younger, "whether a boy or a people," to "the right of primogeniture." Paul is here figuring contemporary relations between Gentiles and Jews. But in doing so, he insists that God has not cast away

the remnant of the people he had chosen, the remnant who do not reject God (Rom. 11:1–8, 25–32). In this context, Milton observes, "I
do indeed hear a purpose of election here, but none of reprobation"
(109). In a well-justified comment on the whole exegetical tradition he
is challenging, Milton asks, "Why do we try further to extract from
these words a bitter and ferocious sense which they do not have
[Quid nos amplius ex his verbis acerbum et truculentum quod non
habent, exprimere conamur]" (108–9)? He goes on to say that when
Paul talks about the elder serving the younger ("surely this is said
rather of people") he says *nothing* about eternal reprobation. Furthermore, Milton remembers, Esau himself also received a blessing (Gen.
27:40) and his descendants "were called to faith with other Gentiles"
(109). If readers insist on mistaking Esau's servitude as reprobation,
then they had better understand reprobation as Milton does: a temporary state of disobedience to God that need not be permanent but is
open to penitence and return to God (109) just as "the word of the
Lord" taught Ezekiel.

But what about the endlessly repeated phrase, "Jacob I loved, but
Esau I hated" (Rom. 9:13)? Doesn't this cut the throat of his argument
("At hoc iugulat; Iacobum dilexi, Esauum autem odio habui" [108–9])?
Milton asks the commonplace objector a question: "in what respect did
God love or hate?" (109). The answer is given in the very text from
which Paul himself was quoting (Mal. 1:2–3). In Malachi, "the word
of the Lord" had informed the prophet that "he hated Esau in that he
consigned his mountains to wilderness" (*DDC* I.4, 109). And, Milton
writes, he loved Jacob "in that he led him back to the fatherland out of
Babylon; according to the same election by which he now invites Gentiles but forsakes Jews" (109–11). Milton also observes that Paul's phrase
is "rather casually appended [*quasi obiter adiiciatur*]" to illuminate the
statement "the elder will serve the younger" (111). Unlike the earlier reference to unborn twins, this refers to them "when long since dead"
(111). Milton says this because in Malachi 1:2–3, the word of the Lord
to Israel is that Esau's heritage will be waste for dragons of the wilderness. Nevertheless, the merciful God's grace is given to undeserving humans, as Paul himself habitually confesses and as the Gentiles (figured
by Esau) have themselves experienced. Contrary to Augustinian and

Calvinist theology, God's justice does not include divine reprobation and hatred of the unborn (111).

What then of Paul's words about God hardening Pharaoh's heart? Milton comments that scripture shows God hardening the hearts of the "markedly impious," those who have freely and persistently chosen to reject him. In a striking phrase I have already quoted, Milton tells us that humans reprobate themselves (*reprobantes*) before they are reprobated (*reprobati*) by God, and then only after God's "long forbearance" (110–11, 116–17). This leads Milton into another passage from Romans 9 that had also become a "hinge [*cardo*]" in discussions of predestination and reprobation from Augustine through the seventeenth century, as we have seen in chapters 2 and 3 above. Paul states that God has mercy on whom he wills, and he hardens the heart of whom he wills (Rom. 9:18). Paul imagines an objection that such a version of divine action hollows out human responsibility. He seeks to answer this criticism.

> Thou wilt say then unto me, Why doth he yet find fault? For who hath resisted his will? Nay but, O man, who art thou that repliest against God? Shall the thing formed say to him that formed it, Why hast thou made me thus? Hath not the potter power over the clay, of the same lump to make one vessel unto honour, and another unto dishonour? (Rom. 9:19–21, A. V.)

With its image of God making some creatures to honor, some to dishonor, and its rejection of any possibility of dialogue with God's decree, it is hardly surprising that Calvinists such as William Twisse sought to use this passage as a proof text of their version of God, election, and reprobation.[23]

Milton's own reading of this text gives us another memorable moment in his engagement with his Calvinist heritage, its theology, and its exegesis of Romans 9. He continues to deny that the verses just quoted or the passages from which they have been extracted concern a divine decree of reprobation. Paul, Milton tells us, is actually discussing the way that after great toleration of human disobedience God finally, as the punishment for pertinacious wickedness, hardens the hearts of such malicious sinners (1.4, 111). As for the potter's power over the clay: yes,

working with suitable material, he can grace with honor whomsoever
he wills. But not, Milton says, "the recalcitrant [*immorigeros*]" (110–11).
He quotes 2 Timothy 2:21: "if anyone purges himself of these things, he
will be a vessel for honourable purposes." God does indeed harden—
that is, punish—rebels, according to the next verse in Romans 9: "he
endured with much long-suffering the vessels of wrath, fixed together
for ruin [*interitum*]." Milton asks what "fixed together" means. He replies that it means those who remorselessly disobey God are fixed together by "their own hardness." This completes the trajectory of their
own freely chosen iniquity. According to Milton, Paul intended nothing in this passage but "to show God's free and gratuitous mercy in
calling and saving the Gentiles, who had been hearers of the faith, and
his just judgment in hardening the Jews and others" who clung "perti-
naciously" to "the law of works" (citing Rom. 9:30–33). There is simply
nothing here concerning "a decree of reprobation" independent of humans rejecting God (113). He concludes his long engagement with this
important text by observing that having "sailed past this rock," other
passages deployed by Augustinian and Calvinist traditions will easily
be negotiated (113).

Milton's remarkable engagement with this "hinge of the question"
illustrates his conviction that nothing in scripture or Christian theology warrants Calvinists' version of God's election, predestination,
and reprobation. As he had argued years earlier in the *Doctrine and Discipline of Divorce*, God is *for us*—unequivocally supportive of human
flourishing. In Milton's version of medieval GE, God's election of humanity involves such commitment to free human agency that he restored the drastic losses in human resources caused by the fall (I.4, together with I.14). God's call to all people (1 Tim. 2:4) is thus one that
enables fallen humans to respond and follow. Milton thus keeps the received language of reprobation but translates it to fit the paradigm of
GE or PG. There is no eternal and individual reprobation. But if one rejects or reprobates God, opposing oneself to the ends of human flourishing, then, in the end, God will fix one's own fixed choices irrevocably.
He will, that is, harden one's heart according to one's own obstinate
will. Habituated in sin, one is finally reprobated when the time of grace
is past. God echoes and compresses this teaching in *Paradise Lost*

(III.173–202).[24] Paul's simile involves utterly inert, passive clay. The Dominican Robert Holcot had commented on the limitations of this model for exploring the relations between divine and human agency as he sketched a model of GE, as we saw in chapter 2. Milton has gone beyond Holcot in ascribing agency and responsibility to what had been imaged as inert clay, agency bestowed by the potter who is himself committed to his vessels' relative autonomy. Genuine autonomy but only relative: in both *De Doctrina Christiana* and *Paradise Lost* Milton is an anti-Pelagian theologian.

As he promised, after sailing around the rocks of the Augustinian version of Jacob and Esau, and of the potter with his clay, the remainder of Milton's journey through the battery of scriptural texts appropriated by Augustinians and Calvinists is an easy passage (I.4, 112–19). There is much fascinating exegesis and argument in these pages, but I think that what I have been describing suffices to show both Milton's version of GE and his modes of critical exegesis. Indeed, Milton's strident criticism of so many of the dogmatic glosses that had become an impediment to thought on the subject of predestination within the Calvinist tradition is an apt demonstration of Milton's view of the dangers of *all* tradition. At the end of this gripping chapter Milton suggests that Calvinist traditions actually "accuse God, although they strenuously deny it; and they are superbly confuted by the pagan Homer [*ab Homero etiam ethnico*]" in the *Odyssey* (I.4, 116–19). Speaking through the "persona" of Jupiter, Homer writes:

> Oh dear! how indeed mortals reproach gods! For they say that evils come out of us, yet they themselves by their own outrages suffer sorrows beyond fate. (*DDC* I.4, 117–19; see *Odyssey* I.7 and I.32–34)

To conclude his discussion by placing Calvinists like William Twisse under the corrective rod of the "pagan Homer" is the final grim joke in this account of Christian doctrine on predestination and reprobation. It is a joke Robert Holcot, himself a powerful critic of Augustinian uses of Paul's potter and clay and one of Beryl Smalley's paradigmatic "classicizing friars," would have appreciated.[25]

In chapter 8 of the first book of *De Doctrina Christiana*, Milton discusses divine providence.[26] As we would expect from the chapters on the decree and predestination, Milton's account of God's providence includes a strong commitment to showing how divine and human agency must not be envisaged as rivals. Divine sovereignty is responsible for creating and sustaining human beings who have been given the gifts of intellect and will, the constituents of human agency and freedom enabled by God (I.8). When Jeremiah writes that "man's way is not under his own control" (Jer. 10:23), Milton comments that this is true so long as we understand that "freedom of the will [*voluntatis libertate*]" is always preserved by God himself (I.8, 320–21). Calvin unambiguously denied the distinction between divine will and divine permission in human action, rejecting the idea that the wicked perish by the permission of God but not by his will (*Institutes* III.23.8). He claimed that God did not merely permit humans to destroy themselves. Perish the thought! Rather, God *ordained* such self-destruction. God *determined* the fall. Calvin exults, "I confess with Augustine that the will of God is necessity" and that "those things will certainly happen which he has foreseen." Adam fell "because the Lord deemed it meet that he should: why he deemed it meet, we know not" (III.23.8).[27] Here is the classic Augustinian/Calvinist *O altitudo!* Divine ordination to sin is, along with punitive divine justice, unambiguously affirmed as an incomprehensible mystery. Milton, however, considers such common Calvinist arguments blasphemous, the very fruit of wickedness, if their makers really understood what they were saying about God (I.3, 66–67). Considering God's providence, he reaffirms that "God who is supremely good cannot bring about evilness [Malitiam autem seu malum culpae, Deus qui summe bonus est efficere non potest]" (*DDC* I.8, 322–23). His chapter on God's providence systematically distributes agency between God and fallen humans. It is only after humans have chosen against God's desire for their flourishing that God, as we have noted, may harden their hearts in these habitual choices (326–28; similar to many arguments earlier in I.3 and I.4). Milton exemplifies such a process through David's pride and the census (I.8, 326–29; 2 Sam. 24). This is a classic example of doubled agency, human and divine, with no sense that the divine coerces or crushes the human. Indeed, out of malevolent, destructive human choices, which God *permits* rather than *ordains*, God "always creates and draws forth something good and just, like light out of darkness" (329; with *PL* XII.467–73). Milton thinks here of the crucifixion and God's redemption of sinful humanity in Christ (331). Here I will leave Milton's exploration of predestination and reprobation, an exploration that has composed a paradigm—*Praedestinatio Generalis*—with perhaps surprising affinities to the model of general election formed by some late medieval theologians.

✳ ✳ ✳

I will now address Milton's engagement with an aspect of Calvinist accounts of predestination and reprobation considered in chapters 3 and 4 above. This is the Calvinist teaching on assurance. Milton titles his own inquiry here as *De certitudine* (*DDC* I.25). In chapter 3, I discussed some of the anxious double binds and some of the possible exhilarations into which such teaching led Calvinists. Milton only considers this topic after he has written chapters on justification, adoption, union and communion with Christ, and membership in the invisible church. The chapter is headed, "On unfinished Glorification: in which are also discussed the Assurance of salvation [*de certitudine salutis*] and the perseverance of the saints" (650–51).

Milton treats assurance, *certitudo salutis,* as a stage (*gradus*) of faith. In it, a Christian believes that if he persists in faith and charity, having been justified and adopted by Christ, he is beginning the process of glorification that will culminate in beatitude (I.25, 652–53). Milton begins with one of the core texts of Calvinist teaching on assurance— "take the trouble, rather, to make your calling and election firm" (655; 2 Pet. 1:10)—but sets his discussion in a context that is incompatible with its Calvinist appropriations. The context is the paradigm we have been following in *DDC* I.3 and 4: GE or, in Milton's Latin, PG. He is perfectly logical when he argues that this paradigm would eschew versions of assurance that cultivated acute anxieties about one's eternal state, including one's possible reprobation. This was as true of its fourteenth-century version as of its Miltonic version in the seventeenth.

Milton emphasizes that election and calling are as certain as they are past (I.25, 655). God has faithfully fulfilled his part of the covenant.

This leaves humans, all elected, to make "firm" their election and calling by practicing virtue in their lives (655; 2 Pet. 1:5–9, 10). Once more
Milton's approach has affinities with Langland's Conscience: God's
gifts of election are faithful, but they come with a "*si* [if]," with a recip-
rocal condition. This approach had profound and critical implications
for the Calvinist doctrine of perseverance and the impossibility of the
elect's final lapse, a doctrine recently affirmed at the Synod of Dort
(1618–19). Calvinists dismissed such challenges to their versions of assurance and perseverance as "papist." Although this was a generalized
term of abuse, it correctly named patristic, medieval, and early modern
Catholic teaching as incongruent with Calvinist ideas in this area.
However, anti-Calvinists within the Church of England had also espoused these "papist" ideas, and the virulently anti-Catholic Milton
joined forces with them over these issues.[28] In Milton's view, God
leaves it in the power he himself gives us to make our election sure by
obeying his teaching, or to reject our election by sustaining practices
and beliefs contrary to the covenant (I.25, 654–57). Milton makes this
very clear: without our laboring to fulfill our calling, our calling ("vocation") will not save us. It becomes nothing ("nihil hoc valeat," 654–55).
We are ordered to examine our faith, to find Christ dwelling within
(655; 2 Cor. 13:5). But we are *not* ordered to examine our election, already given to all humanity in Christ. As for reprobation, the chapter
on assurance and perseverance confirms Milton's teaching on the decree and on predestination in I.3 and I.4: humans can choose a path
against divine election, rejecting the grace of God; this is reprobation
(I.25, 654–57). Milton argues that the assurance we need comes not
from endless introspective searching for signs of election or reprobation but rather from our sustained decision to practice the virtues of
faith and charity, a practice replete with the consolations of hope (654–
59). Perseverance is not remotely like the Calvinist version formulated
at Dort, one insisting that the elect could not finally fail. Milton knew
that the elect could reject God and be finally rejected: we are all given
the power to quench the spirit of God that has sealed us, but as a result
"our assurance of salvation must at the same time be quenched" (657).
With that quenching, we lose the certainty of salvation and joy (657).
God is faithful to his general election of humanity, and we are free to
fail our own selves (659).

Milton's model continues to be one of a covenantal theology of agency within an anti-Pelagian doctrine of grace. This is affirmed as clearly in *Paradise Lost* as in *De Doctrina Christiana*. God promises all we need to deduce the love of God in us.

> God does indeed promise here to put reverence for himself in their mind, so that they shall not depart from him, for he promises what is his own contribution, namely a sufficiency of grace to prevent their departing. Nevertheless he is concluding a covenant [*attamen foedus pangit*]; and in a covenant some [condition] must be fulfilled not by one party alone but by both. (I.25, 660–61)

This pellucid statement characterizes Milton's teaching on this topic. He precedes it by quoting Jeremiah: "I shall conclude a perpetual covenant [*pangam ipsis foedus perpetuum*] for them, that I shall not turn away from following after them, by doing good to them; and I shall put reverence for me in their mind, so that they shall not depart from me" (*DDC* I.25, 658–59; Jer. 32:40). Milton again expresses his confidence that his own teaching corresponds to "the whole tenor of scripture," and he illustrates this with characteristic copiousness (658–61). He displays his habitual commitment to a model of double agency, simultaneously divine initiative and human cooperation—a model in which divine agency and grace never overwhelm human choice. As he reads the history of Israel in relation to these reflections, he observes, "Those very people in whom God promised to put reverence for himself so that they should not depart [from him] did in fact depart" (691). He finds Jesus offers the same warning in his analogy of the vine and its branches (661–63; John 15:1–7). God does not repent of his gifts and promises. But if those who receive the gifts change, if they reject the conditions of the covenant, then (in Milton's words) they fail themselves (663; 658–63).

So Calvinist versions of assurance and perseverance are carefully rejected. We have seen that Milton replaces them by versions compatible with his paradigm of election (GE or PG), and with his model of the delicate relations between human and divine agency within the covenant of grace (I.3–4, I.25, I.26). The elect, and true believers among the elect, *can* "lapse utterly" (663). God did and does speak through Ezekiel, whom Milton quotes more than once, saying, "when the righteous person [*iustus*] turns away from his righteousness . . . he shall die" (661; Ezek. 18:26). And he cites Ezekiel 33:12–13 to the same effect. Also relevant to these issues for Milton is the fact that Christ prayed to the Father that Peter's *faith*—and not God's ordinary grace (*gratia Dei ordinaria*)—should not fail (Luke 22:32). He argues that Christ prayed as he did because "Peter's faith could have failed" despite the gift of God's "ordinary grace." In this most testing of times, Christ prayed that God's extraordinary grace (*gratia Dei extraordinaria*) be given (664–65). In the paradigm of GE/PG, not election but only perseverance paves the pathway to salvation: "For this reason not *the chosen* but *those who persevere* are said to attain salvation," "many people's love will grow cold, but that person who persists right to the end will be saved" (664, my emphasis; Matt. 24:12–13).

In the first translation of *DDC*, Sumner represents Calvin himself as Milton's direct adversary here and cites some relevant passages from the *Institutes*.[29] These passages illustrate Calvin's reading of the text that, as we saw in chapter 1, so troubled Langland's Wille: "many are called, but few are chosen" (Matt. 22:14). For Calvin this statement refers to the paucity of the elect, a position totally rejected in any version of GE. Like Milton, Calvin thinks that calling and faith are of little consequence without perseverance. Unlike Milton, however, he asserts that perseverance is a gift only given to the few elect chosen in God's eternal decree (*Institutes* III.24.7, one of Sumner's texts). Such is the paradigm of double predestination. Milton's adversary here is thus not only Calvin himself, but a whole tradition that Calvin's followers promoted within the Church of England and at Christ's College Cambridge where Milton himself had received his Christian formation. By the time he wrote *DDC*, Milton had found his way to a rather "papist" version of perseverance and assurance, anathema to Calvinists but intrinsic to the paradigm of GE or PG. So, perhaps, in tracing the paradigms of GE from Holcot to Milton, or of double predestination from Gregory of Rimini to Peter Martyr Vermigli and John Calvin, we glimpse the unpredictable wanderings of tradition. We should not allow the habitual invocation of Arminius to occlude this tradition and its strange life in seventeenth-century Reformed theology.

＊ ＊ ＊

Before leaving *De Doctrina Christiana*, I want to briefly discuss a central area of theology considered in chapter 3: Christ's crucifixion. There I addressed Calvin's allegorization of Christ's descent into hell together with the image of a wrathful, punitive Father that he composed. In the present chapter, I have shown how Milton found in the Calvinist doctrine of double predestination a blasphemous picture of God that actually made him the author of the sins he punished. As repulsive as he found this implication of Calvinist dogmatics, Milton charitably put it down to "error rather than wickedness" (I.3, 64–67). Here, Milton was very happy to break with the tradition he inherited, as he was in his doctrine of God (I.5–6), his defenses of divorce and polygamy (I.10), his doctrine of creation (I.7), and his mortalism (I.13). Did he make any such break in his account of Christ's crucifixion? Did his rejection of Nicene Trinitarianism make him rethink this, too?

Milton had tried to write about Christ's crucifixion in an early poem, "The Passion." When the poem was published, Milton included a note saying that he found the subject "to be above the years he had when he wrote it, and nothing satisfied with what was begun, left it unfinished."[30] Many Miltonists have ruminated on this "unfinished" work, which he continued to publish and republish though "nothing satisfied" with it. They have noted the scant few lines devoted to the crucifixion in Michael's version of salvation and history in *Paradise Lost* (XII.412–19), and they have noticed that when he finally wrote a long poem on Christ's saving work, *Paradise Regained*, the crucifixion is a future event referred to as such, and is alluded to in various images only indirectly. Recently the editors of *The Complete Prose and Essential Poetry of John Milton* remarked that "unlike Richard Crashaw or even George Herbert, Milton never warmed to the subject of Christ's blood."[31]

Fascinating as it is to explore versions of Christ (preexistent and incarnate) in Milton's poetry, here I limit my comments to the relations between the crucifixion in *De Doctrina Christiana* and in Calvin's *Institutes*. Unlike Socinians, Milton followed the Protestant tradition he inherited and saw the crucifixion as an essential moment in the atonement.[32] Chapter 16 of Book I focuses on the enactment of Christ's mediatorial office and his exaltation. Christ as God-man (*Theanthropos*) "submitted himself to divine justice in order to undergo all things by which our redemption was to be accomplished" (511). Taken on its own, this is a conventional formulation of the theology of the atonement favored by Reformed theologians. It also contains, however, a major break with both Reformation and medieval accounts of the Incarnation. Medieval theologians had maintained that Jesus Christ suffered in his humanity but not in his divinity. The orthodox model here had its roots in Chalcedonian language and theology: the incarnate Christ was two natures but one divine person; there was no confusion of the two natures, and the divine nature remained impassible.[33] In *Piers Plowman,* Langland brings on the figure of Faith to explain the vision of Christ as Piers the Plowman just given to the dreamer, Wille:

> "*Liberum-dei-arbitrium* for loue hath vndertake
> That this Iesus of his gentrice shal iouste in Pers armes,
> In his helm and in his haberion, *humana natura;*
> That Crist be nat yknowe for *consummatus deus,*
> In Pers plates the plouhman this prikiare shal ryde
> For no dynt shal hym dere as *in deitate patris.*"
>
> (XX.20–25)

> ["*Liberum-dei-arbitrium* has for love undertaken
> That this Jesus for his gentility will joust in Piers's armor,
> In his helmet and in his mail, *humana natura;*
> So that Christ not be known as *consummatus deus,*
> In the plate-armor of Piers the plowman this cavalier will ride,
> For no dent will damage him as *in deitate patris.*"]

The divine nature is hidden and remains impassible, free from suffering in the crucifixion. Calvin and Reformed churches affirmed this tradition. The famous *extra calvinisticum* of Calvinist teaching does so explicitly:

> For even if the Word in his immeasurable essence united with the nature of man into one person, we do not imagine that he was confined therein. Here is something marvelous: the Son of God descended from heaven in such a way that, without leaving heaven, he willed to be conceived in the virgin's womb, to go about the

earth, and to hang upon the cross; yet he continually filled the world even as he had done from the beginning. (*Institutes* II.13.4)[34]

Milton himself retains some elements of Chalcedonian concepts and language while discarding all that he found incompatible with his rejection of Nicene Trinitarianism earlier in *DDC* (I.2, 5–6). The redemption of humanity is achieved by the God-man (I.16, 510–17 with I.14, 474–83).

Unlike the errant and unscriptural Nicene doctrine of the Trinity, the union of divine and human nature in Christ is a genuine and great "mystery" (*mysterium*), one given this description in scripture (I.14, 476–77). A mystery but not one that can quite be described in traditional terms. Two natures, human and divine: *yes*. One divine person with no human person: *no*. For in Milton's view "the union of two natures in Christ" was the union of "two essences" and therefore of "two hypostases." If Christ's human nature did not possess "a subsistence of its own," that is, a person, Christ would not have assumed "true manhood." Christ is the union of two natures *and* a union of two persons. Yet in this union, the two natures remain distinct (as Chalcedon affirmed) and the two persons also remain distinct (against an orthodox tradition that affirmed one person, the Logos). Such is the twofold nature of Christ, most aptly called God-man (I.14, 474–83).

There may be some irony in these paragraphs that seems to have escaped Milton, having just rebuked and mocked the Protestant theologian Zanchius for writing about the natures of Christ in language that is nowhere in Scripture. This rebuke is of a piece with Milton's reiterated claim to be doing a uniquely scriptural theology, a claim discussed earlier in this chapter. He proclaims his liberation of Christian theology from disastrous traditions of metaphysics, yet in this passage from I.14 he himself writes within just such metaphysical traditions, with their often shifty relations between Greek terms and their Latin translations.[35] These observations are certainly not intended as a criticism of Milton for doing metaphysics and deploying concepts that belong to centuries of Christian theology, traditions written by his fellow Christians seeking to understand what they and their church believed. Rather, my remarks draw attention to inconsistencies in his claims to eschew all metaphysics. The confidence of such claims seems to have generated a certain lack of self-reflection, which occluded from him his own participation in traditions he condemned. It also encouraged confident abuse of adversaries such as the Protestant Zanchius (I.14, 479) and of the unspecified but "enormous tomes of Theologasters [Theologastrorum]" whom he exuberantly promised to "throw out from God's temple like pollutants and dust-heaps" (I.14, 476–77; see, too, 480, 482). Be that as it may, Milton concludes his discussion of the unity of Christ's two natures and the unity of his two persons, a unity that preserves the distinction of the properties, with a warning (I.14, 481): we do not know *how* this is so. God himself has left us with a "mystery" (476, 481). Given this, Milton submits that "it is assuredly best that what God wills to be unknown should not be known" (481).[36]

I think we now have a sufficient guide to the contexts in which *De Doctrina Christiana* addresses Christ's crucifixion and the doctrine of atonement in I.16. Although he never acknowledges this, Milton's account is a version of a distinctly Reformation tradition, partly adjusted to accommodate his own dismissal of Nicene Trinitarianism and his theory of mortalism (I.5; I.13). That is, he hands on what had long since become the traditional Protestant dogma of penal substitution that I discussed in chapter 3 when considering Calvin on the crucifixion of Christ. God the Father curses Jesus Christ: "the curse due to us is transferred to him" (I.16, 512–13). As in Calvin and the tradition Milton (on this topic) unquestioningly assumes, the Father's wrath is poured onto and into the Son of God. He suffers "a horrifying awareness of divine anger [*iraeque divinae in se effusae horribili sensu*]" (512–13). In his often brilliantly searching commentary on Romans, Abelard raised profound ethical questions about the kind of God emerging from accounts of the crucifixion such as that elaborated by Anselm a few years earlier in *Cur Deus Homo* ["Why God Became a God-Man"]. In the seventeenth century, Socinians, in a work Milton knew and licensed for publication (the *Racovian Catechism*), raised similar ethical questions about the Protestant version of the atonement. These ethical questions might be especially difficult for those who, like Milton, deny the Trinitarian theology of God and make the Son a creature made in time by the Father.[37] But Milton, unlike Aquinas in the *Summa Theologiae* (III.47.3, obj. 1, ad 1), does not raise any ethical questions concerning the Father's treatment of the Son. For a thinker as scornful of tradition as Milton, this seems a remarkable failure in ethical inquiry and imagination, especially given the contemporary probing offered in the *Racovian Catechism*. Without question he follows Calvin and Protestant tradition by abstracting the cry of dereliction (Matt. 27:46) from all the other sayings of Christ on the cross (I.16, 513). This abstraction directly contravenes his own criticism of those who abstract scriptural texts from their contexts and from the totality of scripture (e.g., I.25, 665–66). It seems that his unexamined espousal of this aspect of Protestant tradition impedes his habitual critical thinking. He assumes that the Reformation's invention of the penal substitution and penal satisfaction theory must be the only possible way of theologizing the crucifixion and atonement. Because of this assumption, he doesn't notice the very different versions of the Father in different models and narratives of the atonement. There is a world of difference between the representation of the Father in Anselm or Aquinas or Langland and the representation in Calvin and Reformed tradition. One might expect the author of *Paradise Lost* to be sensitive to such differences, but such expectations would be without warrant.

From his account of the Father's wrath poured onto and into the Son, Milton moves to the descent of Christ into hell, an article of the Apostles' Creed (related to 1 Pet. 3:18–20). He swiftly dismisses the theological and ethical riches that medieval traditions had found in this descent, riches sublimely displayed in *Piers Plowman* (Passus XX). Milton reduces these traditions to a merely "capricious controversy [*morosa . . . controversia*]" (I.16, 512). He thinks he has "solved" this discourse through his own mortalist doctrine (I.13). Christ's soul, he tells us, died exactly the same death as Christ's body (I.16, 513). For all his elaborate metaphysical arguments about the divine and human nature of the God-man (*Theanthropos*), he simply asserts that Christ's "divine nature" died on the cross under the Father's wrath while experiencing his own "horrifying awareness of divine anger poured out upon him" (I.16, 513). True enough, Christ's "divine nature" did not mean to Milton what it meant to Augustine, Aquinas, or Calvin since his "God-man" was a creature made by the Father (I.5). Yet in the light of the alleged death of Christ's "divine nature," it is slightly puzzling that Milton should have seen fit to deploy at length traditional language and concepts concerning relations within Christ's "duplex [twofold]" nature (I.14, 475–87).

Be that as it may, Anselm, Aquinas, Langland, and most pre-Reformation Christians did not imagine that the God who raised Jesus from the tomb and whom Christians worship subjected Jesus to his own violent wrath as the substitute for the punishment due to the humanity he had chosen to curse with death and damnation. Medieval Christians knew that Jesus suffered the consequences of human wickedness, the consequences of embodying divine love and truth in a world where such love is likely to elicit violent opposition and cruel hatred. They also knew that Jesus Christ did not take on our guilt and sin in the identificatory way envisaged by the Reformation. They all knew that the Father loved the Son, as the New Testament frequently affirms ("This is my beloved Son, in whom I am well pleased" [2 Pet. 1:17; Luke 9:35]), and they all knew that the crucifixion was a work of wicked injustice enacted on the innocent Christ who was the embodiment of perfect love of God and perfect love of neighbor. Of course, Milton and Protestant tradition also used the language of love when describing the Father's decision to expose Christ to his own persecutory wrath and torture, both in body and in soul.[38] But then a butcher who kills and sells lambs may well claim he loves them.

The great reviler of tradition thus wrote about the crucifixion from within a very distinctive tradition that he never identifies as such. In *Paradise Lost*, Milton has God the Father propound the tradition, a veritable deification of this strand of Calvinist ideology:

> Die he [humankind] or Justice must; unless for him
> Some other able, and as willing pay
> The rigid satisfaction, death for death.

(PL III.210–13)

In the *Summa Theologiae* Aquinas had argued against this claim, finding its logic inadequate: "Simply and absolutely speaking, God could have freed man otherwise than by Christ's passion. *For nothing is impossible with God* [Luke 1:37]" (*ST* III.46.2, resp.). How so? Had God desired to save humans from sin without any "satisfaction," he could have done so; moreover, to do so would not be acting against justice. Contrary to Milton's surprisingly unexamined assumptions on this topic, both in *De Doctrina Christiana* and in *Paradise Lost*, God is not in the position of a human judge. The latter is an official of a particular system of justice with its rules of crime and punishment. However, "God has no one above him, for he is himself the supreme and common good of the entire universe. If then he forgives sin, which is a crime in that it is committed against him, he does injury to nobody." Rather he acts mercifully *and* without injustice (*ST* III.46.2, ad 3).[39] Aquinas does accept the traditions of scripture and church that taught that God liberated humankind through the passion of Christ, through the crucifixion. The triune God acted in a manner that was utterly fitting and perfectly designed to save and convert human beings toward a life in which they would participate in God (III.46.2, ad 3). Although he could certainly have found many other ways to save humankind, the one he actually chose was the most fitting. Just why this was so, Aquinas specifies at length (III.1.2). In this carefully argued perspective, the claims of Milton and Protestant tradition—"die he or Justice must" within a transcendental system that demands "rigid satisfaction, death for death"—are shown to be seriously mistaken.

Nevertheless, Milton and his God assume Reformation tradition here, an assumption that impedes consideration of arguments such as those Aquinas developed four hundred years earlier. Confronted with God's dogmatic formulation in *Paradise Lost*, none of the listening angels are willing to offer themselves as penal substitutions for humankind under this mysterious divine curse. But the first of God's creatures, the newly promoted head of angels (*PL* V.600–615), the Son, agrees to do just this: "Behold me then, me for him, life for life / I offer, on me let thine anger fall" (III.236–37). And on him the Father's "anger" will indeed fall, although, as so many Miltonists have remarked, this is not an event that Milton was willing to address directly (as distinct from through prophecy and symbol) after abandoning his early attempt in "The Passion." My own guess is that his unwillingness here represents a theological and ethical resistance to the very tradition of penal substitution theory that he so uncritically hands on in *DDC* I.16 and in *Paradise Lost* III. Ironically, in this case, tradition and custom blocked his critical powers, stifled his ethical imagination. Given his generalized hostility to tradition and custom, Milton would be the first to appreciate my suggestions here. And then he could acknowledge that Christian tradition actually includes resources which could free his critical powers from the alien encrustation of Calvinist theories of the atonement.

* * *

It seems appropriate to conclude this chapter by considering the way Milton's Calvinist model of atonement glides into his anti-Calvinist paradigm of election, predestination, and reprobation (GE or PG). Against the Calvinist dogma of *limited atonement*, Milton argues that Christ died for all, for the whole world, citing John 3:16–17 and John 6:15. Calvinists, as at the Synod of Dort, maintained that Christ only died for the elect few. Milton explicitly rejects this doctrine, ridiculing its supporting exegesis (I.16, 522–23). He refers to his earlier chapter on predestination (I.4) and reaffirms its paradigm of general election (I.16, 522–25). Yet once more he foregrounds Paul's affirmation that God wills all humans to be saved (1 Tim. 2:4; I.16, 522–27). Christ, Milton says, made satisfaction "for all [*pro omnibus*]," and he granted "sufficient grace" for the salvation of all humans, "sufficiently [*sufficienter*] and efficaciously [*efficaciter*]," at least according to God's electing will (522–25). By emphasizing "efficaciously," Milton stresses that the Calvinist qualification of their position by "hypothetical universalism" fails to save the dogma of limited atonement.[40] In Milton's view, God gives sufficient grace for those customarily called "reprobates" to find salvation (525). Against Augustinian and Calvinist traditions, he yet again affirms that when Paul wrote that God wills salvation for all humankind (*pro omnibus hominibus*) he meant just what he wrote: for all humankind, not just for a few from all classes of people (527; 525). Invoking Christ's words in Matthew 23:37 likening himself to a hen who had often willed to gather all her chickens under her wings but had been resisted by her offspring, Milton reminds his reader "how often did [Christ] wish . . . and you did not wish." Grace is resistible. Milton's hen, then, is Samuel Hoard's hen rather than the cruel hen imposed on Christ's analogy by the Calvinist William Twisse (discussed in chapter 3). The paradigm of GE is again referred to in the following chapter,

"On Renewal and also on Calling [*de Vocatione*]" (*DDC* I.17). Here, Milton asserts that even those who don't know Christ are called, including reprobates (I.17, 542, 544). The paradigm of GE (or PG) pervades the rest of *DDC*.

This commitment to general election carries over into *Paradise Lost*, despite the difference of genre and the difference of language. The position declared by Milton's God in Book III is the same as that elaborated and defended in *De Doctrina Christiana*. From "the pure Empyrian where he sits / High throned above all highth," God the Father addresses his Son and "all the Sanctities of Heaven" (III.56–64). Divine vindication for Milton's theology of election so elaborately articulated and defended in *DDC* follows (III.80–343). God seeks to help Milton in the task he announces at the beginning of *Paradise Lost*. There Milton prays for divine illumination so that he may "justify the ways of God to men" (I.22–26). This echoes a phrase in the chapter in *DDC* on the punishment of sin where Milton considers what is needed "to vindicate the justice of God [ad asserendam iustitiam Dei]" (I.12, 436–37). At the heart of his response is the affirmation of humanity's God-given freedom: freedom of judgment ("aliquid liberi arbitrii"), freedom to choose moral good or evil ("voluntatem hominis ad morale bonum vel malum") (*DDC* I.12, 436–37). If, however, God "bends man's will" and then rewards or punishes the outcome he himself has compelled, there will be "outcry against divine justice" (437). Nor, without the gift of human "power and choice," could God have been able "to enter into a covenant with us, nor would we have been able to fulfill it, let alone swear that we would fulfill it" (437). True enough. Not surprisingly, then, Milton makes the model of human freedom within the covenant central to his theological ethics in *DDC* and in *Paradise Lost*.[41]

In *Paradise Lost* God justifies himself as he considers the imminent catastrophe of the fall. He does so by asserting that he created angels and humans with all they needed "to have stood." In this creation, the identity of angels and humans included the gifts of original justice and freedom. God insists that those who "stood" did so freely and those who "failed" did so freely (III.93–102). The gifts of "will and reason" entailed active choice and practice, free from "necessity." Hence, fallen angels and humans cannot "justly" accuse God, nor have they any justification for inventing theologies that lament and excuse their fallen state as the product of "fate" or of predestination, "As if predestination overruled / Their will, disposed by absolute decree / Or high foreknowledge" (III.114–16). Here God unequivocally supports the work of Samuel Hoard considered in chapter 3: *Gods Love To Mankind Manifested, By Dis-Prooving his Absolute Decree for their Damnation* (1633). God also supports Milton's anti-Calvinist version of predestination and reprobation in *DDC*. Milton's God, like Milton himself, also opposes the Augustinian and Calvinist traditions of understanding divine foreknowledge (III.116–23). Indeed, God uses the language of the "decree" in a derisory way, making humans its agents rather than its objects: "they themselves decreed / Their own revolt, not I" (III.116–17). He repeats this striking mockery of the Calvinist lexicon by stating that not God but creatures "ordained their fall" (III.128). As Benjamin Myers has observed in *Milton's Theology of Freedom*, "the word 'ordained' was commonly used in post-Reformation predestinarian discourse; but in a striking appropriation of this term, the Father shifts its reference from a divine to a human context." God turns the divine decree of human salvation and damnation "to an eternal and unchangeable decree of *human* freedom."[42]

God's metaphysical declaration precedes Adam and Eve choosing to reject God. In this way, Milton shows how God's foreknowledge has no influence on the future contingent events of the fall. Neither here nor even in *DDC* does Milton practice the extraordinary logical and metaphysical subtlety of late medieval explorations of the relations between divine omnipotence and contingency, yet he inhabits the same field of inquiry as fourteenth-century theologians, such as Holcot, who developed the new paradigm of GE.[43] He also shares their commitments to both human freedom and divine freedom. As Myers and others have remarked, only the devils in *Paradise Lost* deny such freedom. The fallen angels propound a "Satanic Calvinism" and compose a pagan epic ruled by fate and tragedy.[44]

God, however, unfolds a clear defense of what Milton elsewhere called *Praedestinatio Generalis* (*DDC* I.4, 78), a version of general election. Myers calls God's teaching in *Paradise Lost*, "Universal Election" (74–81). Whether we call it GE or PG or Myers's UE, God unequivocally vindicates Milton's theology of election in *De Doctrina Christiana*:

Some I have chosen of peculiar grace
Elect above the rest; so is my will:
The rest shall hear me call, and oft be warned
Their sinful state, and to appease betimes
Th' incensed Deity, while offered grace
Invites; for I will clear their senses dark,
What may suffice, and soften stony hearts
To pray, repent, and bring obedience due.
To prayer, repentance, and obedience due,
Though but endeavored with sincere intent,
Mine ear shall not be slow, mine eye not shut.
And I will place within them as a guide
My umpire conscience, whom if they will hear,
Light after light well used they shall attain,
And to the end persisting, safe arrive.
This my long sufferance and my day of grace
They who neglect and scorn, shall never taste;
But hard be hardened, blind be blinded more,
That they may stumble on, and deeper fall;
And none but such from mercy I exclude.
(*PL* III.183–202)

These twenty lines are a compressed but lucid account of the treatment of election, predestination, and reprobation in *DDC*. God elects humanity to salvation. After the fall, such election means that he will offer sufficient grace to restore the lost powers of humans. He promises to accept their attempts to repent and obey the covenant as long as they are "sincere."[45] As in *DDC*, God gives all humans all the resources they need to keep the conditions of the covenant and "to the end persisting, safe arrive." This is Milton's anti-Calvinist version of perseverance. Some people, however, will resist divine grace and reject the covenant. As in *DDC*, grace is resistible. The consequence of sustaining such choices, without repentance, without attending to the voice of God's "umpire conscience," is habituation in sin. Those who pursue these practices will find their hearts "hardened." In the language of *DDC*, having reprobated God, such people will finally be reprobated. Thus, their final exclusion from divine mercy is the contingent consequence of their choices.

Some Miltonists seem to have trouble with the first two lines of this long quotation (i.e., III.183–84). As a result, some have imposed on these lines a thoroughly anti-Miltonic version of double predestination, while others have seen the lines hewing out a category for Milton himself in a display of Satanic pride.[46] Such interpretations seem more "peculiar" than the grace Milton is addressing. For here Milton merely reiterates one of his positions in *De Doctrina Christiana*, one actually shared by patristic, medieval, and Reformation Christianity alike: namely, that grace is not undifferentiated, not egalitarian. God, Milton argues, imparts "sufficient" grace to all (*omnibus*) but not "equal" grace to all (*DDC* I.4, 100–103). In medieval versions of GE, theologians might wonder about the hierarchical nature of God's gifts. Did some people have a special vocation "above the rest"? They thought about the Blessed Virgin Mary, about St. Paul. In his commentary on Lombard's *Sentences*, William of Ockham, for example, wondered whether the Blessed Virgin could, like others given the grace of election, choose to sin and lose eternal life. Or was she "ordered to eternal life by a special grace," one that prevented her from "putting any obstacle" of sin in the way of her vocation? Tentatively enough, Ockham thought that "the Blessed Virgin and certain others" were given what Milton's God calls "peculiar grace / Elect above the rest." This, said Ockham, "prevented them from sinning and losing eternal life."[47] I am not suggesting that Milton was reading Ockham's commentary on Lombard's *Sentences*. I am only indicating, for the final time in this book, that Milton's paradigm of GE (or PG or UE) had a longer and more complex history than Miltonists may recognize. In the contexts of late medieval Christianity, GE would suggest some different questions to its advocates than it would in seventeenth-century England. That much is obvious. But there are also discernible family resemblances—discernible, at least, within a diachronic inquiry.

✳ ✳ ✳

These seem apt reflections with which to conclude this book, for it has throughout attempted to develop a diachronic approach to an important cluster of Christian teachings. It has done so across different genres and different languages while seeking to read some complex texts with the kind of specificity they demand and surely deserve. It has also traversed the great divide between medieval and Reformation studies in contemporary universities, a divide that may make it harder for us to grasp the strange mixture of revolutionary transformation and often delayed, hidden continuities that characterize traditions across time. Some of my motivations for attempting such a study have been indicated in the preface and highlighted at various points in the book. I see no need to rehearse these again now, or any reason to offer a summary of arguments woven through the book. Any force these have will be embodied in the range of readings emerging from attention to particular texts. Instead of any kind of grand narrative or survey, this work has attempted to explore some of the ways in which Christian traditions unfold. Often resistant to assimilation to evolutionary and unilinear models of development, these unfoldings may well include the return of a past that had been defeated or forgotten except in some marginal or subordinate forms in the communities constituting the church in history. Such returns will take place in transformed circumstances and may well not be recognized as returnings. Here I recall some lines from T. S. Eliot's *Four Quartets*: "We had the experience but missed the meanings / And approach to the meaning restores the experience / In a different form."[48]

This might be one of the ways to reflect on the late medieval paradigm I have called general election. Anathema to theologians of the magisterial Reformation, hyper-Augustinian as they tended to be, it nevertheless reemerged within the reformation Church of England and was cultivated by John Milton, an avowed reviler of tradition, as *Praedestinatio Generalis*. Thus we may discern how, even in what may well be revolutionary changes, there will yet be unpredictable continuities. Likewise, those vocally hostile to tradition (often dismissed as mere "human traditions") are not through their espousal of innovations and iconoclasm freed from participation in tradition.[49] I have come to see this model of occlusion and reemergence, of proclaimed ruptures that contain unacknowledged continuities, not as anomalous, but as representative of the vital and meandering pathways of Christian tradition.

Appendix

Outline of the Story Langland Tells in the Final Version of *Piers Plow-man*, from Derek Pearsall's edition of *Piers Plowman: A New Annotated Edition of the C-text* (Exeter: University of Exeter Press, 2010), 4–6

The C version of the poem begins with a Prologue, the dreamer's vision of the world in its corrupted state as a 'field full of folk,' dominated by self-seeking. A 'Westminster interlude' shows the higher levels of church and state subjected to the same turbulent misrule. In Passus I, Holy Church explains the dreamer's vision to him, shows him how a right use of worldly goods would be in accord with God's Law, and answers his urgent entreaty, How may I save my soul? (I.80), which in a sense initiates the whole movement of the poem, with a preliminary outline of the doctrine of Charity. But the dreamer wishes to understand more of the ways of the world, and is presented in Passus II–IV with the vision of Meed the Maid, a brilliant allegorical portrayal of the corruption of every estate and activity of society through the influence of perverted ideas of reward and of money. The king (an ideal king) wins a measure of control over Meed with the help of Conscience and Reason, whom he takes as his chief advisers, and a golden age, it seems is about to begin. But administrative reform alone cannot bring this about: men's hearts must be purged of sin so that they may be reformed inwardly. After offering his own 'confession', therefore, the dreamer shows us Reason calling on the folk to repent and to seek Truth (V). The confessions of the Seven Deadly Sins follow (VI–VII), wound up by the prayer of Repentance for general forgiveness. The people rush forth in high enthusiasm to seek for Truth, but find no way until they meet Piers Plowman, who tells them where Truth may be found (in obedience to God's Law) and promises to lead them there when he has finished his ploughing (i.e. the well-organized Christian community must be based on a well-organized economy). All the folk, of all estates, are to help him. But not everyone works with a will: wasters and layabouts refuse to do their share and Piers has to call in Hunger to force them to work, an admission of defeat, since outward coercion is no substitute for inward and voluntary reformation. The passus (VIII) ends with Piers's programme of reform in some disarray, but he receives in the next (IX) a pardon from Truth granted to all those who help him: its terms as they apply to all estates of society are related in detail, but it is not in the end a satisfactory answer to the quest for Truth. It promises salvation for those who do well but does not explain what doing well consists of. Piers Plowman disappears at this point, and the dreamer, pondering on his dream and on dreams in general, takes up the search for Dowel.

At this point the poem makes a new beginning, as if to signal the movement from the outer to the inner, from the outward reform of society to the inward reform of the individual. The dreamer's search for Dowel is first within himself (X), for the answers provided by his own intellectual faculties (Thought, Wit). These answers are not fallacious, but they are partial, and as he goes on to meet a series of personifications of learning (Study, Clergy, Scripture) the dreamer, initially stubborn and complacent, becomes increasingly bewildered (XI). The answers he receives concerning Dowel and salvation are conflicting and confusing, and he falls into a stupor of worldliness, a fast subservience to Fortune, in which his life is dreamed away. The dreamer temporarily loses his identity, his place being taken by Rechelesnesse, who solaces the gnawing of doubt with his easy answers, crude simplifications and bold disparagement of what he does not understand. Witnesses of Truth, like Trajan and Leaute, are glimpsed briefly before being submerged in the prevailing murk, and hints of understanding on the part of Rechelesnesse, as of the virtue of poverty, are swallowed in presumption and vociferous anti-clericalism. This is without doubt the most difficult and in many ways the most profound part of the poem (XII). The dreamer resumes his identity only to make a grotesque misinterpretation of the vision of Middle-Earth (XIII) that he is granted, giving continued evidence of his unredeemed pride and presumption. At last he meets Imaginatyf, the sum of all the intellect can do. Imaginatyf provides interim answers to his questions about salvation and learning as they relate to the life of Dowel, but also, more importantly, embodies the first full and explicit recognition that Dowel consists precisely in not asking the kinds of question he has been asking, but in preparing the self, through humility and patience and voluntary submission of the will to the will of God, for the admission of Charity (XIV).

In the next passus, the dreamer is given an opportunity to exercise this active virtue of patience when he is invited to the feast with the learned and gluttonous friar (XV); for the first time speculation gives way to action, and talking about doing well gives way to doing well. After a momentary intervention by Piers Plowman, an epiphany of Truth and promise of grace for the dreamer, Patience takes on the role of guide and instructs the dreamer and Activa Vita (another *alter ego* for the dreamer, through whom something of the life of common humanity is brought into the search for truth) in the true nature of patient poverty and the voluntary acceptance of God's will (XV–XVI). The achievement of this understanding of God's will is for man true freedom, and the next guide is appropriately Liberum Arbitrium (Free Will), the highest faculty of man as he lives in concord with God. Liberum Arbitrium offers the fullest understanding of true Charity that is accessible to man in his human state, unaided by grace or revelation, and shows the relation of the clergy and the Church to this true Charity (XVI–XVII). He also shows, in the vision of the Tree of Charity (XVIII), how man's growth towards charity is thwarted by the devil's work. Man stands in need of an act of divine grace, and the dreamer glimpses what form this will take in a brief account of the life of Christ. But before this vision of grace can be fully granted, Langland must show how the ascent of the soul to the full life of Charity in the reception of Christ re-enacts and embodies the processes of Christian history. So we return to Abraham (Faith) and Moses (Hope) and see how their partial understanding under the Old Law, of divine truth and specifically of the Trinity is to be crowned in the New Law of mercy and love as it is expounded (XIX) by the Good Samaritan (Charity), a figure who subsequently merges in Piers Plowman and into Christ.

The world and the dreamer's soul are now prepared for the great act of divine intervention, the fulfillment of the promise of redemption, and Passus XX is devoted to an account of the Crucifixion and Harrowing of Hell. From this high climax the poem returns to a vision of the establishment of Christ's Church on earth through the gift of grace; the dreamer, suffused with the glory of revelation, must still doggedly pursue the truth and be shown how the machinery of redemption is to operate, and how it has operated in the centuries of Christian history since the Redemption (XXI). The descent to the world of fourteenth-century England is swift, and the poem ends (XXII) with the Church of Unity besieged by the forces of Antichrist, the deadly sins, and infiltrated by the subtler temptations of the friars. The end of the poem is a resumption of the search for the true Christian life, as it is embodied in Piers Plowman.

NOTES

PREFACE

1. This role of the Middle Ages, together with the effects of institutionally fostered ignorance across the divide between medieval and early modern, has preoccupied me for many years: David Aers, "A Whisper in the Ear of Early Modernists," in *Culture and History, 1350–1600: Essays on English Communities, Identities, and Writing*, ed. David Aers, 177–202 (Hemel Hempstead: Harvester Wheatsheaf, 1992). The most learned, aspiring, and pertinacious advocate for work that is committed to going across received divisions between medieval and early modern cultures, often subjecting the latter to a sharply critical analysis enabled by years of studying medieval culture, is James Simpson. Most relevant to the present work are four books that he published over the past seventeen years: *The Oxford English Literary History*, vol. 2, *1350–1547: Reform and Cultural Revolution* (Oxford: Oxford University Press, 2002); *Burning to Read: English Fundamentalism and Its Reformation Opponents* (Cambridge, MA: Harvard University Press, 2007); *Under the Hammer: Iconoclasm in the Anglo-American Tradition* (Oxford: Oxford University Press, 2010); and *Permanent Revolution: The Reformation and the Illiberal Roots of Liberalism* (Cambridge, MA: Harvard University Press, 2019). I received a copy of *Permanent Revolution* after I had already completed the present work, and Harvard University placed a tiny part of my admiring response on the cover of that book. When I have been most struck by overlaps in our materials I have added notes drawing attention to *Permanent Revolution*, but there are substantial continuities between our concerns despite differences in the approach to theology. Anyone who reads the present book should certainly read *Permanent Revolution*. Congenial to Simpson's projects but in a different mode is Sarah Beckwith's *Signifying God: Social Relation and Symbolic Act in the York Corpus Christi Plays* (Chicago: University of Chicago Press, 2001). For examples of grand narratives of modernity in which the Middle Ages play a significant part, see Michael A. Gillespie, *The Theological Origins of Modernity* (Chicago: University of Chicago Press, 2008); Thomas Pfau, *Minding the Modern: Human Agency,*

Intellectual Traditions, and Responsible Knowledge (Notre Dame, IN: University of Notre Dame Press, 2013). The writer whose modes of inquiry and vision have most influenced what I try to do remains Alasdair MacIntyre. The epigraphs to this preface are drawn from his *After Virtue: A Study in Moral Theory*, 3rd ed. (Notre Dame, IN: University of Notre Dame Press, 2007), 208; and *Ethics in the Conflicts of Modernity: An Essay on Desire, Practical Reasoning and Narrative* (Cambridge: Cambridge University Press, 2017), 76–77. Besides these works, see especially MacIntyre's *Three Rival Versions of Moral Enquiry: Encyclopaedia, Genealogy and Tradition* (London: Duckworth, 1990); *Whose Justice? Which Rationality?* (London: Duckworth, 1988); *God, Philosophy, Universities: A Selective History of the Catholic Philosophical Tradition* (London: Rowman and Littlefield, 2009). I still also return to the first book I read by MacIntyre when I was an undergraduate: *A Short History of Ethics: A History of Moral Philosophy from the Homeric Age to the Twentieth Century* (London: Routledge, 1966).

2. MacIntyre, *After Virtue*, 222.

3. See St. Thomas's exposition of the Pater Noster in his *Opuscula Theologica*, ed. R. A. Verardo, R. M. Spiazzi, and M. Calcaterra (Rome: Marietti, 1954), vol. 2, 228 (para. 1066): "ex modo loquendi datur nobis doctrina."

4. Ibid., 264; emphasis in original.

5. The version of Langland's poem I refer to here is *Piers Plowman: A New Annotated Edition of the C-text*, ed. Derek Pearsall (Exeter: University of Exeter Press, 2010). For the editions of *Piers Plowman* I use throughout this book, consult the first note to chapter 1.

CHAPTER ONE. "Predestinaet" or "Prescit"

1. Unless otherwise stated, all quotations of *Piers Plowman* are from *Piers Plowman: A New Annotated Edition of the C-text*, ed. Derek Pearsall (Exeter: Exeter University Press, 2008). I modernize *u/v*. English translations are mainly from George Economou's *William Langland's "Piers Plowman": The C Version* (Philadelphia: University of Pennsylvania Press, 1996). I have made constant use of the edition of the C version in *Piers Plowman: The C Version; Will's Vision of Piers Plowman, Do-Well, Do-Better, and Do-Best*, ed. George Russell and George Kane (London: Athlone, 1997). For the second version of the poem, I have used *Piers Plowman: The B Version*, rev. ed., ed. George Kane and E. Talbot Donaldson (London: Athlone, 1988). I have also constantly consulted the great nineteenth-century edition of all three versions, *The Vision of William concerning Piers the Plowman, in Three Parallel Texts: Together with Richard the Redeles*, 2 vols., ed. Walter W. Skeat (1886; repr. Oxford: Oxford University Press, 1968). I have also consulted the edition by A. V. C. Schmidt, *Piers Plow-*

man: A Parallel-Text Edition of the A, B, C and Z Versions, 2 vols. (Kalamazoo: Medieval Institute Publications, 2008). On dating the C version, I am persuaded by W. W. Skeat's argument for a date of "about 1393," and more recently by Ralph Hanna: "Langland completed the C version around 1390." See Skeat's edition, vol. 1, xv; Hanna, *Introducing English Medieval Book History: Manuscripts, Their Production, and Their Reading* (Liverpool: Liverpool University Press, 2013), 156. In his edition, Derek Pearsall similarly writes that the C version was not finished until after 1388 (*Piers Plowman*, 1). See, too, Ralph Hanna, *William Langland* (Aldershot: Variorum, 1993). On authorship debates: George Kane, *Piers Plowman: The Evidence for Authorship* (London: Athlone, 1965).

2. Scriptural quotations and references in chapters 1 and 2 are from the Vulgate: *Biblia Sacra iuxta Vulgatem Clementinam: Nova Editio*, 4th ed., ed. Alberto Colunga and Laurentio Turrado (Matriti: Biblioteca de Autores Cristianos, 1965); I also make use of the Douay Rheims translation, *The Holy Bible*, rev. Richard Challoner (Rockford, IL: Tan Books, 1989).

3. In this book, I mostly quote the parallel Latin-English text of the *Summa Theologiae*, trans. Laurence Shapcote, ed. John Mortensen and Enrique Alarcón, from the Leonine Edition (Lander, WY: Aquinas Institute, 2012). I have also used the Blackfriars parallel text in 61 volumes (London: Blackfriars 1964–81). I give references in my text to Part, Question, Article, and part of the article: so here I.1.10, resp.

4. Heiko Oberman has written a very helpful account of the relations between scripture, tradition, and church in late medieval theology: *The Harvest of Medieval Theology* (Cambridge, MA: Harvard University Press, 1963), 365–412.

5. For work as representative as it was influential, see William Whitaker, *A Disputation on Holy Scripture, Against the Papists* (Cambridge: Cambridge University Press, 1849). For an analysis as lively as it is relevant to the present book, see James Simpson, *Burning to Read: English Fundamentalism and Its Reformation Opponents* (Cambridge, MA: Harvard University Press, 2007), esp. ch. 4, "The Literal Sense and Predestination."

6. I refer to *Summa Theologiae* II–II.5.3, ad 3; on Langland's enigmatic ecclesiology in Passus XXI–XXII, see David Aers, *Beyond Reformation? An Essay on William Langland's "Piers Plowman" at the End of Constantinian Christianity* (Notre Dame, IN: University of Notre Dame Press, 2015), 91–93, 126–27, 140–41, 210–11.

7. For important discussions of Chaucer's Wife of Bath, gender, and hermeneutics, see Carolyn Dinshaw, *Chaucer's Sexual Poetics* (Madison: University of Wisconsin Press, 1989), ch. 4; Lee Patterson, *Chaucer and the Subject of History* (Madison: University of Wisconsin Press, 1991), ch. 6. For Langland, see

esp. Elizabeth Fowler, *Literary Character: The Human Figure in Early English Writing* (Ithaca, NY: Cornell University Press, 2003), ch. 2.

8. Not, at least, in the final version of the poem. The B version does give many reasons! See Pearsall's note to C XI.160.

9. Chaucer, "General Prologue," *Canterbury Tales*, I.187. All quotations of Chaucer are from *The Wadsworth Chaucer* [formerly *The Riverside Chaucer*], 3rd ed., ed. Larry Benson (Boston: Wadsworth, 1987). I refer to fragment and line number in my citations of the *Canterbury Tales*.

10. Augustine, *Confessions*, trans. Henry Chadwick (Oxford: Oxford University Press, 1991), VII.10.16. For the Latin text with a fine commentary, I use *Confessions*, ed. James J. O'Donnell, 3 vols. (Oxford: Clarendon Press, 1992); here the illuminating commentary is in III, 438–39. References to *Confessions* henceforth are given in my text, by book, section, and paragraph numbers. For a particularly helpful commentary on this part of *Piers Plowman*, see Joseph Wittig, "*Piers Plowman* B, Passus IX–XII: Elements in the Design of the Inward Journey," *Traditio* 28 (1972): 211–80.

11. There is an immense literature on the theology of grace and conversion in Augustine. For my own use of what I have found most helpful in this, see David Aers, *Salvation and Sin: Augustine, Langland, and Fourteenth-Century Theology* (Notre Dame, IN: University of Notre Dame Press, 2009), ch. 1. For self-knowledge and the Trinitarian image of God in the human person, see *De Trinitate* XV.6.9–9.16, in *The Trinity*, trans. Stephen McKenna (Washington, DC: Catholic University of America Press, 1988).

12. See Wittig, "*Piers Plowman*," 232–36, 245–47.

13. The best introduction to the theology of medieval exegesis, accompanied by massive exemplification of the practice, remains Henri de Lubac, *Exégèse médiévale: Les quatre sens de l'Écriture*, 4 vols. (Paris: Aubier, 1959–64).

14. The exegetes I refer to here on Luke 15:11–32 and the specific editions I have consulted are as follows: Nicholas of Gorran, *In Quatuor Evangelia* (Cologne, 1537), Cambridge University Library (UL), shelfmark C.9.11, 415r–418r; Nicholas of Lyra, *Glossa Ordinaria*, *Biblia Sacra cum Glossa Ordinaria* (Antwerp, 1634), Cambridge UL, shelfmark 1.20.16, vol. 5, 893–904; Denis the Carthusian, *In Quatuor Evangelistas Enarrationes* (Paris, 1552), Cambridge UL, shelfmark F*.8.30(B), 203r–207r.

15. On Elde, see Aers, *Beyond Reformation*, 108–12.

16. See the commentaries on Luke 15:11–32 by Nicholas of Gorran, Nicholas of Lyra, and Denis the Carthusian cited above, n. 14.

17. Thomas Aquinas, *Catena Aurea: Commentary on the Four Gospels Collected out of the Works of the Fathers*, 4 vols., trans. and ed. John Henry Newman (London: Saint Austin Press, 1999), vol. 3, 532.

18. *Piers Plowman* C.XIX.

19. Augustine, *The City of God against the Pagans*, trans. R.W. Dyson (Cambridge: Cambridge University Press, 1998), XI.28.

20. Nicholas of Lyra, *Glossa Ordinaria*, 898.

21. Nicholas of Gorran, *In Quatuor Evangelia*, 416v.

22. Denis the Carthusian, *In Quatuor Evangelistas*, 205ᵛ.

23. Ibid. This exemplifies what Oberman analyzes in his *Harvest of Theology* and in an earlier essay, "*Facientibus quod in se est Deus non denegat Gratiam*: Robert Holcot, O.P. and the Beginnings of Luther's Theology," *Harvard Theological Review* 55, no. 4 (1962): 317–42.

24. Augustine, *City of God*, XI.2.

25. For my attempt to show this, see *Beyond Reformation*.

26. On Rechelesnesse, see Pearsall's note to XI.193.

27. For the relevant passages in Skeat: A XI.250–84; B X.372–441; C XII.204–73a; in Schmidt: A XI.258–92; B X.371–440; C XI.204–75a.

28. On "wanhope" and sloth, see Siegfried Wenzel, *The Sin of Sloth: Acedia in Medieval Thought and Literature* (Chapel Hill: University of North Carolina Press, 1960); Nicholas Watson, "Despair," in *Cultural Reformations: Medieval and Renaissance in Literary History*, ed. James Simpson and Brian Cummings (Oxford: Oxford University Press, 2010), 342–60.

29. Pamela Gradon, "Langland and the Ideology of Dissent," *Proceedings of the British Academy* 66 (1980): 179–208, at 201.

30. Greta Hort, *Piers Plowman and Contemporary Religious Thought* (London: SPCK, 1938), 98, 116. See ch. 5 on predestination.

31. James Simpson, *"Piers Plowman": An Introduction*, 2nd ed. (Exeter: Exeter University Press, 2007); similarly, Watson, "Despair," 344, 354–55.

32. An excellent introduction to the training of theologians and their subject matter is W.J. Courtenay, *Schools and Scholars in Fourteenth-Century England* (Princeton, NJ: Princeton University Press, 1987). Also extremely informative on this topic is J.L. Catto and Ralph Evans, eds., *The History of the University of Oxford*, vol. 2, *Late Medieval Oxford* (Oxford: Clarendon Press, 1992), see pts. 1 and 3.

33. For a lucid and rich account of this historiography combined with a very distinctive exploration of prewar preaching, see Arnold Hunt, *The Art of Hearing: English Preachers and Their Audiences 1590–1640* (Cambridge: Cambridge University Press, 2010).

34. For Wyclif preaching around this topic, see the following examples from his *Sermones*, ed. J. Loserth, 4 vols. (London: Trübner, 1887–90). From vol. 1, see nos. 34 (second Sunday after Trinity, Matthew 22, the wedding feast); 52 (twentieth Sunday after Trinity, Luke 19:41, Christ weeps over Jerusalem);

54 (twenty-second Sunday after Trinity, Matthew 18, parable of the talents). On Robert Rypon, see Siegfried Wenzel, *Latin Sermons from Later Medieval Collections* (Cambridge: Cambridge University Press, 2005), ch. 10. I am very grateful to Siegfried Wenzel for sending me a transcript of Rypon's sermon on predestination, British Library, MS Harley 4894, ff. 9–12.

35. Anne Hudson and Pamela Gradon observe that the topic of "pre-destination and free will" is frequently treated in *English Wycliffite Sermons*, 5 vols. (Oxford: Oxford University Press, 1983–96), here vol. 4, 57. For examples of English texts that diminish Wyclif's attention to predestination, see the following in *English Wycliffite Sermons*: nos. 2 (second Sunday after Trinity); 10 (tenth Sunday after Trinity); 20 (twentieth Sunday after Trinity); 37 (Septuagesima Sunday); 48 (second Sunday after Easter). Wyclif writes a section on predestination in his *Trialogus*, II.14. Later, in IV.24, he claims that only the *predestinate* are contrite for sins in which the *foreknown* lack contrition: *Trialogus cum supplemento tralogi*, ed. G. V. Lechler (Oxford: Clarendon Press, 1869).

36. Aquinas treats the book of life after predestination, and I analyze this in chapter 2. For the Question on predestination, I also use vol. 5 of the Blackfriars *ST* edited by Thomas Gilby, as well as the Aquinas Institute edition.

37. Pearsall's note to XI.207a; Schmidt, note to XI.209a (vol. 2, 594). Contrast Hort, *Piers Plowman*, 103.

38. Pearsall, note to XI.218. Consult John Marenbom, *Pagans and Philosophers: The Problem of Paganism from Augustine to Leibniz* (Princeton, NJ: Princeton University Press, 2015), chs. 9–11.

39. There is an interesting discussion of this scene in French writing of the thirteenth century in Claire M. Waters, *Translating "Clergie": Status, Education and Salvation in Thirteenth-Century Vernacular Texts* (Philadelphia: University of Pennsylvania Press, 2016), 97–105.

40. I quote from *The Predestination of the Saints*, trans. Roland J. Teske, in *Answer to the Pelagians IV*, The Works of Saint Augustine: A Translation for the 21st Century [hereafter cited as WSA], pt. 1, vol. 26 (Hyde Park, NY: New City Press, 1999).

41. For Langland and non-Christians, see Cindy L. Vitto, *The Virtuous Pagan in Middle English Literature* (Philadelphia: American Philosophical Society, 1989), sec. 5; Frank Grady, *Representing Righteous Heathens in Late Medieval England* (New York: Palgrave Macmillan, 2005), esp. 20–40; Nicolette Zeeman, *Piers Plowman and the Medieval Discourse of Desire* (Cambridge: Cambridge University Press, 2006), 228–34; Marenbom, *Pagans and Philosophers*.

42. I refer to Iris Murdoch, *The Sovereignty of Good* (1970; repr. London: Routledge, 2001), 33.

43. Ibid., 33, 39.

44. Karl Barth, "The Vocation of Man," in *The Doctrine of Reconciliation*, in *The Church Dogmatics*, 4 pts. in 12 vols., trans. Geoffrey W. Bromiley (Edinburgh: T&T Clark, 1962), vol. 4, pt. 3.2, 485.

45. On Matthew 22:1–14, I follow and summarize the exegetes cited above: Nicholas of Lyra (with *Glossa Ordinaria*), *Biblia Sacra*, vol. 5, cols. 363–68; Nicholas of Gorran, *Commentaria*, 110v–112r; also, Hugh of St. Cher, *Opera Omnia* (Venice, 1600), vol. 6, 69v–70v; Aquinas, *Catena*, I.739–48. For Augustine and early medieval exegesis, see D. W. Robertson and B. F. Huppé, *Piers Plowman and Scriptural Tradition* (Princeton, NJ: Princeton University Press, 1951), 134–35.

46. See above for references to Aquinas, Nicholas of Gorran, and Nicholas of Lyra. For Denis the Carthusian, *In Quatuor Evangelistas Enarrationes*, 70r–v. For a late medieval sermon on the text, see W. O. Ross, ed., *Middle English Sermons*, EETS 209 (London: Oxford University Press, 1940), 17–19.

47. Simpson, *"Piers Plowman": An Introduction*, 104.

48. See Augustine's exposition on Psalm 61.6 in *Expositions of the Psalms*, trans. Maria Boulding, in WSA, pt. 3, vol. 17, 207–8. See, too, the reading of Matthew 22:10–14 in Augustine's Sermon 90, secs. 4–9, in WSA, pt. 3, vol. 3, at 449–55.

49. "Sola est autem adversus omnes errores via munitissima ut idea ipse sit Deus et homo; quo itur Deus, qua itur homo." *De civitate Dei*, ed. B. Dombart and A. Kalb, 2 vols. (Stuttgart: Teubner, 1993), XI.1 at 463. For English translation, consult Dyson.

50. For an attempt to address the latter, see my part of the introduction to the special issue edited by David Aers and Russ Leo in *JMEMS* 46, no. 3 (2016): 455–83. Managing to offer attention to particularities despite the scale of the story are Eamon Duffy, *The Stripping of the Altars: Traditional Religion in England, 1400–1580*, 2nd ed. (New Haven, CT: Yale University Press, 2005); Simpson, *Reform and Cultural Revolution*; Pfau, *Minding the Modern*.

51. Gradon, "Langland and the Ideology of Dissent," 201; Simpson, *"Piers Plowman": An Introduction*, 164; Zeeman, *Piers Plowman*, 220.

52. The intriguing comparison of Chaucer and Langland is in Simpson, *"Piers Plowman": An Introduction*, 104–5. For Simpson's discussion of Langland's treatment of the many and the few in Jesus's parable of the marriage in Matthew 22, see his essay "Desire and the Scriptural Text: Will as Reader in *Piers Plowman*," in *Criticism and Dissent in the Middle Ages*, ed. Rita Copeland

(Cambridge: Cambridge University Press, 1996), 215–43. On Chaucer, predestination, and the Reformation, see James Simpson, "Not Yet: Chaucer and Anagogy," *Studies in the Age of Chaucer* 37 (2015): 31–54, esp. 43–47.

53. Simpson, *"Piers Plowman": An Introduction*, 104; see Chaucer, *Nun's Priest's Tale, Canterbury Tales* VII.3234–50. For an example of the habitual way intellectual historians use this passage, see Chris Schabel, *Theology at Paris, 1316–1345: Peter Auriol and the Problem of Divine Foreknowledge and Future Contingents* (Aldershot: Ashgate, 2000), 257. As usual, no interest is shown in the contexts and modes of writing.

54. Most recently, Peter Travis, *Disseminal Chaucer: Rereading the Nun's Priest's Tale* (Notre Dame, IN: University of Notre Dame Press, 2010). This book has no interest in theology, but it does offer a useful anthology of the kind of "altercacioun" in modern "scole," or at least in English departments housed there, ca. 1980–2010.

55. See esp. chs. 4–6 and 8 of Hester Gelber, *It Could Have Been Otherwise: Contingency and Necessity in Dominican Theology at Oxford, 1300–1350* (Leiden: Brill, 2004).

56. Simpson, *"Piers Plowman": An Introduction*, 104. I use the edition of *Troilus and Criseyde* in the Wadsworth (Riverside) edition of Chaucer. Chaucer describes his great work as a "tragedye" at V.1784. On the complexity of this term in medieval cultures, see H. A. Kelly, *Chaucerian Tragedy* (Cambridge: Brewer, 1997).

57. Simpson, *"Piers Plowman": An Introduction*, 105.

58. For Chaucer's political life and experience, the most helpful introductions are Derek Pearsall's *The Life of Geoffrey Chaucer* (Oxford: Blackwell, 1992), here esp. chs. 4 and 5; and Paul Strohm, *Social Chaucer* (Cambridge, MA: Harvard University Press, 1989).

59. I attempted to describe this in *Beyond Reformation*.

60. On Criseyde in this context, see David Aers, *Chaucer, Langland and the Creative Imagination* (London: Routledge, 1980), ch. 5.

61. See especially Kelly, *Chaucerian Tragedy*, as well as his *Ideas and Forms of Tragedy from Aristotle to the Middle Ages* (Cambridge: Cambridge University Press, 2005).

62. See *ST* I–II.94.4, resp. (citing Caesar, *De bello Gallico*); with *ST* I–II.94.6, resp.; I–II.96.4, resp.; I–II.99.2, ad 2.

63. For examples of such conversions, see I.610–952; I.1079–86; II.897–903.

64. For Langland's much-discussed pagan emperor, *Piers Plowman* XII.74–88. I discuss this figure and cite much relevant literature on Trajan in *Salvation and Sin*, 119–30 and notes. Most helpful I have found Gordon What-

ley, "The Uses of Hagiography: The Legend of Pope Gregory and the Emperor Trajan in the Middle Ages," *Viator* 15 (1984): 25–63; and Alastair Minnis, "Looking for a Sign: The Quest for Nominalism in Chaucer and Langland," in *Essays in Ricardian Literature*, ed. A. J. Minnis and Charlotte Morse (Oxford: Clarendon Press, 1997), ch. 7.

65. See *Sentences*, chs. 38–41. I use Peter Lombard, *The Sentences: Book I*, trans. Giulio Silano (Toronto: Pontifical Institute of Medieval Studies, 2007). For a fine introduction to Peter Lombard and his contexts, see Marcia Colish, *Peter Lombard*, 2 vols. (Leiden: Brill, 1994).

66. I refer to Aquinas's *Catena Aurea*, vol. 4, 273; and to Augustine, *Homilies on the Gospel of John*, ed. Philip Schaff (Edinburgh: Clark, 1986), xxxii (193).

67. For disputed interpretations here, see Pearsall's note to XII.59a.

68. For the contemporary *laicus litteratus*, see Anne Hudson, "*Laicus Litteratus*: The Paradox of Lollardy," in *Heresy and Literature 1100–1530*, ed. Peter Biller and Anne Hudson (Cambridge: Cambridge University Press, 1994), 222–36.

69. See Aers, *Beyond Reformation*.

70. For an introduction to this conflicting literature, see Pearsall's annotations to IX.3, IX.5, IX.284, and IX.290; and his Introduction, 37–38; see also Ralph Hanna, *The Penn Commentary on Piers Plowman*, 2 vols. (Philadelphia: University of Pennsylvania Press, 2017), vol. 2, 327–48.

71. Langland has the speaker quote from Peter's first epistle, "quasi modo geniti" (XII.111; 1 Peter 2:2), used in the liturgy on the first Sunday after Easter; see Skeat's note to C XIII.110 (vol. 2, 170), a note followed by all later commentators. There is considerable doubt about who speaks these lines; see Pearsall's note to XII.89.

72. For an instructive contrast, see Aquinas's account of the new covenant and Christian liberty in *ST* I–II.106 and 108. For Ockham's rather different account of evangelical liberty, see William of Ockham, *On the Power of Emperors and Popes*, ed. and trans. Annabel S. Brett (Bristol: Thoemmes Press, 1998), ch. 9; with this, see Arthur McGrade, *The Political Thought of William of Ockham* (Cambridge: Cambridge University Press, 2002), 140–49; and Takashi Shogimen, *Ockham and Political Discourse in the Late Middle Ages* (Cambridge: Cambridge University Press, 2007), ch. 6.

73. I quote from *ST* I–II.108.4, resp. See with this, I–II.106.1, resp. The New Law is the law of perfection, the law of charity: I–II.107.1, resp., and 107.1, ad 2, ad 3; and I–II.108.1, sed contra and resp.

74. Augustine, *The Predestination of the Saints*, 11.21.

75. On Piers Plowman and "kynde," see esp. Mary Clemente Davlin, *A Game of Heuene: Word Play and the Meaning of Piers Plowman* (Cambridge: Brewer, 1989), 105–6; Rebecca Davis, *Piers Plowman and the Book of Nature* (Oxford: Oxford University Press, 2016).

76. See XII.75–88.

77. See Pearsall, "Introduction," 38.

78. See Aers, *Salvation and Sin*, 122–31.

79. Wittig, *Piers Plowman*, 252 n. 135; Whatley, "The Uses of Hagiography," n. 64.

80. In my view, the best starting place for thinking about the meanings of *liberum arbitrium* and its relations with *voluntas* is *ST* I.83, with I.82.

81. For a fine example of medieval reading of Canticles 2:3, see St. Bernard's homily, Sermon 48 in Bernard of Clairvaux, *On the Song of Songs*, trans. Killian Walsh and Irene Edmonds (Kalamazoo, MI: Cistercian Publications, 1979), vol. 3, sermon 48.2, 3–5, and 48.3, 6–7.

82. On the exegetical traditions on which Langland draws, see esp. Ben Smith, *Traditional Imagery of Charity in Piers Plowman* (The Hague: Mouton, 1966), ch. 4; Robertson and Huppé, *Piers Plowman*, 204–8; Aers, *Salvation and Sin*, 88–101.

83. Pearsall's note on XX.114.

84. There is a potentially fascinating comparison to be made between Wille's descent into to hell and Dante's *Inferno* 1–3.

85. I quote Julian of Norwich from *Book of Showings to the Anchoress Julian of Norwich*, 2 vols., ed. James Walsh and Edmund Colledge (Toronto: Toronto Pontifical Institute, 1978); here the Long Text, chap. 31 (Revelation 13) at 418. I modernize *u* to *v* and *þ* to *th*. There is an annotated edition by Nicholas Watson and Jacqueline Jenkins, *The Writings of Julian of Norwich* (University Park: Pennsylvania State University Press, 2006).

86. On enigma in *Piers Plowman*, consult Curtis Gruenler, *Piers Plowman and the Poetics of Enigma: Riddles, Rhetoric, and Theology* (Notre Dame, IN: University of Notre Dame Press, 2017), esp. chs. 6 and 7.

87. See XX.417–19, 435–42a. On the dense wordplay here and its theological significance, see Davlin, *Game of Heuene*, 105–6; Nicholas Watson, "Visions of Inclusion: Universal Salvation and Vernacular Theology in Pre-Reformation England," *JMEMS* 27, no. 2 (1997): 145–87, at 157–60.

88. So much so that some readers cannot believe that Christ and Langland mean what they say; for example, Schmidt, *Piers Plowman*, vol. 2, 699. Contrast Watson, "Visions."

89. See Pearsall, notes to XX.430 and 440 with Watson; Hort, *Piers Plowman*, 125–26; Gruenler, *Piers Plowman and the Poetics of Enigma*, 355–57.

90. See the summary by J. N. D. Kelly, *Early Christian Doctrines*, rev. ed. (Peabody, MA: Prince Press, [1960] 2004), 472, 474, 483–85. For Augustine's unequivocal judgment, *City of God* XX.22 with XXI.9–10. For examples of scriptural encouragement, see Robert W. Jenson, *Systematic Theology*, 2 vols. (New York: Oxford University Press, 1999), vol. 2, 360–65.

91. Not to be confused with the tortures of purgatory, themselves dreadful enough. See Duffy, *Stripping of the Altars*, ch. 10.

92. Kelly, *Early Christian Doctrines*, 474, 483–84.

93. Pearsall, note to XX.440.

94. See Gruenler, *Piers Plowman and the Poetics of Enigma*.

95. See George Hunsinger's notes on "Universal Salvation: The Minority Report," in *Disruptive Grace: Studies in the Theology of Karl Barth* (Grand Rapids, MI: Eerdmans, 2000), 234–39.

96. Robert Bolton, *The Last Conflicts and Death of Mr. Thomas Peacock Batchelour of Divinity, and fellow of Brasen-nose Colledge in Oxford* (London, 1646); on this, see Leif Dixon, *Practical Predestinarians in England c. 1590–1640* (Farnham: Ashgate, 2014), 345–49.

97. Ludwig Wittgenstein, *Culture and Value*, ed. G. H. von Wright, trans. Peter Winch (Oxford: Blackwell, 1994), 39e.

98. I quote from Karl Barth, *Church Dogmatics*, vol. 2, pt. 2, 24.

99. Here I refer to XXII.51–75, 1212–28, 199–213, 380–86. I have discussed Passus XXII in *Beyond Reformation*, 110–14, 125–28, 151–60, 171–72.

CHAPTER TWO. Wille Returns "to scole"

1. For an unequivocal account of the innovations in the Reformation here, see Simpson, *Burning to Read*, chs. 4 and 5. See, too, the sweeping narrative so forcefully told in Simpson's *Reform and Cultural Revolution* and in a grippingly compressed and particularized way in the later study, *Under the Hammer*. These themes are followed through in their seventeenth-century lives in Simpson's recent study, *Permanent Revolution*. For the editions of *Piers Plowman* used in the present book, see ch. 1, n. 1.

2. A helpful introduction to this aspect of Augustine's theology is Gerald Bonner, *Freedom and Necessity: St. Augustine's Teaching on Divine and Human Freedom* (Washington, DC: Catholic University of America Press, 2007), esp. Introd., ch. 1, and pp. 130–32.

3. Marilyn McCord Adams, *William of Ockham*, 2 vols. (Notre Dame, IN: University of Notre Dame Press, 1987), vol. 2, 1299; consult ch. 31 on predestination and reprobation.

4. For Lombard's *Sentences*, I quote from the translation by Giulio Silano, *Book 1* (Toronto: Pontifical Institute of Mediaeval Studies, 2007); for the Latin text, see *Sententiae in IV Libris Distinctae*, 3rd ed., ed. Ignatius Brady, 2 vols. (Grottaferrata: Editiones Collegii S. Bonaventurae ad Claras Aquas, 1971, 1981). For Lombard's treatment of predestination, see Colish, *Peter Lombard*, vol. 1, 268–90. For the kinds of continuity that early modernists habitually occlude, see the use of Lombard on predestination and reprobation by the widely read Protestant theologian Wolfgang Musculus, *Common places of Christian religion*, trans. John Man (London, 1563); e.g., 210r and 213v, using Lombard, *Sententiae*, I.d.40. For Musculus's *Common places,* I use the edition in Cambridge University Library, shelfmark Syn.4.56.1.

5. Augustine, *The Predestination of the Saints*, 10.19.

6. Colish, *Peter Lombard,* vol. 1, 288–89.

7. In William Shakespeare, *The Complete Works*, 2nd ed., ed. Stanley Wells and Gary Taylor (Oxford: Clarendon Press, 2005).

8. *To Simplician*, I.2.13, in Augustine, *Earlier Writings*, trans. John H. S. Burleigh (London: SCM Press, 1953).

9. Augustine frequently uses this text; here Lombard is looking at his letter to Sixtus, *Epistles*, 4 vols., trans. Roland J. Teske, ed. Boniface Ramsey (Hyde Park, NY: New City Press, 2001–5), 194.2.5, WSA II/3, 290–91.

10. I quote from *The Augustine Catechism: The Enchiridion on Faith, Hope, and Love*, trans. Bruce Harbert (Hyde Park, NY: New City Press, 1999), sec. 103, pp. 118–20.

11. *Rebuke and Grace*, 14.44 (in WSA I/26, 139).

12. Further references to *Enchiridion* are cited in my text.

13. James Wetzel, "Snares of Truth: Augustine on Free Will and Predestination," in *Augustine and His Critics*, ed. Robert Dodaro and George Lawless (London: Routledge, 2000), 129.

14. For recognitions of Langland's critical and prophetic relations to the Reformation, see Simpson, *Reform and Cultural Revolution*; and Aers, *Beyond Reformation*.

15. See Zeeman, *Piers Plowman*, 220.

16. Jan van Ruusbroec, *The Chastising of God's Children and The Treatise on Perfection*, ed. Joyce Bazire and Edmund College (Oxford: Blackwell, 1957), 119. On the work's date, see 34–37; and its sources, 41–48. I give references to this edition in my text with some modernization of letters. Bazire and College track one of the work's sources to *Stimulus Amoris*, which was translated into Middle English as *The Prickynge of Love*, ed. Harold Kane, 2 vols. (Salzburg: Salzburg University Press, 1983); on anxieties concerning predesti

nation and the remedies, see ch. 33, vol. 1, 166–70. There is a fascinating explo-
ration of these issues in the fifteenth-century translation of Thomas à Kempis,
The Imitation of Christ, ed. B. J. H. Biggs, EETS, o.s., 309 (Oxford: Oxford
University Press, 1997), I.25 (pp. 36–37) and III.63 (p. 143).

17. For editions of Aquinas used and quoted in this book, see ch. 1, n. 3.
For some totally immanent accounts of Aquinas's teaching on election and
reprobation, see the essays by Steven Long and Thomas White in Steven Long,
Roger Nutt, and Thomas White, O.P., eds., *Thomism and Predestination* (Ave
Maria, FL: Sapientia Press, 2016). I have more sympathy with the cautions of-
fered by Barry David in that volume, "Thomas Aquinas's *De Praedestinatione* as
Confessio," ch. 13, esp. 295–98. On Aquinas's rejection of the free will defense,
and the relation of this to Calvin, see Brian Davies, *Thomas Aquinas on God and
Evil* (Oxford: Oxford University Press, 2011), 72–75; see, too, Davies's discus-
sion of providence and predestination in ch. 8 of the same work.

18. For Aquinas's defense of the death penalty, *Summa Theologiae* II–
II.64.2.

19. For an uncritical, learned discussion of Aquinas's exegesis on 1 Timothy 2:4, see John Saward, "The Grace of Christ in His Principal Members:
St. Thomas Aquinas on the Pastoral Epistles," in *Aquinas on Scripture*, ed.
Thomas G. Weinandy, David Keating, and John Yocum (London: Clark,
2005), 202–4.

20. See *Summa Theologiae* I.23.1, resp., with I.12.4. There has been much
debate about such statements in Aquinas, a debate about our natural desire and
capacity for God. By far the best work on this book is the second edition of
Lawrence Feingold's *The Natural Desire to See God according to St. Thomas
Aquinas and His Interpreters* (Naples, FL: Sapientia Press, 2010). For a wild
attack on this book (in which even Feingold's name is constantly misrepre-
sented), see John Milbank, *The Suspended Middle: Henri de Lubac and the
Debate concerning the Supernatural* (Grand Rapids, MI: Eerdmans, 2005). This
has been decisively criticized by Reinhard Hütter, *Dust Bound for Heaven:
Explorations in the Theology of Thomas Aquinas* (Grand Rapids, MI: Eerdmans, 2012), ch. 5. There is a thoughtful review of Feingold's work by Thomas
White in *The Thomist* 79 (2010): 161–67.

21. Herbert McCabe, *God Still Matters*, ed. Brian Davies, introd. Alasdair
MacIntyre (London: Continuum, 2002), ch. 16. Here I quote from pp. 182–83.

22. For *Paradise Lost*, I refer to the edition by John Leonard in John Milton, *The Complete Poems* (London: Penguin, 1998).

23. For a good example of this argument, see Ken Surin, *Theodicy and the
Problem of Evil* (Eugene, OR: Wipf and Stock, 1986).

24. See D. Catherine Brown, *Pastor and Laity in the Theology of Jean Gerson* (Cambridge: Cambridge University Press, 1987), 112–15.

25. See, e.g., Adams, *William Ockham*, vol. 2, 1300, 1337.

26. This analogy is his version of Paul's much-rehearsed one of the potter, the clay, and the pots, Rom. 9:20–23. He also uses this in *Summa Theologiae* I.25.5, ad 3.

27. *De Causa Dei contra Pelagium et de Virtute Causarum* (London, 1618). I am not persuaded that Bradwardine's model of divine/human agency is Augustinian; see Aers, *Salvation and Sin*, ch. 3.

28. See James Halverson, *Peter Aureol on Predestination: A Challenge to Late Medieval Thought* (Leiden: Brill, 1998), 79–81. This book's research and analysis have become central to my own work.

29. Heiko Oberman translates this passage in his section on Bradwardine in his anthology, *Forerunners of the Reformation: The Shape of Late Medieval Thought* (Philadelphia: Fortress Press, 1981), 151–64, here 161–62.

30. On this, see Joseph P. Wawrykow, *God's Grace and Human Action: Merit in the Theology of Thomas Aquinas* (Notre Dame, IN: University of Notre Dame Press, 1995), esp. ch. 4.

31. There are two fine studies in this area which I have found extremely helpful: Paul Gondreau, *The Passions of Christ's Soul in the Theology of St Thomas Aquinas* (Scranton, PA: University of Scranton Press, 2009); Kevin Madigan, *The Passions of Christ in High-Medieval Thought* (New York: Oxford University Press, 2007). For the Chalcedonian core of orthodox teaching in the Middle Ages and the Reformation, consult Kelly, *Early Christian Doctrines*, 338–43.

32. See the essay by Paul Streveler on Holcot's treatment of Peter Lombard's question (II *Sentences* 2.6): "This alone belongs to God: Not to be able to do the best he can do. Robert Holcot O.P. [*ST* I.24.3, resp.] (Some musings, modo Holcoti, on necessity, contingency, and the power of God)," in *Studies in Later Medieval Intellectual History in Honor of William J. Courtenay*, ed. William O. Duba, Russell Friedman, and Chris Schabel (Louven: Peeters, 2017), 393–415.

33. There is a substantial literature on the distinction within God's unitary power, *potentia absoluta* and *potentia ordinata*. The best place to start is with William of Ockham's careful definition in his *Opus Nonaginta Dierum*, ch. 95 in *Work of Ninety Days*, 2 vols., trans. John Kilcullen and John Scott (Lewiston, NY: Mellen Press, 2001); and *Quodlibetal Questions*, 2 vols., trans. Alfred Freddoso and Francis Kelley (New Haven, CT: Yale University Press, 1991), VI.1.1. With these careful definitions, see Adams, *William Ockham*, vol. 2, ch. 28; Eugenio Randi, "A Scotist Way of Distinguishing between God's Ab-

solute and Ordained Powers" in *From Ockham to Wyclif*, ed. Anne Hudson and Michael Wilks (Oxford: Blackwell, 1987), 43–50.

34. Halverson, *Peter Aureol*. I am deeply indebted to much in this work, as I remain to Oberman's *Harvest of Medieval Theology*, though I am persuaded by Halverson's different understanding of Ockham's model of election and of Holcot's.

35. Halverson, *Peter Aureol*, 90.

36. Ibid., 104–7.

37. For an introduction to fascinating and largely unexplored continuities between medieval theology and the Reformation, see Frank James, "A Late Medieval Parallel in Reformation Thought: *Gemina Praedestinatio* in Gregory of Rimini and Peter Martyr Vermigli," in *Via Augustini: Augustine in the Later Middle Ages, Renaissance and Reformation*, ed. Heiko A. Oberman and Frank E. James (Leiden: Brill, 1991), 157–88.

38. For Gregory of Rimini and the *Sentences*, I use the edition by Damasus Trapp and Venicio Marcolino, *Lectura Super Primum et Secundum Sententiarum*, 7 vols. (Berlin: de Gruyter, 1979): here see I.d.40–41, q 1, in vol. 3 (1984), 320. Besides Halverson's discussion of Gregory in *Peter Aureol*, 143–57, I have been helped by the following: Paul Vignaux, *Justification et prédestination au XIVᵉ siècle* (Paris: Leroux, 1934), ch. 4, esp. 165–75; M. Schüler, *Prädestination, Sünde und Freiheit bei Gregor von Rimini* (Stuttgart: Kohlhammer, 1934), 25–69; Chris Schabel, "Parisian Commentaries from Peter Aureol to Gregory of Rimini and the Problem of Predestination," in *Medieval Commentaries on Peter Lombard's Sentences*, ed. G. R. Evans (Leiden: Brill, 2002), 221–65; Gordon Leff, *Gregory of Rimini* (Manchester: Manchester University Press, 1961), 196–204.

39. *Lectura*, vol. 3, 323, 326, 337–39, 342–43, 347–48.

40. *Lectura*, I.d.40–41, a l (vol. 3, 323–24), and again I.d.40–41, a 2 (vol. 3, 338–40).

41. *Lectura*, vol. 3, 347–48. Gregory cites Augustine's *The Predesination of the Saints* 8.14 and *Enchiridion* 27.103. In fact, Gregory's use of Augustine in his rethinking of predestination against Aureol and modern pelagianizing is copious. On Gregory's reading of 1 Timothy 2:4, see Leff, *Gregory of Rimini*, 199–204.

42. *Lectura*, vol. 3, 339, 344–45, 354.

43. *Lectura*, vol. 3, 321.

44. Halverson, *Peter Aureol*, 127.

45. From the impressive recent scholarship on Robert Holcot, I found the following especially helpful to the questions I pursue in this book: Gelber, *It Could Have Been Otherwise*, esp. chs. 4, 5, 7, 8; Halverson, *Peter Aureol*,

122–29; Oberman, *Harvest of Medieval Theology*, 235–48; Katherine Tachau, *Vision and Certitude in the Age of Ockham* (Leiden: Brill, 1988), 243–55; Russell G. Friedman, *Intellectual Traditions at Medieval Universities: The Use of Philosophical Psychology in Trinitarian Theology among the Franciscans and Dominicans, 1250–1350*, 2 vols. (Leiden: Brill, 2013), vol. 2, 732–38; Beryl Smalley, *English Friars and Antiquity in the Early Fourteenth Century* (Oxford: Blackwell, 1965), ch. 7. There is now also an excellent introduction to Holcot's work across all its genres by John T. Slotemaker and Jeffrey C. Witt, *Robert Holcot* (Oxford: Oxford University Press, 2016). For the earlier "skeptical fideist" Holcot, see Gordon Leff, *Bradwardine and the Pelagians* (Cambridge: Cambridge University Press, 1957), 216–27, together with Leonard Kennedy, *The Philosophy of Robert Holcot: Fourteenth-Century Skeptic* (Lewiston, NY: Mellen Press, 1993).

46. Slotemaker and Witt, *Holcot*, 9–10; see ch. 8 on these lectures.

47. See Robert M. Correale and Mary Hammel, eds., *Sources and Analogues of the Canterbury Tales*, 2 vols. (Cambridge: Brewer, 2003), vol. 1, 451, 486–89.

48. I use the edition printed at Basel in 1586: *In Librum Sapientiae Regis Salomonis*. I use the copy in Cambridge University Library, shelfmark B*.1.9 (B). I give references to lecture and page.

49. Oberman's early essay on Holcot remains invaluable: "*Facientibus quod in se est Deus non denegat gratiam.*"

50. See the discussion of Holcot's covenant theology in the opening chapter of Slotemaker and Witt, *Holcot*. They discuss part of this *lectio* on pp. 30–32.

51. Slotemaker and Witt, *Holcot*, 286 n. 65.

52. I quote from Halverson, *Peter Aureol*, 143.

53. As I have noted, rethinking also went in hyper-Augustinian directions from Gregory of Rimini to Beza and Twisse.

54. On John Bromyard, a Dominican in the Hereford Convent, see A. B. Emden, *A Biographical Register of the University of Oxford to A.D. 1500* (Oxford: Clarendon Press, 1957), vol. 1, 278. Emden explains how there had been confusion over two Dominicans named John Bromyard in the Hereford Convent in the fourteenth century. The author of *Summa Praedicantium* "probably died by 1352" (278), while the younger Bromyard became chancellor of Cambridge University in 1382, attended the second session of the Blackfriars Council against Wylif (June 1382), and was an assessor to the bishop of Hereford at the trial of Walter Brut in October 1383. I quote from the Antwerp edition of the *Summa Praedicantium* (1614; hereafter *SP*) held in Cambridge University Library, shelfmark G*-1-28 (B). References to this edition are given in the text by page number.

55. G. R. Owst, *Literature and Pulpit in Medieval England*, 2nd ed. (Oxford: Blackwell, 1966).

56. Halverson, *Peter Aureol*, 2–3, 143–44, 158–59, 170–73.

57. William of Ockham, *Scriptum in librum primum senentiarum ordinatio distinction 19–48*, ed. G. I. Etzkorn and F. E. Kelley, in vol. 4 of the *Opera Philosophia et Theologica* (St. Bonaventure, NY: St. Bonaventure University Press, 1979): d. 41, quaestio unica, p. 597. For Ockham's treatment of predestination and reprobation, see I d. 41, quaestio unica, pp. 597–610. With this, see his *Predestination, God's Foreknowledge, and Future Contingents*, ed. and trans. Marilyn McCord Adams and Norman Kretzmann (New York: Appleton-Century Crofts, 1969).

58. Aquinas uses this analogy in his *Summa Contra Gentiles* III.160.5. It is worth noting that in III.152.2 he did not use 1 Timothy 2:4 as he did in the passage I have discussed from the *Summa Theologiae* or in his comments on Paul's epistle. I use the translation of *Summa Contra Gentiles* by Vernon J. Bourke, vol. 3, pt. 2 (Notre Dame, IN: University of Notre Dame Press, 1975).

59. He and his readers would have to engage here with one of the main topics in medieval theology. From the considerable literature on this, I have found the following especially instructive: Gelber, *It Could Have Been Otherwise*, esp. chs. 4–6; Adams, *William Ockham*, vol. 2, chs. 27–31.

60. I discussed these strikingly different models in *Salvation and Sin*, ch. 1. On the justification for killing those deemed by ecclesiastic judges to be heretics, see *Summa Theologiae* II–II.11.3–4.

61. For Aquinas's treatment of the traditional question about prayer and predestination, see *Summa Theologiae* I.23.8. Aquinas decides that predestination cannot be helped by prayers of the saints, but the predestinate can be helped because God has predestined this help. God uses secondary causes: see *Summa Theologiae* I.22.2–3; I.23.8.

62. See the exegesis discussed in chapter 1 with citations in notes 42 and 43. See, too, Aquinas's *Catena Aurea* on Matthew 22:1–14, vol. 1, 746–47. Here we find the garment as the precepts of God as well as charity.

63. "Sicut praedictus dominus . . . propter bonitatem suam vult multis convivium parare vult quod ipsi *cooperentur* seipsos praeperando & significando & quod aliter non intrent: sed expellantur. Ita Deus: sicut patet de non habente vestem nuptialem" (248; my emphasis).

64. Once again, consult the exposition of Holcot's covenantal theology, the *pactum*, in Slotemaker and Witt, *Holcot*, ch. 1.

65. Nor did it, of course, to Aureol and those Halverson describes in shaping the new paradigm he calls GE; see Halverson, *Peter Aureol*, ch. 3 and pp. 97–98, 103–6, 127, 137–39, 171.

66. There is a long tradition of Catholic scholarship lamenting an allegedly disastrous rupture between Aquinas and theology after Scotus. This is a classic decline and fall narrative. It is associated with the work of Etienne Gilson. It can be seen vividly even in an excellent recent survey, Rik van Nieuwenhove, *An Introduction to Medieval Theology* (Cambridge: Cambridge University Press, 2012), and in its companion, Declan Marmione and Rik van Nieuwenhove, *An Introduction to the Trinity* (Cambridge: Cambridge University Press, 2012). On this paradigm, see the comments by Friedman, *Intellectual Traditions at the Medieval University*, vol. 2, 652–60; but see esp. Bonnie Kent, *Virtues of the Will* (Washington, DC: Catholic University of America Press, 1995), 5–34.

67. *Catena Aurea* (on the denarius), vol. 1, 680, 683, 684, 685.

68. See *Summa Theologiae* I.1.1; I.1.8; I.1.10.

69. See Halverson (who does not mention Bromyard), *Peter Aureol*, 115 n. 14, 122 n. 31, 126–28.

70. Oberman, *Harvest of Medieval Theology*, 187.

71. Unlike the situation within Calvinism, it seems rare for medieval theologians to reject the distinction between permission and causation in God's agency and the sinner's agency; see J. A. Robson, *Wyclif and the Oxford Schools* (Cambridge: Cambridge University Press, 1961), 64.

72. McCabe, *God Still Matters*, 182.

73. Halverson, *Peter Aureol*, 143.

74. In this summary, I draw on three works of Ockham: I *Sent* d. 40 ("Utrum sit possible aliquem praedestinatum et praescitum salvari," pp. 592–97); I *Sent* d. 41 ("Utrum in praedestinatione sit aliqua causae suae praedestinationis et in reprobatione aliqua causa suae reprobationis," pp. 597–610). Second, I draw on *Predestination*. Third, there is a passing mention of Jacob and Esau in relation to God's power in *Quaestiones Variae, Opera Theologica*, vol. 8, 22. There is reasonable disagreement about details of Ockham's favored paradigm for understanding predestination and reprobation—between Halverson (*Peter Aureol*, 111–22) and Adams (*William Ockham*, ch. 31)—but no disagreement that he breaks with the thirteenth-century consensus represented by Aquinas. On Ockham's treatment of Jacob and Esau, see Adams, *William of Ockham*, 1264–65. The whole of Adams's chapter 31 (on predestination, reprobation, and divine and human freedom) is relevant, as is much in chapter 30 (on grace, merit, and God's freedom).

75. I quote from Ockham, *Predestination*, 50; see the similar statement in *Ordinatio, I Sentences* 38 in this volume, pp. 89–90. It is worth noting that Ockham determines that Aquinas's analogy of the stones and the builder *cannot*

protect God from the charge that he intends sin, an argument made by Henry of Ghent and Scotus; see Scotus on predestination and reprobation in his commentary on I *Sentences* d. 41, quaestio unica, at pp. 492–509, in *The Examined Report of Paris Lecture: Reportato I-A*, ed. Allan Wolter and Oleg Bychkov, vol. 2 (St. Bonaventure, NY: St. Bonaventure University Press, 2007). On Scotus and predestination, see Richard Cross, *Duns Scotus* (Oxford: Oxford University Press, 1999), ch. 8.

CHAPTER THREE.   Crossing a Great Divide?

1. See my discussion of Gregory of Rimini in chapter 2.

2. Wetzel, "Snares of Truth," 129, 130. For further explorations by James Wetzel, see especially the following: *Augustine and the Limits of Virtue* (Cambridge: Cambridge University Press, 1992); *Augustine: A Guide for the Perplexed* (London: Continuum, 2010); *Parting Knowledge: Essays after Augustine* (Eugene, OR: Cascade, 2013). Chapter 9 of *Parting Knowledge* would make extremely fruitful reading alongside Christ's oration in hell in *Piers Plowman* XX, discussed in chapter 2 above, as well as alongside Calvin's version of Christ's descent into hell considered later in this chapter. For my own account of Augustine's theology of grace and its various understandings of human agency see Aers, *Salvation and Sin*, ch. 1.

3. Wetzel, "Snares of Truth," 130; see 128–30.

4. Julian of Eclanum is quoted in Augustine's *Opus imperfectum*, as cited in Bonner, *Freedom and Necessity*, 7; see also 1–27, 100, 118–30. I have modified one grammatical slip in Bonner's translation.

5. For Crowley's editions of *Piers Plowman*, I have used *The Vision of Pierce Plowman: now the second tyme imprinted by Roberte Crowley* (1550), Cambridge University Library, shelfmark Syn. 7.55.25. On Crowley, see especially D. Andrew Penny, *Freewill or Predestination: The Battle over Saving Grace in Mid-Tudor England* (Woodbridge: Boydell, 1990), 195–204.

6. The main edition and translation of Calvin's *Institutes* used in this book is John Calvin, *Institutes of the Christian Religion*, 2 vols., ed. John T. McNeil, trans. Ford L. Battles (Philadelphia: Westminster Press, John Knox Press, 1960). I have also consulted the Latin text of the 1559 edition in *Johannis Calvin Opera Selecta*, ed. P. Barth and W. Niesel, vols. 3–5 (Munich: Kaiser, 1928–36), with 2nd ed. vol. 3 (1957) and vol. 4 (1959). I have also made abundant use of the admirably accurate translation by Henry Beveridge, *Institutes of the Christian Religion* (Peabody, MA: Hendrickson, 2009). I give references in my text

to book, chapter, and section of the *Institutes*. The quotation here is found at III.2.15; the two epigraphs to this chapter come from III.21.5 and III.2.11.

7. For an informative introduction to the topic of assurance in Reformed Christianity, written from within Calvinist ideology, see Joel R. Beeke, *Assurance of Faith: Calvin, English Puritanism, and the Dutch Second Reformation* (New York: Lang, 1996), esp. ch. 4 (on Calvin and Beza) and ch. 5 (on Perkins). See, too, Beeke's apologia for the doctrine of personal assurance in seventeenth-century Calvinism, "Personal Assurance of Faith: The Puritans and Chapter 18.2 of the *Westminster Confession*," *Westminster Theological Journal* 55 (1993): 1–30. I have found the recent work of Keith Stanglin especially helpful: Keith Stanglin, *Arminius on the Assurance of Salvation: The Context, Roots, and Shape of the Leiden Debate, 1603–1609* (Leiden: Brill, 2007); Keith Stanglin and Thomas H. McCall, *Jacob Arminius: Theologian of Grace* (Oxford: Oxford University Press, 2012), 176–88. Both works include good discussions of "temporary faith": Stanglin and McCall, *Jacob Arminius*, 178–79; Stanglin, *Arminius on the Assurance*, 182–87.

8. The best introduction to this ministry in theology and practice remains Eamon Duffy's eloquent work, *Stripping of the Altars*, chs. 1–4. Alongside this, one should read John Bossy's fine work, such as "The Mass as a Social Institution 1200–1700," *Past and Present* 100 (1983): 29–61; and *Christianity in the West, 1400–1700* (Oxford: Oxford University Press, 1985).

9. With Calvin, contrast the exposition of this theological virtue in Aquinas's *Summa Theologiae* II-II.1–16, together with the very different but equally beautiful unfolding of faith in *Piers Plowman* XVIII–XXI.

10. See Beeke's brief account, *Assurance of Faith*, 15–16, 70–71.

11. I return to these issues throughout this chapter, but the following works have been especially informative in my own approach: Anthony Milton, *Catholic and Reformed: The Roman and Protestant Churches in English Protestant Thought, 1600–1640* (Cambridge: Cambridge University Press, 1995), 211; Nicholas Tyacke, *Anti-Calvinists: The Rise of English Arminianism c. 1590–1640* (Oxford: Oxford University Press, 1987), 72–79, 248–58; Hunt, *Art of Hearing*, 347–49; on this topic, see also Dixon, *Practical Predestinarians*, 293–302.

12. Aquinas, *ST*, I.prol.; Calvin, "John Calvin to the Reader (1559)," in *Institutes*, vol. 1, p. 4.

13. See François Wendel, *Calvin: The Origins of His Religious Thought* (London: Collins, 1969), 264–69. For the argument that more has been made of the shifts in location than is justifiable, see Paul Helms, *John Calvin's Ideas* (Oxford: Oxford University Press, 2009), 93–99.

14. Wendel, *Calvin*, 264, 269.

15. The quotation here is from Richard Muller's influential work, *Christ and the Decrees: Christology and Predestination in Reformed Theology from Calvin to Perkins* (Grand Rapids, MI: Baker, 1986), quoted by Hunt, *Art of Hearing*, 343. Chapter 7 of Hunt's work is an exceptionally rich description of preaching predestination in seventeenth-century England. The best survey on this topic remains Dewey Wallace, *Puritans and Predestination: Grace in English Protestant Theology 1525–1695* (Eugene, OR: Wipf and Stock, 1982). For an attempt to deny both the Calvinism of the Church of England in the early seventeenth century and Tyacke's demonstration of an emergent anti-Calvinism, see Peter White, *Predestination, Policy and Polemic: Conflict and Consensus in the English Church from the Reformation to the Civil War* (Cambridge: Cambridge University Press, 1992); together with Julian Davies, *The Caroline Captivity of the Church: Charles I and the Remoulding of Anglicanism 1625–1641* (Oxford: Oxford University Press, 1992), esp. 87–125. On Nicholas Tyacke's response to White's arguments (elaborated in his later book), see "The Rise of Arminianism Reconsidered," *Past and Present* 115 (1987): 201–16; see too Tyacke's later observations on defining Arminianism in his *Aspects of English Protestantism c. 1530–1700* (Manchester: Manchester University Press, 2001), 155–59; see also Peter Lake, "Calvinism and the English Church 1570–1635," *Past and Present* 114 (1987): 32–76. It should be noted that H. C. Porter clearly identified "Arminianism *avant la lettre*" at Cambridge in the 1590s and at the Hampton Court Conference (1604) in his magisterial work *Reformation and Reaction in Tudor Cambridge* (Cambridge: Cambridge University Press, 1985), 281 passim. Long ago this work confirmed my hunch that many early modernist literary historians tend to use the term "Arminianism" in a rather unhistorical and imprecise way as they discuss seventeenth-century writers. For reflections on such issues, see Keith Stanglin, "Arminius Avant La Lettre: Peter Baro, Jacob Arminius, and the Bond of Predestinarian Polemic," *Westminster Theological Journal* 71, no. 1 (2005): 51–74. See too the studies by Stanglin cited above in note 7. For Arminius's theology in relation to both Reformation and medieval traditions, see Richard Muller, *God, Creation, and Providence in the Thought of Jacob Arminius* (Grand Rapids, MI: Baker, 1991). A recent work by Freya Sierhuis is also relevant here: *The Literature of the Arminian Controversy: Religion, Politics, and the Stage in the Dutch Republic* (Oxford: Oxford University Press, 2015). This is an immensely informative work, but like so many synchronic early modernist works it does include confident assertions about medieval theology that are often strangely inaccurate; see, e.g., 43–44.

16. For a careful consideration of Calvin and the natural law tradition, see Paul Helm, *Calvin's Ideas*, 367–88. Peter Lake provides a reading of Hooker

that is relevant to the concerns of the present chapter in *Anglicans and Puritans? Presbyterianism and English Conformist Thought from Whitgift to Hooker* (London: Unwin, 1988), ch. 7.

17. Richard Crakanthorp, *Sermon of Predestination, Preached at Saint Maries in Oxford* (1620), quoted by Dixon, *Practical Predestinarians*, 220–21.

18. See Milton, *Paradise Lost* V.797–828; V.1–136.

19. See John Stachniewski, *The Persecutory Imagination: English Protestantism and the Literature of Religious Despair* (Oxford: Clarendon Press, 1991), chs. 2 and 3. For a different perspective with a much deeper archive, see Alec Ryrie, *Being Protestant in Reformation Britain* (Oxford: Oxford University Press, 2015), chs 2, 4, and 5.

20. Here I quote from Dixon, *Practical Predestinarians*, 293; he makes a similar statement at 287.

21. Edmund Spenser, *The Faerie Queene*, 2nd ed., ed. A. C. Hamilton (London: Longmans, 2007), quoting here I.i.2 and I.arg. For examples of the inability of either the Red Crosse Knight or Una to recognize Archimago, see I.i.29–50; I.ii.1–11; I.iii.24–40. Further references to *The Faerie Queene* refer to this edition and will be given in text by book, canto, and stanza numbers.

22. For an account of Augustine's subtle exploration of agency and conversion, see Aers, *Salvation and Sin*, ch. 1. In this exploration I observe that elsewhere Augustine does deploy the model of Paul on the road to Damascus, and I seek to show the malign political and ecclesiastical consequences of this. For *Paradise Lost*, see X.1013–1104, XI.1–72, 90–98. On the peculiar ideal of passivity in Lutheran and Calvinist ideas of conversion, see the illuminating study by Jennifer Herdt, *Putting on Virtue: The Legacy of the Splendid Vices* (Chicago: University of Chicago Press, 2008), esp. pt. 3.

23. See, e.g., Stachniewski, *Persecutory Imagination*, 46–52.

24. Augustine, "Predestination of the Saints," in *Answer to the Pelagians IV*, vol. I/26 of WSA, at 166–67.

25. For a fine example of this, see Aquinas, *ST* II–II.1–16.

26. Paul Hacker, *Faith in Luther: Martin Luther and the Origin of Anthropocentric Religion* (Steubenville, OH: Emmaus Academic, 2017 [originally in German, 1966]), 8–10.

27. I quote from Beeke, *Assurance of Faith*, 24. What I see as self-contradiction, Beeke celebrates as "paradoxical" (*Assurance of Faith*, 22–26).

28. Hacker, *Faith in Luther*, 8–10, 25, ch. 1; also relevant are chs. 3–4.

29. Richard Montague, *A Gagg for the Gospel? No. A New Gagg for an Old Goose* (1624), set in the context I am currently discussing by Milton, *Catholic and Reformed*, 110–19, ch. 2 passim; with this, see Tyacke, *Anti-*

Calvinists, 149, 172. There is a chapter on Montague in White, *Predestination, Policy, and Polemic*, ch. 11.

30. Milton, *Catholic and Reformed*, 103. The quotation comes from the exploration in chapter 2 of how this puritan and Calvinist tradition was rejected by increasingly confident anti-Calvinists in the 1620s and 1630s.

31. Tyacke, *Anti-Calvinists*, 150–57.

32. *Roman de la Rose*, lines 11,053–12,002. I have consulted both the French text edited by Felix Lecoy, 3 vols. (Paris: Champion, 1965–1970); and the English translation by Francis Horgan, *The Romance of the Rose* (Oxford: Oxford University Press, 1994), 70–185. There is a fascinating account of the transformations of "hypocrisy" from Augustine and Aquinas to Mandeville, Hume, and Rousseau in Herdt, *Putting on Virtue*, 58–61, 80–82, 179–80, 198–99, 262–72, 307–8, 314–16. For an absorbing exploration of Langland's transformative innovations in his versions of hypocrisy and personification in *Piers Plowman*, see Nicolette Zeeman, *Arts of Disruption: The Work of Allegory and Piers Plowman* (Oxford: Oxford University Press, 2020), chs. 1, 2.

33. On Aquinas, see Herdt, *Putting on Virtue*, 80–82; on Luther's version, 178–79.

34. Stachniewski writes eloquently on this nexus; see *Persecutory Imagination*, 19–22, 268–69. Stanglin and McCall show how Arminius identified just what Calvinists were inventing in their version of hypocrisy; see *Jacob Arminius*, 115–16, 118–19, 126.

35. Stachniewski, *Persecutory Imagination*, 91–93, ch. 3; Dixon, *Practical Predestinarians*, 287–92.

36. The quotation is from Robert Bolton, *Discourse about the state of true happiness* (London, 1611), in Ryrie, *Being Protestant*, 105; with this, see Dixon, *Practical Predestinarians*, 289–90, 292–93, 295, 345.

37. Ryrie, *Being Protestant*, 189.

38. Ibid., 188. Chaucer, it seems to me, displays the dominant teaching on hypocrisy in the Middle Ages in *The Parson's Tale*, X.394.

39. For an example of such anxiety, see Richard Norwood's account of his spiritual life discussed by Stachniewski, *Persecutory Imagination*, ch. 2, esp. 123–25.

40. From *Reliquiae Baxterianae*, ed. M. Sylvester (1696), quoted in Stachniewski, *Persecutory Imagination*, 92. Relevant to my discussion of Calvinist epistemophilia in this and the next chapter is Susan Schreiner, *Are You Alone Wise? The Search for Certainty in the Early Modern Era* (Oxford: Oxford University Press, 2011), esp. chs. 2, 3; on Calvin, see 66–70. For a very different approach, see Robert Muller, *Christ and the Decree*, 25–27.

41. The quotations are from William Sclater, *Sermons Experiential* (1638), and Bolton, *Discourse about the state of true happiness* (1611), quoted in Dixon, *Practical Predestinarians*, 300, 289.

42. I am of course rehearsing aspects of Stanley Cavell's reading of Othello and his concomitant arguments about skepticism in *The Claim of Reason: Wittgenstein, Skepticism, Morality, and Tragedy* (New York: Oxford University Press, 1999); the essay on Othello is reprinted in Cavell, *Disowning Knowledge in Seven Plays of Shakespeare* (Cambridge: Cambridge University Press, 1987), ch. 3.

43. William Twisse, *The Riches of God's Love unto the Vessells of Mercy, Consistent with His Absolute Hatred or Reprobation of the Vessells of Wrath; Or An Answer unto a book entituled God's Love unto Mankind, Manifested by Disproving His Absolute Decree for their Damnation*, ed. Henry Jeanes (Oxford: Thomas Robinson, 1653), 293. I use the copy in the Cambridge University Library, shelfmark E*-9-33. Twisse died in 1646. For some comments on Twisse's relations with Joseph Mead and the difficulties of the "godly" clergy in working out their response to ritual and ceremony in the ecclesiology favored by Laud in the 1630s, see Tom Webster, *Godly Clergy in Early Stuart England: The Caroline Puritan Movement, c. 1620–1643* (Cambridge: Cambridge University Press, 1997), 174–79. Thinking about tradition and the Protestant rhetoric of freedom from tradition, it is worth recalling that Twisse helped in the preparation of Thomas Bradwardine's *De Causa Dei* for publication in 1618 as an aid to Calvinist ideology around the Synod of Dort. On Twisse in these contexts, see Sarah Hutton, "Thomas Jackson, Oxford Platonist, and William Twisse, Aristotelian," *Journal of the History of Ideas* 39 (1978): 635–52, esp. 647, 650. Hutton describes Twisse as "a man of narrow supralapsarian outlook," illustrating this comment with the following quote from his *Doctrine of the Synod of Dort*: "God by an absolute decree, hath elected and chosen a very small number of persons, without regard either to their faith or obedience, and excluded all the rest of mankind from all saving grace, destined by the same decree unto eternal damnation, without consideration of their incredulities or impenitence" (Hutton, "Thomas Jackson," 650–51). Also relevant here is the account of Gomarus, another influential supralapsarian Calvinist, by Russ Leo, *Tragedy as Philosophy in the Reformation World* (Princeton, NJ: Princeton University Press, 2018), ch. 4, esp. 180–81.

44. Lucy Hutchinson, *Theological Writings and Translations*, vol. 2 of *The Works of Lucy Hutchinson*, ed. Elizabeth Clarke, David Norbrook, and Jane Stevenson, 2 vols. (Oxford: Oxford University Press, 2018), 111–12. Page references are given in my text. The Westminster Assembly's Confession of

Faith devoted a chapter to assurance (ch. 18), and David Norbrook discusses its influence on Hutchinson's reflections in vol. 1, 35.

45. Bolton, *The Last Conflicts and Death of Mr. Thomas Peacock*. Page references are given in my text. The work was brought to my attention by Leif Dixon in *Practical Predestinarians*, 345–49. For a study that does not mention Mr. Peacock but is both relevant to the discussion here and especially informative, see Ralph Houlbrooke, "The Puritan Death-bed, c. 1560–c. 1660," in *The Culture of English Puritanism, 1560–1700*, ed. Christopher Durston and Jacqueline Eales (New York: St. Martin's Press, 1996), 122–44. See especially the example of the wife of Sir Simonds D'Ewes in 1641, pp. 128–29, an example of a Calvinist struggling with assurance and its lack. See too the example of the Lancashire lady Katherine Bettergh, pp. 133–36. Like Mr. Peacock, this godly lady comes to see herself as a "hypocrite" and doubts that she is one of the elect, wishing she had been born as anything but a woman. Houlbrooke assures us that "a spiritual crisis during the last illness was a relatively rare experience" (135). One hopes so. For an informative account of the Harley family who had appointed Mr. Peacock as their rector in 1611, see Jacqueline Eales, *Puritans and Roundheads: The Harleys of Brempton Bryan and the Outbreak of the English Civil War* (Cambridge: Cambridge University Press, 1990), ch. 3, esp. 43–51. Eales shows the centrality of Calvinist teaching on predestination and reprobation in this gentry family. The Harleys participated in the Calvinist quest for assurance and confidence of predestination, finding the requisite signs in their own experiences and those of their friends and allies in "the godly community" to which Mr. Peacock belonged.

46. Ryrie, *Being Protestant*, 461, quoting Henry Valentine, *Private Devotions, Digested in Six Letanies* (1635), 265–66. See also on this topic, Dixon, *Practical Predestinarians*, ch. 7.

47. Ryrie, *Being Protestant*, 461, 460–68; Dixon, *Practical Predestinarians*, ch. 7. For a work that actually studies medieval texts and contexts (unlike Ryrie and Dixon), see Amy Appleford's *Learning to Die in London 1380–1540* (Philadelphia: University of Pennsylvania Press, 2014).

48. Ryrie, *Being Protestant*, 30.

49. Ibid., with chs. 2, 16.

50. On this, consult Ryrie, *Being Protestant*, 38.

51. Ibid., 40–41, 44. On the denial of the relevance of Francis Spira to Calvinsist experience, see Twisse, *Riches of God's Love*, 275–78. On Spira and his role in "religious despair," see Stachniewski, *Persecutory Imagination*, 37–39, 229–30.

52. Twisse, *Riches of God's Love*, 144, 253.

53. John Dod and Robert Cleaver, *Foure Godlie and Fruitful Sermons* (London, 1611), discussed by Ryrie, *Being Protestant*, 36.

54. See also Mr. Peacock's reflections on his teaching in Bolton, *Last Conflicts*, 23–24, 28–29.

55. Ryrie, *Being Protestant*, 40. The whole discussion at 39–48 is relevant here.

56. Ibid., 41.

57. Ibid.

58. For an especially lucid and full comparison of medieval theologies of atonement with Protestant teaching on Christ's penal substitution and satisfaction, see Thomas White, "The Crucified Lord: Thomistic Reflections on the Communication of Idioms and the Theology of the Cross," in *Thomas Aquinas and Karl Barth: An Unofficial Catholic-Protestant Dialogue*, ed. Bruce McCormack and Thomas White (Grand Rapids, MI: Eerdmans, 2013), 157–89; together with his later study, *The Light of Christ: An Introduction to Catholicism* (Washington, DC: Catholic University of America Press, 2017), 168–72. As illuminating is an essay by Rik van Nieuwenhove, "St. Anselm and St. Thomas Aquinas on 'Satisfaction': or How Catholic and Protestant Understandings of the Cross Differ," *Angelicum* 80 (2003): 159–76, together with his later commentary on Anselm's soteriology in *An Introduction to Medieval Theology*, 93–97.

59. See *Piers Plowman* VII.1–68; Chaucer, *Parson's Tale* X.677–738.

60. On the traditionalism of the Calvinist "extra," see E. David Willis, *Calvin's Catholic Christology: The Function of the So-Called Extra Calvinisticum in Calvin's Theology* (Leiden: Brill, 1966).

61. Two excellent discussions of these difficulties are Madigan, *The Passions of Christ in High-Medieval Thought*; Gondreau, *The Passions of Christ's Soul in the Theology of St. Thomas Aquinas*, ch. 1.

62. See the translation of *Cur Deus Homo* (*Why God Became Man*) in Anselm of Canterbury, *The Major Works*, ed. Brian Davies and G. R. Evans (Oxford: Oxford University Press, 1998), 260–356. On Anselm in this context, see the works cited in note 57 above.

63. I quote here from Richardson's sermon as included in Appendix I, "From Calvinist to Arminian: The Doctrinal Tenor of the Paul's Cross Sermons, 1570–1638," in Tyacke, *Anti-Calvinists*, 248–65, at 257–58.

64. Tyacke, *Anti-Calvinists*, 258. For an exemplification of a Calvinist sermon on this topic, see Humphrey Sydenham, *Jacob and Esau*, preached at St. Paul's Cross in March 1622 and included as the second item in his *Five Sermons, upon several occasions preach'd at Paul's Crosse, and at St. Maries in Oxford* (London, 1627), Cambridge University Library, shelfmark Peterborough K.1.20.

65. In Tyacke, "The Rise of Arminiamism Reconsidered," 203.

66. Quoted and discussed by Lake in "Calvinism and the English Church," 35–36.

67. Lake, "Calvinism and the English Church," 59.

68. Samuel Hoard, *Gods Love To Mankind Manifested, By Dis-Prooving his Absolute Decree for their Damnation* (1633). I use the copy in Cambridge University Library, shelfmark BG*.11.9. I give references to this in my text. The reply I consider is by William Twisse, published posthumously and fully cited in note 42 above. It is instructive to consider Hoard alongside the critique of the theory of original sin by Simon Episcopius; see Mark Ellis, *Simon Episcopius' Doctrine of Original Sin* (New York: Lang, 2006), ch. 4.

69. On the Synod of Dort in these contexts, consult Milton, *Catholic and Reformed*, 418–27, together with Tyacke, *Anti-Calvinists*, 87–105.

70. William Laud, "Answer to the Lord Say's Speech Touching the Liturgy," in *The Works of the Most Revered Father in God William Laud D.D.*, vol. 6, pt. 1, *Miscellaneous Papers-Letters* (Oxford: Oxford University Press, 1847–60), 132–33. Peter White's attack on Tyacke's invocation of the passage oddly overlooks the fact that in it Laud was specifically concerned with Calvinism in Brownist theology; see White, "Arminianism Reconsidered: A Rejoinder," *Past and Present* 115, no. 1 (1987): 228; contrast Tyacke, *Anti-Calvinists*, 209–70, a discussion White ignores, referring only to Tyacke's later essay in *Past and Present* 115 (1987): 215.

71. See Athanasius, *On the Incarnation* (Crestwood, NY: St. Vladimir's Seminary Press, 1993).

72. For the image of Christ as Mother, see Julian of Norwich, *A Book of Showings*, ed. College and Walsh, vol. 2, chs. 54–63 of the Long Text.

73. See the marginal commentary on the verse, as well as Nicholas of Lyra's literal and moral commentary, in *Biblia Sacra cum glossa ordinaria*, vol. 5, col. 385.

74. Denis the Carthusian, *In Quatuor Evangelistas Enarrationes*, 74v.

75. On the sources of Antinomianism in pre–civil war England, see David Como, *Blown by the Spirit: Puritanism and the Emergence of an Antinomian Underground in Pre-Civil-War England* (Stanford: Stanford University Press, 2004). Although I will not pursue this here, I note that the exhilarating writing of the Antinomian and Ranter Abiezer Coppe includes an invocation of Jesus's image of the hen and chicks but one in which Coppe himself stands in for Jesus and London is substituted for Jerusalem. How this would have confirmed Twisse's worst fears about Samuel Hoard's invocation of Jesus's self-representation as a hen! Coppe's reference can be found on the title page of his *A Fiery Flying Roll* (1649); a modern edition of the work is included in Nigel Smith, ed., *A Collection of Ranter Writings from the Seventeenth Century* (London:

Junction Books, 1983), 80–116. Arminius himself had deployed Jesus's words in Matthew 23:37 in his dispute over predestination and reprobation with William Perkins in 1602; see *The Works of James Arminius*, 3 vols. (n.p.: Lamp Post, 2015), 253.

76. Twisse, *Riches of God's Love*. Owens's preface is at sig. ¶1v. All further page references are given in my text.

77. Milton, *Catholic and Reformed*, 423 ("high" Calvinism); 419, 420, 435 ("hyper-Calvinist"); 419 ("extreme Calvinist").

78. Arminius is quoted here from his critique of Perkins (published posthumously in 1612) in Tyacke, *Anti-Calvinists*, 39.

79. John Gore is discussed by Tyacke, *Anti-Calvinists*, 216–17, and I quote from p. 217. For further examples of Calvinist insistence on the irresistibility of grace, see Tyacke, *Anti-Calvinists*, 40, 73–74. For anybody approaching these disputes from the perspective of medieval theology, much of what was, and is, labeled "Arminian" in fact seems congruent with prominent strands of medieval teaching.

80. Tyacke, *Anti-Calvinists*, 56–57.

81. I discuss Bradwardine's version of grace and of human and divine agency in *Salvation and Sin*, ch. 3. See, too, note 42 above for the relevance of Bradwardine in the battles around the Synod of Dort.

82. Hoard, *Gods Love*, 100–110.

83. William Perkins, *A Golden Chaine* (Cambridge, 1597); also included in *The Workes of that famous and Worthy Minister of Christ in the Universitie of Cambridge, Mr. William Perkins*, 3 vols. (London: John Leggatt [printer to the University of Cambridge], 1612–613), I.9–116.

84. See especially Perkins, *A Case of Conscience the greatest that ever was: how a man may know whether he be the childe of God or no*, in *Workes*, I.421–28.

85. Arthur Dent, *The Plaine Man's Path-way to Heaven. Wherein every man may clearly see whether he shall be saved or damned. Set forth Dialogue wise for the better understanding of the simple* (London, 1601); discussed at length in ch. 4.

86. Ryrie, *Being Protestant*, 27.

87. Tyacke, *Anti-Calvinists*, 1, 7.

88. Ibid., 164–65.

89. Samuel Harsnett, *A Sermon Preached at S. Paul's Cross in London, the 27 day of October Anno Reginae Elizabethae 26*, significantly enough not printed until 1656 as "A Fourth Sermon" in Richard Steward, *Three Sermons* (London, 1656), 121–65. References to this edition are given in my text.

90. See ch. 2 for my discussion of medieval discourses of general election.

91. Tyacke, *Anti-Calvinists*, 164.

92. Here I have been following and quoting from Milton, *Catholic and Reformed*, ch. 6, at 281, 283–84, 286–87, 292, 231. The work of Kenneth Fincham and Nicholas Tyacke is *Altars Restored: The Changing Face of English Religious Worship 1547–c. 1700* (Oxford: Oxford University Press, 2008); for this story, see chs. 3–6.

93. John Henry Cardinal Newman, *An Essay in the Development of Christian Doctrine*, ed. Ian Ker (Notre Dame, IN: University of Notre Dame Press, 1989); text from the second revised edition of 1878.

CHAPTER FOUR. Conversion in Arthur Dent's
The Plaine Man's Path-way to Heaven

1. Dent, *The Plaine Man's Path-way to Heaven*. I use the copy in Cambridge University Library, Peterborough E.2.42, and I modernize *u* to *v*. References in my text are to page numbers in this edition. The importance of this work was first drawn to my attention by Christopher Hill's *Society and Puritanism in Pre-Revolutionary England* (London: Panther, [1964] 1969), 135–36, 433; and by Keith Wrightson's *English Society 1580–1680* (London: Hutchinson, 1982), 168, 205, 215–16. One of the works I have found most illuminating to read alongside Dent's is by the famous theologian referred to by Dent, William Perkins; see Perkins, *A Treatise tending unto a declaration, whether a man be in the estate of damnation, or in the estate of grace* (London, 1591), in vol. 1 of *Workes*, 356–420. I use the copy in the Cambridge University Library, CCA.6.22. I have also consulted the 1591 edition of the *Treatise* together with the 1595 edition corrected by Perkins (Cambridge University Library, shelfmark Syn. 7.59.53). For the epigraph to this chapter, see Robert Cawdrey, *A Treasurie or Store-House of Similies* (1600), quoted in Hunt, *Art of Hearing*, 244.

2. Christopher Haigh, *The Plain Man's Pathways to Heaven: Kinds of Christianity in Post-Reformation England* (Oxford: Oxford University Press, 2007), 1. There were twenty-five editions of Dent's work between 1601 and 1640. Dent's text has been much used by historians of popular culture, at most length in Haigh, *Plain Man's Pathways*. For another recent example of historians' ways of reading Dent and their use of the *Plaine Man's Path-way*, see John Craig, *Reformation, Politics and Polemics: The Growth of Protestantism in East Anglian Market Towns, 1500–1610* (Aldershot: Ashgate, 2001), introd. and ch. 1 (esp. pp. 1–5, 12–14, 17–21). Despite her analysis of the way Calvinists

sidelined the "human life" of Jesus Christ and neglected the humanity of Christ, Helen White offered some disappointingly superficial comments on Dent's work as a "humane" transformation of despair. As we shall see, "superficial," because Dent, true to his Calvinist ministry, actually seeks to *create* despair together with uncritical dependence on the minister, all as part of the process of conversion to Calvinist Christianity. See Helen C. White, *English Devotional Literature, 1600–1640* (Madison: University of Wisconsin Press, 1931). A book I read after completing the present chapter includes some brief comments on Dent in a relevant context: see Ethan H. Shagan, *The Birth of Modern Belief: Faith and Judgment from the Middle Ages to the Enlightenment* (Princeton, NJ: Princeton University Press, 2018), 135–36, together with the comments on Bunyan's *Grace Abounding* in ch. 4, "The Unbearable Weight of Believing."

3. Haigh, *Plain Man's Pathways*, 1, 12.

4. This was, of course, a central concern in the work of R. H. Tawney, Max Weber, Christopher Hill, and Keith Wrightson. I have found David Underdown's *Revel, Riot, and Rebellion: Popular Politics and Culture in England 1603–1660* (Oxford: Clarendon Press, 1985) especially illuminating, along with Keith Wrightson's *Earthly Necessities: Economic Lives in Early Modern Britain* (New Haven, CT: Yale University Press, 2000); and Ronald Hutton, *The Rise and Fall of Merry England: The Ritual Year, 1400–1700* (Oxford: Oxford University Press, 1994). Eamon Duffy has recently attempted to oppose arguments made by historians such as Wrightson which claim the Calvinist mission of Dent and his colleagues was bound up with a mission to transform the dominant forms of culture among the landless, the small holders, the people outside the groups which ruled England at national and local levels. For this essay, see his *Reformation Divided: Catholics, Protestants and the Conversion of England* (London: Bloomsbury, 2017), ch. 12, "The Godly and the Multitude." Duffy claims that "puritan polemic against the profane culture they saw around them," polemic amply illustrated in Dent's work, was not a polemic against "'popular culture' in the straightforward sense of the culture of the lower orders" (353)! However Duffy's broad claims fare in the study of religion and culture in Reformation England, his attempt to produce the gentry as Dent's real target seems to me as implausible as it is lacking in evidence. Duffy's strategy seems the rather desperate one of apparently identifying "the gentry" with all those who could own the "merry books" Antilegon commends in the face of the Calvinist preacher's contempt (354). I see nothing in the work of Underdown or Wrightson to make me think that they have identified anti-Calvinist popular culture only with those Duffy calls "the poor." Dent and his colleagues be-

longed to a long cultural and political war that is clearly identifiable in the late Middle Ages but took on very particular inflections in the Calvinist strands of the Reformation. For outstanding work on these long cultural wars, very unusual in its commitment to serious study across the great divide between medieval and early modern historians, see Marjorie McIntosh, *Controlling Misbehavior in England 1370–1600* (Cambridge: Cambridge University Press, 2002), together with her study of ideology and practice in poor relief, *Poor Relief in England 1350–1600* (Cambridge: Cambridge University Press, 2012). I also found an earlier essay by Christopher Durston especially illuminating both in its arguments and its rigorous documentation: "Puritan Rule and the Failure of Cultural Revolution, 1645–1660," in Durston and Eales, *The Culture of English Puritanism*, 210–33.

    5. Wrightson, *English Society*, 209. See also Duffy, *Stripping of the Altars*; Webster, *Godly Clergy in Early Stuart England*; Charles Prior, *Defining the Jacobean Church: The Politics of Religious Controversy 1603–1625* (Cambridge: Cambridge University Press, 2012). Still extremely informative in this area is Rosemary O'Day, *English Clergy: The Emergence and Consolidation of a Profession 1558–1642* (Leicester: Leicester University Press, 1979). Gerrard Winstanley, writing during the revolution, has many extremely sharp observations on the learned clergy of the Church of England: "the old Kingly Clergy, that are seated in Parishes for lucre of Tythes, are continually distilling their blind Principles into the people, and do thereby nurse up Ignorance in them; for they observe the bent of the peoples minds, and make Sermons to please sickly minds of ignorant people, to preserve their riches and esteem among a charmed, befooled and besotted people." See *The Law of Freedom in a Platform or True Magistracy Restored* (1651), in *The Works of Gerrard Winstanley*, ed. George H. Sabine (New York: Russell and Russell, 1965). In Dent's model, Theologus achieves a conversion that makes of Asunetius a Calvinist tithe-paying conformist who abandons the dissenting reflections of his friend and neighbor, Antilegon. There is related, critical material in William Walwyn's *The Compassionate Samaritan* (1644) and *A Whisper in the Eare of Mr. Thomas Edwards* (1645/6), in *The Writings of William Walwyn*, ed. Jack R. McMichael and Barbara Taft (Athens: University of Georgia Press, 1989).

    6. Wrightson, *English Society*, 209. Contrast this with the picture of late medieval parishes given in Duffy, *Stripping of the Altars*, chs. 1–4.

    7. Langland, *Piers Plowman*, VII.155–59; see also VI.1–VII.181. See chapter 1 above for Langland's treatments of predestination and reprobation. For a reading of *Piers Plowman* that puts it in a broad conversation that implies aspects of early modern Christianities, see Aers, *Beyond Reformation?*

8. For a fine account of the ideology and practice of preaching in Calvinist tradition, together with shifts during the early and mid-seventeenth century, see Hunt, *The Art of Hearing.*

9. See George Gifford, *A Brief Discourse on Certain Points of Religion which is among the Common Sort of Christians which May be Termed Country Divinity* (London, 1581); Dewey Wallace, "George Gifford, Puritan Propaganda and Popular Religion in Elizabethan England," *Sixteenth Century Journal* 9, no. 1 (1978): 27–49; Timothy S. McGinnis, *George Gifford and the Reformation of the Common Sort* (Kirksville, MO: Truman State University Press, 2004), 151–52. William Perkins himself includes pastoral directions that sometimes seem closer to Gifford than to Dent: see, e.g., "Consolations for the troubled consciences of repentant sinners," in *A treatise tending unto a declaration*, 118–29.

10. See Peter Clark, *The English Alehouse: A Social History, 1200–1830* (London: Longman, 1983); and Haigh, *The Plain Man's Pathways*, 85–86, 90–92, 145–47.

11. William Shakespeare, *Twelfth Night*, in *The Riverside Shakespeare*, 2nd ed., ed. G. Blakemore Evans (Boston: Houghton Mifflin, 1997); see esp. II.3, II.5, and III.4.

12. William Blake, "The Little Vagabond," in *Songs of Experience*, in *The Complete Poetry and Prose of William Blake*, ed. David V. Erdman (Garden City, NY: Anchor Books, 1982).

13. *Piers Plowman*, VI.350–442.

14. *Piers Plowman*, VI.425.

15. For recurrent use of the language of "good providence" in the minute particulars of life, see Ralph Josselin, *The Diary of Ralph Josselin 1606–1683*, ed. Alan Macfarlane (London: British Academy and Oxford University Press, 1976, 1991).

16. For my discussion of Hutchinson, see ch. 3.

17. References in my text to Calvin's *Institutes* refer to the 1559 edition edited and translated by John T. McNeill and Ford L. Battles, *Institutes of the Christian Religion*, 2 vols. (Louisville, KY: Knox Press, 1965), and are given by book, chapter, and section number.

18. This passage, from a chapter explaining how a reprobate may be made "partaker of all that is contained in the Religion of the Church of Rome: and a Papist by his Religion cannot go beyond a Reprobate," can be found in Perkins, *A treatise tending unto a declaration*, 88–106, at 92. Similarly, in a sermon preached in 1571, John Bridges, later bishop of Oxford, asserted that Catholic teaching brings a person "to the pit brink of desperation that maketh a man al

ways mistrusting lest he shall be damned." When Calvinists reiterate this re-
frain, they do so without any doubts about their own doctrine's proclivity to
sow doubt and despair. I quote Bridges here from Peter Lake's essay, "Calvinism and the English Church 1570–1635," 37. See my discussion of assurance in
chapter 3. Calvin might think that his own line on assurance is shaped and disciplined by his Christology (see, e.g., *Institutes* II.24.4–11), but my discussion
of this in chapter 3 shows why I think this is true neither of him nor of Calvinists teaching this doctrine.

19. This is an area that fascinated Stachniewski in *The Persecutory Imagination*; see esp. chs. 1 and 3. Contrast the treatment of "despair" in Ryrie, *Being
Protestant*, ch. 2. More specific than Ryrie on the issues of election and its psychological potentials is a work referred to in a previous chapter, Dixon's *Practical Predestinarians*; here see esp. ch. 2, "William Perkins and the Search for
Certainty," and the discussion of Robert Bolton's account of the existential
hazards of his Calvinist doctrine of election, *The Last Conflicts and Death of
Mr. Thomas Peacock* (London, 1646), in ch. 7, 345–49, a text discussed at some
length in chapter 3 of the present study. Particularly relevant here (as in ch. 3)
is the work of Schreiner, *Are You Alone Wise?*, esp. 66–77. Anthony Milton
has argued that after the 1590s "there was an increasing process of elaboration
and diversification in English Calvinists' treatment of predestinarian issues,
and fewer translations were published of foreign Calvinist works of grace"; see
Catholic and Reformed, 412–13. Milton also rightly emphasizes the "tension"
within the English Calvinists' theologies of election "already evident" in the
reign of James (413; see esp. 413–18, 426–27). Ryrie's very different work, with
its different archive, seems to concur in his treatment of conversion, though he
is less clear in his narrative than Milton (Ryrie, *Being Protestant*, 35–38). See,
too, Hunt, *The Art of Hearing*.

20. Thomas Brooks, *Heaven on Earth: a treatise on Christian assurance*
(London: Banner of Truth Trust, [1654] 1961), I.1.

21. Stachniewski quotes and discusses some of this passage in his discussion of Bunyan's *The Pilgrim's Progress*; see *Persecutory Imagination*, 184–85.
There are some fascinating overlaps between Bunyan's grim treatment of the
one he names "Ignorance" and Dent's treatment of Antilegon. For an illuminating account of Bunyan's figuration of Ignorance at the end of the first part
of *Pilgrim's Progress*, see Stachniewski, *Persecutory Imagination*, 208–15.

22. Compare George Herbert's rather more Christologically shaped and
benevolent version of this figuration in "Redemption," which begins, "Having
been tenant long to a rich Lord, / Not thriving," in *The Temple: The English
Poems of George Herbert*, ed. Helen Wilcox (Cambridge: Cambridge University

Press, 2007), 132–34. For an introduction to the political and ideological struggles over tenure to which I refer and which Dent fails to make a topic of moral and theological exploration, see Brian Manning, *The English People and the English Revolution: 1640–1649* (London: Heinemann, 1976), 273–74, 293–95, 298, 308–12. Also relevant here is Christopher Hill's "Customary Liberties and Legal Rights," ch. 2 in his *Liberty against the Law* (London: Penguin, 1996). In mentioning Herbert in the context of Calvin and Dent, I should mention a recent work on these writers in which it is affirmed that Calvin's version of predestination is indeed "a doctrine of comfort in trial" in a theology of "breathtaking beauty"; see Daniel Doerksen, *Picturing Religious Experience: George Herbert, Calvin, and the Scriptures* (Newark: Delaware University Press, 2011), 16. Oddly enough, this study does not even cite Stachniewski's *Persecutory Imagination* in its bibliography, let alone address Stachniewski's critical account of Calvin's theology and its victims in seventeenth-century England. The best brief introduction to the historiography on the agrarian transformations in the seventeenth century and beyond is Ellen N. Wood, *The Origin of Capitalism: A Longer View* (London: Verso, 2017), chs. 1–6.

23. See *Institutes*, III.2.2–5; III.2.12, 15, 17, 19. For a sympathetic analysis of these strikingly contradictory strands and the insistence that there is no contradiction here, see Beeke, *Assurance of Faith*, 50–66. For a discussion of Lutheran versions of the cultivation of despair as part of contrition, see Simpson, *Burning to Read*, 86, 106–41.

24. John Bunyan, *Grace Abounding to the Chief of Sinners*, in *Grace Abounding: With Other Spiritual Autobiographies*, ed. John Stachniewski and Anita Pacheco (Oxford: Oxford University Press, 1998), 26, para. 69 [84]. See also Stachniewski, *Persecutory Imagination*, ch. 3, esp. 131–37.

25. For Calvin on the faith of reprobates and the "hypocrisy" this generates, see *Institutes* III.2.11–12, 37–38; III.24.8; and the previous chapter in this study together with the illuminating discussion of Protestant versions of hypocrisy and their sources in Herdt, *Putting on Virtue*, chs. 6 and 7, esp. 198–200, 211–13.

26. For a discussion of this argument, see Hunt, *The Art of Hearing*, 368.

27. See Twisse, *Riches of God's Love*, Book 1, 293. Twisse's work is discussed at length in chapter 3 of the present study.

28. Dent's Antilegon would have much sympathy with Robert Burton's *Anatomy of Melancholy: What it is. With all the kindes, causes, symptoms, prognosticks, and severall cures of it* (Oxford, 1624). Stachniewski does not relate this work to Dent's earlier Antilegon, but he does have a chapter on Burton in *Persecutory Imagination* (ch. 5), which is especially relevant to the current discussion.

29. See, e.g., Phil. 1:25, 3:1, 4:10; Rom. 5:1–2, 12:8; 2 Cor. 2:3, 7:4, 7:13; Col. 1:11.

30. Compare Calvin's attack on Catholic versions of the sacrament of penance in *Institutes* II.4. This could be fruitfully read alongside some of the arguments about transformations within Christianity in Sarah Beckwith's *Shakespeare and the Grammar of Forgiveness* (Ithaca, NY: Cornell University Press, 2011). When one reads through the complete text of the *Institutes* (1559), the continual polemics against late medieval Christianity and the church become very striking: it would be illuminating to have a detailed study of these polemics done by someone who knows the medieval church, its communities and devotion, as well as Eamon Duffy does. In my view, Calvin's polemics often become a smokescreen to conceal contradictions and inadequacies in his own theological reasoning. I have mentioned some profound difficulties or contradictions in Dent, Calvin, and Calvinists around "assurance" and "certainty" in both this chapter and the preceding one. None, in my view, could be more disturbing than Calvin's exultant display of the *peculiarly* Protestant version of Christ's "atonement," the dogma of penal substitution, in his treatment of the crucifixion as the creed's article on Christ's "descent into hell." See *Institutes* II.16.8–12. There are some striking illustrations of Calvinist devotion on these lines in Debora Shuger, *The Renaissance Bible: Scholarship, Sacrifice, and Subjectivity* (Berkeley: University of California Press, 1994), 107–27.

31. Recall Dent's emphasis on the paucity of the saved at, e.g., 283, 285, 287, 290, 292, 294, 324–25.

32. Simpson, *Reform and Cultural Revolution*; Duffy, *Stripping of the Altars*, pt. 2.

CHAPTER FIVE.   John Milton

1. In this chapter I quote Milton's *De Doctrina Christiana* from the fine parallel text edition and translation by John K. Hale and J. Donald Cullington in two parts in volume 8 of *The Complete Works of John Milton*, ed. Thomas Corns and Gordon Campbell (Oxford: Oxford University Press, 2012). I quote here from pp. 81 (English) and 82 (Latin). I give references in my text to book and chapter, followed, where appropriate, by page numbers of the Latin and/or English. The first translation of this work was by Charles R. Sumner in 1825, and I have made use of this in J. A. St. John's edition of *The Prose Works of John Milton*, vols. 4 and 5 (London: Bell and Sons, 1884, 1887). I have also consulted the invaluable introduction, annotations, and translation by John Carey and

Maurice Kelley in volume 6 of *The Complete Prose Works of John Milton*, ed. Don Wolfe (New Haven, CT: Yale University Press, 1973). There is a considerable literature on Milton's theology, but for my own concerns I have found the following the most helpful: Gordon Campbell, Thomas Corns, John Hale, and Fiona Tweedie, *Milton and the Manuscript of "De Doctrina Christiana"* (Oxford: Oxford University Press, 2007); Maurice Kelley, *This Great Argument: A Study of Milton's "De Doctrina Christiana" as a Gloss upon Paradise Lost* (Princeton, NJ: Princeton University Press, 1941); C. A. Patrides, *Milton and the Christian Tradition* (Oxford: Clarendon Press, 1966); Michael Lieb, *Theological Milton: Deity, Discourse, and Heresy in the Miltonic Canon* (Pittsburgh, PA: Duquesne University Press, 2006); Dennis Danielson, *Milton's Good God: A Study of Literary Theodicy* (Cambridge: Cambridge University Press, 1982); Russell M. Hillier, *Milton's Messiah: The Son of God in the Works of John Milton* (Oxford: Oxford University Press, 2011); Benjamin Myers, *Milton's Theology of Freedom* (Berlin: de Gruyter, 2006); Phillip Donnelly, *Milton's Scriptural Reasoning: Narrative and Protestant Toleration* (Cambridge: Cambridge University Press, 2009); Stephen M. Fallon, *Milton's Peculiar Grace: Self-Representation and Authority* (Ithaca, NY: Cornell University Press, 2007). In a later essay Stephen Fallon addresses some of the issues discussed in this chapter, albeit without considering earlier traditions than "Arminianism," which Milton recovers in his teaching on predestination and reprobation; see Fallon, "Milton and Literary Virtues," *Journal of Medieval and Early Modern Studies* 42, no. 1 (2012): 181–200, esp. 182, 184–87. For a careful account of Milton's Arminianism, see also Fallon, "Milton's Arminianism and the Authorship of De Doctrina Christiana," *Texas Studies in Literature and Language* 41 (1999): 103–27. Warren Chernaik's recent study, *Milton and the Burden of Freedom* (Cambridge: Cambridge University Press, 2017), presents Milton as a theologian of "Reformed Protestantism" whose theology is "Post-Calvinist," like John Goodwin's in many ways, "firmly within the Reformed tradition" but also coming to oppose Calvinist teaching on predestination and free will (see ch. 1, "Milton's Post-Calvinist Theology"). Still an influence in some recent studies of Milton is William Empson's *Milton's God*, rev. ed. (London: Chatto and Windus, 1965); Empson's explicit loathing of Christianity and its God is a fascinating work with no interest in acknowledging, let alone exploring, the many-stranded, continuously self-reforming and self-criticizing dimensions of Christian tradition. John K. Hale's recent work, *Milton's Scriptural Theology: Confronting "De Doctrina"* (Leeds: Arc Humanities Press, 2019), is surely worth consulting but was unfortunately published after I finished work on the present book.

2. John Milton, *The Ready and Easy Way to Establish a Free Commonwealth*; he published two editions in the rapidly changing situation of February and April 1660. See also the edition by N. H. Keble and Nicholas McDowell, *Vernacular Regicide and Republican Writings*, vol. 6 of *The Complete Works of John Milton* (Oxford: Oxford University Press, 2013).

3. For this, see Hale and Cullington's introduction to their edition of *De Doctrina Christiana* at lvii.

4. Many scholars have seen this as a mark of Ramist dialectic. For the most recent attempt to demonstrate Milton's Ramism and its role in *DDC*, see Hale and Cullington's introduction to *DDC*, lv–lxxiii. For a rather generalizing recent survey of these matters, see Phillip Donnelly's "Logic," in *Milton in Context*, ed. Stephen Dobranski (Cambridge: Cambridge University Press, 2010), ch. 29.

5. On this process, rather more complex than any imagined by Milton or any compatible with his ideology of pure origins followed by corruption, see Lewis Ayres, *Nicaea and Its Legacy: An Approach to Fourth Century Trinitarian Theology* (Oxford: Oxford University Press, 2004).

6. I quote Milton's poetry from *The Complete Poetry and Essential Prose of John Milton*, ed. William Kerrigan, John Rumrich, and Stephen M. Fallon (New York: Modern Library, 2007); here see *Paradise Lost* XII.504–14. Further references to *Paradise Lost* (hereafter cited as *PL*) are given in my text by book and line number.

7. On Milton's hermeneutics, see especially Dayton Haskin, *Milton's Burden of Interpretation* (Philadelphia: University of Pennsylvania Press, 1994).

8. Milton's "Ad Patrem" is an impressive illustration of this; see *The Complete Poetry and Essential Prose*, 220–24.

9. On some of these skills and their uses, see Brian Cummings, *The Literary Culture of the Reformation: Grammar and Grace* (Oxford: Oxford University Press, 2007).

10. One is tempted here to write "Holy Spirit," but this would clarify nothing given Milton's own account of the ambiguities in this language in scripture: *DDC*, I.6. Here Milton's hermeneutics converge with Quakers', a convergence discussed later in this chapter.

11. For a helpful account of the different medieval configurations of scripture, church, and tradition, see Oberman, *The Harvest of Medieval Theology*, ch. 11, esp. sec. 2.

12. For the return of images, liturgy, and sacramental Christianity in the reformed Church of England, see the fine study by Fincham and Tyacke, *Altars Restored*, esp. chs. 3–6. On iconoclasm in this Reformation tradition, see

especially Margaret Aston, *Broken Idols of the English Reformation* (Cambridge: Cambridge University Press, 2016); Simpson, *Under the Hammer*; and Simpson, *Permanent Revolution*, 192–94 (on Milton).

13. The Quakers certainly did not dismiss the usefulness of scripture as a guide to truth, arguing that written scripture should be read and searched with the Spirit. See, e.g., James Nayler, *The Lambs War* (1658); George Fox, *The Great Mystery of the Great Whore Unfolded* (1659); and Robert Barclay's *Catechism and Confession* (1673) in the anthology edited by Hugh Barbour and Arthur Roberts, *Early Quaker Writings, 1650–1700* (Wallingford: Pendle Hill Publications, 2004), at 112, 291, 292, 316–20. Here it seems necessary to recall that although many difficulties and contradictions in Quaker hermeneutics had been identified by Baptist adversaries, Milton never seems to have grasped the importance of such contemporary debates to his own treatment of scripture, its authority, and its interpretation. For an excellent introduction to this subject, see T. L. Underwood, *Primitivism, Radicalism, and the Lamb's War: The Baptist-Quaker Conflicts in Seventeenth-Century England* (Oxford: Oxford University Press, 1997), esp. chs. 2, 4, 7, 8. For illuminating accounts of Milton's profound and unacknowledged changes in his hermeneutic theory and practice in the *Divorce Tracts*, see especially the following: Haskin, *Milton's Burden of Interpretation*, ch. 3; Stanley Fish, *How Milton Works* (Cambridge, MA: Harvard University Press, 2001), ch. 6. Haskin also comments on the ironies inherent in Milton's participation "in a tradition which professes to scorn tradition" (70).

14. For Margery Baxter and Hawisia Mone, see Norman P. Tanner, ed., *Heresy Trials in the Diocese of Norwich, 1428–1431* (London: Royal Historical Society, 1977), 41–51, 138–43. For an excellent introductory anthology to women teaching, preaching, and writing in Milton's England, see Curtis W. Freeman, *A Company of Women Preachers: Baptist Prophetesses in Seventeenth-Century England, A Reader* (Waco, TX: Baylor University Press, 2011). For an illuminating introduction to the writings of Margaret Fell and Quaker women of the later seventeenth century, see Sally Bruyneel, *Margaret Fell and the End of Time: The Theology of the Mother of Quakerism* (Waco, TX: Baylor University Press, 2010), esp. ch. 5; and Teresa Feroli and Margaret Thickstun, eds., *Witness, Warning, and Prophecy: Quaker Women's Writing, 1655–1700* (Tempe, AZ: ACMRS Publications, 2018).

15. See, e.g., *Of True Religion, Haeresie, Schism, Toleration* (1673), in John Milton, *Complete Prose Works* (New Haven, CT: Yale University Press, 1982), vol. 8, 416–40.

16. All quotations of *Piers Plowman* continue to be from *Piers Plowman: A New Annotated Edition of the C-text*, ed. Derek Pearsall; English transla-

ion by George Economou. Of course, by the time Milton wrote *De Doctrina* and *Paradise Lost* many participants in the Reformation had, like Hoard (see ch. 3), rejected the Calvinist account of the absolute, unconditional decree; see the account of John Goodwin's *Redemption Redeemed* (1651), in John Coffey, *John Goodwin and the Puritan Revolution* (Woodbridge: Boydell, 2006), 214–29, esp. 216–18 on the conditionality of divine decrees.

17. For a recent work devoted to this topic, see Myers, *Milton's Theology of Freedom*, especially on the present topic at 86–89.

18. On this, consult Wetzel, "Snares of Truth," here 128–30. Still well worth reading on this "poison" is the work by Norman P. Williams, *The Idea of the Fall and of Original Sin: A Historical and Critical Study* (London: Longmans, Green & Co., 1927), esp. 326–32 and 360–84.

19. See chapter 2, with the work of Halverson, *Peter Aureol*.

20. For some difficulties in Ockham's early theology in this area, see Aers, *Salvation and Sin*, ch. 2; and, in an outstanding grand narrative, Pfau, *Minding the Modern*, chs. 6–8.

21. Consult Hale and Cullington, *DDC* part I, "Translating the Biblical Citations," xlvii–li.

22. On "the ultimate rejection of God" which constitutes damnation, John Paul II wrote, "*Here, it is not so much God who rejects man, but man who rejects God*" (emphasis in original). See *Crossing the Threshold of Hope* (London, Cape: 1994), 73. How interesting to find Milton in total congruence with a Roman Catholic theologian and pope.

23. See my discussion of Twisse in chapter 3 of the present volume.

24. See Kelley, *This Great Argument*, 71–84.

25. Holcot's *Lectiones on the Book of Wisdom* is replete with quotations from Ovid, Virgil, and other Roman writing; see Smalley, *English Friars and Antiquity in the Early Fourteenth Century*.

26. Cf. Calvin's *Institutes* I.16–18. Although she does not discuss the issues of predestination and reprobation that concerned many Protestants, Alexandra Walsham's study of providence is very informative: *Providence in Early Modern England* (Oxford: Oxford University Press, 1999).

27. Here I use Beveridge's translation of the 1559 *Institutes of the Christian Religion*.

28. See Tyacke, *Anti-Calvinists*, 70–74, 156–57, 175–76, 196–97, 216–17, 256–59; White, *Predestination, Policy, and Polemic*, 195–99, 219–21, 225–28. In the discussion of these issues throughout chapter 3 I provide copious references to relevant secondary literature.

29. Sumner's translation, 373 n. 7; he cites *Institutes* III.3.23 and III.24.6–7.

30. Milton, *Complete Poetry and Essential Prose*, 30–33.

31. Ibid., 31. For reflections on the range of political and ideological questions raised by different ways of writing about Christ's Passion, see David Aers and Lynn Staley, *The Powers of the Holy: Religion, Politics, and Gender in Late Medieval English Culture* (University Park: Pennsylvania State University Press, 1996), chs. 1–3 and epilogue; pp. 264–65 mention "The Passion." For an attempt to go against the grain of Milton criticism here, see Hillier, *Milton's Messiah*; unfortunately, Hillier confuses Anselm's account of the redemption in *Cur Deus Homo* with that of Protestant theories of penal substitution (e.g., 166–67, 27).

32. For Socinian rejection of Catholic and Protestant soteriology, see Thomas Rees, ed. and trans., *The Racovian Catechism* (London: Longman, 1818); see Lieb, *Theological Milton*, on Socinianism and some of Milton's differences.

33. J. N. D. Kelly summarizes the decisions of Chalcedon in *Early Christian Doctrines*, 338–43. For two especially illuminating works on the way theologians addressed (or evaded) substantial difficulties here, see Gondreau, *The Passions of Christ's Soul in the Theology of St. Thomas Aquinas*; Madigan, *The Passions of Christ*.

34. See, too, *Institutes* IV.17.30. I have substituted "conceived" for the rather odd "borne in the virgin's womb" in II.13.4 in the Battles edition I habitually use. For Aquinas's teaching on the impassibility of Christ's divinity in the Incarnation, see *ST* III.16.8 with III.46.12.

35. On Milton's own contribution to terminological inconsistency, see Maurice Kelley's notes in Carey's translation of *DDC* (vol. 6 of *Complete Works*) cited by Hale and Cullington, *DDC* 491 n. xx.

36. Hale and Cullington, in their note to this in *DDC*, relate this to *PL* VIII.71–78 and 172–74.

37. For Abelard's critical reflections, see his *Commentary on the Epistle to the Romans*, trans. Steven Cartwright (Washington, DC: Catholic University of America Press, 2011), bk. 2, 164–68. Consult the helpful study by Richard Weingart, *The Logic of Divine Love: A Critical Analysis of the Soteriology of Peter Abelard* (Oxford: Clarendon Press, 1970), chs. 3, 5. For the *Racovian Catechism*, see n. 32 above.

38. For striking examples of Calvinist crucifixion writing, see Shuger, *The Renaissance Bible*, ch. 3, "The Death of Christ." Among scholars of Calvin on this topic I have found the following most helpful: Stephen Edmondson, *Calvin's Christology* (Cambridge: Cambridge University Press, 2004), 96–102.

39. I adjust the translation of the Blackfriars parallel text edition here because it introduces the language of rights gratuitously, a red herring (vol. 54, 10–11).

40. The issues of limited atonement and "hypothetical universalism" were contested topics in the pre–Civil War Church of England; see Tyacke, *Anti-Calvinists*, 94–99, 179–80, 249–57; White, *Predestination, Policy, and Polemic*, 187–92; Milton, *Catholic and Reformed*, 420–24.

41. See Myers on this commitment in Milton's works, *Milton's Theology of Freedom*, chs. 2, 3, 5, 6.

42. Myers, *Milton's Theology of Freedom*, 87; emphasis in the original.

43. For a superb introduction to this tradition of inquiry, see Gelber, *It Could Have Been Otherwise*.

44. See Myers, *Milton's Theology of Freedom*, 78 with ch. 2; on Satan's compositions, see Dennis Burden, *The Logical Epic: A Study of the Argument of Paradise Lost* (London: Routledge, 1967). For Milton's dazzling account of pagan metaphysics and poetry in hell, see *PL* II.546–69. It seems to me that Stachniewski locates Milton's vestigial Calvinism in this place in *The Persecutory Imagination*, ch. 8. He observes that in *DDC* and *Paradise Lost* Milton was "rejecting Calvinism" but claims that he "readmitted it by a back door" in making Satan "the predestined reprobate" of Calvinist ideology (337). This claim ignores the way Milton shows, contrary to demonic fatalism, that Satan and his allies freely chose to reject God. Oddly enough, Stachniewski had nothing to say about *PL* V–VI, the account of the processes through which Satan chooses against God and his covenant with the angels. As in *DDC* so in *Paradise Lost*: rational creatures reprobate God before he reprobates them.

45. On "sinceritas," see *DDC* II.2, 932–37.

46. See the note to these lines in the edition of *Paradise Lost* by John Leonard, *John Milton: The Complete Poems*, 747 n. 183; with the comments in Myers, *Milton's Theology of Freedom*, 77 n. 11 and 79 n. 23. For the essay by Fallon that Myers refers to, see its inclusion in the arguments of Fallon's later book, *Milton's Peculiar Grace*; this concludes a chapter on *DDC* and *Paradise Lost* (ch. 7).

47. Ockham, I *Sentences* ch. 41, q. v., in *Opera Theologica* IV.606, translated and discussed by Adams, *William of Ockham*, vol. 2, 1330; see 1327–34. Halverson, unlike Adams, sees Ockham as a proponent of GE in *Peter Aureol*, 113–22. These issues are discussed in chapter 2 of the present work.

48. "The Dry Salvages," pt. 2.

49. I am, here and widely, influenced by Alasdair MacIntyre, especially his *After Virtue*, ch. 15; *Three Rival Versions of Moral Enquiry*; *Whose Justice? Which Rationality?*; and *Ethics in the Conflicts of Modernity*. See the preface to this volume, which acknowledges and illustrates this relationship in its discussion of the present book's explorations of the ways in which traditions unfold.

BIBLIOGRAPHY

Primary Sources

Abelard, Peter. *Commentary on the Epistle to the Romans*. Translated by Steven Cartwright. Washington, DC: Catholic University of America Press, 2011.

Anselm of Canterbury. *The Major Works*. Edited by Brian Davies and G. R. Evans. Oxford: Oxford University Press, 1998.

Aquinas, Thomas. *Catena Aurea: Commentary on the Four Gospels Collected out of the Works of the Fathers*. 4 vols. Translated and edited by John Henry Newman. London: Saint Austin Press, 1999.

———. *Opuscula Theologica*. 2 vols. Edited by R. A. Verardo, R. M. Spiazzi, and M. Calcaterra. Rome: Marietti, 1954.

———. *Summa Contra Gentiles*. Edited and translated by Vernon J. Bourke. Notre Dame, IN: University of Notre Dame Press, 1975.

———. *Summa Theologiae*. 61 vols. London: Blackfriars, 1964–81.

———. *Summa Theologiae*. 8 vols. Translated by Laurence Shapcote. Edited by John Mortensen and Enrique Alarcón. Lander, WY: Aquinas Institute, 2012.

Arminius, James. *The Works of James Arminius*. 3 vols. n.p.: Lamp Post, 2015.

Athanasius. *On the Incarnation*. Crestwood, NY: St. Vladimir's Seminary Press, 1993.

Augustine. *The Augustine Catechism: The Enchiridion on Faith, Hope, and Love*. Translated by Bruce Harbert. Hyde Park, NY: New City Press, 1999.

———. *The City of God against the Pagans*. Translated by R. W. Dyson. Cambridge: Cambridge University Press, 1998.

———. *Confessions*. Translated by Henry Chadwick. Oxford: Oxford University Press, 1991.

———. *Confessions*. 3 vols. Edited by James J. O'Donnell. Oxford: Clarendon Press, 1992.

———. *De civitate Dei.* 5th ed. 2 vols. Edited by B. Dombart and A. Kalb. Stuttgart: Teubner, 1993.

———. *Earlier Writings.* Translated by John H. S. Burleigh. London: SCM Press, 1953.

———. *Epistles.* 4 vols. Translated by Roland J. Teske. Edited by Boniface Ramsey. The Works of Saint Augustine: A Translation for the 21st Century (hereafter WSA), pt. 2, vols. 1–4. Hyde Park, NY: New City Press, 2001–5.

———. *Expositions of the Psalms.* 6 vols. Translated by Maria Boulding. Edited by John E. Rotelle. WSA, pt. 3, vols. 15–20. Hyde Park, NY: New City Press, 2001–4.

———. *Homilies on the Gospel of John.* Edited by Philip Schaff. Edinburgh: Clark, 1986.

———. *The Predestination of the Saints.* Translated by Roland J. Teske. In *Answer to the Pelagians IV.* WSA, pt. 1, vol. 26. Hyde Park, NY: New City Press, 1999.

———. *Rebuke and Grace.* Translated by Roland J. Teske. In *Answer to the Pelagians IV.* WSA, pt. 1, vol. 26. Hyde Park, NY: New City Press, 1999.

———. *Sermons.* 10 vols. Translated by Edmund Hill. WSA, pt. 3, vols. 1–10. Brooklyn, NY: New City Press, 1990–95.

———. *The Trinity.* Translated by Stephen McKenna. Washington, DC: Catholic University of America Press, 1988.

Barbour, Hugh, and Arthur Roberts, eds. *Early Quaker Writings, 1650–1700.* Wallingford: Pendle Hill Publications, 2004.

Barth, Karl. *Church Dogmatics.* 4 pts. in 12 vols. Translated by Geoffrey W. Bromiley. Edinburgh: T&T Clark, 1956–75.

Baxter, Richard. *Reliquiae Baxterianae.* Edited by M. Sylvester. London, 1696.

Bernard of Clairvaux. *On the Song of Songs.* 4 vols. Translated by Killian Walsh and Irene Edmonds. Kalamazoo, MI: Cistercian Publications, 1979.

Biblia Sacra iuxta Vulgatem Clementinam: Nova Editio. 4th ed. Edited by Alberto Colunga and Laurentio Turrado. Matriti: Biblioteca de Autores Cristianos, 1965.

Blake, William. *Songs of Experience.* In *The Complete Poetry and Prose of William Blake,* edited by David V. Erdman. Garden City, NY: Anchor Books, 1982.

Bolton, Robert. *Discourse about the state of true happiness.* London, 1611.

———. *The Last Conflicts and Death of Mr. Thomas Peacock Batchelour of Divinity, and fellow of Brasen-nose Colledge in Oxford.* London, 1646.

Bradwardine, Thomas. *De Causa Dei contra Pelagium et de Virtute Causarum.* London, 1618.

Bromyard, John. *Summa Praedicantium*. London, 1614. Cambridge University Library, shelfmark G*-1-28 (B).

Brooks, Thomas. *Heaven on Earth: a treatise on Christian assurance*. London: Banner of Truth Trust, [1654] 1961.

Bunyan, John. *Grace Abounding to the Chief of Sinners*. In *Grace Abounding: With Other Spiritual Autobiographies*, edited by John Stachniewski and Anita Pacheco. Oxford: Oxford University Press, 1998.

Burton, Robert. *Anatomy of Melancholy: What it is. With all the kindes, causes, symptoms, prognosticks, and severall cures of it*. Oxford, 1624.

Calvin, John. *Institutes of the Christian Religion*. 2 vols. Edited by John T. McNeil. Translated by Ford L. Battles. Philadelphia: Westminster Press, John Knox Press, 1960.

———. *Institutes of the Christian Religion*. Translated by Henry Beveridge. Peabody, MA: Henrickson, 2009.

———. *Johannis Calvin Opera Selecta*. 5 vols. Edited by P. Barth and W. Niesel. Munich: Kaiser, 1928–36; 2nd ed. 1957–59.

Cawdrey, Robert. *A Treasurie or Store-House of Similies*. London, 1600.

Chaucer, Geoffrey. *The Wadsworth Chaucer*. 3rd ed. Edited by Larry D. Benson. Boston: Wadsworth, 1987.

Denis the Carthusian. *In Quatuor Evangelistas Enarrationes*. Paris, 1552. Cambridge University Library, shelfmark F*.8.30(B).

Dent, Arthur. *The Plaine Man's Path-way to Heaven. Wherein every man may clearly see whether he shall be saved or damned. Set forth Dialoguewise for the better understanding of the simple*. London, 1601. Cambridge University Library, Peterborough E.2.42.

Dod, John, and Robert Cleaver. *Foure Godlie and Fruitful Sermons*. London, 1611.

Feroli, Teresa, and Margaret Thickstun, eds. *Witness, Warning, and Prophecy: Quaker Women's Writing, 1655–1700*. Tempe, AZ: ACMRS Publications, 2018.

Freeman, Curtis W., ed. *A Company of Women Preachers: Baptist Prophetesses in Seventeenth-Century England, a Reader*. Waco, TX: Baylor University Press, 2011.

Gifford, George. *A Brief Discourse on Certain Points of Religion which is among the Common Sort of Christians which May be Termed Country Divinity*. London, 1581.

Gregory of Rimini. *Lectura Super Primum et Secundum Sententiarum*. 7 vols. Edited by Damasus Trapp and Venicio Marcolino. Berlin: de Gruyter, 1979–84.

Harsnett, Samuel. *A Sermon Preached at S. Paul's Cross in London, the 27 day of October Anno Reginae Elizabethae 26.* In Richard Steward, *Three Sermons.* London, 1656.

Herbert, George. *The English Poems of George Herbert.* Edited by Helen Wilcox. Cambridge: Cambridge University Press, 2007.

Hoard, Samuel. *Gods Love To Mankind Manifested, By Dis-Prooving his Absolute Decree for their Damnation.* London, 1633. Cambridge University Library, shelfmark BG*.11.9.

Holcot, Robert. *In Librum Sapientiae Regis Salomonis.* Basel, 1586. Cambridge University Library, shelfmark B*.1.9 (B).

The Holy Bible, Translated from the Latin Vulgate. Revised by Richard Challoner. Rockford, IL: Tan Books, 1989.

Hudson, Anne, and Pamela Gradon, eds. *English Wycliffite Sermons.* 5 vols. Oxford: Oxford University Press, 1983–96.

Hugh of St. Cher. *Opera Omnia.* Venice, 1600.

Hutchinson, Lucy. *The Works of Lucy Hutchinson.* 2 vols. Edited by Elizabeth Clarke, David Norbrook, and Jane Stevenson. Oxford: Oxford University Press, 2018.

John Duns Scotus. *The Examined Report of Paris Lecture: Reportato I-A.* 2 vols. Edited by Allan Wolter and Oleg Bychkov. St. Bonaventure, NY: St. Bonaventure University Press, 2007.

Josselin, Ralph. *The Diary of Ralph Josselin 1606–1683.* Edited by Alan Macfarlane. London: British Academy and Oxford University Press, 1976, 1991.

Julian of Norwich. *Book of Showings to the Anchoress Julian of Norwich.* Edited by James Walsh and Edmund College. 2 vols. Toronto: Pontifical Institute of Mediaeval Studies, 1978.

———. *The Writings of Julian of Norwich.* Edited by Nicholas Watson and Jacqueline Jenkins. University Park: Pennsylvania State University Press, 2006.

Kane, Harold, ed. *The Prickynge of Love.* 2 vols. Salzburg: Salzburg University, 1983.

Langland, William. *Piers Plowman: The B Version.* Rev. ed. Edited by George Kane and E. Talbot Donaldson. London: Athlone, 1988.

———. *Piers Plowman: The C Version; Will's Vision of Piers Plowman, Do-Well, Do-Better, and Do-Best.* Edited by George Russell and George Kane. London: Athlone, 1997.

———. *Piers Plowman: A New Annotated Edition of the C-text.* Edited by Derek Pearsall. Exeter: University of Exeter Press, 2010.

———. *Piers Plowman: A Parallel-Text Edition of the A, B, C and Z Versions.* Edited by A. V. C. Schmidt. 2 vols. Kalamazoo, MI: Medieval Institute Publications, 2008.

———. *The Vision of Pierce Plowman: now the second tyme imprinted by Roberte Crowley.* London, 1550. Cambridge University Library, shelf-mark Syn. 7.55.25.

———. *The Vision of William concerning Piers the Plowman in Three Parallel Texts: Together with Richard the Redeles.* 2 vols. Edited by Walter W. Skeat. Oxford: Clarendon Press, 1886; repr. Oxford: Oxford University Press, 1968.

———. *William Langland's "Piers Plowman": The C Version.* Translated by George Economou. Philadelphia: University of Pennsylvania Press, 1996.

Laud, William. "Answer to the Lord Say's Speech Touching the Liturgy." In *The Works of the Most Revered Father in God William Laud D.D.*, vol. 6, pt. 1, *Miscellaneous Papers-Letters.* Oxford: Oxford University Press, 1847–60.

Lombard, Peter. *The Sentences: Book I.* Translated by Giulio Silano. Toronto: Pontifical Institute of Medieval Studies, 2007.

———. *Sententiae in IV Libris Distinctae.* 3rd ed. 2 vols. Edited by Ignatius Brady. Grottaferrata: Editiones Collegii S. Bonaventurae ad Claras Aquas, 1971–81.

Milton, John. *The Complete Poems.* Edited by John Leonard. London: Penguin, 1998.

———. *The Complete Poetry and Essential Prose of John Milton.* Edited by William Kerrigan, John Rumrich, and Stephen M. Fallon. New York: Modern Library, 2007.

———. *The Complete Prose Works of John Milton.* 8 vols. Edited by Don Wolfe. New Haven, CT: Yale University Press, 1953–82.

———. *De Doctrina Christiana.* 2 vols. Edited and translated by John K. Hale and J. Donald Cullington. Vol. 8 of *The Complete Works of John Milton.* Oxford: Oxford University Press, 2012.

———. *De Doctrina Christiana.* Translated by Charles R. Sumner. Vols. 4 and 5 of *The Prose Works of John Milton*, edited by J. A. St. John. London: Bell and Sons, 1884, 1887.

———. *The Ready and Easy Way to Establish a Free Commonwealth.* London, 1660.

———. *Vernacular Regicide and Republican Writings.* Edited by N. H. Keeble and Nicholas McDowell. Vol. 6 of *The Complete Works of John Milton.* Oxford: Oxford University Press, 2013.

Montague, Richard. *A Gagg for the Gospel? No. A New Gagg for an Old Goose*. London, 1624.

Musculus, Wolfgang. *Common places of Christian religion*. Translated by John Man. London, 1563.

Nicholas of Gorran. *In Quatuor Evangelia*. Cologne, 1537. Cambridge University Library, shelfmark C.9.11.

Nicholas of Lyra. *Glossa Ordinaria, Biblia Sacra cum Glossa Ordinaria*. Antwerp, 1634. Cambridge University Library, shelfmark 1.20.16.

Perkins, William. *A Golden Chaine: Or, The description of theologie: containing the order of the causes of salvation and damnation*. Cambridge, 1597.

———. *A treatise tending unto a declaration, whether a man be in the estate of damnation, or in the estate of grace*. London, 1591.

———. *The Workes of that famous and Worthy Minister of Christ in the Universitie of Cambridge, Mr. William Perkins*. 3 vols. London: John Leggatt [printer to the University of Cambridge], 1612–13.

Pierce, Thomas. *A Correct Copy of Some Notes Concerning God's Decrees, Especially of Reprobation*. London, 1657.

Rees, Thomas, ed. and trans. *The Racovian Catechism*. London: Longman, 1818.

Roman de la Rose. 3 vols. Edited by Felix Lecoy. Paris: Champion, 1965–70.

The Romance of the Rose. Translated by Francis Horgan. Oxford: Oxford University Press, 1994.

Ross, W. O., ed. *Middle English Sermons*. Early English Text Society (hereafter EETS), o.s., 209. London: Oxford University Press, 1940.

Ruusbroec, Jan van. *The Chastising of God's Children and The Treatise on Perfection*. Edited by Joyce Bazire and Edmund College. Oxford: Blackwell, 1957.

Sclater, William. *Sermons Experiential*. London, 1638.

Shakespeare, William. *The Complete Works*. 2nd ed. Edited by Stanley Wells and Gary Taylor. Oxford: Clarendon Press, 2005.

———. *The Riverside Shakespeare*. 2nd ed. Edited by G. Blakemore Evans. Boston: Houghton Mifflin, 1997.

Smith, Nigel, ed. *A Collection of Ranter Writings from the Seventeenth Century*. London: Junction Books, 1983.

Spenser, Edmund. *The Faerie Queene*. 2nd ed. Edited by A. C. Hamilton. London: Longmans, 2007.

Sydenham, Humphrey. *Five Sermons, upon several occasions preach'd at Paul's Crosse, and at St. Maries in Oxford*. London, 1627. Cambridge University Library, shelfmark Peterborough K.1.20.

Tanner, Norman P., ed. *Heresy Trials in the Diocese of Norwich, 1428–1431*. London: Royal Historical Society, 1977.

Thomas à Kempis. *The Imitation of Christ*. Edited by B. J. H. Biggs. EETS, o.s., 309. Oxford: Oxford University Press, EETS, 1997.

Twisse, William. *The Riches of God's Love unto the Vessells of Mercy, Consistent with His Absolute Hatred or Reprobation of the Vessells of Wrath; Or An Answer unto a book entituled God's Love unto Mankind, Manifested by Disproving His Absolute Decree for their Damnation*. Edited by Henry Jeanes. Oxford: Thomas Robinson, 1653. Cambridge University Library, shelfmark E*-9-33.

Valentine, Henry. *Private Devotions, Digested in Six Letanies*. London, 1635.

Walwyn, William. *The Writings of William Walwyn*. Edited by Jack R. McMichael and Barbara Taft. Athens: University of Georgia Press, 1989.

Whitaker, William. *A Disputation on Holy Scripture, Against the Papists*. Cambridge: Cambridge University Press, 1849.

William of Ockham. *On the Power of Emperors and Popes*. Edited and translated by Annabel S. Brett. Bristol: Thoemmes Press, 1998.

———. *Predestination, God's Foreknowledge, and Future Contingents*. Edited and translated by Marilyn McCord Adams and Norman Kretzmann. New York: Appleton-Century Crofts, 1969.

———. *Quaestiones Variae*. In *Opera Philosophica et Theologica*, edited by G. I. Etzkorn and F. E. Kelley. St. Bonaventure, NY: St. Bonaventure University Press, 1979.

———. *Quodlibetal Questions*. 2 vols. Translated by Alfred Freddoso and Francis Kelley. New Haven, CT: Yale University Press, 1991.

———. *Scriptum in librum primum senentiarum (ordinatio). Distinctiones 19–48*. In *Opera Philosophica et Theologica*, edited by G. I. Etzkorn and F. E. Kelley. St. Bonaventure, NY: St. Bonaventure University Press, 1979.

———. *Work of Ninety Days*. Translated by John Kilcullen and John Scott. 2 vols. Lewiston, NY: Mellen Press, 2001.

Winstanley, Gerrard. *The Law of Freedom in a Platform or True Magistracy Restored* (1651). In *The Works of Gerrard Winstanley*, edited by George H. Sabine. New York: Russell and Russell, 1965.

Wyclif, John. *Sermones*. 4 vols. Edited by J. Loserth. London: Trübner, 1887–90.

———. *Trialogus cum supplemento tralogi*. Edited by G. V. Lechler. Oxford: Clarendon Press, 1869.

SECONDARY SOURCES

Adams, Marilyn McCord. *William of Ockham*. 2 vols. Notre Dame, IN: University of Notre Dame Press, 1987.

Aers, David. *Beyond Reformation? An Essay on William Langland's "Piers Plowman" and the End of Constantinian Christianity.* Notre Dame, IN: University of Notre Dame Press, 2015.

———. *Chaucer, Langland and the Creative Imagination.* London: Routledge, 1980.

———. *Salvation and Sin: Augustine, Langland, and Fourteenth-Century Theology.* Notre Dame, IN: University of Notre Dame Press, 2009.

———. "A Whisper in the Ear of Early Modernists." In *Culture and History, 1350–1600: Essays on English Communities, Identities, and Writing,* edited by David Aers, 177–202. Hemel Hempstead: Harvester Wheatsheaf, 1992.

Aers, David, and Russ Leo. "Unintended Reformations?" *Journal of Medieval and Early Modern Studies* 46, no. 3 (2016): 455–83.

Aers, David, and Lynn Staley. *The Powers of the Holy: Religion, Politics, and Gender in Late Medieval English Culture.* University Park: Pennsylvania State University Press, 1996.

Appleford, Amy. *Learning to Die in London 1380–1540.* Philadelphia: University of Pennsylvania Press, 2014.

Aston, Margaret. *Broken Idols of the English Reformation.* Cambridge: Cambridge University Press, 2016.

Ayres, Lewis. *Nicaea and Its Legacy: An Approach to Fourth Century Trinitarian Theology.* Oxford: Oxford University Press, 2004.

Beckwith, Sarah. *Shakespeare and the Grammar of Forgiveness.* Ithaca, NY: Cornell University Press, 2011.

———. *Signifying God: Social Relation and Symbolic Act in the York Corpus Christi Plays.* Chicago: University of Chicago Press, 2001.

Beeke, Joel R. *Assurance of Faith: Calvin, English Puritanism, and the Dutch Second Reformation.* New York: Lang, 1996.

———. "Personal Assurance of Faith: The Puritans and Chapter 18.2 of the Westminster Confession." *Westminster Theological Journal* 55 (1993): 1–30.

Bonner, Gerald. *Freedom and Necessity: St. Augustine's Teaching on Divine and Human Freedom.* Washington, DC: Catholic University of America Press, 2007.

Bossy, John. *Christianity in the West, 1400–1700.* Oxford: Oxford University Press, 1985.

———. "The Mass as a Social Institution 1200–1700." *Past and Present* 100 (1983): 29–61.

Brown, D. Catherine. *Pastor and Laity in the Theology of Jean Gerson.* Cambridge: Cambridge University Press, 1987.

Bruyneel, Sally. *Margaret Fell and the End of Time. The Theology of the Mother of Quakerism.* Waco, TX: Baylor University Press, 2010.

Burden, Dennis. *The Logical Epic: A Study of the Argument of Paradise Lost.* London: Routledge, 1967.

Campbell, Gordon, Thomas Corns, John Hale, and Fiona Tweedie. *Milton and the Manuscript of "De Doctrina Christiana."* Oxford: Oxford University Press, 2007.

Catto, J. L., and Ralph Evans, eds. *The History of the University of Oxford,* vol. 2, *Late Medieval Oxford.* Oxford: Clarendon Press, 1992.

Cavell, Stanley. *The Claim of Reason: Wittgenstein, Skepticism, Morality and Tragedy.* New York: Oxford University Press, 1999.

———. *Disowning Knowledge in Seven Plays of Shakespeare.* Cambridge: Cambridge University Press, 1987.

Chernaik, Warren. *Milton and the Burden of Freedom.* Cambridge: Cambridge University Press, 2017.

Clark, Peter. *The English Alehouse: A Social History, 1200–1830.* London: Longman, 1983.

Coffey, John. *John Goodwin and the Puritan Revolution.* Woodbridge: Boydell, 2006.

Colish, Marcia. *Peter Lombard.* 2 vols. Leiden: Brill, 1994.

Como, David. *Blown by the Spirit: Puritanism and the Emergence of an Antinomian Underground in Pre-Civil-War England.* Stanford, CA: Stanford University Press, 2004.

Correale, Robert M., and Mary Hammel. *Sources and Analogues of the Canterbury Tales.* 2 vols. Cambridge: Brewer, 2003.

Courtenay, W. J. *Schools and Scholars in Fourteenth-Century England.* Princeton, NJ: Princeton University Press, 1987.

Craig, John. *Reformation, Politics and Polemics: The Growth of Protestantism in East Anglian Market Towns, 1500–1610.* Aldershot: Ashgate, 2001.

Cross, Richard. *Duns Scotus.* Oxford: Oxford University Press, 1999.

Cummings, Brian. *The Literary Culture of the Reformation: Grammar and Grace.* Oxford: Oxford University Press, 2007.

Danielson, Dennis. *Milton's Good God: A Study of Literary Theodicy.* Cambridge: Cambridge University Press, 1982.

Davies, Brian. *Thomas Aquinas on God and Evil.* Oxford: Oxford University Press, 2011.

Davies, Julian. *The Caroline Captivity of the Church: Charles I and the Remoulding of Anglicanism 1625–1641.* Oxford: Oxford University Press, 1992.

Davis, Rebecca. *Piers Plowman and the Book of Nature.* Oxford: Oxford University Press, 2016.

Davlin, Mary Clement. *A Game of Heuene: Word Play and the Meaning of Piers Plowman.* Cambridge: Brewer, 1989.

Dinshaw, Carolyn. *Chaucer's Sexual Poetics*. Madison: University of Wisconsin Press, 1989.

Dixon, Leif. *Practical Predestinarians in England c. 1590–1640*. Farnham: Ashgate, 2014.

Doerksen, Daniel. *Picturing Religious Experience: George Herbert, Calvin, and the Scriptures*. Newark: Delaware University Press, 2011.

Donnelly, Phillip. "Logic." In *Milton in Context*, edited by Stephen Dobranski, 349–60. Cambridge: Cambridge University Press, 2010.

———. *Milton's Scriptural Reasoning: Narrative and Protestant Toleration*. Cambridge: Cambridge University Press, 2009.

Duffy, Eamon. *Reformation Divided: Catholics, Protestants and the Conversion of England*. London: Bloomsbury, 2017.

———. *The Stripping of the Altars: Traditional Religion in England, 1400–1580*. 2nd ed. New Haven, CT: Yale University Press, 2005.

Durston, Christopher. "Puritan Rule and the Failure of Cultural Revolution, 1645–1660." In *The Culture of English Puritanism, 1560–1700*, edited by Christopher Durston and Jacqueline Eales, 210–33. New York: St. Martin's Press, 1996.

Eales, Jacqueline. *Puritans and Roundheads: The Harleys of Brempton Bryan and the Outbreak of the English Civil War*. Cambridge: Cambridge University Press, 1990.

Edmondson, Stephen. *Calvin's Christology*. Cambridge: Cambridge University Press, 2004.

Ellis, Mark. *Simon Episcopius' Doctrine of Original Sin*. New York: Lang, 2006.

Emden, A. B. *A Biographical Register of the University of Oxford to A.D. 1500*. Oxford: Clarendon Press, 1957.

Empson, William. *Milton's God*. Rev. ed. London: Chatto and Windus, 1965.

Fallon, Stephen M. "Milton and Literary Virtue." *Journal of Medieval and Early Modern Studies* 42, no. 1 (2012): 181–200.

———. "Milton's Arminianism and the Authorship of *De Doctrina Christiana*." *Texas Studies in Literature and Language* 41 (1999): 103–27.

———. *Milton's Peculiar Grace: Self-Representation and Authority*. Ithaca, NY: Cornell University Press, 2007.

Feingold, Lawrence. *The Natural Desire to See God according to St. Thomas Aquinas and His Interpreters*. 2nd ed. Naples, FL: Sapientia Press, 2010.

Fincham, Kenneth, and Nicholas Tyacke. *Altars Restored: The Changing Face of English Religious Worship 1547–c. 1700*. Oxford: Oxford University Press, 2008.

Fish, Stanley. *How Milton Works*. Cambridge, MA: Harvard University Press, 2001.

Fowler, Elizabeth. *Literary Character: The Human Figure in Early English Writing*. Ithaca, NY: Cornell University Press, 2003.

Friedman, Russell G. *Intellectual Traditions at the Medieval University: The Use of Philosophical Psychology in Trinitarian Theology among the Franciscans and Dominicans, 1250–1350*. 2 vols. Leiden: Brill, 2013.

Gelber, Hester. *It Could Have Been Otherwise*: Contingency and Necessity in Dominican Theology at Oxford, 1300–1350. Leiden: Brill, 2004.

Gillespie, Michael A. *The Theological Origins of Modernity*. Chicago: University of Chicago Press, 2008.

Gondreau, Paul. *The Passions of Christ's Soul in the Theology of St. Thomas Aquinas*. Scranton, PA: University of Scranton Press, 2009.

Gradon, Pamela. "Langland and the Ideology of Dissent." *Proceedings of the British Academy* 66 (1980): 179–208.

Grady, Frank. *Representing Righteous Heathens in Late Medieval England*. New York: Palgrave Macmillan, 2005.

Gruenler, Chris. *Piers Plowman and the Poetics of Enigma: Riddles, Rhetoric, and Theology*. Notre Dame, IN: University of Notre Dame Press, 2017.

Hacker, Paul. *Faith in Luther: Martin Luther and the Origin of Anthropocentric Religion*. Steubenville, OH: Emmaus Academic, 2017.

Haigh, Christopher. *The Plain Man's Pathways to Heaven: Kinds of Christianity in Post-Reformation England*. Oxford: Oxford University Press, 2007.

Hale, John K. *Milton's Scriptural Theology: Confronting "De Doctrina."* Leeds: Arc Humanities Press, 2019.

Halverson, James. *Peter Aureol on Predestination*: A Challenge to Late Medieval Thought. Leiden: Brill, 1998.

Hanna, Ralph. *Introducing English Medieval Book History: Manuscripts, Their Production, and Their Reading*. Liverpool: Liverpool University Press, 2013.

———. *The Penn Commentary on Piers Plowman*. Vol. 2. Philadelphia: University of Pennsylvania Press, 2017.

———. *William Langland*. Aldershot: Variorum, 1993.

Haskin, Dayton. *Milton's Burden of Interpretation*. Philadelphia: University of Pennsylvania Press, 1994.

Helms, Paul. *John Calvin's Ideas*. Oxford: Oxford University Press, 2009.

Herdt, Jennifer. *Putting on Virtue: The Legacy of the Splendid Vices*. Chicago: University of Chicago Press, 2008.

Hill, Christopher. *Liberty against the Law: Some Seventeenth-Century Controversies*. London: Penguin, 1996.

———. *Society and Puritanism in Pre-Revolutionary England*. London: Panther, [1964] 1969.

Hillier, Russell M. *Milton's Messiah: The Son of God in the Works of John Milton*. Oxford: Oxford University Press, 2011.

Hort, Greta. *Piers Plowman and Contemporary Religious Thought*. London: SPCK, 1938.

Houlbrooke, Ralph. "The Puritan Death-bed, c. 1560–c. 1660." In *The Culture of English Puritanism, 1560–1700*, edited by Christopher Durston and Jacqueline Eales, 122–44. New York: St. Martin's Press, 1996.

Hudson, Anne. "*Laicus Litteratus*: The Paradox of Lollardy." In *Heresy and Literature 1100–1530*, edited by Peter Biller and Anne Hudson, 222–36. Cambridge: Cambridge University Press, 1994.

Hunsinger, George. *Disruptive Grace: Studies in the Theology of Karl Barth*. Grand Rapids, MI: Eerdmans, 2000.

Hunt, Arnold. *The Art of Hearing: English Preachers and Their Audiences 1590–1640*. Cambridge: Cambridge University Press, 2010.

Hütter, Reinhard. *Dust Bound for Heaven: Explorations in the Theology of Thomas Aquinas*. Grand Rapids, MI: Eerdmans, 2012.

Hutton, Ronald. *The Rise and Fall of Merry England: The Ritual Year, 1400–1700*. Oxford: Oxford University Press, 1994.

Hutton, Sarah. "Thomas Jackson, Oxford Platonist, and William Twisse, Aristotelian." *Journal of the History of Ideas* 39 (1978): 635–52.

James, Frank. "A Late Medieval Parallel in Reformation Thought: *Gemina Praedestinatio* in Gregory of Rimini and Peter Martyr Vermigli." In *Via Augustini: Augustine in the Later Middle Ages, Renaissance, and Reformation*, edited by Heiko A. Oberman and Frank E. James, 157–88. Leiden: Brill, 1991.

Jenson, Robert W. *Systematic Theology*. 2 vols. New York: Oxford University Press, 1999.

John Paul II. *Crossing the Threshold of Hope*. London: Cape, 1994.

Kane, George. *Piers Plowman: The Evidence for Authorship*. London: Athlone, 1965.

Kelley, Maurice. *This Great Argument: A Study of Milton's "De Doctrina Christiana" as a Gloss upon Paradise Lost*. Princeton, NJ: Princeton University Press, 1941.

Kelly, H. A. *Chaucerian Tragedy*. Cambridge: Brewer, 1997.

———. *Ideas and Forms of Tragedy from Aristotle to the Middle Ages*. Cambridge: Cambridge University Press, 2005.

Kelly, J. N. D. *Early Christian Doctrines*. Rev. ed. Peabody, MA: Hendrickson, 2004.

Kennedy, Leonard. *The Philosophy of Robert Holcot: Fourteenth-Century Skeptic*. Lewiston, NY: Mellen Press, 1993.

Kent, Bonnie. *Virtues of the Will.* Washington, DC: Catholic University of America Press, 1995.

Lake, Peter. *Anglicans and Puritans? Presbyterianism and English Conformist Thought from Whitgift to Hooker.* London: Unwin, 1988.

———. "Calvinism and the English Church 1570–1635." *Past and Present* 114 (1987): 32–76.

Leff, Gordon. *Bradwardine and the Pelagians.* Cambridge: Cambridge University Press, 1957.

———. *Gregory of Rimini.* Manchester: Manchester University Press, 1961.

Leo, Russ. *Tragedy as Philosophy in the Reformation World.* Princeton, NJ: Princeton University Press, 2018.

Lieb, Michael. *Theological Milton: Deity, Discourse, and Heresy in the Miltonic Canon.* Pittsburgh, PA: Duquesne University Press, 2006.

Long, Steven, Roger Nutt, and Thomas White, O.P., eds. *Thomism and Predestination: Principles and Disputations.* Ave Maria, FL: Sapientia Press, 2016.

Lubac, Henri de. *Exégèse médiévale: Les quatre sens de l'Écriture.* 4 vols. Paris: Aubier, 1959–64.

MacIntyre, Alasdair. *After Virtue: A Study in Moral Theory.* 3rd ed. Notre Dame, IN: University of Notre Dame Press, 2007.

———. *Ethics in the Conflicts of Modernity: An Essay on Desire, Practical Reasoning and Narrative.* Cambridge: Cambridge University Press, 2017.

———. *God, Philosophy, Universities: A Selective History of the Catholic Philosophical Tradition.* London: Rowman and Littlefield, 2009.

———. *A Short History of Ethics: A History of Moral Philosophy from the Homeric Age to the Twentieth Century.* London: Routledge, 1966.

———. *Three Rival Versions of Moral Inquiry: Encyclopaedia, Genealogy and Tradition.* London: Duckworth, 1990.

———. *Whose Justice? Which Rationality?* London: Duckworth, 1998.

Madigan, Kevin. *The Passions of Christ in High-Medieval Thought.* New York: Oxford University Press, 2007.

Manning, Brian. *The English People and the English Revolution: 1640–1649.* London: Heinemann, 1976.

Marenbom, John. *Pagans and Philosophers: The Problem of Paganism from Augustine to Leibniz.* Princeton, NJ: Princeton University Press, 2015.

Marmione, Declan, and Rik van Nieuwenhove. *An Introduction to the Trinity.* Cambridge: Cambridge University Press, 2012.

McCabe, Herbert. *God Still Matters.* Edited by Brian Davies. Introduction by Alasdair MacIntyre. London: Continuum, 2002.

McGinnis, Timothy S. *George Gifford and the Reformation of the Common Sort.* Kirksville, MO: Truman State University Press, 2004.

McGrade, Arthur. *The Political Thought of William of Ockham*. Cambridge: Cambridge University Press, 2002.

McIntosh, Marjorie. *Controlling Misbehavior in England 1370–1600*. Cambridge: Cambridge University Press, 2002.

———. *Poor Relief in England 1350–1600*. Cambridge: Cambridge University Press, 2012.

Milbank, John. *The Suspended Middle: Henri de Lubac and the Debate concerning the Supernatural*. Grand Rapids, MI: Eerdmans, 2005.

Milton, Anthony. *Catholic and Reformed: The Roman and Protestant Churches in English Protestant Thought, 1600–1640*. Cambridge: Cambridge University Press, 1995.

Minnis, Alastair. "Looking for a Sign: The Quest for Nominalism in Chaucer and Langland." In *Essays on Ricardian Literature*, edited by A. J. Minnis and Charlotte Morse, 142–78. Oxford: Clarendon Press, 1997.

Muller, Richard. *Christ and the Decrees: Christology and Predestination in Reformed Theology from Calvin to Perkins*. Grand Rapids, MI: Baker, 1986.

———. *God, Creation, and Providence in the Thought of Jacob Arminius*. Grand Rapids, MI: Baker, 1991.

Murdoch, Iris. *The Sovereignty of Good*. London: Routledge, 1970; repr. 2001.

Myers, Benjamin. *Milton's Theology of Freedom*. Berlin: de Gruyter, 2006.

Newman, John Henry, C. O. *An Essay in the Development of Christian Doctrine*. Edited by Ian Ker. Notre Dame, IN: University of Notre Dame Press, 1989.

Nieuwenhove, Rik van. *An Introduction to Medieval Theology*. Cambridge: Cambridge University Press, 2012.

———. "St. Anselm and St. Thomas Aquinas on 'Satisfaction': or How Catholic and Protestant Understandings of the Cross Differ." *Angelicum* 80 (2003): 159–76.

Oberman, Heiko. "*Facientibus quod in se est Deus non denegat Gratiam*: Robert Holcot, O.P. and the Beginnings of Luther's Theology." *Harvard Theological Review* 55, no. 4 (1962): 317–42.

———. *Forerunners of the Reformation: The Shape of Late Medieval Thought*. Philadelphia: Fortress Press, 1981.

———. *The Harvest of Medieval Theology*. Cambridge, MA: Harvard University Press, 1963.

O'Day, Rosemary. *English Clergy: The Emergence and Consolidation of a Profession 1558–1642*. Leicester: Leicester University Press, 1979.

Owst, G. R. *Literature and Pulpit in Medieval England*. 2nd ed. Oxford: Blackwell, 1966.

Patrides, C. A. *Milton and the Christian Tradition*. Oxford: Clarendon Press, 1966.

Patterson, Lee. *Chaucer and the Subject of History*. Madison: University of Wisconsin Press, 1991.

Pearsall, Derek. *The Life of Geoffrey Chaucer*. Oxford: Blackwell, 1992.

Penny, D. Andrew. *Freewill or Predestination: The Battle over Saving Grace in Mid-Tudor England*. Woodbridge: Boydell, 1990.

Pfau, Thomas. *Minding the Modern: Human Agency, Intellectual Traditions, and Responsible Knowledge*. Notre Dame, IN: University of Notre Dame Press, 2013.

Porter, H. C. *Reformation and Reaction in Tudor Cambridge*. Cambridge: Cambridge University Press, 1985.

Prior, Charles. *Defining the Jacobean Church: The Politics of Religious Controversy 1603–1625*. Cambridge: Cambridge University Press, 2012.

Randi, Eugenio. "A Scotist Way of Distinguishing between God's Absolute and Ordained Powers." In *From Ockham to Wyclif*, edited by Anne Hudson and Michael Wilks, 43–50. Oxford: Blackwell, 1987.

Robertson, D. W., and B. F. Huppé. *Piers Plowman and Scriptural Tradition*. Princeton, NJ: Princeton University Press, 1951.

Robson, J. A. *Wyclif and the Oxford School*. Cambridge: Cambridge University Press, 1961.

Ryrie, Alec. *Being Protestant in Reformation Britain*. Oxford: Oxford University Press, 2015.

Saward, John. "The Grace of Christ in His Principal Members: St. Thomas Aquinas on the Pastoral Epistles." In *Aquinas on Scripture: An Introduction to His Biblical Commentaries*, edited by Thomas G. Weinandy, David Keating, and John Yocum, 197–222. London: Clark, 2005.

Schabel, Chris. "Parisian Commentaries from Peter Aureol to Gregory of Rimini and the Problem of Predestination." In *Medieval Commentaries on Peter Lombard's Sentences*, edited by G. R. Evans, 221–65. Leiden: Brill, 2002.

———. *Theology at Paris, 1316–1345: Peter Auriol and the Problem of Divine Foreknowledge and Future Contingents*. Aldershot: Ashgate, 2000.

Schreiner, Susan. *Are You Alone Wise? The Search for Certainty in the Early Modern Era*. Oxford: Oxford University Press, 2011.

Schüler, M. *Prädestination, Sünde und Freiheit bei Gregor von Rimini*. Stuttgart: Kohlhammer, 1934.

Shagan, Ethan H. *The Birth of Modern Belief: Faith and Judgment from the Middle Ages to the Enlightenment*. Princeton, NJ: Princeton University Press, 2018.

Shogimen, Takashi. *Ockham and Political Discourse in the Late Middle Ages.* Cambridge: Cambridge University Press, 2007.

Shuger, Debora. *The Renaissance Bible: Scholarship, Sacrifice, and Subjectivity.* Berkeley: University of California Press, 1994.

Sierhuis, Freya. *The Literature of the Arminian Controversy: Religion, Politics and the Stage in the Dutch Republic.* Oxford: Oxford University Press, 2015.

Simpson, James. *Burning to Read: English Fundamentalism and Its Reformation Opponents.* Cambridge, MA: Harvard University Press, 2007.

———. "Desire and the Scriptural Text: Will as Reader in *Piers Plowman.*" In *Criticism and Dissent in the Middle Ages,* edited by Rita Copeland, 215–43. Cambridge: Cambridge University Press, 1996.

———. "Not Yet: Chaucer and Anagogy." *Studies in the Age of Chaucer* 37 (2015): 31–54.

———. *The Oxford English Literary History,* vol. 2, *1350–1547: Reform and Cultural Revolution.* Oxford: Oxford University Press, 2002.

———. *Permanent Revolution: The Reformation and the Illiberal Roots of Liberalism.* Cambridge, MA: Harvard University Press, 2019.

———. *"Piers Plowman": An Introduction.* 2nd ed. Exeter: University of Exeter Press, 2007.

———. *Under the Hammer: Iconoclasm in the Anglo-American Tradition.* Oxford: Oxford University Press, 2010.

Slotemaker, John T., and Jeffrey C. Witt. *Robert Holcot.* Oxford: Oxford University Press, 2016.

Smalley, Beryl. *English Friars and Antiquity in the Early Fourteenth Century.* Oxford: Blackwell, 1965.

Smith, Ben. *Traditional Imagery of Charity in Piers Plowman.* The Hague: Mouton, 1966.

Stachniewski, John. *The Persecutory Imagination: English Protestantism and the Literature of Religious Despair.* Oxford: Clarendon Press, 1991.

Stanglin, Keith. "Arminianism Avant La Lettre: Peter Baro, Jacob Arminius, and the Bond of Predestinarian Polemic." *Westminster Theological Journal* 71, no. 1 (2005): 51–74.

———. *Arminius on the Assurance of Salvation: The Context, Roots, and Shape of the Leiden Debate, 1603–1609.* Leiden: Brill, 2007.

Stanglin, Keith, and Thomas H. McCall. *Jacob Arminius: Theologian of Grace.* Oxford: Oxford University Press, 2012.

Streveler, Paul. "This alone belongs to God: not to be able to do the best that he can do: Robert Holcot O.P. (Some musings, modo Holcoti, on necessity, contingency, and the power of God)." In *Studies in Later Medi-*

eval Intellectual History in Honor of William J. Courtenay, edited by William O. Duba, Russell Friedman, and Chris Schabel, 393–415. Louven: Peeters, 2017.

Strohm, Paul. *Social Chaucer.* Cambridge, MA: Harvard University Press, 1989.

Surin, Ken. *Theodicy and the Problem of Evil.* Eugene, OR: Wipf and Stock, 1986.

Tachau, Katherine. *Vision and Certitude in the Age of Ockham.* Leiden: Brill, 1988.

Travis, Peter. *Disseminal Chaucer: Rereading the Nun's Priest's Tale.* Notre Dame, IN: University of Notre Dame Press, 2010.

Tyacke, Nicholas. *Anti-Calvinists: The Rise of English Arminianism c. 1590–1640.* Oxford: Oxford University Press, 1987.

———. *Aspects of English Protestantism c. 1530–1700.* Manchester: Manchester University Press, 2001.

———. "The Rise of Arminianism Reconsidered." *Past and Present* 115 (1987): 201–16.

Underdown, David. *Revel, Riot and Rebellion: Popular Politics and Culture in England 1603–1660.* Oxford: Clarendon Press, 1985.

Underwood, T. L. *Primitivism, Radicalism and the Lamb's War: The Baptist-Quaker Conflicts in Seventeenth-Century England.* Oxford: Oxford University Press, 1997.

Van Niuewenhove, Rik. *Introduction to Medieval Theology.* Cambridge: Cambridge University Press, 2012.

Vignaux, Paul. *Justification et prédestination au XIVᵉ siècle.* Paris: Leroux, 1934.

Vitto, Cindy L. *The Virtuous Pagan in Middle English Literature.* Philadelphia: American Philosophical Society, 1989.

Wallace, Dewey. "George Gifford, Puritan Propaganda and Popular Religion in Elizabethan England." *Sixteenth Century Journal* 9, no. 1 (1978): 27–49.

———. *Puritans and Predestination: Grace in English Protestant Theology 1525–1695.* Eugene, OR: Wipf and Stock, 1982.

Walsham, Alexandra. *Providence in Early Modern England.* Oxford: Oxford University Press, 1999.

Waters, Claire M. *Translating "Clergie": Status, Education, and Salvation in Thirteenth-Century Vernacular Texts.* Philadelphia: University of Pennsylvania Press, 2016.

Watson, Nicholas. "Despair." In *Cultural Reformations: Medieval and Renaissance in Literary History*, edited by James Simpson and Brian Cummings, 342–60. Oxford: Oxford University Press, 2010.

———. "Visions of Inclusion: Universal Salvation and Vernacular Theology in Pre-Reformation England." *JMEMS* 27, no. 2 (1997): 145–87.

Wawrykow, Joseph P. *God's Grace and Human Action: Merit in the Theology of Thomas Aquinas*. Notre Dame, IN: University of Notre Dame Press, 1995.

Webster, Tom. *Godly Clergy in Early Stuart England: The Caroline Puritan Movement, c. 1620–1643*. Cambridge: Cambridge University Press, 1997.

Weingart, Richard. *The Logic of Divine Love: A Critical Analysis of the Soteriology of Peter Abelard*. Oxford: Clarendon Press, 1970.

Wendel, François. *Calvin: The Origins of His Religious Thought*. London: Collins, 1969.

Wenzel, Siegfried. *Latin Sermons from Later Medieval Collections*. Cambridge: Cambridge University Press, 2005.

———. *The Sin of Sloth: Acedia in Medieval Thought and Literature*. Chapel Hill: University of North Carolina Press, 1960.

Wetzel, James. *Augustine: A Guide for the Perplexed*. London: Continuum, 2010.

———. *Augustine and the Limits of Virtue*. Cambridge: Cambridge University Press, 1992.

———. *Parting Knowledge: Essays after Augustine*. Eugene, OR: Cascade, 2013.

———. "Snares of Truth: Augustine on Free Will and Predestination." In *Augustine and His Critics*, edited by Robert Dodaro and George Lawless, 123–40. London: Routledge, 2000.

Whatley, Gordon. "The Uses of Hagiography: The Legend of Pope Gregory and the Emperor Trajan in the Middle Ages." *Viator* 15 (1984): 25–63.

White, Helen C. *English Devotional Literature, 1600–1640*. Madison: University of Wisconsin Press, 1931.

White, Peter. "Arminianism Reconsidered: A Rejoinder." *Past and Present* 115, no. 1 (1987): 217–29.

———. *Predestination, Policy and Polemic: Conflict and Consensus in the English Church from the Reformation to the Civil War*. Cambridge: Cambridge University Press, 1992.

White, Thomas. "The Crucified Lord: Thomistic Reflections on the Communication of Idioms and the Theology of the Cross." In *Thomas Aquinas and Karl Barth: An Unofficial Catholic-Protestant Dialogue*, edited by Bruce McCormack and Thomas White, 157–89. Grand Rapids, MI: Eerdmans, 2013.

———. *The Light of Christ: An Introduction to Catholicism*. Washington, DC: Catholic University of America Press, 2017.

Williams, Norman P. *The Idea of the Fall and of Original Sin: A Historical and Critical Study*. London: Longmans, Green & Co., 1927.

Willis, E. David. *Calvin's Catholic Christology: The Function of the So-Called Extra Calvinisticum in Calvin's Theology*. Leiden: Brill, 1966.

Wittgenstein, Ludwig. *Culture and Value*. Edited by G. H. von Wright. Translated by Peter Winch. Oxford: Blackwell, 1994.

Wittig, Joseph. "*Piers Plowman* B, Passus IX–XII: Elements in the Design of the Inward Journey." *Traditio* 28 (1972): 211–80.

Wood, Ellen N. *The Origin of Capitalism: A Longer View*. London: Verso, 2017.

Wrightson, Keith. *Earthly Necessities: Economic Lives in Early Modern Britain*. New Haven, CT: Yale University Press, 2000.

———. *English Society 1580–1680*. London: Hutchinson, 1982.

Zeeman, Nicolette. *Arts of Disruption: The Work of Allegory and Piers Plowman*. Oxford: Oxford University Press, 2020.

———. *Piers Plowman and the Medieval Discourse of Desire*. Cambridge: Cambridge University Press, 2006.

INDEX OF BIBLICAL CITATIONS

GENERAL INDEX

Titles of authored works will be found under the author's name, unless otherwise indicated.

Barth, Karl, 23, 52

Baxter, Margery, 192

Baxter, Richard, 125, 126

Beckwith, Sarah, 261n30

Bernard of Clairvaux, 5

Bettergh, Katherine, 251n45

Beza, Theodore, 144, 188, 189,
242n53

Bible. *See* Scripture; *separate index
of biblical citations*

Biel, Gabriel, 82, 89, 93

Blake, William: "The Little
Vagabond," 168

Blessed Virgin Mary, 221

Boethius: *Consolation of Philosophy*,
28, 30

Bolton, Robert: *The Last Conflicts
and Death of Mr. Thomas
Peacock*

Calvinist versions of election and,
48, 127–34, 139, 141, 142, 143,
157, 251n45

Dent and, 172, 176, 259n19

book of life

in *Piers Plowman*, 16–18, 20, 102

Thomas Aquinas on, 16–18, 101–2

Bradwardine, Thomas: *De Causa
Dei*, 28, 74–75, 153–54, 250n43

bridesmaids (wise and foolish
virgins), parable of, 92–93

Bridges, John, 142–43, 258n18

Bromyard, John: *Summa
Praedicantium*, 73, 87–106

Augustine and, 88, 91, 92, 95–96,
98, 100, 103, 104, 106

biographical information, 87–88,
242n54

concausality and cooperation, use
of, 91, 94–96

doubled agency model, use of,
91–93

exegesis of Ephesians, Romans,
and 1 Timothy, 88–91

on free will, 88–90, 92, 95, 96, 101

general election in, 87, 93, 100, 106

on God as author of sin, 100–101

Holcot compared, 89, 92, 93, 106

hope, emphasis on, 103–5

Milton compared, 195

parables, metaphors, and exempla
used by, 92–95, 96–97

pastoral concerns of, 88, 98–99

Piers Plowman and, 11

on quest for certainty, 101–3

rise of sacramental theology
against Calvinism in
seventeenth century and, 181

Thomas Aquinas and, 88, 92,
95–100, 106

on *vocatio*, 105–6

Brook, Thomas: *Heaven on Earth*,
173

Brownists, 145, 253n70

Brut, Walter, 242n54

Bunyan, Paul, 103

Grace Abounding, 74, 83, 118, 126,
139, 173, 175–76

The Pilgrim's Progress, 259n21

Burton, Robert: *Anatomy of
Melancholy*, 260n28

Cain, 26

Calamy, Edmund, 127

Calvin, John

certainty of predestined status as
obsession of, 85

Dent compared, 170, 172, 175,
261n30

mother, God viewed as, 148–49,
154–55. *See also* hen, Christ
comparing himself to
Muller, Richard, 247n15
murderer acting under influence of
alcohol, metaphor of, 89–90
Murdoch, Iris, 22, 25
Myers, Benjamin: *Milton's Theology
of Freedom*, 219

Nayler, James, 264n13
Nebuchadnezzar, 95–96, 155
Neoplatonism, 30, 32, 68
Nero, 69
Newman, John Henry Cardinal: *An
Essay on the Development of
Christian Doctrine*, xii, 162
Nicene Christianity/Trinitarianism,
185, 210, 212, 213
Nicene Creed, 54
Nicholas of Gorran, 7, 8, 10–11, 23
Nicholas of Lyra, 7, 10, 11, 23, 149
Norton, Thomas, 114
Norwood, Richard, 249n39

O altitudo, 59, 83, 205
Oberman, Heiko, 100, 229n4
Ockham. *See* William of Ockham
Origen, 47, 48, 93, 100
original sin, 71, 79, 89, 152–53
Owen, John, 150
Owst, G. R.: *Literature and the
Pulpit in Medieval England*, 87

Paul (apostle), xi, 19, 56, 59, 102, 119,
173, 174, 200–201, 221, 248n22
Peacock, Thomas. *See* Bolton,
Robert: *The Last Conflicts and
Death of Mr. Thomas Peacock*

Pearsall, Derek, xvi, 2, 16, 18, 42, 44,
47–48, 223–26, 228–29n1
Pelagianism/semi-Pelagianism/
anti-Pelagianism
Calvinist versions of election and,
110, 120, 153–54
Dent on, 177
medieval versions of election and,
62, 73, 81, 85, 92, 100
Milton on, 199, 204, 208
Piers Plowman and, 27, 42
penal substitution/satisfaction, 135,
137, 138, 213–14, 216, 252n58,
261n30, 266n31
Perkins, William
A Golden Chaine, 157–58
*A Treatise tending unto a
declaration...*, 170, 175, 255n1,
258n9, 258n18
Peter (apostle), 15, 72, 192
Peter Abelard, 213
Peter Aureol, 81–82, 83, 89, 181, 196
Peter Lombard: *Sentences*, x, 14, 33,
49, 54–59, 61, 80, 82, 83, 88, 98,
106, 136, 220
PG. *See Praedestinatio Generalis*
Pharaoh, unrepentant (in Exodus
story), 95–96, 202
Piers Plowman (Langland), 1–52
allegorical visions of tree of
Charity, Trinity, and salvation
history in, 43–44, 49–50
ambivalence of Langland
regarding contemporary
theology in, 33–34
anxiety over predestination in,
26–28, 37, 41, 48–49, 51, 55, 58,
62–63, 74, 87, 101–3, 104, 111, 125
on atonement, 139–41

DAVID AERS

is James B. Duke Professor of English and Historical Theology with appointments in both the English Department and in the Divinity School at Duke University. His many publications include *Salvation and Sin: Augustine, Langland, and Fourteenth-Century Theology* (2009) and *Beyond Reformation?: An Essay on William Langland's Piers Plowman and the End of Constantinian Christianity* (2015), both published by the University of Notre Dame Press.

www.ingramcontent.com/pod-product-compliance
Lightning Source LLC
Chambersburg PA
CBHW022121220325
23870CB00026B/517